THE ROAD

D0188352

TO HELL

HOW THE BIKER GANGS ARE CONQUERING CANADA

JULIAN SHER

AND

WILLIAM MARSDEN

SEAL BOOKS

Seal Books and colophon are trademarks of
Random House of Canada Limited.

THE ROAD TO HELL
Seal Books/published by arrangement with Alfred A. Knopf Canada
Alfred A. Knopf Canada edition published 2003
Vintage Canada edition published 2004
Seal Books edition published July 2005

ISBN: 0-7704-2984-X

Cover image: Tony Arruza/Corbis

Seal Books are published by Random House of Canada Limited.
"Seal Books" and the portrayal of a seal are the property of
Random House of Canada Limited.

Visit Random House of Canada Limited's website:
www.randomhouse.ca

PRINTED AND BOUND IN THE USA

OPM 10 9 8 7 6 5 4 3 2 1

CONTENTS

To Lisa and Janet,
our partners in crime

PROLOGUE

Source C-2994

"The source is very close to the bikers and has a very good knowledge of the milieu. His potential is unlimited."
RCMP CONFIDENTIAL REPORT, OCTOBER 19, 1994

The killers left the eighteen-month-old baby alive, crying in his crib. His parents were not so lucky.

It was a peaceful rural Sunday, September 10, 2000. The house was quiet. Too quiet, in fact. So a neighbour came up the dirt driveway to check on the family home, which sat off an isolated stretch of Cogmagun Road in Hants County, Nova Scotia, about seventy-five miles southwest of Halifax. She found the sobbing infant inside. In the living room lay the bodies of Kirk Mersereau, forty-eight, and his wife, Nancy, forty-seven. Both had been slain execution-style. They had a four-year-old daughter, who was at her grandmother's for the night. Had she been home she likely would have been executed too; hitmen don't leave witnesses around. Only his tender age saved her younger sibling.

Kirk's brother, Randy, a former Hells Angel who broke with the gang and dared to set up his own drug network, had vanished about a year earlier and was presumed dead.

A small-time drug dealer in his own right, Kirk had put out a bounty of $50,000 on the head of anyone connected to his brother's murder. "He made it known that he believed the Hells Angels were behind Randy's disappearance and he was going to do something about it," says Bruce Macdonald of the RCMP. Instead, he ended up paying the ultimate price for crossing the Hells.

To this date, police have not laid any charges in the case, and have no suspects. Only now, in this book, are details of a plot by the Hells Angels to execute Kirk Mersereau revealed for the first time, including vows by a top leader from Montreal that Mersereau "must be killed"; discussions at the Halifax clubhouse with the local chapter president about the need to eliminate Kirk; decisions that a biker hangaround—and eventually the newest member of the Halifax Angel club—should get the "mandate to kill" Mersereau.

When the bikers were calmly planning Mersereau's elimination, they didn't know that among them was a police informant.

His name was Dany Kane, and for years he had been walking a deadly tightrope between police and the Hells Angels, filing daily intelligence briefings. His reports reveal the Hells Angels' most intimate secrets and follow the brutal, cold-blooded expansion of an outlaw biker gang that has grown into the most powerful criminal force in Canada. They show the degree to which police had a detailed knowledge of what was happening inside the Hells Angels as they blasted their way to power.

Rarely has the curtain been pulled back on police intelligence. Rarer still are the opportunities to tell the story of a deep-cover RCMP informant. The RCMP encases its informants in such a high level of secrecy that not even the bosses know their true identities.

The rise to power of leading Hells Angels such as

Maurice "Mom" Boucher, David "Wolf" Carroll and Walter "Nurget" Stadnick—and their ties to their brethren in Nova Scotia, Ontario, Manitoba and British Columbia—unfolds in thousands of pages of these intelligence reports entered into court records. This book tells the real story behind a small group of bikers who grew so powerful they shook the foundations of our justice system.

And it all revolves around one man who six years before the Mersereau murder made a telephone call to Mountie headquarters.

Sgt. Jean-Pierre Lévesque had been in his third-floor office at RCMP headquarters in Ottawa, riffling through the accordion file folder he had jammed full of photographs of bikers. He had dozens of them. Some were individual shots taken at biker rallies. Lévesque thought that if only one of these bikers would talk, it would break the seal on a world that police—so far—had totally failed to penetrate.

Lévesque was the chief analyst for the Criminal Intelligence Service Canada (CISC), an RCMP-led coordinating group of more than a hundred national, regional and local police intelligence officers. It was October 17, 1994, and for several years, CISC had warned of the rising strength of biker gangs, especially the most powerful: the Hells Angels. Across the country, they were eclipsing Asian gangs, the Russian mob and even the traditional Italian Mafia as the top organized crime group.

Lévesque knew the police were losing the war. For years, they had neglected the bikers. Now that they were scrambling to catch up, they had no idea who the real power brokers were, how the organizations worked, how they moved their drugs and how they laundered their profits. Half the time, they didn't even know for certain who among the growing number of leather-jacketed Harley riders was an outlaw biker and who was not.

To make matters worse, in Quebec, where the bikers were fighting an all-out war, the police were embroiled in scandal, corruption and embarrassing infighting. What's more, nobody in authority seemed to care. Bombs were going off across the city almost weekly and yet police simply shrugged them off as a "settling of accounts."

"I'll tell you honestly, the department didn't give two shits," Montreal police Comdr. André Bouchard admitted. "They're killing each other. I give a hell if some guy pops somebody who just got out of jail? No. We didn't give a shit."

Lévesque had recently started Project Spotlight. The idea was to gather as much pure intelligence as possible on the bikers. Maybe then police could better focus their investigations, shake things up a bit and see if they couldn't scare up a few informers. But other than clipping newspapers and filing police reports, he wasn't really getting anywhere.

And now here he was again flipping through colour pictures. Oddly, one particular photo always seemed to catch his eye. It was of a ragtag group of bikers, a short-lived Hells Angels puppet club from Belleville, Ontario, who called themselves the Demon Keepers. In the centre, crouching with one knee on the ground, was Dany Kane. His hair was cropped short and neat, his wire-rimmed glasses gave a schoolboyish look to his round face. It was as though the young man from a small village in Quebec couldn't quite manage the tough, dead-eye biker look.

"He looked so like a librarian with his little glasses," Lévesque recalled. "For some reason I just kept looking at the guy—and then suddenly, who phones!"

After seven frustrating years in the biker world and a short, miserable stint in prison, Dany Kane, once he'd decided he wanted to turn informer, went right to the top. He had no intention of dealing with the Quebec police, whom he didn't trust, or the Montreal police, whom he thought were small time. He found Interpol in the telephone listings in Ottawa, assuming—wrongly—that the world police coordinating agency was sort of a joint operation of the FBI, the American Drug Enforcement Agency and the RCMP.

Luck can sometimes play a surprisingly large role in police work. As it happened, the Interpol office was just down the hall from Lévesque's office on the third floor of the RCMP headquarters. By a further stroke of luck, Lévesque happened to be in when the phone call came for Interpol.

"I want to speak to someone who works on the bikers," Kane said, never identifying himself. The RCMP officer assigned to Interpol put Kane on hold and walked over to Lévesque's office: "There's someone who wants to talk to you."

Lévesque picked up the line and, after listening to Kane's offer of assistance, started posing a few basic questions. "Do you know the bikers?" he asked. The man said yes.

"Do you know Stadnick? Mom?" Lévesque continued, rattling off the names of some of the prominent Angels— Quebec leader Maurice "Mom" Boucher, his fellow Angel and national organizer Walter Stadnick—bikers who are well known now but weren't at the time. The phone caller said he knew them all.

"Where are the chapters?" the RCMP officer queried. And the man on the other end of the line listed their locations.

Lévesque wasn't overly impressed. Getting calls from people who want to inform on their associates wasn't unusual. Still, he felt there was definitely something worth exploring. The man said he would call back the next day. Lévesque said fine and hung up the phone.

As soon as he got off the line, Lévesque called Corp. Pierre Verdon, a veteran RCMP interrogator and intelligence officer in Montreal whom he knew and trusted. He described his conversation with the unknown caller and

Verdon agreed to join Lévesque for a meeting if the man called back.

The man was true to his word. He phoned the next day at 1:30 p.m., and Lévesque set up a meeting for that evening at six. "Pointe Claire shopping centre. East door," Lévesque said. "Meet me there with a copy of *Le Devoir* under your left arm. Not your right arm. Not *La Presse*. Not the *Journal de Montréal*. *Le Devoir*."

Once again, Lévesque called Verdon, who booked a room at the International Best Western Hotel near Dorval Airport. At 6:00 p.m., with a third officer in a backup car running surveillance, they approached the west-end Montreal shopping mall in a van. Lévesque spotted the source at the designated meeting place. The guy was right on time. A good sign. But Lévesque still couldn't see who it was. He went into the mall through another door and came up behind the man.

"Follow me," the RCMP officer said.

When they got into the van, Lévesque turned to the person he now recognized from the photo of the Demon Keepers.

"How's it going, Dany?" Lévesque said. Kane turned and smiled, showing lots of poise.

Lévesque and Verdon drove their new-found biker acquaintance to the hotel, taking a roundabout route to make sure they weren't followed. By seven-fifteen, they were inside the room. After introductions were made, Kane took control. He told them he had an intimate knowledge of the biker world and access to the top Hells Angels. He then described his seven-year history with different biker gangs, the Condors, Evil Ones and the Demon Keepers. He told them about his drug trafficking and gun dealing as well as his operation of a stripper agency called Aventure. He told them he was an expert in explosives and was used by the bikers to make bombs. He gave them a who's who of the biker world in Montreal and a rundown on Ontario, describing which gangs wanted to join the Hells Angels and which wanted to remain independent or join the rival Outlaws.

The two officers took copious notes, trying to hide their delight. The way he laid it all out, nice and orderly, it was almost as if he had rehearsed the whole thing. He seemed intelligent and straight. The cops questioned him about his intentions. He wanted the relationship to be long term, as in years, and he told them about his plan to become a Hells Angel. Why was he doing it? Revenge and money, he said. He expected to be well paid. Did he want to become an agent, sign a contract, carry a body pack? No, not right now.

Kane was shown surveillance pictures of Hells Angels. Many of the bikers he knew only by their street names— nicknames like "Gyrator" and "Toots," "Crow" and "Zappa." But he knew them all. The meeting finally broke up at ten-thirty that night. The interview had lasted three and a quarter hours. Verdon would put in an expense claim for $7.13 of "non-alcoholic" drinks plus $88.88 for the room. They made arrangements for Kane to call the first week of November to set up a second meeting. Then they said their goodbyes. "We'll get in touch with you," the officers told him, trying not to look too enthusiastic.

Would anything come of it? Lévesque and Verdon didn't know, but right now they wanted to believe they had struck gold, that they finally had the chance to penetrate to the heart of the Hells Angels. Pierre Verdon turned to Lévesque and said simply, "Good man."

The next day, Verdon sat down and wrote a ten-page debriefing report. He gave it the second-highest security classification, Protection B. The report shows Kane's efforts to impress the RCMP had paid off in spades. "The source is very close to the bikers and has a very good knowledge of the milieu," Verdon wrote. "His potential is unlimited and we are of the opinion that this opportunity would probably never again arise. . . . Such a source would be able to serve not only as an intelligence source in the biker milieu but also could be used in all the illegal activities the bikers get mixed up in—and we all know how diverse those activities are."

The RCMP officers had not checked out Kane on any police database. They were afraid to leave footprints or trigger a "silent hit"—an instant computer message to any officer watching Kane that someone else had run his name. For security reasons, they didn't want to tip off any other police force that the intelligence branch had an interest in Kane. But Verdon and Lévesque were eager to accept their new acquaintance at face value and to capitalize on his position within the biker community, as well as his obvious involvement in a wide variety of crimes. They had no idea—or at least didn't want to imagine—how serious and deadly that involvement was. They would learn all about that in the years to come, when their relationship would be blown violently apart. For now they just wanted to sign the marriage contract.

In order to cement the relationship and get Kane on the payroll, they needed the financial backing of their superiors. The bosses bit. At least for the moment, Verdon's superiors were equally keen to infiltrate the bikers. Jealousy, backstabbing, ass covering and career saving would come later.

The next encounter with Kane was twelve days later, on October 30, in Ottawa. Verdon and Lévesque met Kane in an underground parking lot and then drove to the Welcome Inn, where Lévesque had booked a room. They paid Kane $500 in cash. He accepted the money but made it clear he wanted a lot more. Verdon told him he would have to earn it. Kane was now known simply as Source C-2994.

Both the RCMP and Kane had got what they wanted. Kane had his steady income and was on the path to sweet revenge against the Angels for taking advantage of him for years without rewarding his efforts. And the cops were finally inside the bikers. That was the easy part.

The RCMP and then the police in Montreal would run Kane as one of the most successful—and secretive—agents ever to infiltrate organized crime. Kane would climb all the way to the top: from a lowly hangaround to a trusted confidant of the Quebec Nomads, the elite chapter led by the top lieutenants of Maurice "Mom" Boucher. And through his entire six-year career as a spy, few people—even inside the police—would ever know about his dangerous double life.

Kane's infiltration would be instrumental in helping the police strike a blow against the powerful Hells empire in Quebec, but in many ways it would come too late. By the time police finally moved against the Angels in that province, the bikers had already doubled their strength in the rest of the country. When Mom Boucher was finally imprisoned for life in the spring of 2002, the Hells had 597 official members spread across thirty-seven chapters from one end of the country to the other.

In Ontario, police compiled a list of the top ten organized crime groups—traditional Mafia, Russian mobsters, Asian gangs, Jamaican gangs and bikers. And at the top of the list stood the Hells Angels. "They are the number-one priority," says Don Bell of the province's special Biker Enforcement Unit (BEU). "They're more sophisticated. Right now the Hells Angels are the greatest threat to public safety." It's the same story across the country. In Nova Scotia, the Angels secured their monopoly over the cocaine trade in a murderous elimination of their enemies. In Manitoba, gang warfare turned ugly with drive-by shootings in downtown Winnipeg and the firebombing of a police officer's home. In British Columbia, which numbers some of the wealthiest Angels on the continent, the Hells profited from RCMP bungling and political blindness to strengthen their infiltration of the stock market and their stranglehold on smuggling in the all-important Vancouver and area ports. Across the country, the bikers have set up sophisticated money-laundering operations with the help of bankers, stockbrokers and shady lawyers, earning Canada the well-deserved reputation as one of the best places in the world to hide dirty money.

"The Hells Angels succeeded in doing what no crime organization has in the past," says one top RCMP officer who monitors national syndicates. "This is the first time Canada has seen an organized crime organization coast to coast." Narcotics trafficking, prostitution rings, protection rackets, loan sharking—they control almost all of it, directly or indirectly.

The Hells Angels are stronger here than in any other country. More than one in four of the Hells Angels' worldwide members calls Canada his home. Unlike any previous organized crime group, they have never hidden their affiliation. They sport their "Filthy Few" tattoos and Death Head patches with pride and arrogance.

Why, then, has it taken so long for police forces and politicians to get a grip on such a public enemy? If the road to hell is paved with good intentions, in Canada it is also pitted by neglect, corruption and downright stupidity. The story of how the bikers conquered Canada's crime world is a tale of how politicians dithered while overburdened and understaffed prosecutors burned out and lost major cases; how errors by certain judges and a tragically complacent justice system at times severely crippled attempts to convict bikers; how police brass squabbled while a handful of dedicated cops worked years to bring down the bikers; how a few brave citizens stood up to the bikers and how some of them paid for it with their lives.

Now for the first time that story, with its murder plots, drug deals, money laundering and assassinations can be told in full, through never-before-revealed police wire-taps, surveillance videos, court transcripts and interviews with dozens of eyewitnesses. We will also learn the secret strategies the police used to finally trap Mom Boucher and his associates.

Yet the bikers keep rolling on, their chapters and membership expanding across the country, while the death toll rises along the road to Hell.

PART I

THE NOMADS AND THE MOLE

ONE

The Hellraiser

"He rules by fear. People respect him because they fear him.
They don't respect him because he's respectable."
COMDR. ANDRÉ BOUCHARD

Air conditioning.

Ask André Bouchard what most ails policing today, and
that's the two-word answer from the head of Montreal's
Major Crimes Squad. The thirty-two-year police veteran
remembers the old days when his cruiser rumbled through
the hot city's streets with the windows rolled down.

"We prowled, we didn't patrol," he says, through the
wafts of smoke from the two packs of cigarettes he smokes
every day. "And we listened."

Bouchard feels police have become too soft, too comfortable—and too isolated behind their sealed, cooled
police cars. "We don't have tough cops any more," he
laments. "I don't want to sound like a dinosaur, but they
have taken that physical aspect out of it. Today we have to
be the 'smiley little cop.' "

That's fine for the suburbs, Bouchard says, but not for
the inner city. Like Mom Boucher, André Bouchard grew
up in blue-collar east-end Montreal. They were both tough

kids who never walked away from a good fight. But by the time they were out of their teens, the two men took radically different paths that would set them on a collision course for more than a decade.

At 149 pounds and with the toned body of a swimmer, Bouchard was a compact, lean recruit when he first joined the Montreal police in 1970, at the age of twenty. One of his first postings was as a bodyguard for the station commander—and enforcer on the police hockey team. "I wasn't the best hockey player. I was a fighter," he admits. Bouchard's role as designated goon was to take out the best player on the opposing team—often during warm-ups even before the game had started.

In the early 1970s when Bouchard walked the Main, Montreal's famous mile-long drag of bars and restaurants, taking care of the bikers was easy. "Don't forget this was before the Charter of Rights," he says. "You saw a guy walking up the street in his colours, you kicked the shit out of him and that was it."

The Popeyes were the first biker gang in Quebec, running prostitution rings and providing the collection muscle for the Mafia and the French gangs such as the Dubois brothers. They sported grey jackets—and for the blue-uniformed police, that meant a no-holds-barred colour war.

"What did we tell you last time?" Bouchard would yell when he spotted a grey-patched Popeye. "We'd rip the shit out of his colours and throw them on the floor. And then we'd walk away. That was the way it worked. It was [biker] grey or [police] blue."

Bouchard had little time for the sensitivity training the police had initiated with the early bikers. The idea was to get the cops and the motorcycle gangs to understand each other. So Montreal police created a biker liaison officer who was solely responsible for chumming with the motorcycle gangs. Police gave him a Harley-Davidson, and he grew his hair long so he could fit in. He even wore his Montreal police badge as a patch on his leather jacket. Once during Bouchard's academy days, the liaison officer showed up with fifteen long-haired members of a biker gang to meet a classroom of recruits.

"I want to know what would you do if it was one o'clock in the morning and we're revving our motors and having a beer and you tell us we have to leave and I tell you to go fuck yourself," one biker asked the class. "What would you do?"

Bouchard was at the rear of the hall, waving his hand madly. "Yeah, you in the back," the biker said.

"Sir," Bouchard started politely, "if you told me to go fuck myself, I'd take the little wooden stick that they give us and I'd shove it so far up your ass that you'd remember me for a long time."

"They threw me out of the hall," Bouchard recalls with a chuckle. "So that was my beginning. The bikers didn't like me since, and I don't like them since. I always hated these guys. I would see them on the streets and they'd piss me off. I just didn't like them."

Bouchard had lots of pedigree. His father was an MP (military police) in the air force before joining the Sûreté du Québec (SQ). His two older brothers had joined the Montreal police force before Bouchard followed suit in June 1970.

Over the years, the fast-rising recruit learned to use his brain and not just his brawn as he moved steadily through the ranks. He tackled break-ins and stolen cars, confronted Mafia dons during his stint on the morality squad, mastered surveillance and solved homicides. The one nagging problem that always lingered was the bikers. By the mid-eighties, the greasy, long-haired bums Bouchard had confronted on the Main had morphed into the tightly organized, disciplined Hells Angels. But the authorities had not adjusted.

"We had trouble with the motorcycle guys because the bosses didn't take them seriously," says Bouchard. "When they got their Hells Angels patches, we looked at them and said, 'What the fuck are the bosses waiting for?' I mean, they were walking downtown with patches on. We couldn't do what we used to do—rip the patches off—because you have legal rights and everything now. But we didn't have special units or teams to look at these guys. They let them go."

There was one biker Bouchard remembers hearing about back then—a sometime thief and heavy drug user from the east end of the city named Maurice Boucher. "He was muscle. He was a crazy fucker," Bouchard recalls. "They'd send him out to beat up some guy. He was stoned half of the time."

The scraggly punk with shoulder-length hair and a bandana atop his head quickly cleaned up his act as he gravitated toward the elite circle of the Hells Angels. Maurice "Mom" Boucher had his eyes on becoming leader of the pack.

"Mom at that time had aspirations," says Bouchard. "He was ambitious—and vicious."

The man who became the most feared hellraiser in Canada was born in the tiny Gaspé village of Causapscal on June 21, 1953—one of eight children. When he was only two, his parents moved the family to the working-class neighbourhood of Hochelaga-Maisonneuve in Montreal.

These were tough streets, and Maurice grew up tough. A court-ordered psychological profile of the young Boucher prepared by a criminologist in 1975, when he got into trouble with the law, offers a revealing glimpse of a gang leader in the making.

Boucher's father was an ironworker, described as a "severe man who tolerated no lip from his children." When his father drank, he became "hot-tempered and violent" and imposed "an iron discipline." Maurice was indifferent to his father's outbursts and would simply walk out when his temper flared.

Described as a "mediocre" student, Boucher left school at age seventeen in Grade 9. The next year, at eighteen, he left home—but he never did cut ties with his mother and visited her often.

Hochelaga-Maisonneuve is a sprawling patchwork of streets and alleyways that spreads out from the shadow of the Olympic Stadium—south toward the incessant noise and grimy smoke of the factories and warehouses along the St. Lawrence River and eastward to the fumes of the oil refineries. Its residents are overwhelmingly white, French and poor, but it is no slum; the residents keep their small balconies trim and the tiny yards tidy.

For a young, uneducated boy on the street, drugs and crime offered an easy escape, and Boucher excelled in both. By his late teens, he was using such a dizzying cocktail of drugs—hash, LSD, amphetamines, heroin and cocaine—that he became "suspicious and paranoid."

"He was afraid of everything," the court report says, "and even went to bed with a .303 [rifle]."

His first official run-in with the law came in April 1973, when at age nineteen he was charged with shoplifting. By the end of the next year, he was nailed for breaking and entering—by his own admission, he was so pumped up on Valium that he hardly remembered what he had done.

Guy Pellerin, the criminologist who examined him in February 1975, reported that Boucher was trying to get a job in construction but not having much luck. "He appears quite depressed. He suffers from insomnia and never stops asking questions about what's to become of him. . . . It's normal that trapped in such a situation an individual is ready to do anything he can to get out."

Pellerin noted Boucher's girlfriend was eight months pregnant, and Boucher was worried about his child's future with his father behind bars. More prison time would likely make Boucher even more aggressive, Pellerin warned prophetically. "The future for him will be even more sombre and perhaps he will not hesitate to turn to more virulent means to escape from his cage. . . . He has come, we believe, to the hour of choice."

Boucher made that choice—more crime and drugs. In January 1976 he was found guilty of armed robbery. He racked up more petty crimes in the next few years—possession of a stolen credit card and theft. Then in September 1984 he sexually assaulted a woman while he held a knife to her throat. He got twenty-three months in prison.

He was riding with a loose gang of bikers who called themselves the SS. The Hitlerian reference was more symbolic than real—Mom's group was not affiliated with any neo-Nazi movement—but the racial overtones were not accidental. Still, Mom and his fellow SS riders were little more than thugs on bikes, and the group disbanded in 1984. Boucher was hooked on the power and camaraderie that came from riding with the boys, however, and he set his eyes on another, more prominent, biker group that was making inroads into Quebec—the most powerful of them all. The Hells Angels.

The name came from a B-17 Bomber Group stationed in England during the Second World War; one of their planes was nicknamed "Hell's Angels." By the war's end, more than a dozen other units had adopted the name, including a United States Marine Corps fighter squadron in Asia. On his return to California, one of the pilots suggested that his biker buddies carry on the tradition. A motley crew of biker clubs had sprung up in southern California after the war with in-your-face names like the Booze Fighters and

Satan's Sinners. On the July 4 weekend in 1947, two thousand bikers invaded the small California town of Hollister.

The mayhem grabbed national attention, and the American Motorcycle Association quickly dissociated itself from the "hoodlums and troublemakers," insisting that 99 percent of cyclists were clean-cut and law abiding. The rebels seized on that notoriety and called themselves "the one percenters"—a minority label to which Hells Angels members to this day proudly cling.

In 1948, the first chapter of the Hells Angels was born, in San Bernardino. Their rebel image flourished in the 1950s, mythologized in Hollywood movies such as *The Wild One*, starring Marlon Brando. In 1957, a Grade 10 dropout named Ralph "Sonny" Barger formed the Oakland chapter. The next year, the Angels relocated their headquarters there, and to this day Barger remains the inspirational leader of Angels in Canada and around the world.

What started as motorcycle mayhem became a vehicle for money—money derived from crime and drugs. They trademarked their name, their winged Death Head emblem—a screaming skeleton with a helmet and feathers streaming behind him—and their red and white colours. The right to be a "full patch"—to wear the official colours—belongs only to members.

By the late sixties, the Angels claimed a membership of about five hundred, most of them still in California but with chapters in the northeastern States and in Switzerland, England and West Germany. Up until that point, the Angels had not crossed the border into Canada. Here, the Satan's Choice was the country's largest gang, with chapters throughout southern Ontario and in Montreal. Their rivals in Quebec were the Popeyes—the grey-jacketed bikers André Bouchard was so fond of beating up. The rivalry between the two gangs could be deadly: at one point, a Popeye member was found hanging in a graveyard.

The biker landscape in Canada changed forever on December 5, 1977, when the Hells Angels made their first official entry into the country. They took over about thirty-five members of the Popeyes in Quebec and opened up a Hells Angels chapter in Sorel, just outside Montreal. Almost thirty years after their birth in California, the Angels had finally set up shop north of the border.

From that first foothold in Quebec, the Angels spread across the country—slowly at first, but relentlessly. By 1984, they had one more chapter in Sherbrooke, one in Halifax and four in British Columbia. Looking back on those critical early years—and even well into the 1980s and 1990s—veteran police officers agree that authorities ignored the Hells Angels for too long, dismissing them as boozing ruffians.

"No one was targeting them from an enforcement perspective," recalls Andy Richards. Richards would become an inspector with British Columbia's Organized Crime Agency set up to take on the bikers in the late 1990s, but back in the early eighties he was a rookie cop with the Vancouver Police Department. "By the time we all collectively woke up in the early nineties, we're going, 'Holy shit, we have a problem here.'"

While the police worked on other priorities, the Hells Angels out west grew steadily stronger—and wealthier. They began by taking over three other biker clubs in British Columbia to form chapters in Vancouver, Nanaimo and White Rock on July 23, 1983; the East End chapter in Vancouver followed a few months later. By August 1986, the Hells Angels out west were rich enough to sponsor a party at Angels Acres—a seventeen-acre spread equipped with several campsites and a large swimming pool, bought by Nanaimo chapter members. Angels came from as far away as Switzerland—and from other gangs within Canada as well. The out-of-province guest list was indicative of the

Angels' strategy. They always had an eye out for corporate expansion; they preferred a takeover to a knockdown battle but were prepared for either. And they were patient. It would take more than a decade before the Angels swallowed up two of the groups at the party—Alberta's Grim Reapers and Ontario's Para-Dice Riders.

The Angels began to polish their public image, not just their bikes. They made charitable donations through Toys for Tots, even raising funds for a child who needed a liver transplant.

The easy ride the bikers seemed to be getting from the media and even the police irked Vancouver street cops such as Andy Richards. He got his start on the seedy streets of Vancouver's Downtown Eastside—not far from the Angels' East End clubhouse. "It really bothered me because we had been given the lectures by biker experts at the police academy that these guys were organized crime and involved in murders, extortions, drug trafficking—and nobody seemed to be doing anything about them," he recalls. "[The Angels] were slowly building and building and gathering strength and amassing wealth and becoming quite sophisticated. They were in my backyard and I saw them every day. It was frustrating." Richards would have to wait more than a decade for his first serious crack at taking down the Angels—and even then he would learn the hard way just how formidable a foe they were.

Meanwhile, out east, a violent Nova Scotia gang known as the Thirteenth Tribe had always enjoyed close ties to Montreal. The Thirteenth Tribe became full HA members by 1984. They took control of Halifax's cocaine trade and moved into street prostitution. One woman who fled their network after a severe beating told police the Angels were pocketing 40 percent of the girls' gross earnings.

By the mid-eighties, the RCMP estimated that "hardcore" bikers—from all the gangs—numbered about 400 in

Ontario and Quebec, another 100 in B.C. and Alberta, and 150 in the other provinces. But it was in Quebec—the Angels' home base in Canada—that they were always the strongest and the fastest growing. The Hells Angels took over yet another club called the Gitans in late 1984 and opened a new chapter in Sherbrooke. They appeared unstoppable.

But then in 1985 police fished five bloated and beaten bodies out of the St. Lawrence River. They had been wrapped in chains and weighted down with bricks. The Hells Angels from Lennoxville had invited five members from the Laval chapter over to their clubhouse on March 24, 1985—and then promptly executed them. A sixth biker was found beaten to death in a motel room two weeks later. The Lennoxville boys simply didn't like the way their Laval partners were handling the drug trade—too much of the coke was ending up in their noses instead of on the streets.

The police got a break when a biker named Yves "Apache" Trudeau—one of the few members of the Laval chapter to survive the Lennoxville massacre—turned informant. Trudeau was a paid assassin who admitted to having had a hand in no fewer than forty-three murders. In exchange for his testimony, he was convicted only of manslaughter and sentenced to eleven years. Upon release, he was given a new identity under the witness protection program. Eighteen years later, in 2004, he was arrested on ten counts of sexual assault on a minor and witness protection was dropped. Trudeau would be just the first in a long line of snitches, not always trustworthy, who would dutifully file through courtrooms to rat on their former biker pals in return for the protection of the state.

The police moved in and eventually charged twenty-one bikers—almost half of the fifty-member contingent of the Hells Angels in Quebec. The prosecution of this first major biker trial in Canada fell to two up-and-coming

Crown attorneys from Montreal—André Vincent and René Domingue. The judge was Jean-Guy Boilard, a tough magistrate with a reputation for berating lawyers. Still, the prosecutors were young and eager: here was a chance to nail the nascent Angels for good. Vincent could never have imagined that almost two decades later he would be immersed in yet another biker mega-trial battle—and that the same Judge Boilard would wreak havoc on two more high-profile biker cases.

Prosecutor René Domingue recalls that back in 1985, even with good police work and solid evidence, it was an uphill battle against the bikers. "They had better sources of income. And it all boils down to what is your budget. They were able to pay the best lawyers."

Twelve days into one of the trials, a juror confessed that the Hells Angels had offered him a bribe of $100,000 if there was an acquittal; the juror had already received $25,000. He was charged and the trial continued with only eleven jurors.

Domingue and Vincent pulled it off. It would take three years for the cases to wind their way through the courts, but the Crown lawyers secured guilty verdicts for all but one of the bikers; five of them got life sentences. The politicians were quick to declare victory; as far as they were concerned, the bikers in Quebec were all but washed up.

"It seems that police and politicians were happy with the result," says Domingue. "Being naive or not wishing to put any money in a half-decent budget to fight crime, they seemed to think that it was the end of the road for the Hells Angels."

It would not be the last time the authorities would seriously and tragically underestimate the bikers. Depleted by informers, massacres and jailings, the Hells Angels in Quebec were definitely in trouble. But their future was saved by two people—a young punk from east-end

Montreal weaning himself from drugs and a diminutive but determined street fighter from Hamilton.

Maurice Boucher and his fellow bikers learned their lesson well from the massacre that prompted the court case: if they wanted to make it with the HA, drug abuse was out of the question. "He got the message and a lot of them got the message," says André Bouchard. "It scared the shit out of them."

Boucher cleaned up his act. Booze was fine, but drugs were out. After his SS gang dissolved, he gravitated toward the Sorel chapter of the Hells Angels, and on May 1, 1987, Maurice Boucher became a full-patch member of the most powerful motorcycle club in the world. He was joined by another former SS member, Normand "Biff" Hamel.

But most of Boucher's friends at the time took a different path that would eventually set the stage for a bloody war. Salvatore Cazzetta and his brother Giovanni didn't want to be swallowed up by a huge international club where they would wield little clout. Instead, they went on to form their own motorcycle club—the rival Rock Machine. They were joined by two close pals of Mom Boucher's—a monster of a man nicknamed Paul "Sasquatch" Porter and André Sauvageau.

While the Cazzetta brothers began building their power base, Maurice Boucher was climbing up the ranks within the Angels. His singular drive and ambition were just what the Hells Angels needed. Within a few years, he would lead the powerful Nomad chapter and become the undisputed biker king in Quebec.

From the start, he displayed a flair for publicity. He was always visible, ready for the cameras at the endless series of public biker events. "He'd do it on purpose, come out of the funeral parlour, stand with ten or twelve of the guys, look right into the cameras and smile and wave," André

Bouchard says. "But he never talked. Because I'll tell you honestly, he can't put two words together."

Boucher may not have been a towering intellectual, but the high school dropout was a natural-born leader. He had two vital qualities as a manager. First, he had a shrewd sense for business. "He's very intelligent in the way he runs people," Bouchard says. "He's got a very high leadership quality. If he was straight, he'd be a great manager for any business."

Second, Boucher was also ruthless. As he would show over the ensuing years, he was willing to kill friend or foe to protect his empire. "He rules by fear. People respect him because they fear him. They don't respect him because he's respectable."

Almost all the Quebec Hells Angels surrounding Mom were cut from the same rough cloth: francophones from the tougher neighbourhoods of Montreal and small-town Quebec. They were provincial in every sense of the word: they had rarely travelled outside Quebec and thought little beyond it borders. Three of the nomads, however, wereEnglish Canadians. The most notable among them was a small man named Walter Stadnick—a Hamilton native who had a shrewd business sense and a breathtaking vision: to build a national biker empire.

TWO

The Visionary

————

"He could see this being a big business. This was a big company and he was the CEO. He saw it as a money-making, big international organization."
SGT. JOHN HARRIS, HAMILTON POLICE

He doesn't look very threatening. He is small by biker standards—160 pounds packed into a five-foot-four-inch frame. But nobody crosses Walter "Nurget" Stadnick. He earned the respect of Mafia dons in Ontario and unruly bikers across the country. His fearless reputation for cutthroat discipline and business acumen carried him to the top of the Angels heap.

Most of Mom Boucher's associates—indeed, most bikers across Canada—are by definition local. Bikers did business in one city or region, often not far from where they grew up. They rarely strayed far from their turf. But Stadnick was a true Nomad: he had roots—and fingers—in at least three provinces. He was born and lived in Hamilton, had family and friends in Winnipeg and was a top biker boss in Quebec.

And perhaps more than anyone else, Stadnick fought to build the Hells Angels into a coast-to-coast network, earning grudging admiration even from his police foes. "He took a group of individuals, he maintained very strong relations with them and he groomed them," says Rick Lobban, a detective-sergeant with the Winnipeg police who followed Stadnick's career for two decades.

"He travelled the country. He knew almost everybody," says Jean-Pierre Lévesque, the RCMP's chief biker analyst at national headquarters in Ottawa and the man who took the call from Dany Kane. "He had a country-wide vision. He knows it's good for business—the bigger the name, the better the business."

That vision started young. Wolodumyr Stadnick grew up in a lower-middle-class neighbourhood on East Sixteenth Street. In high school, he and his friends formed a gang called the Cossacks. They ran their ponytails through a hole in the top of their helmets—presumably to give themselves the look of the fearsome Cossack riders—and enjoyed tearing through the fields and open roads of the south end of the city.

But Stadnick quickly moved beyond the fun and games of the street. By 1978, he joined up with the Wild Ones, a small gang with a nonetheless ruthless reputation. Police say they did the dirty work for the Mafia and other traditional crime lords, planting explosives to terrorize bakeries and other small businesses. "It was quite a sophisticated operation," recalls Ken Robertson, a sergeant at the time who worked on the extortion bombings and who would take on Stadnick three decades later as the city's police chief.

Stadnick at first did not stand out. "He was a little short guy. He certainly wasn't the most visible member of the gang. He was just a face in the crowd," recalls John Harris, who first ran into Stadnick and the Wild Ones as a uniformed patrol officer in the late seventies. "He was almost invisible—but he did have a head on his shoulders."

Harris would become Stadnick's nemesis throughout the next decade. At six feet six inches and 270 pounds, Harris looked every inch the Hamilton Tiger Cats defensive end he once was. In 1981, he got the post as the biker specialist for the Hamilton police—not the least because of his imposing size. "I'm sure that helped. It's always nice if you're the biggest guy—at least you can intimidate somebody."

When he was only twenty-six, Stadnick took a bold initiative. A unilingual anglophone from a small town and even smaller bike gang, he and a few of his pals simply got on their bikes and drove to Montreal because that was where the Hells Angels action was in Canada.

But Stadnick learned early about the bloody rules of biker politics. A powerful gang called the Outlaws—then one of the largest biker clubs in Ontario—did not take kindly to the prospect of Stadnick and the Wild Ones cozying up to their long-time rivals, the Hells Angels. The Outlaws sent a hit squad to Montreal; they burst into a bar with guns blazing, killing one of Stadnick's friends and wounding another.

It was hardly any safer back home in Ontario. A Wild One biker was blown to pieces when he turned on the ignition of his car. Two more bikers blew themselves up making a bomb. A fourth gang member lost his leg in another explosion. The Wild Ones were effectively wiped out.

The bloodshed would have convinced many young punks to pack it in. But not Stadnick. "A lot of them are thinking, You know what, maybe I don't want to be a biker any more. But the hard-core ones, they're still thinking they want to become Hells Angels," remembers biker cop Harris. "I think Stadnick thought, 'This will never happen to me. I'm too smart for this. The ones we're losing were the careless ones.' "

Stadnick stuck it out. With his charm and bravado, he wormed his way into the most fearsome—and largely

French—circle of bikers in Quebec. By 1982, Walter "Nurget" Stadnick was a member of the Hells Angels. He partied with a handful of chosen faithful when they celebrated the Angels' fifth anniversary in Quebec at the Sorel clubhouse. The origin of his biker nickname is unclear: one police officer who has known Stadnick for years suggests it began years earlier when, as a hash dealer in high school, he always had a little "nugget" of hash on hand.

Once he became an Angel, Stadnick was almost killed by a man of God. While other bikers faced death in gangland slayings, sanctioned assassinations or police shootouts, Stadnick—always the exception—had a near-fatal run-in with a priest. It happened in September 1984 near Drummondville, Quebec. Stadnick and a procession of bikers were on their way to a party to pay tribute to their slain leader, national president Yves "The Boss" Bluteau, who had been murdered one year earlier. A priest was dashing to pay tribute to his own leader, a very much alive Pope John Paul, on his first visit to Canada. The man of the cloth went through a stop sign and ploughed into the men in leather.

The clash between heaven and hell left one biker dead. Stadnick's gas tank exploded. The heat was so intense that it melted his bike helmet. He put his hands over his head to protect his eyes and face, but the blaze cost him several fingers and scarred him with horrific burns to his arms, nose and cheeks. The priest escaped without a scratch.

When Stadnick's lawyer, Stephan Frankel, walked in to see him at Hamilton's St. Joseph's Hospital, he says Stadnick was so badly burned that he would not have recognized him if it had not been for his wife, Kathy, at his bedside. Stadnick made a long and painful recovery—but he did it with a flair and display of power that was remarkable for a young biker who by this time had only been an Angel for two years. As he lay defenceless in his hospital bed, Stadnick feared he'd be an easy target for the Outlaws.

Mario Parente, the leader of the rival gang, had recently shot up a Greyhound bus in an attempt to kill two visiting Hells from Quebec. So Stadnick came up with a bold plan.

Sgt. John Harris got the call from Stadnick's wife. He met with her and lawyer Frankel.

"We want to know if we can hire officers to protect Walter when he's here in the hospital," they said.

"Well, all you can do is ask the chief," Harris replied.

To his dismay, the chief said yes. "I didn't like it. I thought we were compromising our integrity," recalls Harris. "They said he was a citizen like anybody else. 'Yeah,' I said, 'but let's remember who he is and what he belongs to.'"

When he returned to Quebec Stadnick found a biker club without a leader or direction. Into that power vacuum stepped two unlikely allies—Stadnick himself, the Hamilton boy who was about to become a national leader, and the young thug named Maurice "Mom" Boucher who had just signed up with the Hells Angels.

At first glance, theirs was an unusual partnership. Boucher was tall and beefy; Stadnick short and unimposing. Boucher, the school dropout who spoke only French, had rarely been outside the province. Stadnick, the anglo, was more sophisticated and knew Canada. Perhaps both men recognized in each other the ruthlessness that was needed to stay on top and alive in the Hells Angels. Certainly they realized they needed each other: Boucher would give "les Hells" the power base in the Quebec drug and sex trade that they needed to expand; Stadnick would give them the vision and direction to make that expansion happen.

In 1988, Stadnick got the nod and, according to most media and police accounts, was elected national president. It was a remarkable achievement for an anglophone boy from Hamilton who only six years earlier had joined a group of largely unilingual francophones from Quebec. Doubtless he got the job in part because there simply was not a lot of choice—many of the Angels in Quebec were either dead or behind bars. "He got it by default," says Harris. "He was the last guy that had some seniority and some smarts."

Stadnick himself always denied that he held any kind of official post. "Ah, just because you get more attention than the others, all of a sudden you're named president by the media," he once complained to a police officer. Still, Hamilton police started noticing what they took as one of the perks of Stadnick's new post: a "company car," a shiny black Jaguar with Quebec plates that appeared in Stadnick's driveway every time he was in town.

If Stadnick's title as national president was accurate, it was a lot loftier on paper than in reality: the HA chapters are notoriously autonomous and bristle at taking orders from anyone. He not so much issued commands as pushed and prodded reluctant bikers to work together. As he surveyed the biker landscape across the country, Stadnick knew that the shattered Quebec Hells had to rebuild. That job would fall to Mom Boucher. He also saw that on the two coasts—Halifax and British Columbia—the young chapters were flourishing.

Stadnick realized that if the Hells Angels stood any chance of becoming a truly national empire, they had to fill the huge gap in Central Canada—and that meant Manitoba and Ontario. Manitoba because it was the axis of distribution for any drugs moving east and west in the country; Ontario because it was the Golden Horseshoe, for drugs, prostitution and all other proceeds of crime. If anyone could pull off an expansion in Ontario, it was Stadnick. Though a Quebec member of the Hells Angels, Stadnick always kept a home in Hamilton.

But Canada's richest province stubbornly resisted Stadnick's attempts to implant the Hells Angels trademark. Ontario was home to two main biker gangs—the Outlaws and the Satan's Choice. The Outlaws had no love for the

Angels or Stadnick: in the mid-1980s, some Outlaws got hold of a rocket launcher and were going to blow up a Hamilton bar run by Stadnick. Only an arrest prevented the attack. Satan's Choice, meanwhile, had aligned themselves to the Alberta Grim Reapers and the Los Brovos in Manitoba to ward off the Angels. An RCMP report concluded, "The three gangs, while totally independent, seem to have come to an informal agreement of mutual support against outside aggression."

Stadnick and other emissaries from Quebec tried courting the smaller groups such as the Loners, the Para-Dice Riders (PDRs) and Vagabonds. The Loners were not hostile but rebuffed any formal alliance. "That idea was put on ice for the moment," Dany Kane reported to his RCMP handlers. The Vagabonds held a party attended by Hells Angels representatives from across the country while several Para-Dice Riders acted as security. The PDRs were apparently evenly split on the prospect of rallying to the Angels. Half were in favour, the other half opposed, Kane reported. "When members of the Hells Angels visit them in Toronto, they are welcomed."

Walter Stadnick was a patient man, and he never gave up. In June 1993, he led a brigade of about a hundred Hells Angels and their backers as they rode across the province to Wasaga Beach, a favourite hangout of rival biker gangs. It was just for show—Stadnick was flying the Hells Angels colours, warning his rivals that he was not giving up on the riches of Ontario. "For them to go there was like saying, 'Nobody can tell us where to go. We'll go where we want and when we want.' It was like visiting royalty," says one biker cop.

It would take another seven years for Stadnick to realize his dream—and he would not be free to enjoy the fruits of his labour. But his ultimate triumph in Ontario would be more spectacular than anyone—the police, the rival bikers or even the Hells Angels themselves—could ever have imagined.

The scene in Manitoba was even more complicated than in Ontario and initially not much more welcoming to the Angels. For starters, Winnipeg had more street gangs than any other city in Canada—two thousand young people, many of them teenagers, active in more than two dozen gangs. In addition were two long-standing biker gangs that pre-dated the Angels in Canada by more than a decade: the Spartans and Los Brovos had both been around since 1967. They were traditional bikers, who liked to party and ride. Sure, they frequently crossed the line of legality but with none of the full-time seriousness and sophisticated organization of the Hells Angels.

Rick Lobban, a cop who knows the Winnipeg bikers better than anyone, keeps his grey hair trim and neat today, but back then it was dark and almost shoulder length. He still sports a large tattoo on his left shoulder and speeds into the police parking lot on a motorcycle—a Japanese model, he takes pains to point out, not a Harley. Lobban joined the Winnipeg police force in 1975 when he was seventeen, made detective seven years later—and as quickly as possible went into the vice division. "Uniform never had an appeal for me," he says. "I wanted the freedom to operate."

In 1985, Lobban found himself back in uniform for a while—the Winnipeg police force has a strict policy of rotating officers—and he met up with a twenty-seven-year-old rookie named Ray Parry who had just joined the force the previous year. "Rick got me started with bikers," Parry explains. "He had an interest in it, and I caught the bug."

Uniformed cops out on patrol would often try to avoid the bikers, leaving them to the guys in Vice. But not Lobban and Parry. Lobban wanted to flash his colours to the bikers in black. So every Wednesday night he and Parry would stop by the Grant Hotel in the city's south end, where the Los Brovos gathered for a regular club night. Nothing fancy, just what the police call a bar walkthrough—letting them know that this was their turf too. But never pushing it. "You deal with them fairly and you don't jerk their chains," Lobban says. "You never make it personal."

Lobban knew Winnipeg was too central to a drug distribution network for the Hells Angels to ignore for long. Marijuana is grown in Canada, mainly on the West Coast, and there is plenty of pot easily available in the East as well. Cocaine, however, comes in mainly by sea or by air, to the main ports of Halifax, Montreal and Vancouver. After that, it moves by road—and if you want to move any drugs between Ontario and B.C., you have to go through Winnipeg. It's the drug gateway to the East and the West.

"It's the chokepoint," says Lobban. "We knew the Hells Angels were going to come. It was only a matter of time. Not today, not tomorrow, maybe not next year and years after, but it was going to come."

It came with Walter Stadnick. He was a constant visitor to Winnipeg in the 1990s. He had a girlfriend in town named Tiffany; together they had a son named Damon—Nomad spelled backwards. Stadnick was busy cajoling, courting and cracking down on squabbling bikers.

The Manitoba bikers had a love-hate relationship with the HA. On the one hand, both the Spartans and Los Brovos exhibited a Central Canadian pride, jealously guarding their territory from what they saw as Eastern interlopers. On the other hand, the power and prestige of the Angels held a certain appeal.

"There's always a big resistance [to the HA] and it's always been like that," explains Ernie Dew, a veteran rider with Los Brovos. "We were the top. We held that for years. It was pride more than anything."

Dew grew up on a farm in Snowflake, Manitoba. He left home at thirteen and recalls fondly saving up for his first bike back then—a Keystone minibike—by working at a cannery for $1.75 an hour. In between run-ins with the law, Dew moved up to bigger bikes—a Honda, then a Suzuki and, finally, his first Harley, a 1982 FXR.

He was twenty-two, and he admits his love affair with the biker life cost him his first marriage. "My wife said, 'You got a choice: me or the club.'"

Dew didn't hesitate. "See you later!" he told her.

Dew signed up with Los Brovos in the mid-eighties and never looked back. "The camaraderie is the big thing, the brotherhood, the riding with the guys."

Still, even for a proud Manitoban like Dew, the prospect of joining an international organization like the Hells Angels was enticing: "That is *the* club," he says. "You've gone from the farm team to the major leagues."

And Dew—all six feet four inches of him—was impressed by the diminutive emissary from back east. Though a foot shorter than Dew, Stadnick still loomed large in the eyes of the Winnipeg biker. "He's stayed here many times," Dew recalls. "I always sat down and talked to Walter when he came by the clubhouse. He's a very easy man to talk to. Walter is a very well respected man, a very knowledgeable man."

Stadnick was trying to encourage the Manitoba bikers to unite, or at least stop fighting. But Dew and his fellow Brovos riders never liked or trusted their rivals, the Spartans. In 1984, the two clans merged briefly—boosting their ranks to an impressive 130 members. "But the two groups never blended together," says Lobban.

Some ex-Spartans, disgruntled with being swallowed up by Los Brovos, formed a secret gang called the Silent Riders. Their leader was a thick-bearded thug named Darwin Sylvester. He'd met with the Montreal Hells Angels as far back as 1980 and again in 1983. Now his Riders once more made overtures to the Hells Angels, even travelling to B.C. to visit chapters there. But the courtship was short-lived. The Brovos leaders distrusted the insurgent group in their ranks, and after a brief war the Silent Riders were forced to burn their colours and disband.

Not for long. When Darwin Sylvester emerged from prison in 1990, after serving time on drugs and weapons charges, he took the bold step of reforming the Spartans. He would directly take on Los Brovos—while both groups were also trying to curry favour with the Hells Angels.

For some time, it was not clear whom the Angels would choose as their partners—the Spartans or Los Brovos. Walter Stadnick was right in the thick of things, making frequent trips to Winnipeg and trying to spot the best talent in the warring factions. "By his presence, prior to any official biker involvement with the Hells Angels, he had a big influence," says Ray Parry. "He built up a personal network of associates."

The Spartans seemed to pull further ahead in the war when Los Brovos suffered heavy casualties in September 1993. In the biggest drug seizure in the city's history, police nabbed coke and heroin worth $18 million, raided seventy homes, including the Brovos clubhouse, and arrested sixteen people on numerous drug and money-laundering charges. But the much-ballyhooed bust of the decade was a classic case of short-term publicity for the police and politicians with no real long-term gain—a pattern the authorities would all too often repeat across the country. In the end, it would be three of the sixteen people arrested in the September sweep—and not any of the Spartans—who would go on to form the first Hells Angels chapter in the province.

While the police were busy congratulating themselves for busting the Brovos, Walter Stadnick was busy building his power base. In 1995, Stadnick—ever the control freak—helped set up a third gang, the Redliners. Made up mainly of Spartans dismayed at the erratic leadership of Darwin Sylvester, the Redliners were supposed to become a puppet club of the Rockers, itself a puppet club of the Quebec Nomads. That triple layering—insulating the Hells leaders from the dirty business on the street—was central to the success of Stadnick, Boucher and the other biker bosses. Control the action, take little of the risk.

"The Redliners were his attempt to create a group and give it a pedigree that could become a Hells chapter," says Lobban. And initially it looked as though it could work.

The new protégés began by setting up a clubhouse at 929 Notre Dame that was a tribute to Angel architecture. "It was a showcase," says Parry. "It was the first time we saw them building a clubhouse with the bunker mentality."

Stadnick's Redliners painted their new digs black and grey, the colours of their erstwhile model, the Rockers. They installed electromagnetic doors, a backup power generator and an elaborate camera system. For fortifications, they used cinder blocks, armour plating and sand.

Parry recalls Stadnick's frequent visits to Winnipeg to groom his protégés. He was exacting in his attention to detail, even down to the length of hair. "They were the most polished," says the biker cop. "They were very well groomed. Their hair was well trimmed. . . . The way they conducted themselves was a carbon copy of the Hells Angels' thinking at the time and completely foreign to the way things had operated in the West."

According to Dany Kane's reports that eventually made their way into official court records, Stadnick travelled to Manitoba in April 1995 "in order to establish a corridor for drug sales from Thunder Bay, Ontario, to Winnipeg." Within a year the Angels had the delivery service down to a science. As Kane told his handlers, here's how a delivery transpired on a weekend in mid-April 1996: A courier boarded a train from Montreal with three kilos of coke for Winnipeg (and another 3.5 kilos for Toronto, to be delivered during a stopover on his return trip). He arrived in Winnipeg with a booklet of nine business cards for local hotels, each numbered one to nine. Place Louis Riel is Number 1, the Sheraton is Number 2, the Windsor Park Inn is Number 3 and so on. He chose a hotel, checked in and then dialled a pager number given to him in advance: 204-931-1695. He then punched in the number assigned to the hotel and his room number. It was a code only someone with the list of numbered hotels could understand. Shortly afterwards, a man showed up at his door and picked up a package. "The guy who comes to pick up the coke is just another courier for Stadnick," Kane said. "None of the couriers in this operation knows each other and they don't ask questions." The courier from Montreal then moved on to the next hotel and repeated the cycle.

Good business, though, needs stability, and bikers are notoriously unstable and violent. Stadnick worked hard to keep a handle on the rivalries between the Redliners, the Spartans and the Los Brovos, who were emerging as the most powerful. "That battle went on for years," recalls Brovos veteran Ernie Dew. "There were shootings that went on then, stabbings that went on then [and] bombings." In 1996, three bikers associated with Los Brovos murdered three Redliners in a dispute over drugs and prostitutes. The executions were particularly brutal, even by biker standards: multiple stab wounds, eyes gouged, bodies mutilated.

"Stadnick had to help settle things down," Parry says. "He needed to broker a peace between them because it was bad for business."

In 1997, the Spartans stumbled badly, when in September two members and two supporters gang-raped a teenage girl at their clubhouse. It would hardly do for an aspiring HA chapter in Winnipeg to be tarred with that PR disaster; the rape seemed to put them out of the running. A sure sign that Los Brovos were now the anointed ones came on the weekend of October 18, 1997, with a grand celebration of their thirtieth anniversary. Walter Stadnick arrived on the Tuesday before the big event, and large numbers of Hells Angels from the West and East began to file into town.

The Brovos had taken over a former Filipino church in the Elmwood area of town for their clubhouse. They boarded up the bottom windows, prepared steel plating for the arched windows on top, installed security cameras. They transformed the altar into a more appropriate symbol of biker worship—a bar.

The bikers also turned their weekend celebrations into a neighbourhood bash—and a big PR coup. It was a sign that the Angels across the country were learning that winning the hearts of the public was as important as winning the drug battles on the streets. "Biker kindness" ran one obliging headline in the *Winnipeg Free Press*. One enterprising vendor set up a hot-dog stand—and offered specials for the bikers. "The bikers bought all the kids in the neighbourhood hot dogs," she said.

Older residents seemed equally delighted with their new biker neighbours. "It's the best security I've had here in thirty-three years," an elderly man said. "I know I won't be broken into as long as they are here."

By weekend's end, it was official: two dozen full-fledged Brovos and nine associates entered into a probationary period; they would have to prove their worth to Stadnick and the Angels.

How quickly things had changed in the world of biker politics. Just a few years earlier, Los Brovos had linked up with the Grim Reapers in Alberta and Satan's Choice in

Ontario to try to ward off the Hells Angels. By July 1997, the Angels had swallowed up the Reapers in Alberta and were courting the Choice in Ontario. In Manitoba, Ernie Dew and the boys were now listening carefully to the pitch from the Hells Angels.

"They had already flipped the [Alberta] Grim Reapers," Dew recalls. "So they come to us: 'Come on, guys, jump on the bandwagon. Flip it over, guys, flip it over.' So we had a big powwow and flipped over [to the HA]."

Biker cop Lobban put it less prosaically: "At one stage you either get on the bus or you get run over by the bus."

With Los Brovos on the bus, there was no need for the Redliners. Within a few months, the Redliners had folded, but one Redliner, Stadnick's star disciple—Bernie Dubois, who ran a successful auto scrapyard north of the city—survived. By the spring, the police spotted Bernie riding with Los Brovos. The cream of the bikers, former enemies, were uniting under the HA emblem. The best and the brightest were on their way to becoming full-fledged Angels. The Redliners would soon be replaced by a far more dangerous and violent puppet group—the Zig Zags—that would terrorize Winnipeg's streets. And still, the politicians and police leaders did little.

"When the Hells Angels were coming into Manitoba, there didn't seem to be a recognition that we have to rejig the justice system," complains Gord Mackintosh, at the time justice critic for the opposition NDP. "I remember raising the issue of organized crime and street gangs in the legislature in the mid-nineties and being laughed at by one of the ministers of the day."

But no one would laugh when the firebombs started exploding and drive-by shootings terrorized citizens in the years to come—when Mackintosh would find himself in the hot seat of power.

Stadnick's successes in the streets of Winnipeg were matched by an uncanny ability to avoid major criminal convictions. In his early days, petty crimes and short jail terms typified his rap sheet. His first breach came at age 18 when he was sentenced to four months in jail for trafficking in LSD. Two years later he served seven days for willful damage to property. He managed to stay out of prison for the next five years until 1978 when he joined the Wild Ones and promptly got nailed for carrying a concealed weapon—a pistol—for which he got eight months. But from then on, despite his dominant role over the next two decades in building a massive criminal empire, he demonstrated a remarkable gift for staying out of prison.

On June 16, 1992, the RCMP arrested Stadnick at the Winnipeg airport with more than $81,000 in cash. He was charged under the Narcotics Control Act with possession of the proceeds of crime—in other words, carrying drug money. Nabbing someone with a lot of cash is one thing. Proving it came from crime is a lot harder.

In the meantime, Stadnick got into a tussle with two off-duty Winnipeg police officers. In August, Stadnick and a close biker pal of his, Donald Magnussen, were partying at the Rolling Stone cabaret with some Spartans and Brovos and a couple of call girls. According to witnesses, the officers taunted the bikers but were ejected by bouncers. Once outside, one of the cops pushed tensions over the edge by straddling one of the bikers' wheels. In the ensuing melee, the policeman got the worst of it, ending up in hospital with facial cuts and bruises. Stadnick and Magnussen were arrested, but an embarrassed Crown attorney eventually dropped the charges.

Stadnick's proceeds of crime trial was set to start October 4, 1993, but got sidetracked when the *Winnipeg Sun* ran a story detailing Stadnick's career as a biker leader. Stadnick's lawyer immediately filed for a stay of proceedings, arguing that the story jeopardized his client's right to a fair trial, and tried to get Melanie Verhaeghe, the young crime reporter who wrote the story, to reveal her sources. Outside the court, she discovered Magnussen was tailing her. "Every time I turned around there was a long-blond-haired man in a black Jeep," she says. "I was pretty scared." After the trial, Verhaeghe says Stadnick's lawyer came up to her and boasted, "Have I got a file on you." Apparently, a private investigator had also been hired to follow the journalist around, capturing her movements on video.

In the end, the judge rejected Stadnick's motion to stay the proceedings. But fifteen months later the federal Crown attorney dropped the charges anyway, usually a sign the government lacks evidence. "Mr. Stadnick is pleased there was no conviction," his lawyer said. He would not say what his client had been doing with that much cash.

The police had as much trouble tying drugs to Stadnick as they did cash. Back in his native province of Ontario, they arrested him at the home of the former president of Satan's Choice, Douglas Freeborn, and charged him with possession of 330 grams of hashish for the purpose of trafficking. Freeborn insisted the drugs were his, and Stadnick chalked up another victory against the cops. On another occasion the police were keeping watch on a trailer home that Stadnick kept in a suburb outside Hamilton. A man cutting the grass came upon some Tupperware containers filled with pills: they turned out to be speed. The police sat on the discovery, hoping to catch Stadnick retrieving the stash. He never showed, and the cops had to settle for simply trashing the drugs.

"He's been pretty good at eluding prosecution," says Don Bell of Ontario's Biker Enforcement Unit. "Everyone knew who he was and what he was about, but he was good at what he did. He was good at isolating himself. He worked in the depths of criminal activity and kept himself one step away, which made it very difficult to collect the necessary evidence and charge him.

"To a biker investigator, he sort of epitomized—I hate to say this—the professionalism of the Hells Angels and the way they did business."

If anything, Stadnick was cocky enough to reverse the tables—and charge the police. One day Hamilton police sergeant John Harris got a call at the office.

"I need to speak to Sergeant Harris," the man on the other end said.

"That's me," the officer said.

"This is Walter Stadnick calling."

"Are you sure?" said the skeptical cop. Harris thought someone was pulling his leg.

"Yes, it's Walter Stadnick. Of course it's Walter Stadnick!" the Hells Angel leader insisted, clearly upset at not being believed.

Harris offered to meet Stadnick for a chat. The biker refused; he hated talking to cops, much less being seen with them.

"I want to complain," he said. "My property is damaged. My belt buckle is broken."

Stadnick owned a solid gold belt buckle with an Angels logo—an enormously gaudy piece weighing about one pound. Stadnick insisted the buckle had been broken during an arrest. Harris said he knew nothing about it. The Hells Angel leader sued Harris and the arresting officers for $500 for repairs and for the mental anguish he'd suffered.

The case went to small claims court. Stadnick lost, but his lawyer, Stephan Frankel, says the biker walked away with a moral victory: "I think there was some pleasure at having all those involved in court for the day to answer for what they had done," he says. "There was a principle behind what took place there: 'Let's set the record straight: you can't just push me around because you want to push me around.' "

Stadnick was not going to let anyone push him, or the Hells Angels, around. Having laid down solid roots for the organization in Manitoba, he was on his way to turning the Hells Angels into the national empire he had envisaged.

But one thing was still missing—a solid base in Ontario. He would not give up hope of making a breakthrough—and he made one fatal error.

As he had in Winnipeg with the Redliners, Stadnick and other Quebec Angels decided to set up a puppet group in Ontario. It was a good way to wave the Angels flag in the faces of rivals like the Outlaws who for too long had dominated the province's biker world without a serious challenge.

It was 1993, and the new gang was called the Demon Keepers. As president of the ill-fated club, the Quebec Hells Angels chose a smart, promising biker coming through their ranks: Dany Kane. Perhaps Stadnick saw a bit of himself in the eager Kane, still in his twenties. Perhaps he felt some kinship with the quiet, more reflective biker from a small town.

Whatever the reason for choosing Kane, it was a gamble. You never knew whom you could trust in the dark, dangerous world of bikers. Stadnick trusted Kane. It was the worst mistake of his life.

THREE

Raising Kane

———

"Dany Kane had a James Bond side to him, a sense of adventure."
DET. SGT. BENOIT ROBERGE, MONTREAL POLICE

"Our objective was that he would become an agent and
incriminate the entire Nomad chapter, the hard core."
SGT. GAETAN ST. ONGE, RCMP

About twenty miles due south of Montreal lies the tiny
rural village of L'Acadie, well off almost anybody's beaten
track. Nine times out of ten, if you wind up there you're
lost. Like so many Quebec villages, its only landmark is a
tall grey-stone Catholic church, built in 1802. Its imposing
spire can be seen for quite some distance over the surrounding flat, fertile plain of vegetable and dairy farms. In
winter, it's a windswept, snowbound hamlet. In summer,
it's hot and muggy, with a few old maple trees for shade.
There's a grade school, a grocery store and a post office.

And on the edge of the village there's a small bungalow
with eggshell aluminum siding. That's where Dany Kane
grew up. Not in the gritty neighbourhoods of Hamilton like
Walter Stadnick or the tough streets of east-end Montreal
like Mom Boucher but in the bucolic countryside along the
narrow banks of L'Acadie River, among centuries-old
Breton farmhouses and barns. Still, his background helped
launch him on his own private road to Hell.

Kane, born in October 1968, was the son of Jean-Paul Kane and Gemma Brideau. His father worked as a bricklayer, and his mother, a small Acadian woman from New Brunswick, stayed home to take care of Dany and his two sisters. There was never a lot of money around, and his mother was often ill. So, while his sisters stayed home, Dany was sent to live with a childless uncle in a nearby town. Gemma Kane says Dany came home for weekends and holidays. But being the only child to be sent away must have had a powerful impact, ingraining in the young boy almost from the start the feeling of being a loner.

Weekends and during the summer he was usually seen helping his father. Dany and his father were almost inseparable, recalls Germain Godin, who owned the grocery store and now runs a greenhouse outside town. The skinny little boy was always eagerly playing helper to his dad. When he wasn't with his father, Dany would help out at Godin's store to earn pocket money. "He was always very polite, a good employee," Godin says. "He was easy to deal with. It was a good family."

There wasn't much else to do in the isolated hamlet of L'Acadie. Dany was a restless student who couldn't sit still in the confined space of a country classroom. So at sixteen, he left and took whatever work came his way. He became friends with a neighbour of his parents' named Robert Guimard, who introduced him to motorcycles. Before long, he'd discovered the biker fraternity and the sleazy strip-club life that circulates in the small towns around Montreal and is run by the bikers.

He committed his first crime, a break and enter, at seventeen and then began working for a biker named Patrick Lambert who belonged to a small gang in St-Hubert, just south of Montreal, called the Condors. By age eighteen, Kane had joined the Condors and was almost immediately convicted again of breaking and entering and fined $250.

It was hardly hard-core crime, but it gave him a pedigree and kick-started his biker career. Kane worked six months for Lambert, earning about $700 a week making sure his dealers were well stocked. When the Condors merged with a Hells Angels satellite club called the Evil Ones to control the south shore of Montreal, Kane resented having to prove himself all over again to a new set of bikers. He decided to leave the club and develop his own business selling drugs, contraband cigarettes and guns. He carved out territory in six bars located in small towns south of L'Acadie, close to the U.S. border. He also had regular clients who sent their orders through his pager, and he would deliver directly to their homes.

From 1990 to 1992, he was earning about $3,000 a week clear from the drug trade. He also sold between thirty and fifty machine guns, handguns and silencers, earning another $300 to $400 on each sale. And he taught himself how to make bombs. At one point, he bought ten pounds of C4 plastique explosives for $5,000 and practised blowing up tree stumps in the countryside. But, he later told police, it was "never to blow up anybody or anything." Except maybe the odd bar. He used dynamite to blow up the Bar Delphis in La Prairie, near Montreal. He quickly graduated to more violent crimes to maintain his drug network. He beat up three people who hadn't paid their drug debts, putting his pistol in one man's mouth and threatening to blow his head off. Then in September 1992, he and three henchmen took two men who had stolen some guns from Kane to a sandpit and beat them almost to death with a pistol. During the beating, Kane's gun accidentally went off and wounded one victim in the head. Kane was arrested and pleaded guilty to conspiracy to murder, kidnapping, assault, illegal use of a firearm and possession of a gun with the serial numbers filed off. After serving only ten months of a twenty-five-month sentence and five months in a transition home, he was back on the street by January 1994, with his status as a standup guy greatly enhanced.

Kane, by his own choice, had remained outside the biker fraternity. He soon realized that his power had diminished and his former biker friends had frozen him out. His business languished. Kane was too proud to return to the Evil Ones. It would have been an admission of defeat. So he decided to bypass his former gang members and go straight to the top—to the Angels.

He approached two English-speaking Hells who were to become his main handlers: Walter Stadnick and David "Wolf" Carroll. Carroll came from Halifax, where he controlled the East Coast Hells. He was also, like Stadnick, a senior member of the Hells Angels' Montreal chapter, which controlled the Evil Ones. Kane hoped they would be his entree into the world's most powerful outlaw motorcycle gang. Both men already knew and trusted Kane. He had an engaging, likeable personality. He also had poise. He didn't bitch and whine like many bikers. He didn't drink or take drugs. His only weakness was sex. He regularly bragged about the length of his dick and his prowess with women. Bikers could respect that. What Kane didn't brag about was that he was bisexual. In fact, he kept it a secret. Bikers generally don't like gays. But most of all, Kane was smart and reliable. You asked him to do something and it was done. What's more, he kept his mouth shut.

Working for the Hells was no picnic. Kane found himself on call twenty-four hours a day, seven days a week. It was slave labour. Delivering drugs, guns, women. Chauffeuring Carroll and Stadnick. Playing bodyguard at biker parties. And even picking up the tab. Hells Angels tend not to pay their own way. They have guys like Kane to do that. After more than a year had passed, Kane was growing restless and annoyed that neither Carroll nor

Stadnick had made any move to invite him into the gang. He had once run his own show, calling all the shots. Now he was little more than an underling and glorified gofer.

In the Hells Angels organization, recruits usually start in a satellite club. If they perform well, they graduate to become a hangaround. Although they can't wear an HA patch, they are considered part of the club. The next step up is a prospect. They get a half patch that shows which chapter they belong to. And if they make the grade, they become full-patch Angels and get to wear the winged Death Head emblem. Climbing the ladder can take years. But it's a complicated process that depends largely on what you can bring to the table and whether or not there's an opening. If you're more valuable as an underling, you'll stay that way. If you're not a good earner, you'll also be kept in the lower ranks. And if you don't have a sponsor—some Hells Angel who will go to bat for you—forget it. Most underlings either quit or end up dead or in jail. Only a fraction ever make it to the big leagues.

Kane had worked several years for these guys, and he wasn't even a hangaround yet. His fortunes changed, however, when in 1993 Stadnick and Carroll asked him to set up three chapters of a satellite gang in Cornwall, Ottawa and Toronto. They would be called the Demon Keepers, and Kane would run the show. It would be the beginning of the Hells' move into Ontario, Canada's most lucrative drug market, and Kane would be the spearhead. His first assignment was to carve out territory around Toronto and go to war against the rival Outlaws. Suddenly things were looking up for Dany. Or so he thought.

Kane's Demon Keepers paraded their colours through the streets of small towns like Belleville and tried to intimidate local bikers into allying with the Angels. "While we were there, we put together several murder plots to eliminate the Outlaws," Kane said seven years later in his handwritten confession to police. "We slapped surveillance on them and the bars they frequented," says Det. Sgt. Benoit Roberge, the Montreal police detective who later worked with Kane. "To conquer territory, they wanted to create an impact by killing some Outlaws."

Kane soon found himself alone with what he later described as a bunch of "no-talent imbeciles" who didn't show a lot of respect for their skinny little patchless leader. He wasn't getting any help from Carroll, whose heavy drinking often put him out of commission. As for Stadnick, he was occupied with trying to persuade the Para-Dice Riders and Satan's Choice of Toronto and southern Ontario to become allies of the Hells Angels. This made Kane wonder if the wily Stadnick wasn't using him. Let the police concentrate on Kane and his gang who were trying to take on the tough Outlaws while Stadnick worked to convert the more sympathetic biker gangs of Ontario.

Yet Kane soldiered on without complaint until April Fool's Day in 1994, when, before they could carry out any of their murder plots, the Demon Keepers got a nasty surprise. From the start, the Demon operation was bedevilled by mishaps. The Quebec police had tipped off the Ontario Provincial Police that the Angels were up to something. As Dany Kane and his conspirators pulled into a parking lot in Belleville, not far from Kingston, the police were waiting. Kane had two loaded revolvers in his car and was the only one charged. That the leader gets nailed while his minions walk free wasn't supposed to happen, and Kane found it humiliating. He pleaded guilty to illegal possession of a firearm and possession of the proceeds of crime and got four months in jail. Stadnick immediately shut down the Demon Keepers and severed all ties with most of its members.

When Kane left prison that summer, he found himself without a job or any prospects inside the biker community, but he was still a resourceful guy. He offered his services to Scott Steinert, an ambitious Hells Angels Montreal prospect who Kane thought had star quality. "Steinert started off low, but he gained a lot of power as he got heavily involved in the biker war," explains Roberge. Kane also knew Steinert had powerful backing. His sponsor was Robert "Tiny" Richard, considered, according to Kane, the most feared and respected Angel in Canada at that time. He was also the gang's national president, taking over the post from Stadnick in 1994. (Like many others' nicknames, Tiny's was a joke; at six feet and well over two hundred pounds, he was anything but. He died of a heart attack in 1996.) Kane figured Steinert would become a full-patch Hells Angel within a year and then would clear the way for Kane.

There was one glitch. Wolf Carroll had other plans. He told Kane to return to his old clubmates by joining the Evil Ones. For Kane, that was a major step backwards and another humiliation. Kane suddenly found himself sandwiched between Steinert and Carroll, two violent bikers who he knew disliked each other. As far as Kane was concerned, Carroll was going nowhere. He considered him "a very bad businessman" and a lousy administrator. "Wolf makes a lot of money but can't keep it," Kane said. At one point, Wolf even had to borrow money from the club to buy a car.

Steinert, on the other hand, was bold, aggressive and had big plans for the future. He wanted Kane to go to Kingston, Ontario, and start another club. He planned to make his own move into Ontario as soon as he got his full patch. Even though Steinert was still only a prospect, Kane decided he was his ticket, but he kept the lines open with Carroll. Riding the power plays within the Hells Angels is like trying to master the twisting schemes of ambitious— and sometimes psychotic—medieval princes. A wrong move could get you killed.

"I like that—working for two guys," Kane later told one of his police handlers. "Working for two Hells, that allows me to skate between both of them." That way, he explained, he could keep away from tasks he didn't like or considered too dangerous.

Yet Kane's manoeuvring had deeper motives. He was developing a serious dislike for the Hells Angels, believing they had used him for years without giving anything in return. He thought they had shown him contempt. He could take a lot of abuse but not that. When he left prison and found himself frozen out yet again, he decided it was payback time. Make the Hells never forget Dany Kane. "He told us he wanted revenge," one of his police handlers said. Ever since his parents sent him away to live with his uncle, he had learned to hide his bitter feelings of rejection and just get along. As he would later admit, it gave him a thrill to have secret feelings, to harbour plans nobody else knew about. It empowered him in the same way it empowered him to ride a motorcycle with gang colours stitched to his leather jacket. The road opened up. Dany liked that.

Now he wanted to move even further into the shadows. He had methodically planned his approach. He could have called police right after he got out of prison, but he needed to lay the groundwork. He needed to better position himself first, show the cops he was well connected within the Hells Angels and had a career advancement plan. This would allow him to bring more to the table when he finally made the call. Make him sound intelligent and analytical, as if he had everything figured out and wasn't just some dumb, desperate biker trying to get back at somebody. It would also increase his value and get him a good contract.

That was important. Kane always needed money. He had a wife and three kids to look after. As he later told police, he wanted to establish a long-term relationship that paid in cash. He wanted to make sure that within two or three years he'd be at the top of the Hells Angels. Wouldn't that be a treat! The top guy in the Hells Angels' Montreal chapter, the most powerful outlaw gang in Canada, a police informer. Now, after months of manoeuvring, he felt ready.

It may have helped that Kane, the solitary boy from L'Acadie, was cut from a different cloth than most Quebec bikers. He didn't come from a family steeped in crime. Roberge says, "In that milieu, maybe Kane didn't have the criminal roots to say, 'Me, I'll never talk to the cops.' Because for many bikers, it's almost like a religion, it's so strong." What Kane did have was "a James Bond side to him, a sense of adventure."

On October 17, 1994, at 2 p.m.—six months after his arrest in the Belleville parking lot—Kane placed the call that led him into the arms of Jean-Pierre Lévesque and Pierre Verdon of the RCMP.

After four meetings in Montreal hotel rooms with the RCMP's new star informant, Lévesque had to bow out. He was too busy in Ottawa as a national coordinator and was not supposed to work full time running informants. So Verdon's boss, Gaetan St. Onge, a small bulldog of a man nicknamed "Fonzie" because of his pompadour hairstyle, took over. For the next three years, he and Verdon would handle Dany Kane.

Kane and his Mountie handlers never looked back. From then on, Kane either phoned or met with them once, twice, sometimes three times a week. In November, they had ten meetings. In December, nine. In January, eighteen. The money quickly increased from $500 to $1,000 a week. By April 1995, the RCMP were paying Kane $2,000 a week. He kept them informed about what the top bikers in his circle were up to: where they were travelling; whom they were talking to; who had murdered whom and who was next; the

Hells' war plans against their Quebec rivals, the Rock Machine; their expansion plans into Ontario and Manitoba; and weapons and explosives purchases. Each week, the RCMP got a detailed record of events inside the Hells Angels and their satellite gangs. Verdon would record it all in 842 pages of mostly handwritten intelligence reports.

Kane's association with both Steinert and Carroll (and via Carroll to Stadnick) gave him access to three of the most brutal and ambitious Hells Angels in Canada. By December 1994, Kane had told Corporal Verdon and Sergeant St. Onge about murder plots and illicit business dealings, bombings and expansion plans, and the Hells' business connections with top members of the Italian Mafia. For the first time, police had a glimpse into the real power structure of the Angels.

"Biff Hamel, another HA Montreal member, is the main associate of 'Mom' Boucher," Verdon wrote in his November 14, 1994, report. "These two have very good relations with the top level of the Italians and are considered the richest members of the HA Montreal." Kane listed the bars they controlled in Montreal, the Laurentians and Sorel. He told them what bars they were strong-arming their way into in Ottawa and the Gatineaux. He talked about the Quebec Angels' trips to Toronto to try to negotiate alliances with local clubs there. He delivered phone numbers and pager numbers of the bikers so police could begin tapping phones. In telephone calls on secure lines and during meetings in hotel rooms at the Ramada Inn in Longueuil, just south of Montreal, Kane unravelled the mysteries of the bikers, and in return Verdon would hand him $500 a week in crisp $100 bills.

Kane returned from the Hells' annual party in Sherbrooke on December 4, 1994, with a basketful of diverse information about who did or did not attend and who was inducted into the gang. It was a special event for

Walter Stadnick, Kane told his handlers, who had marked his tenth anniversary as an Angel by getting a gold Hells Angels belt buckle (the same one he would later sue police for damaging). Kane recounted biker gossip and described drug deals. An excited Verdon could not resist making a jab at his clueless counterparts in the Sûreté du Québec: "They didn't get half the information that we got on the 'party' in Sherbrooke, and they were covering the event," he wrote in his report. "Because of our source, the total cost of our coverage was only $250."

The most ominous news from Kane, however, was the Hells Angels' plan to form an elite group based in Montreal called the Nomads. Traditionally, the bikers had set up their clubhouses outside the major urban centres—in part because they knew the rural cops of the SQ were a lot easier to fool than the large municipal forces in the big cities. HA bunkers dotted the countryside like medieval fortresses. In Sherbrooke, the large red-and-white building crowned with a death's head weather vane and surrounded by a tall chain-link fence sat on a hillside overlooking the St. François River valley. Across the river from Quebec City in the bedroom suburb of St-Nicolas, the Hells bunker was equipped with steel-plated doors, security cameras and cement barriers. Trois-Rivières had its chapter; and the nearest clubs to Montreal were in Sorel and St-Basile-le-Grand.

These five once-autonomous outlaw clubs soon found themselves paying homage to the elite Nomads, who controlled the flow of drugs throughout the province. The Nomads also represented the dominance of Montreal as the centre of Hells power. Having conquered the countryside, the Hells were vanquishing the city. It was such a historic shift in the biker war that it's worth quoting Verdon's report at length:

> The HA Mtl. are going to split in two to form the Nomads. . . . They'll have about a dozen members and will control all of Quebec as their territory. They'll put pressure on clubs that aren't doing a good job selling drugs. Only a few Hells know about this. C-2994 learned about it because he was around when it was discussed. The Hells want to change the biker mentality because the day is approaching when they will be declared a criminal organization and they want a unit to remain united.

The Nomad leader would be Maurice "Mom" Boucher. Membership would include Scott Steinert, David "Wolf" Carroll, Walter "Nurget" Stadnick, Donald "Pup" Stockford, Gilles "Trooper" Mathieu, Normand "Biff" Hamel, Louis "Melou" Roy and maybe a few others added later.

Mom would set up headquarters in an ugly, three-storey grey building on Bennett Street, topped with three satellite dishes, surrounded by floodlights and guarded by a German shepherd. In the shadow of the Olympic Stadium, Boucher's new bunker was across from a daycare centre and just down the street from police station 23. Right near the cop shop was the Pro-Gym, the favourite hangout for Mom and the boys.

These were the streets of Hochelaga-Maisonneuve where Boucher had wandered as a kid and a drugged-up teenager. Except now he was king and he owned the streets.

The Nomads would be, as they said in the finest Quebec French, *plus rock 'n' roll* than any other chapter—meaning they would be dangerous even by biker standards. Thanks to Kane, the RCMP was the first to know about them—two months before they started wearing their Nomad patches in February 1995, which gave Verdon and St. Onge time to plan Kane's infiltration into this elite group.

They knew Mom Boucher was doing more than just restructuring for business. This was war. Kane warned his handlers that the Hells Angels intended to crank up its battle with the Rock Machine, which was led by some of Boucher's former SS gang friends, now his deadly foes. With bombs going off around Montreal almost weekly, the biggest and most immediate payback was Kane's information on the bomb makers. Until Kane came along, police had no idea who within the biker gangs was responsible. The RCMP were eager to get their hands on any information about the source of explosives, about where they were being stored, who was making the bombs and planting them. Kane came through on all counts.

He told them that Steinert led a team of bomb makers and had purchased twenty pounds of C4 plastique explosives. Among the members of his crew was Kane's old pal Patrick Lambert. Kane said Lambert had twenty-four remote control "boxes" rigged up to trigger bombs. He told them Lambert purchased the remote control devices from toy stores around Montreal. Kane also claimed Lambert had detonators in his apartment at 2289 Hochelaga Street in east-end Montreal. Trouble was, he claimed not to know the apartment number. It was the first sign that Kane would not be entirely forthcoming. He would lead the RCMP only so far and then stop. Later Kane's hesitancy would become a major problem—in fact, a deadly one. But for the time being, Verdon and St. Onge were simply glad they were getting leads. They were reluctant to push him. They expected Kane would be careful about exposing himself, and the last thing St. Onge and Verdon wanted now was to blow a source as rich as Kane.

Then on December 2, 1994, Kane disclosed that Steinert and two of his crew had installed "two to eight bombs in

Montreal." He said each bomb had five yellow sticks of dynamite, marked "Super Frac 7000." "The goal of the bombs is to make the Rock Machine and their sympathizers realize that the HA are serious in their bid to take control of Montreal," Verdon warned in his report.

It was alarming information. Bombs had simply been scattered around the city ready to go off. This time the Montreal police had been tipped off. With Kane's leads, they found two homemade bombs on busy streets in the east end. The police were late but lucky. The detonators had already exploded, but they were not powerful enough to ignite the dynamite.

The incident showed, however, that there was, in effect, another ticking time bomb: Dany Kane. Verdon and St. Onge were not running an enforcement operation, where the police send in a paid informant to nail organized crime targets specified in advance. They felt the rich vein of intelligence they intended to mine was too valuable to be wasted on a few arrests. Maybe later when Kane was firmly in place at the top he could be used in an operational function for targeted investigations. In an effort to protect Kane and their long-term plans, St. Onge and Verdon had to be careful about the information they passed along and how it was used. They didn't want to nab a few low-level bombers. They wanted the entire top echelon.

What made things tricky was that the information Kane provided was almost too detailed and specific (a conundrum that would only grow worse over the next three years). Who killed whom and who planted what bomb. Hard to ignore. It raised, however, numerous uncomfortable questions. The killings had to be stopped and the perpetrators arrested. But releasing too much information leading to too many arrests could kill the source—literally. Kane's bomb tips lit a fuse right under the Mounties—how much could they release and whom could they trust to release it to?

Two days later, Kane gave Verdon information that showed the RCMP's fears were justified: word was fast spreading—among cops and even bikers—that there was a traitor among the Angels. Kane reported that he overheard two SQ officers claiming the RCMP had a source inside the bikers. It was all St. Onge and Verdon needed to remind them to be vigilant. But as the killings accelerated, the RCMP would find it increasingly difficult to hold back Kane's information or ask police to back off.

Kane's explosive intelligence dragged another nagging moral issue to the surface. He claimed to be one of only four people who knew about the bombs. That would put him right inside Steinert's bomb-making team. To what degree was he engaged in making and planting them? He had told the RCMP he knew how to obtain explosives and make bombs. Now suddenly he had inside information about bombs hidden around the city. Clearly he was deeply involved. The RCMP knew the bikers would never have shared such detailed information with Kane unless he had played an important role in the crime. But it wasn't a question the RCMP cared to ask their paid informant, and the issue never comes up in the intelligence reports.

The only time the RCMP came close to addressing Kane's obvious participation in criminal activity was when they periodically noted in their reports that they warned Kane not to commit crimes. The notation seems more self-serving than real. Of course, both Kane and his handlers knew that the only way to become a Hells Angels Nomad was to commit crimes—serious crimes. And Kane's steady climb up the Hells ladder to the Nomads was, from the beginning, the long-term goal. There was no other plan. The RCMP wanted their source inside the inner circle of the Hells Angels. Everything else was moot. When, three years later, the whole thing blew up in their faces, St. Onge clearly stated as much in a report to his bosses: "Our short-term objective (5 years) was for C-2994 to become a 'hangaround' Nomad. . . . The long-term objective was to become a 'prospect,' which had almost all the rights of a full member. . . . Our objective was that he would become an agent and incriminate the entire Nomad chapter, the hard core." St. Onge, at least, had no illusions about what Kane's climb inside the Hells ranks meant: "In this environment, to climb the ladder you must help the club in an important way," he wrote, "which is to say you have to commit some serious crimes or enrich the club."

Kane had been spying for the RCMP for less than two months, and already, by the end of 1994, it was clear the RCMP were playing a dangerous spy game with a licence to kill, with C-2994 their own 007. From the moment Kane signed on as a source, the RCMP was committed to that plan. They needed a thief to catch a thief. Or, as things turned out, a murderer to catch murderers. Turning a blind eye became the force's modus operandi.

Mom Boucher and his Angels began stepping up plans for their attack on the Rock Machine in December 1994, and Kane gave his handlers a front-row seat. Kane told them that Steinert wanted him to get aerial photographs of the entire city so the Angels could plot territorial strikes. The plan was to eliminate the Rock Machine and their allies the Outlaws with bombs and machine guns early in the new year. The HA chose Kane to oversee the collecting of intelligence on the Rock Machine. He conducted surveillance by renting apartments close to Rock Machine clubs, allowing the Angels to monitor their comings and goings.

Kane also told police the HA had a secret motor pool of stolen vans to use as car bombs. They had already used one to kill a Rock Machine member on December 5. Another was to be used to attack a Rock Machine clubhouse, but that scheme was cancelled because there were children playing in the area—a concern the bikers would not show in a few months' time. Kane's reports to the RCMP showed hurried activity among the Hells Angels and their satellite clubs to assemble an arsenal of handguns, machine guns, dynamite and plastique explosives. They blew up a car along a country road to test the explosives and fired the machine guns in a bar they owned in Sorel called the Polo Ranch.

Mom Boucher had put his army on a war footing, setting up execution squads. "Mom Boucher hands out the execution orders for the current war with the Rock Machine. Steinert is the executioner," Verdon wrote. Boucher and his Angels were also securing their own ranks. They weren't pleased with some of the latest recruits, claiming their lives were "too beautiful and tranquil." Boucher thought there were too many floaters in the club. He didn't trust members reluctant to risk their lives for the war. So the Montreal chapter decided to close its membership and lengthened the probation for existing hangarounds.

Verdon and St. Onge determined that they had to see first-hand some of the clubhouses and bomb storage areas Kane had been talking about. So on December 19, Kane took them on a tour of biker homes and bomb plants throughout Montreal, the South Shore and Sorel. They passed on some of the intelligence to the Montreal police, who clamped surveillance on a garage where Kane claimed the Hells stored vehicles. Two weeks later, police seized two vans, each containing fifty sticks of dynamite. "This seizure saved lives," St. Onge later boasted in a report. As a mark of appreciation, the Montreal police gave the RCMP $2,000 toward Kane's salary. A sort of Christmas present to a ghost, since no one on the Montreal force knew who Kane was.

The new year pushed the biker war to new heights— and beyond the borders of Canada. Normand Baker, a Rock Machine biker who was suspected of murdering a Hells Angel the previous summer, was taking a holiday in

Acapulco, Mexico. Late in the evening of January 4, 1995, he was drinking at a bar with friends when François Hinse, a Hells Angel prospect from Trois-Rivières, walked up to him. "Happy New Year," Hinse said, and shot him. Customers at first thought it was a joke. Then they saw the blood and dove for cover. A friend of Baker's chased after Hinse and, with the help of some waiters, caught him. Police seized the weapon and arrested Hinse. It looked as if the Quebec Hells Angel was going away for a long time.

But four days later, Kane confidently told his handlers the Hells would fix it and Hinse would walk free in no time. He said Hinse would spend his time in the Mexican prison infirmary with access to drugs and prostitutes. Boucher, Kane said, had direct contacts with Acapulco police and was organizing Hinse's release for $5,000. "The Hells have many contacts everywhere in Acapulco and everybody there can be bought," Verdon reported.

Sure enough, on January 15, at 5 p.m., a week after Kane's prediction, Hinse walked out of prison a free man. The gun had disappeared and so had the two main witnesses. Verdon wrote in his report, "The source was not able to say how the witnesses suddenly clammed up. He did not say if they had been killed (which is always a possibility. . . .) Mexico has informed us of the liberation of Hinse despite all the evidence. It's a clear case of corruption."

Yet, for Verdon and St. Onge, the Mexican standoff was, in a sense, a victory. If there were ever any doubts about C-2994's information, they'd vanished in the sleaze of the Mexican justice system. As Verdon put it in an intelligence report, Mexico not only showed the "power and importance of the Hells Angels" but also the reliability of source C-2994. "We understand that the HA invested a million Mexican pesos to buy the Mexican authorities," Verdon wrote. "Events have proved [C-2994] right and once again demonstrated the reliability and importance of our source." Verdon's entry into the file was less a matter of intelligence than a message to his bosses. Kane was demanding more money, and Verdon wanted the bosses to pay up or lose their super source.

The RCMP also had to worry about police corruption closer to home. Kane told them there were leaks in the Sûreté du Québec and in the police forces of Greenfield Park and Brossard, two cities south of Montreal. According to Kane's intelligence reports filed in court records, "The Evil Ones are really friendly with the Brossard police." Kane claimed the Hells had obtained police photographs of each member of the Rock Machine's allies, the Outlaws. The RCMP were not only facing an expanding biker war, but they also had to deal with the possibility that police were leaking like a sieve. They could not be sure whom to trust.

There was also the nagging dilemma about what to do with Kane's information—save lives or save the source? On January 20, St. Onge and Verdon went for another ride with Kane. He showed them the apartment where Patrick Lambert hid dynamite for Steinert, in a wardrobe in a small storage room to the left of the entrance foyer. It was in this room that the bikers prepared their bombs and remote control boxes. Lambert paid a stripper $250 a month to rent the apartment. Normally, with such reliable information, the police would have immediately set up surveillance and raided the place, if only to protect the lives of the other tenants.

The RCMP did give the information to the Montreal police. But no arrests were made. Police didn't want to expose the source. RCMP Staff Sgt. Pierre Lemire, who was in charge of intelligence, wrote the following directive: "With the ongoing war, all the members of the different clubs involved are aware of the dangers. We will act only in the case of a direct and precise threat against an individual."

The security of the people who lived in the apartment building with the explosives would have to be sacrificed to a greater good.

Even the promise to act against a "precise threat against an individual" proved hollow. Kane drove his handlers to a building on Desery Street in Montreal and told them the man who lived in apartment 1 was a priority target. That same month Kane gave police sixteen more targets in the Rock Machine alliance. Police decided that if they were too stupid to realize they were targets in their own war, it was pointless to warn them now.

The war slowed to a halt briefly when Mom Boucher took a March vacation in Mexico, where Kane said he owned considerable property. According to a police affidavit, Boucher owned 50 percent of a hotel in Ixtapa. Kane reported that Mom had ordered a ceasefire until he got back.

Once back home, Boucher—and an increasingly squeezed Kane—had to deal with an internal war within the Angels as well. Scott Steinert, Kane's occasional benefactor, was making enemies within the Hells hierarchy. Though still only a prospect member, he had assembled what he called his "Groupe de Cinq"—his Crew of Five—to take over bars on Crescent Street, one of downtown Montreal's most popular nightlife districts, and along Ottawa's York Street. This was Wolf Carroll's territory. Steinert also planned to carve out his own niche in Kingston, Toronto and Winnipeg. This was Stadnick country.

In addition, Steinert wanted to control all the stripper agencies in Quebec through his company, Sensation—a direct challenge to Carroll, who controlled the rival Aventure agency. The bikers were making huge money operating roadside bordellos and supplying strippers not just in Quebec but also everywhere else in Canada and in the Caribbean. Recently a New York Mafia soldier had come to Montreal looking for a steady stream of strippers to supply a new mob-owned club in the Dominican Republic. The club, which included a marina and condos, was simply a front for money laundering, according to Kane's report to the RCMP. Steinert wanted a piece of this action too. Hell, he wanted it all. He wanted anything that had a good profit tied to it.

He was a strong money-maker, boldly shipping large quantities of cocaine and hash through the Hells' Canadian network. Mom Boucher liked Steinert just for that reason. Boucher considered himself all business. He went to bed early and got up before sunrise because business, he would say, can best be conducted in the light of day, when it's hardest for your enemies to track you. Steinert thought the same way, and Boucher respected that.

Carroll, on the other hand, liked profits, but he yearned for more partying. "He's the type of guy who believes that a biker gang is drinking beer and having fun. They're criminals, but it's important to have fun," says one police officer who got to know Carroll well through hours of electronic surveillance. "And he's disappointed to see the money end of it has taken over. The Nomads were business, business, business."

With Mom siding with Steinert, Carroll would just have to back off—for now. Kane's handlers were still worried: they didn't want C-2994 to get caught in the middle of a potentially lethal Hells civil war. But like it or not, Kane inevitably found himself wedged between his two patrons, Carroll and Steinert. When Carroll asked Kane to drive him to Halifax in March 1995, Steinert refused to allow it, and the two men almost came to blows. Steinert was the bolder—or simply crazier—personality. He was a killer and cared nothing for the privileges of rank if they got in the way of his ambitions. Carroll was less confrontational. He backed off, so Dany Kane stayed home.

C-2994, meanwhile, seemed to enjoy playing the two off against each other. He told the RCMP that Steinert was an American who never took out Canadian citizenship, even though he had lived in Canada most of his life. Because he had a criminal record, Canadian authorities had the right to deport him. Verdon and St. Onge immediately informed immigration officials, who instigated deportation proceedings. Steinert—unaware that his own underling was behind this sudden hassle—hired an immigration lawyer to fight it. Kane spent the next three years having a good time reporting to his handlers how Steinert constantly complained about his immigration problems. Steinert frequently wondered where he would go if Canada tossed him out. Boucher, the man with property and police connections down south, had a suggestion: Mexico. Mom said he could get Steinert citizenship for $30,000.

That spring, Kane learned how dangerous his spy games could be. Kane told the Mounties in his intelligence reports that Richard Lock, one of Steinert's enforcers, along with a Mafia thug, had badly beaten the owners of the Crescent Bar—a well-known middle-class bar in downtown Montreal—for refusing to pay protection money plus 10 percent of the bar take. The RCMP passed the story on to the Montreal police. When one of the anti-gang detectives ran into Lock at a Montreal restaurant, according to the intelligence file, he carelessly told him, "You and your boys beat up the owners of the Crescent." Lock knew that nobody else was present at the beating. He doubted the owners would have talked. The incident got back to a furious Kane, who complained to his handlers that they were talking too much. The RCMP complained to the Montreal anti-gang cops, but it didn't do much good.

Things got even more perilous for Kane when, in the final week of March, the SQ arrested Mom Boucher for possession of a weapon, for which he was sent to prison.

Kane learned from a Hells Angel that an SQ officer had stupidly bragged to Boucher that the police had a "coded informer" inside the Hells' inner circle. Verdon and St. Onge were stunned. They took special note of the situation in their report, relating what Kane told them: "After some hard thinking, Mom reached the conclusion that it could only be [one of] six people," Kane reported. Mom's suspects were Scott Steinert, two members of the Rockers, a Hells sympathizer, a prospect—or Kane himself. Kane told his handlers he was "very nervous" because, as the Mounties reported, "he was the least known to Boucher and therefore . . . was the main suspect." Kane also told the RCMP that the Hells had barred anybody who was not a prospect or full patch from entering their clubhouses. Paranoia, he said, was setting in. Nobody trusted anybody.

The RCMP felt helpless. Verdon and St. Onge waited to see if their man was blown. After a few days, they breathed easier. "There is no indication to make us seriously believe C-2994 is identified," St. Onge wrote in the intelligence file. He tried to put the best spin on things, hoping the event "may only spread mistrust" among the bikers. The handlers told Kane to go back to work.

A cocky Steinert dismissed Boucher's suspicions as "babble," but Kane was concerned and so were the RCMP. Over the next months, indeed years, they would continue to receive frequent reports about police leaks to the bikers. Kane several times gave the RCMP copies of police photos of Rock Machine members that somehow found their way into the hands of the Hells Angels and Rockers. The RCMP consequently closed ranks around Kane, exerting a tighter control of the information flow to other police forces.

The heat came off Kane when the SQ arrested several Hells Angels based on information from a newly-turned biker informant named Serge Quesnel. Kane and his handlers relaxed for a while. But what the police didn't realize was that the SQ police officer's leak about a coded informant had seriously affected Mom Boucher. He didn't believe for a moment that Quesnel was the snitch because he was not a true insider. Mom became obsessed with not only ferreting out the coded source but also putting in place a scheme to discourage any other biker from becoming an informant. He told friends he would "raise a lot of shit" to find the informant. Whiling away his time in prison, he began replaying in his mind past arrests and seizures. He finally focused on the Montreal police seizure of a minivan full of explosives that winter, which convinced him that what the SQ officer had told him was true.

There was a mole inside the Hells. Boucher began plotting a deadly scheme to ensure it never happened again. The slip by an all too talkative SQ officer would eventually have lethal consequences for two law enforcement workers.

It was 12:40 p.m. on Wednesday, August 9, 1995. A clear, warm summer day. Eleven-year-old Daniel Desrochers was playing on the grass in front of Saint-Nom-de-Jésus School with his friend Yan Villeneuve, ten, when the car bomb exploded. It ripped apart the Jeep, killing its twenty-year-old driver, Marc Dubé, and sending shrapnel tearing through the quiet tree-lined neighbourhood in east-end Montreal. Yan instinctively covered his head. When he looked up, he saw Daniel lying on the ground, tucked into the fetal position. A piece of metal the size of a baby's little finger had penetrated the rear of his skull and lodged deep in his brain. Doctors would later measure it: 3.4 cm by 1.9 cm by 1 cm. Frightened and crying, Yan ran home to tell his mother. His friend Daniel sank deep into a coma and four days later died in hospital.

"When I left for work that morning, my three children were still asleep," his mother, Josée-Anne, said later. "When I got home, I didn't even have time to say goodbye to my son—he was no longer there." The Hells Angels insisted they had nothing to do with the bomb, but even bikers understand that killing a child is bad PR. So they offered the boy's mother cash to help ease the loss. She refused it and vented her anger against them and the authorities. "It disgusts me. I'll never forgive the act. . . . This has been going on for five years, and the government has done nothing."

More than any other single event in the biker war, the killing of Daniel Desrochers galvanized public opinion. Images of the carnage on the street and his funeral packed with tearful schoolchildren were flashed on TV screens across the country. The public outcry was aimed more at the police than at the bikers. Why couldn't the police and the government protect citizens from a handful of thugs? Suddenly, it was no longer good enough for police to shrug off the latest gang killing as a "settling of accounts." Calls swamped the office of the Montreal police chief, Jacques Duchesneau. "People are asking why this is happening— they're not living in Beirut," Duchesneau told a press conference at the time. But the best police could do for the moment was to announce a twenty-four-hour hotline for anybody with information about gang warfare.

The boy's killing rattled even hard-bitten cops like André Bouchard, the Montreal police commander who had grown used to seeing—and largely ignoring—bikers killing other bikers. Suddenly, the game had changed. "I'm convinced today that the person who pressed the button to have the bomb explode saw the children across the street. There was no way he could not see the children across the street."

Panicked, the Montreal police called the RCMP to see if their source had any information on the murder. St. Onge called Kane at six that evening. Kane told the RCMP that nobody knew why Dubé had been murdered: he was loosely associated with the Angels as a small-time drug runner. Nobody could figure out why anybody would bother to kill such a minor player. For the next few days, Kane came up with surprisingly little information. He talked about the Evil Ones' preparation for a party and Wolf Carroll's trip to Halifax and the holiday plans of Rocker Paul Fontaine. But nothing about the bombing that killed Daniel Desrochers.

Two weeks later, Kane came through. He told the RCMP that the Hells Angels had definitely planted the bomb, and he pointed a finger at Steinert. The day before the bombing that killed Daniel Desrochers, Steinert had ordered three remote control bomb kits from Patrick Lambert. Steinert was eager to get his hands on them that evening. He didn't want to wait until the next day, Kane said. "Steinert was really excited and bragging that he was really going to do something that would 'rock 'n' roll,' " Kane said. The next day Montreal learned what that was.

Kane described Steinert as uncharacteristically silent after the Desrochers murder. "Since that day, Steinert no longer talked about the bombs he had ordered and never again spoke about using bombs," he told his handlers. "Steinert asked some of his crew what they thought of the bombing. . . . When told they thought the murderer should be liqui- dated, Steinert didn't respond and became very pensive."

That still didn't answer the question why. Dubé, the biker victim, was tied to the Angels. Why would the HA blow up one of their own? Kane provided a clue when he reported earlier in the year that Mom Boucher was impa- tient with the Hells. He felt they were not aggressively pur- suing the war. He even suggested that somebody take out a Hells Angel and blame it on the Rock Machine. It would be a call to arms, Boucher thought.

And Steinert was crazy enough to do it. Verdon and St. Onge viewed him as a "very violent and cruel psychopath who can't control himself." Of course he would never sac- rifice a full-patch Hells. That would be too dangerous. But a low-level drug runner like Dubé, well, who would miss him? The fact that the trigger man blew the bomb with children close by seemed to indicate a willingness to create havoc and do it deep in Mom Boucher's territory—exactly what was needed to anger the Hells. Verdon and St. Onge wrote in their reports that Steinert's strange conduct indicated he could have been behind the bomb.

But what about Kane himself? He was one of Steinert's closest associates and a self-declared bomber for the Hells. There's nothing in the reports to suggest the RCMP ever questioned Kane closely about his actions or whereabouts the day Daniel Desrochers was killed. To this day, neither Verdon nor St. Onge will talk about it. One thing, however, is absolutely certain. Kane never told the RCMP about his own murderous criminal activities inside the bikers. And the RCMP didn't ask.

The record shows that from 1994 to 1997, Kane participated in at least eleven killings of rival Rock Machine members. He made bombs and remote control devices. He planted a bomb that blew up the Green Stop restaurant in Châteauguay. He planted two other bombs in two bars controlled by the Rock Machine (though he didn't trigger them because there were too many innocent bystanders). It would not have been impossible or improbable for Kane to have assisted his mentor Steinert in setting off the bomb that killed the eleven-year-old boy. Kane was also part of a group called the Commandos, whose mandate was to destroy the Rock Machine in south-end Montreal. Finally, he never told his handlers that on March 3, 1996, he drove Roland Labrasseur, a drug addict who had stolen from Kane, to Brossard, just south of Montreal, shot him and dumped his body on the roadside.

Kane had mentioned Labrasseur to Verdon and St. Onge shortly after Daniel Desrochers was killed. He told them Labrasseur had been a soldier in the Canadian army and knew how to make remote control bombs with pagers and car alarms. Verdon checked with the armed forces and discovered that while he had served in the army, he had never taken any explosives training. He basically knew how to throw a hand grenade. Labrasseur was a sad character, a bit of a simpleton with a cocaine addiction. As Kane later described in his confession, after a while, Wolf Carroll didn't want him around. So Kane murdered him but pointed the finger at someone else. He told his handlers it was Daniel Bouchard, a Hells drug dealer, who killed Labrasseur. The RCMP in Sept-Îles had been investigating Bouchard for trafficking, so on April 3, St. Onge hopped on an RCMP plane with four other police officers and flew to Sept-Îles to discuss Kane's information with the investigating officer. It was a wild-goose chase—but St. Onge wouldn't know that until years later.

Kane also never told them he had been involved after the fact in the September 1995 murder of biker Stéphane Boire. Police found the body in a shallow grave north of Trois-Rivières in July 1996. It was badly decomposed and only a tattoo was recognizable. St. Onge phoned Kane and asked if he knew anything about it. "He told me that there's a good chance it's Stéphane Boire who disappeared in Sept. 95," St. Onge wrote in an intelligence report dated June 11, 1996. Five years later Kane confessed to police that he had disposed of Boire's body—but insisted he was not the trigger man; as in the murder of Labrasseur, he implicated Bouchard. St. Onge still maintains that while Kane may not always have told the whole story, he never lied to the police. Yet he certainly lied about Labrasseur, and likely about Boire as well. So the lingering question is, how many other people did the super source kill? As police would soon find out, Kane often made a fine but erroneous moral and legal distinction between pulling the trigger and going along for the ride—helping to set up the hit or dispose of the body.

Kane was more truthful about his personal involvement in day-to-day biker crimes, such as drug trafficking. For example, on November 9, 1995, he told his handlers he was leaving that day for Thunder Bay to set up cocaine deals for Steinert. The goal, St. Onge duly noted, was to take advantage of the price spread: in northern Ontario, cocaine was going for $50,000 a kilo compared with $32,000 in Montreal. The RCMP had to have known that drugs sales weren't the only misdeeds their source was committing.

"One of the problems was wondering if Kane was the one who was doing the crimes," St. Onge says today. "His information was hot, but if he wasn't the guy doing the crimes, how did he know so much?" This was a common problem with sources, but with Kane it was particularly acute. His information often involved murders, attempted murders and bombings. So, again and again, with each Kane debriefing the question hung in the air like a ghost: How much blood did Kane have on his own hands?

The RCMP simply danced around it: they felt it just had to be that way. "During those days a bomb went off every week, and Kane was able to explain it all," St. Onge says. Kane was their only road into the Hells. That road was about to get a lot more treacherous. In September 1995, Kane gave St. Onge and Verdon exciting news: he had just been invited to join the Rockers, the enforcement squad run by the Nomads.

The invitation, the Mounties gleefully reported, came from "none other than Maurice 'Mom' Boucher himself."

FOUR

Hell in Halifax

"We've got Kane cold, trapped, cooked."
CONST. TOM TOWNSEND, HALIFAX RCMP

Six weeks after Daniel Desrochers died, on September 23, 1995, Quebec Public Security Minister Serge Ménard announced the creation of a special police task force. They called it Wolverine, perhaps hoping the sharp-toothed animal with a reputation for viciousness would inspire the Quebec police finally to get their act together against the bikers.

Quebec—indeed the rest of the country—had never seen anything like it. Joint police operations, especially between the RCMP and regional forces, were common across Canada, but not such a massive squad dedicated solely to fighting the bikers. Before the decade was over, two other provinces faced with a mounting threat from the Hells Angels would follow suit.

Initially composed of thirty investigators from the Montreal police and an equal number from the Sûreté du Québec, the Wolverine team grew to more than seventy investigators, with extra bodies from the RCMP. The task force would have an almost unlimited budget. Its mandate was clear: take down the bikers. SQ director Serge Barbeau vowed to reporters that the new squad of "top investigators" would "terminate the wave of violence that we're having right now."

At first, the new squad captured the imagination of a Quebec population weary of the almost daily carnage of bombs, bullets and body bags. One enthusiastic citizen dug out of his garage a slightly moth-eaten stuffed wolverine he had once shot and sent it to the new squad—with the bullet hole plainly visible in its underbelly. The dusty mascot still sits at the entrance to the squad's current Montreal headquarters on the fourth floor of the east-end SQ building.

But hunting animals was easier than hunting bikers. It would not take long for Wolverine to collapse under the weight of corruption and infighting. And just when the police needed Dany Kane's steady flow of intelligence more than ever, scandal would cripple the Mounties' man inside the Angels.

SQ boss Serge Barbeau had bigger problems on his hands than the bikers. His provincial police force was crumbling into disarray. For decades, the SQ had the reputation of being a rogue force that answered to nobody. Rumours swirled that its officers took too many shortcuts and acted like cowboys. The Montreal police didn't trust them and were reluctant to share information or conduct joint investigations. "They'd steal your information, take credit for your busts and lie to you about their own informants," recalls Kevin McGarr, a veteran Montreal police detective who is now retired.

A year before the creation of Wolverine, the SQ thought they had done what no other force had succeeded in doing, which was to take down Gerry Matticks, an Irish gangster with close ties to the Hells Angels. He controlled the drug smuggling through the port of Montreal, but in May 1994 the SQ charged him with importing 26.5 tonnes of hashish in three shipping containers. The smart money was on Matticks going to jail for a long time.

It looked like a solid case, but in court, allegations surfaced that police planted incriminating documents at the offices of Matticks' associate—an unfortunate display of overzealousness since Matticks happened to be illiterate. A furious judge freed Matticks and called for a criminal investigation into the SQ. Four SQ officers were charged with fabricating evidence, perjury and obstructing justice. They were eventually acquitted, but the SQ could not shake the stink of scandal. Stories emerged that top SQ officers close to Barbeau were intimidating the force's internal investigators who were probing police corruption in the "Matticks affair." Then came reports of witness tampering, obstruction of justice, illegal wiretapping and perjury. By 1996, Barbeau was forced to resign, and the government appointed a three-member Royal Commission headed by Lawrence Poitras, a former chief justice of the Quebec Superior Court.

Two years and $20 million later, Poitras produced a ruthlessly critical report whose 1,700 pages described an incompetent, corrupt and unprofessional police force in need of major reforms. It accused senior officers of obstruction of justice, evidence tampering and threatening witnesses. The commission noted that the SQ even stooped to plagiarizing a report on organized crime published by the Montreal police. Poitras's probe also led right to the man who'd become chief of the Wolverine squad— Michel Arcand, one of two senior Sûreté officers questioned for impeding an internal investigation into three of his officers. Even though he was never charged, Poitras deplored his "contemptuous" attitude and concluded that making him head of the anti-biker strike force was "totally inappropriate."

The provincial government reacted by retiring senior officers—including Arcand—and naming a civilian to head the force. But the damage had been done. While it was clear that the bumbling police were the authors of their own undoing, it was also evident that Mom Boucher profited from the scandal.

A former SQ officer named Gaetan Rivest became a media darling when he hit the airwaves with allegations that SQ officers beat confessions out of suspects. Rivest's revelations even earned him a private meeting with Quebec's public security minister. But Rivest went from whistle-blower to wiseguy when it turned out he had close ties to biker associates. He published an anti-police rag called *Le Juste Milieu* that was partially owned by a Hells Angels loan shark named Robert Savard. Rivest himself eventually pleaded guilty to charges of loan sharking and extortion.

Mom Boucher was privately snickering about the havoc he was causing. Soon after the Poitras report came out, Kane and Boucher were chatting in the showers at the Pro-Gym in Montreal. According to Kane's personal diary, which he wrote every day for the police, Boucher complained about how much money he had to pay to publicize dirt on the SQ and get the government to start the Poitras Commission. "He told me he was the person behind the Poitras inquiry, and not even the Matticks brothers know that and that he paid the lawyers for getting the shit out for the Poitras inquiry."

The Wolverine squad was pushed to the edge of collapse. Yet the SQ's downfall was not a surprise to veteran officers in the Montreal police force like André Bouchard. Things hadn't changed much since the wily street cop had fought bikers on the streets as a beat cop, only to watch Boucher and the bikers soar to unchallenged supremacy in Quebec.

Bouchard had gained a few pounds and a few ranks, but his attitude was the same: hit them hard and hit them often.

Bouchard joined Wolverine almost at its inception in 1995 and took command of a squad that investigated the Rock Machine and other biker gangs in Quebec City and Sherbrooke. He'd had lots of experience with the SQ, watching as internal conflicts between senior SQ and Montreal officers over budgets and glory—not to mention questionable police methods—destroyed the effectiveness of his men and hamstrung the entire Wolverine squad.

Bouchard started stirring things up in Quebec City and Sherbrooke by raiding biker clubhouses and bars. The strategy was to make a few arrests and hope somebody started talking. The bosses sent Montreal cops in because the bikers often intimidated the local cops. "They used to tell the cops down there when they raided a place, 'Hey, your wife still working at the beauty parlour down there on the corner?'" Bouchard was one cop who wouldn't put up with intimidation. He'd wear his full dress uniform and his blue hat with its shiny black brim and gold braid. Make sure he stood out from all the other cops in their blue jeans and windbreakers with POLICE in big gold letters on the back. "We'd go down there and line the guys up on the floor and I'd say, 'Everybody shut the fuck up!' I wanted them to know who I was. We come from Montreal. So don't talk about my wife and my kids 'cause I'll shoot ya."

At first, Bouchard liked what he saw when he arrived at Wolverine. There seemed to be money for everything: new cars, planes, the best surveillance equipment, wiretaps and lots of eager cops. Anything they wanted, they got. Bouchard got a brand-new Taurus to replace his old K-car. But it wasn't long before he started to suspect that things weren't going as planned. All that money and media attention seemed to go to the heads of the SQ officers. Bouchard recalled that when he went to Quebec City to introduce himself to some of the SQ investigators, they threw him a lavish party at a local restaurant. He was incredulous. As a vice-squad cop over the years, he, like many other officers, was not above dropping by a local bar and accepting a free Scotch from an owner grateful for the police presence. But the Quebec City bash went way beyond that. "I walk in and they got a party going on in there. This was sit-down supper, you know—booze and wine at $50 a bottle. Nobody's paying. And you're starting to think, What the fuck's going on here? Is this a protected bar? Ah, okay. So they never take down a Hells Angel or a Rock Machine or someone who's in the bar. They let him alone. That's not good."

SQ officers would hand in huge expense accounts. Bouchard refused to sign them. "My guys from Montreal are interrogating a source at some motel, and they order a pizza and four Cokes or whatever, talk to the guy for a couple of hours and then they order a club sandwich. But the SQ guys were coming in [with accounts for the] Ritz Carlton, steak dinner, wine. I was asked to sign bills for $800. I go, 'Fuck you, I'm not signing this. You interrogate a piece of shit, you interrogate him in a motel—you don't bring him to the fucking Ritz.' " He then got doubly angry when he discovered that the SQ officers would take the rejected expense claim to an SQ boss who signed off on it.

But conflicts arose over more serious things than expense accounts and free meals. The Montreal police had problems with the way the SQ conducted investigations. Bouchard got a first-hand look at its methods when an SQ investigator called him one night about the imminent seizure of a shipment of dynamite. Bouchard drove into Wolverine headquarters and wanted to set up a SWAT team, but the SQ told him it wasn't necessary. Bouchard immediately grew suspicious. Why not? he asked. The SQ told him not to worry because it was their own source who was transporting the dynamite.

"You don't do that!" Bouchard lost his temper. "A source cannot be involved in a crime." He told them they were setting somebody up for a frame, and he wouldn't be part of that.

They went ahead and did it anyway. After a while the SQ simply stopped telling the Montreal force what they were up to. "They were doing secret jobs. We didn't know. We found out the next morning: there'd be seven guys in the cells. Where the fuck did they come from? That's when it got a little rough."

Bouchard, who at the time was a detective lieutenant, left Wolverine in 1996 to study for his commander's exams. A year and a half later, Montreal police chief Jacques Duchesneau pulled all his men out of the force. The Poitras Commission, not surprisingly, declared that a "virtual police war was being waged" inside Wolverine. Poitras noted that the SQ blamed other police forces for the mess to make its own contribution seem more significant.

Amid all the sound and fury, however, one man kept his nose to the ground. Dany Kane, the best biker source the police would ever have, was burrowing deeper and deeper into the Hells Angels.

Soon after Wolverine got off the ground, the RCMP assigned Kane's handler Staff Sergeant St. Onge to be one of their intelligence representatives and liaison officers. He moved over to Wolverine's expansive offices on Montreal's waterfront. Across the desk from him sat Det. Sgt. Benoit Roberge of the Montreal police.

The two men hit it off immediately. Like St. Onge, Roberge was smart and aggressive. And he had little love for the SQ. As an intelligence analyst back in 1989—when most Quebec police were dismissing the bikers as bad dressers—he began piecing together information on the nascent Rock Machine and the trouble brewing between them and the Hells Angels. "I had to convince them there was a war. The SQ laughed at me," he recalls. For two years St. Onge had been feeding Roberge intelligence gathered from Kane. Roberge knew his friend had a great source—he just never knew his name. Nor did he suspect that eventually he not only would help destroy the RCMP source but also, in a divine twist of fate, resurrect and run Dany Kane in the most dangerous assignment the police source would ever pursue.

St. Onge and Verdon continued to meet with Kane two or three times a week and fed whatever information they thought necessary—and safe—to Wolverine investigators. Kane was the only real inside source Wolverine had. He continued to give the RCMP weekly updates on the Hells Angels' nationwide telephone directory, complete with cell and pager numbers. He gave them the coded pager number for each Hells Angel as well as the codes for meeting places in hotels and restaurants. He gave them the addresses of biker safehouses where they hid drugs, guns and explosives. When Rocker André "Toots" Tousignant was driving around with two bodies in his trunk, the RCMP learned about it. When he bought thirty units of a new "cone" explosive, they learned about that too. Kane even told them the Hells got the recipe for making chemical bombs off the Internet—the same type used in the bombing of the federal building in Oklahoma City—and that they were storing the chemicals in an apartment in Longueuil. The RCMP knew who killed whom and why. It all came from C-2994.

Often Kane's most significant intelligence was not facts but rather painting the broad picture. He explained to police how the Hells organization functioned and its daily ebbs and flows. He described how the bikers formed partnerships among themselves and their associates on various drug deals. Inclusion depended on what money, skills or contacts a biker could bring to the table. Each group became a cell unto itself, keeping its own profits and its own secrets. He then kept the RCMP abreast of what various cells were up to.

St. Onge constantly had to ward off Wolverine investigators from the SQ and Montreal who asked him point-blank for the name of his source. In April 1995, a Montreal police detective sergeant asked him to reveal the identity of C-2994. As always, St. Onge refused; the officer was later suspended from the force under suspicion of "going over to the other side" and taking kickbacks from a police source.

Warned repeatedly by Kane that the police leaked like a sieve, St. Onge was worried that too many members of the Wolverine squad seemed far too eager to uncover the real identity of C-2994. "[Wolverine] was a total circus," he says. "The SQ was jealous of the RCMP source. They were always asking his name. The SQ used to give out the names of their sources all the time. They didn't care if they were blown. They treated them like dirt. At meetings they would just blurt out their source's name and expect everybody to keep it quiet."

The SQ didn't believe St. Onge when he insisted that even his own RCMP bosses didn't know his source's identity. "In the RCMP," St. Onge says adamantly, "the source belongs to the agent."

Belonging, of course, meant nurturing and taking care of. It meant doing your best to protect them and forgiving them their trespasses. Money was always a crucial part of Kane's complicated charade. From the RCMP, Kane got $2,000 cash every week. The RCMP didn't know—or didn't want to know—if he was making thousands more selling drugs, bombing and killing people.

Whatever the source of his money, Kane needed a financial front to maintain credibility with the bikers. After all, the best bikers had a method of laundering their illicit earnings. Kane had to have one too.

So in July 1996, the RCMP gave him $30,325 to set up *Rencontres Selectes*, a sex magazine with personal ads for strippers, phone sex and escort services. Kane envisaged the magazine as a meeting place for gays and as a launch pad for his gay dating agency. The masthead had two adjoining red hearts serving as the *o* in *Rencontres*. It described itself on the cover as the journal of "mail sex."

A good Mountie is nothing if not creative and Staff Sergeant St. Onge showed surprising zest in nudging the force into the gay dating business. He justified the expense to his bosses by arguing—or perhaps hoping—that Kane's salary from the magazine "meant he didn't have to commit serious crimes and thus could avoid getting himself arrested or killed and could continue to feed us information."

So, the Royal Canadian Mounted Police got into the sex magazine trade. Taxpayers' money financed Kane's weekly magazine. The force laundered its investment through a bank and notary. St. Onge and Verdon prepared an analysis of why a previous sex magazine had failed and tried to come up with a better business plan. "The reasons for the failure were bad advice from the graphic artist and the poor quality of the magazine," St. Onge told his bosses, attaching copies of the proposed first cover for the new magazine.

The Mounties should have stayed in the police business. In the end, Kane's RCMP-funded venture survived only a few issues. But Kane's short-lived magazine would have a lasting impact: it led him into the arms of a man who would unravel not only his life but the entire Mountie penetration of the Hells Angels.

Aimé Simard first came to the attention of the RCMP on February 12, 1997, when Verdon and St. Onge asked

Kane if he knew anything about a shooting near Quebec City. Earlier that month, somebody severely injured a man and woman with a high-calibre handgun. Kane certainly did know about it. He told his handlers the shooter was Simard and told them this story: Five people connected to the Rock Machine were in a car and opened fire on Simard; he returned fire, hitting two of them with his .44 Magnum. He then got rid of the gun. Once again, nothing in the intelligence report indicates the RCMP asked how Kane knew any of this.

The story Kane told was bogus. It was true his new pal Simard had shot the two people. But there was never any car chase or shootout. Kane seems to have made that up. In fact, Simard went to Quebec City with a friend who owed money to a drug dealer and shot both the dealer and his girlfriend on a sidewalk. They wouldn't be the only murders Simard committed that month.

This odd concoction of conflicting fairy tales was sparked by the fact that three months earlier Kane and Simard had become lovers. Simard was trying to impress his new boyfriend with what a tough guy he was, and Kane was trying to impress his handlers with an even better account of a shootout. Verdon and St. Onge knew Kane had left his wife, but they had no idea that Kane had a relationship with Simard. "We didn't even know Kane was bisexual," St. Onge says.

Why Kane would choose Simard as a lover is one of the great Kane mysteries. They were total opposites. In Quebec City, Simard studied management, accounting and police administration and at one point wanted to become a cop—though his 350 pounds put him slightly over the weight limit. He later had his stomach stapled, but he still looked like a teardrop with legs. In between jobs and his studies, he committed crimes. He was convicted for more than eighty petty crimes, including theft, writing bad cheques and shoplifting. He went to prison for using a gun to threaten someone. A psychologist might blame it all on his alcoholic father, whom ten-year-old Aimé found dead one day on the living-room couch. Whatever drove his criminal behaviour, Aimé wasn't good at it. Police say he often acted in such a brazen manner that it was as if he wanted to be caught—or just didn't care.

When he got out of prison, he moved to Montreal. He was twenty-nine years old and thought he might study forensics. He took out an ad in Kane's gay dating service—and guess who answered? Simard later testified that Kane called him one November day to say he was driving to Halifax and could stop off and meet Simard in Quebec City. (Kane never told his handlers about the Halifax trip. He did, however, tell them that Wolf Carroll had sent some henchmen to Nova Scotia to muscle bars and establish drug territory, and it's likely that Kane was one of Carroll's shock troops. Kane's next unreported trip to Halifax would have much more impact.)

With his mother holidaying in Florida, Simard took Kane to her vacant home and showed him around. As Simard later testified, when Kane spotted a whirlpool in the basement he asked Simard if he could use it. "Sure," Simard said. Both men stripped and climbed in. Simard spotted a Hells Angels tattoo on Kane's arm, and Kane lied that he was a Hells prospect—he was still only a Rocker at the time. Simard was impressed and decided to pump up his own criminal past by claiming that he had once done jail time for shooting a cop. Kane asked Simard if he wanted to sleep with him. "I said yes," Simard recalled.

Perhaps it was a case of opposites attracting. Simard was totally out of control while Kane was a control freak. Everything had to be neat and tidy. He left his wife in part because she had too many animals, and Kane claimed they gave him a rash. Kane prided himself on his clean-cut, lean, muscular appearance. St. Onge remembers Kane as an impeccable dresser with carefully shined alligator boots and expensive leather jackets, black designer jeans and glasses. Kane was obsessed with keeping his body taut and healthy, although by the time he met up with Simard he was taking steroids. "He was always showing us his muscles," St. Onge says. "He'd take off his jacket and flex his biceps: 'See how big I'm getting.'"

And Kane loved sex. He once dialled St. Onge's number and then handed the phone to a stripper who told St. Onge with a loving voice exactly what Kane was doing to her and how impressed she was with his sexual prowess. Throughout the whole encounter, St. Onge was listening at the other end of the line, wondering what the hell was going on. "Kane was quite hyper during this time," St. Onge says.

These were indeed tense times for Kane. The steroids made him jumpy. More seriously, his long-standing balancing act in the middle of a fierce standoff between two Hells Angels factions—Scott Steinert vs. the Carroll/Stadnick group—had reached a deadly climax. Steinert, who was now a full-patch Hells Angel with the Montreal chapter, had persisted in his bid to carve out territory in Quebec, Ontario and Manitoba, which Wolf Carroll and Walter Stadnick considered rightfully theirs. Tensions had been growing for years. But they boiled over into bloodshed when Steinert's closest partner, Donald Magnussen, acting on a personal grudge, killed a visiting biker from the Winnipeg Los Brovos gang at a Hells Angels party in Halifax in May 1996.

Killing an invited guest is frowned upon even by the Angels. But this murder was particularly problematic. Carroll regarded Halifax as his territory. Nobody kills there without his permission, especially one of Steinert's gang. Worse still, for some time Stadnick had been wooing Winnipeg bikers, especially Ernie Dew and Los Brovos, to patch over to the Hells. Killing a Los Brovos was not a good calling card, and Stadnick was furious. Kane told the RCMP that both Carroll and Stadnick wanted Magnussen dead. Verdon's intelligence reports during this time are filled with references to the growing rift between Hells Angels factions in Montreal and the plan to murder not only Magnussen but also Steinert. Kane claimed Carroll hired Mom Boucher's bodyguard, Toots Tousignant, to kill Magnussen.

After almost five months, Tousignant had still not done the job. So, according to Verdon's intelligence reports filed in the court record, in October 1996 Carroll, Stadnick and Pup Stockford offered to pay Kane $10,000 to hit Magnussen. They figured that because Magnussen trusted Kane, Kane could get close to him. But the contract from three of the most powerful Nomads put Kane in a tough spot. He could hardly say no. But Steinert was Kane's youngest son's godfather. And Kane knew that if he murdered Steinert's best friend, that would be the end of him. He had to get out of it.

So he turned to the RCMP. Kane didn't typically reveal his murder plots to his handlers, but this time, he made an exception. It indicated both Kane's desperation and his conviction that the police probably could fix it so that he wouldn't have to kill Magnussen. He wanted them to warn the biker. Detective Sergeant Roberge visited Magnussen twice and tipped him off about the contract, hoping he might turn. Magnussen later told Kane he laughed at the cops. Roberge tells a slightly different story: Magnussen was indeed scared but refused protection.

Kane was running out of options. Then Mom Boucher stepped in to save him. As Nomads president, Boucher declared that since Magnussen was the right-hand man of a full-patch Hells Angel, only another full patch—and not a simple Rocker such as Kane—could dispatch him. Boucher said Stadnick had to do it because he had the most to gain from Magnussen's death, Verdon wrote in an intelligence report. Kane was off the hook—and Magnussen edged one step closer to death.

Magnussen's luck worsened when in February 1997 he and two other bikers severely beat the son of Montreal Mafia boss Vito Rizzuto outside a bar on St. Laurent Boulevard. Magnussen claimed he didn't know who the young man was. Kane told his handlers that the rumour was that Rizzuto vowed revenge. Whether it was upset Italian mobsters or angry Nomads, Magnussen was a dead man. In 1998, police fished his body out of what they called the Hells Angels' favourite graveyard: the St. Lawrence River. His killers were likely the Nomads because a year later they found his boss Steinert's body just a bit farther downriver. Both men had been hammered to death.

Simard began hanging around full time with Kane's biker friends. By then, Kane had moved into his new girlfriend's Montreal apartment. Simard often stayed with them. He became Kane's driver, although he wasn't a very good one. He smashed up two cars. Kane liked the distinction of having a chauffeur, which showed he was moving up in biker society. Simard even chauffeured Kane to the hotels where he secretly met with Verdon and St. Onge.

Kane thought it was all kind of funny. Simard had no idea whom Kane was meeting; the RCMP had no idea Simard was his driver. Kane seemed to view Simard as a goofy sort of toy—somebody he could play with or employ as the need arose. Then just after Simard shot the two people in Quebec City, Kane figured out the perfect use for Simard.

Robert MacFarlane, at thirty-four, was nominally a Halifax businessman who owned a security and cellphone company. But more than anything, MacFarlane was a troublemaker. An associate of the Halifax Hells Angels, he was the kind of braggart that even bikers tire of. He used coke, he used steroids and he was huge—he used to beat people up just because he knew he could. "If you were walking a beat downtown and you saw Bob MacFarlane, you knew within hours you'd be called to that bar. It was just a matter of time," recalls one veteran city cop. "Very obnoxious, very loud, very much full of himself."

Too full. Out in Vancouver, he got into a fight in a Hells-controlled bar, nearly biting the finger off one of the bouncers, all the while boasting of his ties to the East Coast bikers. But back home in Halifax, he would also get on people's nerves at a popular downtown bar run by Paul Wilson, a good friend of Wolf Carroll's.

"I think his demise was because he was such an ass-hole," says Bruce Macdonald, one of the RCMP officers charged with keeping an eye on the local bikers.

There was a $25,000 contract to kill MacFarlane, and Kane got the job.

Kane decided to take Simard along and have him do the hit. "You'll get some pocket money and I'll be able to see you operate," Kane told him. "If you do this job, the organization won't forget you; they'll remember that you did this for them."

The two men headed down east in a rented white four-door Buick LeSabre, stopping off in Quebec City to visit Simard's sister. But they didn't make it past Oromocto, just outside Fredericton, New Brunswick, before they ran into trouble. The Trans-Canada Highway through the Maritimes is an asphalt conveyor belt for illicit drugs, from the ports of Nova Scotia to Montreal. Hoping to at least slow the traffic, the RCMP initiated Operation Pipeline to spot-check strangers who didn't look as though they belonged. When Const. Gilles Blinn and his partner, Auxiliary Const. Dale Hutley, saw Kane and Simard, with their Quebec licence plate and trimmed goatees, leather jackets, jewellery and tattoos, they thought these guys fitted the bill—and pulled them over.

Blinn dealt with Simard, the driver, while Hutley spoke to Kane. Blinn ran both their names through CPIC, the central police database; the constable thought Kane was the spookier of the two, with his cold, unflinching manner. Simard was travelling under an alias, so nothing came up, but Kane's name registered a hit. When Kane's biker ties lit up Blinn's computer screen, he decided to search the car.

The highway patrolmen never saw the gun Simard had tucked in his belt under his shirt. Simard just seemed like a nice guy, chattering away, with a big grin on his face, trying to be friendly as he opened the trunk. Inside Blinn found two walkie-talkies, a police scanner and a large amount of luggage. At that point, Kane told Blinn to leave the equipment alone and refused to allow him to search any further without a warrant. Blinn lacked reasonable cause and had to let them go. It probably saved the constable's life. According to Kane, Simard often said he wanted to kill a cop.

Meanwhile, back at RCMP headquarters in Montreal, Blinn's CPIC search of Kane had registered on St. Onge's computer screen as a "silent hit." RCMP officers routinely put a source's name on observation status in CPIC. This means that every time any police officer in Canada checks out the name, it registers on the handler's computer. If another police officer is snooping around a source, the handler wants to know why. When St. Onge came in to work the next day, he was surprised to see Constable Blinn's background check on Kane. What was Kane doing in New Brunswick, St. Onge asked himself, as he picked up the phone to call Blinn.

When Blinn came on the line, St. Onge quickly introduced himself and then peppered the constable with questions: who was Kane with, what kind of vehicle was he driving, what was found in the vehicle and in what direction were they travelling? Blinn answered all of his questions and then asked one of his own: why was St. Onge interested? St. Onge told him he was a member of a special team investigating bikers and rang off.

Blinn's information worried St. Onge. He immediately paged Kane. No reply. He paged him four or five times more but still got no reply. St. Onge would just have to wait until Kane got back.

Kane and Simard had reached Halifax and were checking out their target. They had planned to kill Robert MacFarlane after staking out his Halifax store called, ironically, the Spy Shop. But that first night MacFarlane wasn't there. They checked into a motel, telling the receptionist they were in town for a convention. They tried again the following day, but MacFarlane was always with other people, so Kane backed off. He and Simard went to the movies and a local gym.

On Thursday, February 27, 1997, they bought ten lobsters and had the motel chef cook them up. Afterwards they drove over to MacFarlane's store. This time, they saw MacFarlane leaving with two companions and decided to follow. MacFarlane spotted the white car and suspected he was being tailed—probably by the police. He drove to an industrial park on the outskirts of the city, as he wanted to show his friends some antique cars he stored at a warehouse. He pulled in behind the drab grey buildings where forklifts jostled for space with rusted scrap metal.

The white car pulled in as well. Never one to shy away from a fight, MacFarlane walked over to the Buick. "He gets out to confront them—like he would," says Halifax Const. Steve Waterfield. "Everywhere he goes he makes a big scene."

But it turned out to be the last scene of his life. As MacFarlane approached their car, Simard leaned out the passenger window and started firing his .38-calibre pistol.

The gun at first jammed, but Simard kept pulling the trigger and finally got off a shot, wounding MacFarlane. MacFarlane ran screaming from the car, and his companions ran for cover. Simard gave chase, pulling a 9 mm pistol from his waist. At that point the vinyl rain pants he was wearing slipped down to his knees and he almost tripped. He calmly took them off, continued the chase and shot MacFarlane in the neck. As he walked away, Simard heard two shots. He turned and saw Kane standing, gun in hand, near MacFarlane's body. But neither of Kane's shots had hit their target. St. Onge says he believes Kane intentionally missed so he could claim to his handlers that he was not McFarlane's killer.

The two men then fled in their rented Buick all the way back to Montreal, stopping only to throw their guns, a stolen Nova Scotia licence plate and clothes into some roadside woods. But they didn't know a video camera on one of the warehouses caught their car driving in. Police, aided by MacFarlane's surviving companions, later issued a bulletin for two males driving a four-door white sedan.

Murders are infrequent enough occurrences in the Maritimes that a bulletin for the killers of MacFarlane would be noteworthy. But the RCMP seemed strangely silent. Neither Constable Blinn nor Sergeant St. Onge, who both had prior knowledge of a highly suspicious white four-door sedan with two males, responded to the bulletin. What's more, the investigators had linked MacFarlane to bikers. Still, St. Onge did not respond. The RCMP's criminal operations chief in Halifax would later note in a report that St. Onge "did not contact anyone even after Robert MacFarlane was murdered and investigators had disseminated a message advising that two male suspects operating a white four-door vehicle were being sought as suspects." St. Onge later stated that when he asked Kane what he was doing in Halifax, the answer was chauffeuring strippers.

St. Onge had his own problems to worry about. His new boss, Staff Sgt. Pierre "Patame" Bolduc, a stocky, jovial cop with a bulldog face and a nickname nobody understood, was not a fan of source C-2994. Bolduc had been part of a highly successful sting operation in the early nineties that trapped numerous money launderers and drug dealers connected to the Italian Mafia and the Colombian drug cartels and led to the seizure of a boatload of cocaine.

Bolduc believed that sources must lead to major arrests. Otherwise they were useless and a waste of money. What, he asked himself, had source C-2994 done for the $2,000 a week the RCMP was paying him, not to mention the car they had leased for him, the $32,000 they had invested in the magazine and the $10,000 debt they had covered for him? Bolduc began studying the reports, and one thing kept bothering him. Much of C-2994's information was what he called "nice to know" but of little real use to the RCMP as far as criminal investigations were concerned. Bolduc's thinking led him to an uncomfortable question: if C-2994 wasn't producing for the RCMP, for whom was he producing? Was C-2994 an RCMP mole in the bikers or was he a biker mole in the RCMP? Bolduc decided to find out.

Dany Kane checked back with his handlers shortly after returning from Halifax. He met with St. Onge and Pierre Verdon on March 5 in a hotel south of Montreal. Kane had a lot to tell; Verdon scribbled nine pages of notes. Most of it was gossip—precisely of the "nice to know" variety that Bolduc complained about. Stuff like the news that Hells Angels Quebec had bought shares in the Erikson cellphone company. Or that a drug dealer asked Mom Boucher if he could deal heroin—which was against Hells rules—but Boucher had okayed it as long as he kept it a secret and gave Mom a cut.

But nowhere in the report does it indicate that St. Onge and Verdon asked Kane about his trip to Halifax, even though by then it was almost certain that they knew a Halifax cocaine dealer linked to bikers had been murdered and that their Mountie colleagues in Nova Scotia were desperately searching for two men in a white four-door sedan.

Six days later, St. Onge and Verdon again met with Kane. This time Simard's name came up. Kane told them Simard was part of the commandos, the group of Rockers set up to murder members of the rival Rock Machine. Kane called Simard "very unpredictable and dangerous . . . capable of anything." He was right. Once back in Montreal from Nova Scotia, Simard continued his killing spree: he shot and killed a friend who had witnessed him shoot the Quebec City drug dealer and his girlfriend weeks before the MacFarlane hit. Kane was still covering for his lover: he described him as five feet eight inches and weighing 150 pounds—a considerable understatement by at least 100 pounds. Again, there is no mention of Halifax in the RCMP report or whether Kane's handlers asked him anything about the MacFarlane murder.

The RCMP's next meeting with Kane was March 14. This time he told his handlers that the Hells and Rockers no longer trusted Simard because "he's got a big mouth and brags all the time about his exploits." That didn't stop Kane from taking his two sons plus Simard on a week's holiday in Jamaica that month. Again, nothing in the file indicates St. Onge or Verdon asked about Halifax.

Tanned and rested from his Caribbean vacation, Simard returned to Montreal—and on March 28 he killed again. Only this time he got truly sloppy. Simard's victim was Jean-Marc Caissy, a twenty-five-year-old member of the Rock Machine. The murder was classic Simard: cool and cold-blooded. Caissy played in a floor hockey league at an east-end Montreal sports centre. One team included drug traffickers affiliated with the Hells Angels' Rockers. When Caissy threatened them during a game and brandished a gun, the drug-dealing hockey players asked the Rockers for protection. The Rockers sent over their Commandos to deal with Caissy.

As Caissy left the arena, Simard simply walked up to him and shot him point-blank in the face with his cherished Magnum. He then calmly took out his phone and punched in the number of the pager for the head of the Commandos, Pierre Provencher. Then he entered this code: 555 357.

The first digits were the pre-arranged signal that the murder had gone down; the second was the calibre of the weapon. His job done, Simard headed for the Pro-Gym, where all the bikers hung out. He casually left his weapon in a locker and went home.

Two days later Kane called St. Onge and told him Simard was the killer. He added that Simard was going to kill again that night. St. Onge immediately passed the word on to the Montreal police, who tried to locate him. But they failed—and that evening Simard beat a drug dealer half to death with a baseball bat.

Meanwhile, the janitor at the Pro-Gym was cleaning out lockers when he found Simard's gun. Police quickly identified it as the one used in the Caissy killing. They already knew from the RCMP the name of the killer; Kane had also given the police Simard's cellphone number, his address and a description of his vehicle. Montreal police clamped a surveillance team on him and waited for him to retrieve his gun. Sure enough, on April 11, Simard walked into the Pro-Gym, went to his locker and was promptly arrested. Police questioned him over the next three days, but Simard didn't need much grilling. In return for a promise that his statement could not be used against him, he calmly recited the list of people he had shot.

Most of the names didn't surprise them. But there was one victim from outside the province whom they had never heard of—Robert MacFarlane.

On Monday, April 14, Det. Sgt. Benoit Roberge notified Halifax RCMP that they had MacFarlane's killer and were looking for his accomplice. Meanwhile, Verdon and St. Onge were having their 135th debriefing with Kane. They knew Simard had been arrested and had agreed to become a *délateur*—the word used in Quebec for an informer ready to testify against his former companions. They also knew C-2994 knew Simard and had been in Halifax when MacFarlane was murdered. Nevertheless, they remained in denial.

Nothing in their report indicates they asked about MacFarlane. In fact, the report is very upbeat. They met Kane in a hotel on the South Shore at 2 p.m. and paid him his biweekly $4,000. He told them nobody in the Rockers or Hells Angels was worried about Simard because he was such a liar that no jury would believe him. Kane then proudly announced his big news. Gilles "Trooper" Mathieu intended to nominate him to be a hangaround Nomad. Finally, after three years, Dany Kane was about to enter the inner circle. Exactly what the RCMP had wanted. Its substantial investment was about to pay off. Congratulations echoed round the room. But the celebrations were short-lived. Source C-2994 was about to become the most sought-after police target in Canada.

Events quickly spun out of control for Kane and his handlers. Police from all directions were suddenly descending on the RCMP's best-kept secret. Montreal police notified them that they wanted to interview Kane, indicating they knew—or suspected—he was their super source. The SQ also wanted to interrogate Kane. And the Halifax RCMP said they were sending two investigators to be briefed on the Simard confession and carry out further investigations.

C Division in Montreal immediately started battening down the hatches. On Tuesday, April 15, Verdon, St. Onge and Insp. John MacLaughlan, the commissioned officer in charge of intelligence, met in the office of Supt. Rowland Sugrue, head of criminal investigations, to discuss their options. They were caught between protecting what now had become a truly Machiavellian plot to penetrate the bikers and cooperating with a murder investigation. St. Onge insisted that Kane didn't do the shooting and in fact was incapable of killing anybody. St. Onge's statements indicate the degree to which he was out of touch with his source. In a subsequent report, St. Onge claimed to understand why Kane had "voluntarily omitted" to tell him about the MacFarlane murder. St. Onge said Kane didn't think he was doing anything wrong, given the fact that Simard was the trigger man and that he'd decided to participate in the MacFarlane murder because he believed it would get him nominated as a hangaround Nomad, exactly what his handlers wanted. He was, therefore, simply serving the interests of the RCMP. By hiring Simard to do the job, Kane believed he would be blameless. "After three tough years, Corp. Verdon and I believe that C-2994 is . . . not capable of pulling the trigger," St. Onge stated. He was clutching at straws. He still had no idea how wrong he was.

Sugrue, however, was not prepared to risk the RCMP's reputation on C-2994. He decided the RCMP had no choice but to cooperate with the Halifax investigation. Both the Montreal police and the SQ could wait, since they still had no evidence Kane had committed any crime in Quebec. Nevertheless, it was time, he said, to cut Kane loose. Nobody in C Division would have anything more to do with him. Nobody was allowed to contact him or receive calls from him. All payments would immediately be stopped. And Sugrue stressed one more thing: Kane's position as an RCMP source would remain strictly confidential. No outside police force must know.

The RCMP had no intention of allowing Kane to fall into the hands of another police force. The day after the meeting in Sugrue's office, Halifax RCMP investigators Sgt. G. A. Barnett and Const. Tom Townsend arrived at Dorval Airport and were whisked off to RCMP headquarters. That's when they learned the truth about Kane. The Montreal Mounties told them Kane had been a confidential source for the RCMP for three years. But they also warned the Halifax officers that nobody in the Wolverine squad knew Kane was an RCMP source "and, if possible, that this fact should not be disclosed at our meetings."

Sworn to secrecy, Townsend and Barnett then took a trip over to Wolverine headquarters, where tensions were running high. To their dismay, the Halifax Mounties discovered that the Montreal police had made a deal with Simard not to use his confession against him. Halifax investigator Barnett was boiling mad but tried to conceal his anger.

"Why would you make a deal without our knowledge and consent?" he asked.

"You should be happy," one of the Montreal cops retorted, since they now knew who killed MacFarlane.

Barnett and Townsend were definitely not happy. The RCMP men tried to keep their fury in check. They had to work with these guys. The next day they made it clear that they would not be bound by the Montreal deal with Simard and that they intended to charge him after completing their investigation. They also added that they wanted to question Simard; Quebec police politely told them Simard was having a bad day. He was upset, they said, because he had turned in his friend and lover, Dany Kane.

Meanwhile, more than a few cops at Wolverine had growing suspicions that Dany Kane was in fact the RCMP's much-vaunted source. When Barnett told a Wolverine officer that he intended to arrest Kane, the officer looked skeptical and said, "I hope you do, but I don't think your bosses will let you."

Back in Halifax, the prosecutor named to the case stressed to the RCMP that he wanted Kane arrested as soon as possible—if only to make sure he didn't kill again. Craig Botterill also noted that Kane was the only person who could link the Hells Angels to the murder. He wanted to get to him before the Hells Angels did—a problem that didn't seem to occur to the Montreal police, who wanted to bide their time until Simard signed an informant contract.

It wasn't long, however, before the main preoccupation of all three forces—Montreal, SQ and RCMP—was to be the first one to get their hands on Kane. The man who held all the cards, though, was St. Onge. And he played them very close to his chest. He was living by the RCMP dictum that the source belongs to the handler, and he didn't want to let go. At least not yet. He had been around long enough to know that sooner or later sources like Kane screw up and get caught committing a crime. It's the nature of the beast. He was trying to control the situation and protect the identity of C-2994. That was the deal he and Verdon had made with Kane three years earlier, and they were going to stand by it. But it was also self-serving. The RCMP brass knew that "the disclosure . . . has the potential to cause significant negative media attention," as an internal memo delicately put it.

Remarkably, with the approval of his superiors, St. Onge was still in touch with Kane. In fact, Kane gave the RCMP intelligence briefings on April 17 and again on April 25, which St. Onge passed on to Wolverine. Halifax RCMP was pressing for an arrest; St. Onge knew an arrest was inevitable. He just wanted to keep Kane in the RCMP family: that way Kane's role as an agent—and his life—

would be protected. So St. Onge set up one last meeting with the best source of his career.

At 2:30 p.m. on Wednesday, April 30, Verdon and St. Onge entered room 524 at the Ramada Inn in Longueuil and called Kane's pager twice, carefully entering the coded digits that told him his handlers were waiting for him. He arrived soon after the call. St. Onge barely had time to greet him when he got a call from an angry senior officer at Wolverine:

"Gaetan, I know what you are doing and I want you to stop immediately and call your boss, Sugrue."

St. Onge agreed and called Sugrue's office. He spoke to Inspector MacLaughlan and Staff Sergeant Bolduc, who told him to wait before arresting Kane. But by that time it was too late. Verdon was already reading Kane his rights. He searched him, and the two men handed Kane over to Townsend. Townsend took Kane to a waiting RCMP plane at St-Hubert Airport and flew him to Halifax, leaving behind a chorus of furious Wolverines.

Before his departure, Kane turned to St. Onge, his long-time handler who had become somewhat of a father figure to the lone biker spy. "I would have been a hangaround Nomad soon," he said. "I didn't do anything in Halifax."

"If the Halifax investigators have come all the way down here, it's because they have a lot more than just Simard's statement," St. Onge replied. He was right. They had recovered one of the murder weapons precisely where Simard told them he had tossed it; they had the pants he had left at the crime scene; and a video of their white sedan entering the warehouse parking lot.

"We've got Kane cold, trapped, cooked," Townsend told St. Onge, referring to the murder charge.

St. Onge was skeptical. "I wouldn't be so sure. When it's a biker, you never know what's going to happen."

FIVE

Killer Ambition

---

*"They made sure you were covered in blood.
They injected you with it."*
ROBERT PIGEON, SQ POLICE INTERROGATOR

With Dany Kane behind bars, the police were blind and deaf to the inner workings of the Hells Angels for the first time in three years. Source C-2994 had been the eyes and ears of the cops in the biker organization; now the Wolverine squad—already crippled by scandal—was even more in the dark than usual without the pipeline of information and warnings provided by the Mounties' man inside the HA.

The setback came at a bad time. Ever since 1995, when a chatty SQ officer let slip that the police had a "coded informer" deep inside the Angels, Mom Boucher was obsessed with rooting out informants. He'd confided in his closest allies that he would "raise a lot of shit" to put an end to police spies once and for all.

By the late spring of 1997, Boucher began to contemplate waging war on the justice system, killing a few prison guards—maybe even some judges and politicians—so that no one would ever dare challenge his empire again. The

Nomad leader knew his crowd was filled with crackpots who would kill at the snap of his fingers. But he needed somebody cold-blooded and crazy enough to kill someone in uniform.

He found that killer ambition in a small-time drug dealer named Stéphane Gagné.

Stéphane Gagné grew up in the same working-class neighbourhood that had bred Boucher—Hochelaga-Maisonneuve. His father had eked out a living as a professional wrestler in spite of having severed both legs below the knee in an accident. His uncle was a legendary gunman for the Dubois crime family until he was gunned down in 1974 in a late-night shootout.

To a teenager who only made it as far as Grade 7, a conscious choice to follow in his uncle's criminal footsteps seemed the only path to success. And Gagné quickly found that, like his uncle, he was good at it. He started a thriving business selling drugs to students, though a lot of his cash went to financing his own drug habit. Most of his teenage years were spent "*quasiment gelé*," as he put it. Ripped. Semi-conscious. Doped out on daily doses of hash and the occasional PCP. When he wasn't pushing drugs, he robbed homes and businesses, stole cars. Over the next twelve years, he built up a respectable criminal file: convicted nine times for car theft, break and enter, probation violations and drug trafficking.

By age twenty-four, he was making more money from drug sales than he had ever dreamed of. He later testified that he had settled down with his wife, Marie-Claude Nantais, who willingly helped him with his trafficking, driving the car when he made deliveries. He had a son, Harley-David, named after his prized bike. With a partner named Tony Jalbert, Gagné operated crack houses and shooting galleries. In a good week they each cleared up to

$6,000 cash; in a year, they made about $250,000. Gagné had a good set of honed muscles and he knew when to use them. His nickname was "Godasse," meaning "old shoe." He knew how to put the boots to people who didn't pay their drug debts.

He and Jalbert were independent. They didn't belong to any gang. They bought drugs from various suppliers. Then came the summer of 1994, and the entire game changed. The biker war came down hard as a fist. In the truest sense, Gagné and Jalbert were victims of their own success. Their shooting galleries hadn't gone unnoticed. The Rock Machine wanted part of the action. Their rivals, the Hells Angels, wanted it all.

One day Gagné got paged by Paul "Fonfon" Fontaine. Fontaine was with the Rockers, the Hells Angels' puppet club. "Close down your shooting galleries," Fontaine said.

Just like that. No negotiation.

After consulting his partner, Gagné tried to set up a meeting with Mom Boucher. He went to an east-end boutique on Sherbrooke Street called Frank Rock that sold Bell Mobility pagers and left a pager number with the owner. The next morning he got an urgent page to meet Mom at the boutique. Gagné was excited and a little wary: he was on his way to meet the king.

Boucher was waiting in the store when Gagné arrived. Putting a finger to his lips, Boucher cautioned Gagné to say nothing and guided him out onto the street. He called him by his nickname, Godasse. Very friendly. As they sauntered along Sherbrooke Street with one of Boucher's bodyguards tailing behind, the two men talked partly in gestures, partly in the vague language of the underworld, never referring to anything directly and then peppering it with obscenities. Gagné touched his nose to signify cocaine, then touched his arm to signify he wanted Boucher to front him the cocaine. After all the hand signals and discreet talk were over, Gagné had what he wanted. He could go on selling, but he was now working for the Hells Angels, specifically Paul Fontaine.

His first chance to show his loyalty to the Hells came in a volcanic fury of violence and retribution in December 1994. He was tossed in prison for two years less a day for selling 1.5 kilos of coke in a sting operation run by an SQ undercover agent named Robert Pigeon. Neither Gagné nor the unassuming detective could know that this routine takedown would set both men on a collision course that three years later would help destroy the biker king Boucher. For now, Gagné viewed Pigeon as just another forgettable cop trying to improve his arrest record.

Bordeaux prison, in the north end of Montreal, was in effect an armed camp run by rival biker gangs. The Rock Machine controlled the C Wing; Gagné specifically asked not to be placed there, claiming he was with the Angels. The guards checked his file, and it showed no biker connection. So despite his entreaties, they tossed him in C anyway. Within a day, Rock Machine members confronted Gagné in his cell and demanded that he declare his allegiance to them. One of them, a biker named Jean Duquaire, who would later become a leader of the Bandidos, tossed a newspaper photo of Boucher on the floor and ordered Gagné to stomp on it. He refused and was beaten so badly that he had to be taken to the prison hospital.

Gagné's revenge was swift and brutal. With the help of several inmates, he attacked Duquaire with a metal bar and a makeshift knife. When an inmate walked in on the beating, Gagné forced him to stab Duquaire as well so he wouldn't squeal to the guards.

No charges were ever laid, but the guards knew who was responsible. They transferred Gagné to a prison in Sorel, fifty miles east of Montreal on the St. Lawrence River.

There he met Boucher once again. Boucher had just arrived to serve six months for illegal possession of a firearm. Boucher regarded Sorel prison as his personal turf. When prison warden Nicole Quesnel refused him day passes, arsonists burned down her St-Lambert home.

Gagné wasted no time in boasting about defending Boucher's honour at Bordeaux. Mom was pleased. As a reward, he ordered his son Francis to deliver a weekly cash payment to Gagné's wife. The two biker inmates—the Nomad leader at the top of the biker pyramid and the fiery Gagné, who was so insignificant he was not even a hangaround for a puppet club—became constant companions. Even though prison officials refused Gagné's request to be transferred to Boucher's wing, they arranged to meet in the exercise yard and at sessions of Alcoholics Anonymous and Drug Addicts Anonymous, which they attended frequently just so they could talk. Boucher seemed to be obsessed with prison guards and frequently spoke about having big plans for them.

Boucher was released in mid-summer. Gagné had to wait until the following April of 1996 to get out. He immediately contacted Francis Boucher and asked for a meeting with his father. The next day he was told to meet Mom that morning at his Bennett Street headquarters. The two men went to lunch.

"I've got important work for you," Boucher said. "I want you to stick around."

Two days later Boucher suddenly showed up at Gagné's mother's house, where Gagné was living. Mom Boucher was like that. He would appear as if out of nowhere or page someone demanding instant action. Gagné never knew what to expect. This time Mom came with his bodyguard, Toots Tousignant. Mom had Gagné's first assignment.

Mom gave Gagné $1,000 in cash and took him for a drive through Verdun, a blue-collar neighbourhood in south Montreal. The three men drove by a Rock Machine clubhouse and garage. He wanted Gagné to put a bomb in a car parked near the club to create a diversion while some Hells Angels and Rockers ran into the club and machine-gunned its members. But he never mentioned the word "bomb." Instead, he clenched his fist and then opened it like an explosion.

Over the next few weeks the plan changed several times, but each time Gagné's obedient efforts were thwarted by the presence of police. No one realized that Dany Kane had tipped off his handlers about the intention to bomb the Rock Machine clubhouse. On August 23, police seized a van abandoned near the clubhouse—right in the middle of a crowded neighbourhood. Inside were two hundred pounds of dynamite rigged to be set off by remote control. When police later ran a test at an army munitions site, they discovered the bomb was powerful enough to scatter shrapnel more than a thousand feet and damage numerous buildings, potentially killing dozens of innocent bystanders.

Gagné was hungry to become a Rocker, the same farm team for the Angels that Kane had successfully penetrated. That meant cranking up the violence. The Rockers had formed attack teams. The "baseball team" battered heads and destroyed property such as clubs run by rival bikers. At the top of the ladder, however, were the members of the "football team." They killed people, with bombs, guns or by beating them to death. Gagné joined one of several football teams but was frustrated with the lack of action and security. He contacted Rockers Paul Fontaine and Toots Tousignant, hoping to transfer to their football team, which operated in the gay village, just east of downtown Montreal. Gagné found his new team to be far more cautious. An atmosphere of relentless paranoia clung to every encounter. Paranoia over police electronic surveillance. Paranoia over betrayal. The bikers took long walks, discarding all electronic devices for fear that a pager or cellphone might be bugged. They communicated in a sort of crude sign language. To order a hit, an Angel merely made the sign of a pistol. Often they wrote on magnetic boards, then quickly erased the message. Not to speak directly about the crimes was a form of censorship of the crime itself, as if it never happened.

Gagné's first target—and, as it turned out, his first big mistake—was Christian Bellemare, a small-time Hochelaga-Maisonneuve drug dealer who owed Gagné about $12,000 and stubbornly refused to pay. In March 1997, Gagné and Steve Boies, another Hells wannabe, lured the victim to a snowbound chalet in the Laurentians. But Gagné's first murder quickly turned into a grotesque comic opera. As Bellemare climbed over a snowbank, Boies shot him with a revolver. Bellemare fell, but wasn't dead. Gagné tried to shoot him point-blank, but his gun jammed. A frightened and mystified Bellemare kept pleading for his life; Gagné simply gripped Bellemare's throat and strangled him. Bellemare collapsed. Gagné and Boies covered him in snow and headed back to Montreal.

Trouble was, Bellemare wasn't dead. He regained consciousness, dug himself out, stumbled to a nearby chalet where he got help. Gagné and Boies read about their mistake in the newspapers the next day and went into hiding. A month later, out of sheer boredom, they returned to the streets and went back to work for the Hells Angels, who didn't seem to mind that Gagné had screwed up his first murder. They promoted him to hangaround Rocker. Gagné was on his way up the ranks, and he was determined that his next victim would not walk away.

Life for a soldier like Gagné was one of slavish obedience. Between drug deals to earn a living, he served as bodyguard to the Hells. When the Hells went out on the town, he carried the bags. In bars or restaurants, he took a table by himself, watched the door and surveyed the crowd. Nobody was allowed to get near the Angels except women. He was always armed. If someone entered and went directly to the bathroom, he would follow and check him out. "If the guy returned and put his fingerprints everywhere, that's not a killer, that guy, because a killer would not put his fingerprints everywhere," Gagné says.

He was also regularly called on to conduct surveillance. The Hells had their own surveillance vehicles, just like the cops. They had three stored in a garage located south of Montreal: a Mazda pickup P-2000, a Mazda 323, and a twenty-seven-foot van with a sign on the side advertising a plumbing company. The van had cameras, shelves and batteries to keep the cameras working for seventy-two hours. All the vehicles had tinted windows.

The Hells had rigged a Kleenex box with a video camera. They set the box on the dashboard or by the rear window of their spy cars and left the vehicle on a street. Gagné would pick it up a day later and hand the film over to Mom. One time, Mom asked him to film the funeral of the wife of Mafia boss Frank Cotroni. He wanted photos of everybody who showed up. Once he had finished with the Rock Machine, Mom was thinking of waging war against the Italians.

Gagné was more than just an obedient soldier; he was determined to please his Angel bosses every chance he got. "When the Hells went on a bike rally and stopped for a rest, Gagné would jump off his Harley and start polishing the Hells' machines," one Quebec police officer says. "He'd make sure the refrigerator was stocked with beer at biker parties and brought them drinks." No Hells Angel had to ask for another beer when Gagné was around.

In the summer of 1997, Gagné got the chance he'd been waiting for, one he thought would help him in his ambition to become a full-patch Rocker and then a Hells Angel.

As Kane had warned the RCMP, Boucher was determined to stop the leaks, particularly after the SQ had told him about the mole within his circle. He wanted to make it as hazardous as possible for anybody who decided to testify against the Hells. In his twisted thinking, he believed that if they killed guards, policemen, prosecutors and judges, no biker would ever turn stoolie for fear of fast and furious retribution.

In June 1997, Boucher resolved to escalate the violence by turning his war machine on the state. It couldn't have come at a worse time for the police. Kane's arrest and imprisonment meant the flow of insider information that might have alerted police to the approaching disaster had dried up. Had the RCMP kept a closer watch on their super source before he killed MacFarlane, two prison guards might still be alive today.

Boucher told his two right-hand men, Paul "Fonfon" Fontaine and Toots Tousignant that he wanted prison guards killed. They in turn turned to Godasse Gagné, the eager novice in the Rockers. Which is how, on a warm June evening just after sundown, Gagné found himself in the woods near the Rivière-des-Prairies prison.

The small, high-security prison, located in a largely commercial area in east-end Montreal, houses prisoners awaiting trial or other court procedures. Each morning, blue justice department buses take inmates through the streets of Montreal to the downtown courthouse. The prison sits about one hundred yards back from the road, partially surrounded by thick woods. Gagné positioned himself at the edge of the woods with a full view of the prison parking lot. He had parked his car several streets away, walked cautiously along a gravel path and crawled under a chain-link fence. After observing the scene for some time, he left, but several days later repeated the same routine. He was hunting for a target.

At one point he saw a man dressed in white walk toward the prison entrance past the guardhouse and disappear. He figured he had to be a cook or something. Gagné crept nearer the parking lot and noticed another man dressed in a suit, with a valise, climb into an Oldsmobile V8. He was probably a director of some sort because he left just before the guards finished their evening shift. The man was clearly one of the higher-ups and would make an easy target.

One night, Gagné waited in his car for the man in the Oldsmobile to exit the prison grounds. But when he followed him, he discovered that the man turned north instead of south at the first main street, Henri-Bourassa Boulevard. This was no good. North leads away from the highway, and Gagné thought he needed the highway as an escape route. The man in the Oldsmobile was saved. Gagné had to find a prison worker who turned right.

He decided to head back to the prison the following night and check out the man in white. But that day he got a page from Toots Tousignant, ordering him to come to Boucher's headquarters on Bennett Street. Tousignant was waiting on the street when Gagné arrived. Toots knew that Mom Boucher was getting impatient.

"I have a screw [guard] to kill at Bordeaux, and I thought of you because they tore a strip off you," Toots told him. He was referring to the fact that Gagné claimed the guards had once beat him up.

Gagné told him he was working with Paul Fontaine. Tousignant brushed aside his excuse. "I'll arrange that with Paul, and then you'll help me."

That Thursday, June 19, Toots headed out to the prison with Gagné to plot an escape route. The plan was to follow a guard from the prison on a motorcycle, kill the guard on the highway heading north just before the bridge to Laval and drive to the waiting getaway car, where they would leave the motorcycle. They chose the second turnoff in

Laval, leading to a series of large shopping malls, to make the switch.

Now they were ready for the kill. Several days later, Gagné and Tousignant drove to a garage on Rue St-André in the centre of town where the Hells had stored two stolen motorcycles. They chose the '81 Suzuki Katana. They pulled blue motorcycle clothes, pants, jackets and gloves over their street clothes. They put nylon stockings over their heads so there wouldn't be any trace of hair inside their motorcycle helmets. In the pockets of the jackets, someone had already placed three guns, including a semi-automatic and a revolver. With Gagné driving, they headed toward Bordeaux.

But the best-laid plans, even of killers, sometimes go awry. Gagné quickly realized there was a major problem with the bike: Toots was too heavy riding on the back, the clutch slipped and they couldn't get enough speed. So they returned to the garage, and on the evening of Thursday, June 26, they tried again. Both men prepared for the hunt in silence. They had to get to Bordeaux before 9:45 p.m., when the shift changed. Gagné was beginning to feel the stress. He found himself taking deep breaths and wondering if Toots would hold up under the pressure.

Gagné stuck the two revolvers in his front belt, and Tousignant tucked the semi-automatic in his back, giving Gagné—who would ride behind Toots—easy access to all three weapons.

When they got to Bordeaux, the first guard they followed was in a silver-grey Cherokee. They followed him toward the highway but were foiled when the guard turned south. The killers raced back to Bordeaux, hoping to pick up a guard heading north to Laval.

Diane Lavigne was an eleven-year veteran at Bordeaux. She'd followed in the footsteps of her father, who had served almost three decades as a guard, becoming one of the first women hired there. She worked in the front office, classifying prisoners. A small, robust woman with a broad smile and short, curly red hair, she had married young and now had two grown children. She lived in a bungalow in the working-class community of St-Eustache, located north of the prison.

That day in late June, she did as she always did. She punched out, walked out of the main entrance and headed to her white minivan in the parking lot. She usually wore civilian clothes to and from work. Today she wore her uniform. She nodded at the gatekeeper as he raised the barrier and let her pass. She turned left onto Gouin Boulevard, then left again onto Salaberry Street. As she took the north ramp onto the highway, she paid no particular attention to the two men in blue riding the motorcycle behind her. She was taking a route she had taken thousands of times before. In the dying light, Tousignant raised his tinted visor to get a better look. Once on the autoroute, he said to Gagné, "Do it before the bridge."

Meanwhile, a second guard, Danielle Leclair, had left work immediately after Lavigne. Now on the highway, she found herself following Lavigne's minivan. A swiftly moving motorcycle raced past her, and she slowed to avoid a collision.

Gagné was ready. He gave Tousignant two slaps on the thigh and pulled the revolver from his belt. Tousignant brought the bike even with the van. Gagné looked over at the driver and saw the white shoulder patch against the blue shirt of a prison official. He fired one shot. Then another. And another. A bullet went through Lavigne's left forearm, damaging some soft tissue. Another shot penetrated her upper left arm and lung and lodged in her back. That was the shot that would kill her.

Gagné thought he'd hit his target but didn't know where or how badly. The driver didn't seem even to notice him. He signalled to Tousignant, and the bike sped away.

Leclair heard several loud cracks and saw Lavigne's car drift onto the shoulder. Leclair slowed to see if her colleague had a flat tire. Traffic was heavy, and she was going too fast to stop, so she continued on her way. Only the next day did she find out what had happened.

Tousignant and Gagné abandoned the motorcycle in the shopping mall and retrieved the getaway car. Gagné removed his nylon gear as they drove back down the autoroute past the scene of the shooting. They could see the lonely white van on the opposite side with its emergency lights flashing. Cars and trucks streamed by, but nobody paid any attention. Lavigne's van was just another vehicle parked on the shoulder, probably with engine trouble.

The two killers returned to the garage. They put their gear into a sack. Gagné tossed it into his car, then drove to a wooded area in east-end Montreal. He poured five gallons of gasoline on the clothes and helmets and burned them. He then went home to get some sleep.

Back on the highway, a tow truck had finally pulled over next to Lavigne's vehicle. The driver found her slumped against the steering wheel and called 911.

Gagné had no idea he had killed a woman—he had just seen the uniform. It was only from the news reports the next day that he learned about his victim. First thing the next morning, Paul Fontaine came to Gagné's house. Together, they went to the office on Bennett where they saw Mom and Trooper Mathieu. Nobody mentioned the shooting. Instead, the four men went to a florist on Ste-Catherine Street. Boucher went inside and demanded to know where the owner was.

"On his way," the clerk answered.

"Ah, these fags—just like women, always late!" Boucher laughed.

The owner arrived soon after and went directly to the refrigerated storage room. He returned with three bouquets of flowers. He knew the routine. Every Friday morning Mom bought flowers for his wife and his mistress, Louise Mongeau, who frequently spoke to him over the phone, calling him "*minou*" and "*mon p'tit chaton*"—my pet, my little kitten. Mom has never disclosed the recipient of the third bouquet.

The four bikers then went for a walk along Ste-Catherine Street, leaving their pagers and cellphones in the trucks as a security precaution. Gagné and Fontaine trailed behind Mom and the Trooper.

"Me and Toots, we did it," Gagné whispered to Fontaine.

He wanted to get the word to Mom that he had carried out what he knew were the boss's orders. He wanted credit. Fontaine immediately walked ahead to join Mom and whispered in his ear. Mom stopped and waited for Gagné.

"That's great, my Godasse. It's not serious that she had tits," Boucher said, consoling Gagné, since killing a woman might seem less macho. "Don't talk to anybody about this because it means twenty-five years—and if there was a death penalty, they'd hang you." He cricked his neck as if he were hanging from a rope and laughed. Mom then turned to Mathieu: "What do you think, Trooper?"

"That's great, Godasse!"

Gagné was beaming with pride. He was one step closer to getting his full patch. He and Paul dropped back, and the four men continued their walk. They sauntered around the block and then drove back to the Bennett Street office, where several bikers were gathered around the radio. When the announcer began talking about the Diane Lavigne murder, Paul Fontaine motioned for silence. The moment the news reader said Lavigne was dead, the bikers celebrated by slapping one another on the back. Gagné and Toots hugged and smiled. They felt they had done a good job. The gang then went off to Chez Paré, a downtown strip club that serves free roast beef for lunch. They ate heartily.

On July 1, 1997, Fontaine and Tousignant got their rewards. They were made Hells Angels Nomads prospects. Faxes, intercepted by the police, were sent out to all the members, announcing their promotions. The following evening, Tousignant started phoning family and friends to boast about his promotion. The wiretaps offer a glimpse at the banality of biker murder—how the Angels call family to boast about business as if they were car salesmen or accountants.

Tousignant first telephoned his wife. His son Ricky answered the phone and Toots asked him how he'd enjoyed playing in the park that day. Then Tousignant's wife, Eve, came on the line and Tousignant rushed to tell her the good news.

"I got my patch yesterday."

"You did?"

"Yeah! I knew, eh."

"I'm so proud of you."

"Yeah!"

"You're proud of yourself?"

"Yeah!"

"You earned it. Did you tell Ricky yet?"

"No."

"No? Just show it to him, don't tell him."

No sooner had the jubilant biker said goodbye to the wife than he dialled his mistress.

"Hey, I've become a prospect."

"All right! Congratulations!"

"Thanks."

"I'm really happy for you."

Gagné, for his part, had to wait for his reward. He was attacked by a member of the Rock Machine, who rammed his car into Gagné's motorcycle. Battered and bruised, Gagné took about a month to recover. The Hells Angels stationed armed guards outside his hospital room. Once out, Gagné continued selling drugs and acting as a bodyguard.

Then finally, on August 21, he got his prize for the Lavigne murder. During a party thrown for a Rocker vice-president, the club gave him his patch as a striker, one rung below a full-patch Rocker. One more kill should do it.

He renewed his hunt for prison guards and returned to stake out the Rivière-des-Prairies prison. Again, the lives of the prison guards seemed to hang on which way they turned when they left for home. But Mom Boucher was impatient again. By the beginning of September, he wanted to know why Paul Fontaine and Gagné hadn't carried out the second hit. Gagné felt even more pressure when he discovered that after the Lavigne murder, Fontaine didn't want to kill another guard—but Boucher was insistent.

Now Normand Robitaille was also putting pressure on Gagné.

"How's it going with you and Paul?" he asked one day.

They were having trouble finding a good getaway route, Gagné replied.

But the senior Nomad and confidant of Mom wasn't buying it. He told him of a prison bus that takes a route along St-Jean-Baptiste in the east end. Gagné decided to check it out. It sounded promising.

On Wednesday, September 3, Gagné and Fontaine saw a guard leave the prison at 3 p.m. His name was Richard Auclair. Gagné had worked out an escape route and wanted to do the hit as soon as Auclair stopped at a light.

"How do you feel?" Paul asked him.

"I feel fine. You?" Gagné looked over at his partner. He didn't like what he saw. Fontaine looked a bit unhinged.

"Ah!" Fontaine sighed. "I don't want to do it."

"What do you mean you don't want to do it?"

"I know we have to do it, but I don't want to. I don't like the getaway route. Okay? I think there's another way."

So they let Auclair drive off, "I don't want to do twenty-five years for killing guards," Fontaine said as he watched

Auclair disappear into traffic. "They're nothing to me. [Killing a] Rock Machine—that doesn't bother me because they're our enemies."

Fontaine then put the motorcycle in gear and drove back to the garage Steve Boies had rented at 2905 Rue Losch in St-Hubert to store stolen vehicles for the Hells. Fontaine didn't like the idea of using a motorcycle. He wanted a van for the job and a car to make the getaway. He decided to talk to Mom.

The opportunity arose the next day at the Bennett Street office. Fontaine told Boucher he wanted to speak to him. The two went outside, with Gagné following several steps behind.

"I need this," Fontaine said, making the sign of a car with his hands.

"Do what you have to do, and then speak to me afterwards," Boucher said.

The Angels were nothing if not an efficient killing machine. By the end of the day, Gagné was told the required automobiles had been delivered. When he arrived at his mother's house, there was a stolen Dodge Caravan on the street waiting for him.

Gagné was a cautious killer. He had forgotten his gloves, so he took off his running shoes and socks, put his socks on his hands and climbed into the van. No fingerprints. He drove the van to Losch Street, then went out searching the streets for an identical white Dodge Caravan. When he located one in a parking lot, he took a stencilled impression of the licence plate and returned to the garage to make a copy, using the metal skills he had learned in prison. Parked in the garage was the getaway vehicle: a gold Mazda 323 that according to court evidence was supplied by Daniel Foster, an automobile concession owner and friend of Boucher's. Foster was often seen around the Bennett Street office. Two of his companies were registered to that address, and Boucher carried his personal phone numbers in his diary.

On Friday, September 5, Gagné and Fontaine returned to the prison, looking for their prey and a good escape route. They arrived early. That's when they noticed the prison bus. It arrived each morning at about 6:45 to pick up prisoners. But before it got there, it had to stop at a railway level crossing. This would be ideal: plenty of time to ambush the bus and make their escape to some woods out in the east end. There they could burn the van and the weapons and drive off in the getaway car, which would be parked close by. Fontaine liked the plan.

So the following Monday, September 8, they drove the Mazda to the woods and took the van to the level crossing, arriving just after 6:15 a.m. They prepared for the ambush.

Fontaine checked his 357 Magnum revolver. He was supposed to do the job himself. Gagné was simply backup. But then Gagné mentioned that one of the guards might be armed.

"I'll take the driver, you do the other one," Fontaine said. Normally a calm, thoughtful guy, Fontaine was clearly stressed. Gagné nodded and pulled his 9 mm semi-automatic from his belt. The two got out of the car and sauntered over to a bus shelter near the tracks.

Pierre Rondeau, a forty-nine-year-old father of a teenage boy, climbed into the blue prison bus at 6:10 that morning and drove out of the underground parking lot at Montreal's courthouse. It was the second of twelve buses to leave the garage that morning. His assistant, Robert Corriveau, fifty-one, was next to him in a passenger seat that was turned to face the driver. They were doing what they did every morning: driving to Rivière-des-Prairies to pick up prisoners slated to appear in court that day. Occasionally, they stopped in at a doughnut shop. They sometimes varied their route for no other reason than boredom. That day, Rondeau made the fateful decision of taking Du Tricentenaire toward the railway crossing.

The two guards were chatting when Rondeau pulled to a halt at the tracks. That's when Corriveau saw a man dressed in dark clothes pointing a gun in their direction. Paul Fontaine opened fire. He weighed 240 pounds and was only five feet seven inches tall, but the biker was agile enough to pull himself onto the hood of the bus. Through the front window he fired point-blank at Rondeau, hitting him three times. One bullet ricocheted inside his body, fatally damaging his heart, both lungs and his liver.

Now it was Gagné's turn. He fired at Corriveau, but his gun jammed. Corriveau ducked down onto the floor. Gagné cleared the gun chamber, walked to the side of the bus and fired at Corriveau through the door. By this time, Fontaine was already lumbering back to their van. Gagné followed but kept firing in case one of the guards fired back. He had no idea if he had hit his target. He just emptied his gun in the direction of the bus. He didn't realize that one of his bullets had hit Rondeau, lying wounded in the bus. Corriveau, who miraculously had not been hit, dialled 911 on his cellphone.

Gagné gunned the van and headed to the woods, where he emptied five gallons of gas on the floor of the van. When he tossed a match on the gas, the fireball that engulfed the interior badly seared his face. He leaped out of the van and slammed the door. His facial skin turning crimson, Gagné made his way to the getaway car, not realizing he had cut off oxygen to the fire; it died down— allowing police to recover the weapons intact.

As he ran to the car, he noticed a girl standing inside a bus shelter. Nancy Dubé was going to work at an east-end Montreal appliance and furniture store. As Gagné climbed into the Mazda to join Fontaine, he wondered if she had seen him. But there was nothing he could do about it. His weapon was in the van.

"You forgot the licence plate," Paul said, referring to the false plate Gagné had so carefully crafted for the van.

"Yeah, I forgot it," Gagné said impatiently. "Let's go."

The two men sped to Hochelaga-Maisonneuve, where Fontaine retrieved his own car and the two men separated. Before driving away, Paul instructed Gagné to call Steve "Mon Oncle" Boies to help get rid of the evidence.

"Make sure you get rid of everything," Fontaine cautioned.

Gagné didn't have to be told. He had left the guns in the burning van, but he still wanted to get rid of his clothes and shoes. He bundled them up, drove to St-Bruno and burned them in a wood near a bike path. The image of the girl in the bus shelter continued to haunt him. His face was getting redder, and the skin began to hurt. When he got back to the Losch Street garage, he got a call from Fontaine.

"Hey, in the garage there's a box of bullets, a licence plate. Get rid of them. Call Mon Oncle to help you and then stay home. Don't go out."

Fontaine was worried that Gagné's burned face might give him away. Police were scouring the city for biker suspects, and Fontaine didn't want Gagné out in public. That's why he thought Boies should help Gagné destroy the evidence. Boies had already helped Gagné attach the fake licence plate to the van. Of course, he was never told what it was for. Now Boies would help dispose of the box of bullets, clean up the garage and drive the gold Mazda to a junkyard to have it crushed. Again, he would never be told why. And while Boies could speculate all he wanted, he could never prove any connection. It seemed safe to bring him in. A small thing. But it turned into a big mistake. As events unravelled, Fontaine's decision to elicit Boies's assistance would prove disastrous for the Angels.

Gagné's day was not over. When he got home, Tousignant paged him.

"Are you busy?" he asked.

Gagné was tired and just wanted to go to bed. But he couldn't lie to a Hells Angel, not if he wanted to get ahead in their world. So he said no and, on Tousignant's orders, went out and bought several boxes of bolts at a Reno Depot home improvement store. Tousignant wanted the bolts to blow up a Rock Machine meeting to be held at a lawyer's office. Fortunately, a secretary stumbled upon the bomb before it blew up.

Exhausted, Gagné finally went home to sleep—dreaming perhaps of the full patch he was sure was now his. The next morning, Normand Robitaille came to Gagné's house and gave him a roll of five stacks of cash held together by rubber bands. This time there would be no Bennett Street celebrations.

"You are going to take a vacation in Western Canada," Robitaille told him and left.

The vacation plans changed slightly when Fontaine arrived later that day. He took Gagné's magnetic board—so they could "talk" to each other without any police bugs picking up the conversation—and wrote out his new instructions: "You are going to the Dominican Republic. Buy some plane tickets for you, your wife and your kid, and stay for a week because it will disguise your burned face."

When Gagné returned from his Caribbean vacation, he and Fontaine drove over to the Pro-Gym. After Boucher finished his training and drank a coffee in the gym's snack-bar, he finally turned to Gagné.

"So, your trip was good? It's too bad you had to take your wife, 'cause there's some beautiful chicks down there."

Then he looked Gagné in the eye, and became all Hells Angels business:

"You know, it's not Mom that's speaking to you now. It's the Hells. We've done this thing with the prison guards so there won't be any more informants around us because anybody who speaks about this is going to get twenty-five years."

Then the biker leader posed the one question that concerned him the most: "Does anybody else know about this?"

Gagné was about to tell him about Steve Boies, but Fontaine jumped in and calmly assured Mom: "No. Nobody else knows." Gagné tried to conceal his surprise. Boies couldn't connect them to the murders directly, Gagné thought, but Boucher should know that he helped dispose of the evidence. That at least partially brought Boies into the loop. And if Mom ever found out he hadn't been told about Boies, Gagné would be in trouble because telephone records would show Gagné had paged him. Fontaine would then blame Gagné.

But Gagné couldn't call Fontaine on it now that he had just lied to Mom. Doubts would be raised in Boucher's mind. And that was enough to get people killed. Fontaine would probably kill Gagné himself. And Mom might have them both killed. Gagné decided it was better to keep his mouth shut.

Later, Gagné confided in Tousignant about the Boies incident.

Toots tried to assure him: "If you lie to the guys, you're going to be killed. You can't lie to the guys. You can lie to the police, but among the bikers you can't lie."

Another prison worker dead, and police had no leads. But this time the guards themselves were beginning to beat the bushes. That's how Serge Boutin found out that Gagné's name had come up.

Boutin was the Hells paymaster and manager of drug trafficking in Montreal's gay village. Gagné and Steve Boies were his employees. Fontaine was his partner.

He also had his spies. At any given time, several members of Boutin's crew were in prison. When they came out he usually questioned them about what they'd heard inside. Convicts are bored and like to talk. And Boutin liked to listen. It helped him keep track of what was happening on the street. In October 1997, he heard something that deeply disturbed him. The Bordeaux guards were asking every convict entering the prison if they were aware that Stéphane Gagné was involved in the killing of the guards. Boutin had been around long enough to know what was going on. The police were using the guards to flush out the murderers or anybody remotely connected. Rumours pinpointed Gagné, who had been a well-known prison troublemaker. The names of Paul Fontaine and Tousignant were also on the street.

One day Boutin took Gagné and Fontaine aside.

"Listen, I'm hearing that the guards are spreading rumours about you, Stéphane, that you had something to do with the guards' murders."

Both Gagné and Fontaine left without saying a word.

But the news got to Boucher. Three weeks later he called Fontaine and Gagné for a meeting in front of the Lafleur restaurant at Ontario and De Lorimier streets.

"Do you know that there are guys at Bordeaux prison, people who are our allies, who say that when they go through the classification in the prison the guards ask them if they know Godasse. When they say yes, the guards say, 'You know that Godasse killed the prison guards?'"

Gagné smiled and laughed nervously.

But Mom was not amused. "It's because you're so irritating when you're in prison. That must be why the guards think it's you."

The talk ended, but Gagné was unnerved. Boucher was fishing, testing his reactions, and Gagné knew it. Boucher was worried about whether Gagné was a standup guy. Gagné's life was on the line. If Mom thought for a moment he would sing, he knew he was dead.

He decided to stay close to Boucher. A few days later he asked to speak to him at the Bennett Street offices.

"No problem," Boucher said casually, leading him out into the street.

Gagné told him that he always took all the precautions necessary to ensure that his people didn't talk.

"I take the social security numbers and licence numbers of everybody who works for me, just like you," he said.

But Mom didn't seem interested. "We're going to do another screw," he announced.

"Hey," Gagné said, amazed. "The police are all over the place. Everybody is being followed."

"Nothing to worry about," Mom said. "We're going to do a policeman. We're going to do prosecutors, judges. But that's not for you, my Godasse, because you have already done your part."

Gagné left Bennett Street slightly relieved that Mom was still on the hunt and, he hoped, no longer harbouring doubts about his loyalty. Gagné spent the next six weeks trying to expand his drug business and preparing for the twentieth-anniversary celebrations of the Quebec Hells Angels, slated for Saturday, December 6, 1997. Hells Angels from all over the country were flying in for the weekend party. Gagné was to chauffeur the guests from the airport. He was looking forward to it, hoping it would be the occasion for him to get his full patch at last.

It was early Thursday evening, December 4, and Cmdr. André Bouchard was sitting in Big Bertha. That's the affectionate nickname the Montreal police gave to the bus that was their mobile command centre. Police had got nowhere in their investigation of the guards' murders. So they decided it was time to put pressure on the streets. They called it Project HARM. Originally they had called it Project Respect. Respect for police officers. Respect for the system. Except cops like Bouchard didn't like that name. It wasn't tough enough. What do bikers care about respect? So they changed it to Project HARM, which stood for Hells Angels Rock Machine. But it also meant hit them hard. Hurt them. Bouchard's men had T-shirts and caps made with a logo of a shark swallowing a Harley-Davidson. It was corny, but it reminded the cops what they were up to. And they thought it would piss off the bikers.

They started the project by making drug buys from employees of strip clubs, bars and restaurants controlled by the bikers. In the process they closed down about twenty clubs. Surveillance of drug dealers and their runners gave them a list of more than a hundred suspects. By the first week of December, Bouchard was sitting in Big Bertha ready to make mass arrests.

A policeman's voice crackled over the radio, calling for backup.

"I need some help here. Get me some help here."

Bouchard could hear another voice in the background: "You think you have enough guns to shoot all of us?"

That sounds like trouble, Bouchard thought. He had seventeen teams out that night, raiding bars, strip clubs and homes. Every available man in narcotics and vice was on the street, plus hordes of uniformed cops. The distress call was coming from a placement agency for strippers on the second storey of a small commercial building on Rosemount. There shouldn't have been any trouble there. Surveillance had indicated cops could expect no more than three girls working and two bikers. So why was this officer screaming for backup? Bouchard scanned the roster of available men. He radioed for available patrol cars but was getting no reply.

"Well, screw this," he said to no one in particular and jumped into the driver's seat of Big Bertha, cranked up the engine, turned on the flashers and sirens and sent the huge machine hurtling through busy Montreal streets. When he arrived outside the agency, he parked in the middle of the road, grabbed his gold-braided hat, pulled out his revolver and headed up the stairs.

When he walked in, he was greeted by a regular biker convention: fifteen motorcycle guys, four biker girls and his four cops with shotguns out, yelling at them to "get on the floor" and "everybody down." Bouchard was in full uniform, and the other cops were in blue jeans. So all eyes were on him. He was in charge, gun in his hand. One of the bigger bikers started coming toward him.

"You're kidding me," Bouchard growled—and landed a right to the guy's head that sent him reeling back onto the floor. "Anybody else want some?" the burly cop asked. There were no takers. They all got down on the floor and stayed down. As more backup arrived, they searched the bar and the bikers, found drugs and arrested everyone. They found a wall diagram of Montreal that was split into different sections, showing exactly which bars were controlled by which bikers. And surprise, surprise, they found pictures of the bikers having sex not only with the strippers but also with each other. That night, they seized $2.5 million in drugs, eighteen cars, sixty-seven guns and arrested dozens of bikers and low-level dealers. One was Steve Boies.

Det. Mike Vargas had arrested Boies. Vargas had emigrated with his parents from Peru and grew up in Montreal speaking English, French and Spanish. His colleagues used to joke that they didn't understand him in any language. He proved a good cop and rose quickly through the ranks. Vargas had arrested Boies near Parc Lafontaine in downtown

Montreal, a favourite cruising spot for gays and male prostitutes, where drug dealers enjoy a flourishing trade.

Police also raided Boies's home and found a small cooler hidden under a counter in the kitchen containing several kilos of cocaine. Boies was already awaiting sentencing for drug trafficking. Now he was facing possibly fifteen years. He knew he was in serious trouble.

Vargas was processing his arrests when Boies called him over.

"I want to talk to you," he said.

Vargas stared at him, thinking, What's he up to? Then he took him aside into an interrogation room.

"If we make a deal, I can give you the guards' shooter. It's Godasse Gagné."

Vargas said, "Don't tell me anything more; just sit there and be quiet."

He rushed up to Bouchard's office. It was about 5 a.m., Friday, December 5. Bouchard and his officers were having a coffee break and a debriefing when Vargas barged in. Bouchard recalls that Vargas looked as white as a sheet.

"You're not going to believe this," Vargas said. "He wants to give us the shooter."

"What shooter?"

"The guards' shooter."

Bouchard didn't believe it. "That's easy, anybody can say that."

"No," Vargas said. "It's for real."

That morning, Gagné showered and took a cab across the river to a South Shore café, where he bought a coffee and waited for Tousignant. He had no idea that the night before Montreal narcotics agents had arrested his friend Steve Boies. When Tousignant arrived, Gagné jumped into his car and the two headed for Mom's farm in Contrecoeur. Gagné was supposed to spend the day sitting in a helicopter, one of two the Angels had rented that weekend for protection.

Toots was to sit in the other one. Both were to be armed. The idea was that if the Rock Machine attacked the party, the Hells would gun them down from the helicopters before the cops could catch them.

But a snowstorm grounded the helicopters and forced Boucher to cancel the plan. So, at 5:08 p.m., a bored and hungry Gagné borrowed Boucher's cellphone to order himself a club sandwich from a local restaurant. Gagné, Tousignant and Boucher then climbed into Boucher's Dodge Ram and drove to the Hells' Sorel bunker.

Police usually show up in force for biker celebrations, hoping to ID any new members. They often barricade the area. They check and videotape anybody going in or out. Usually Boucher got stopped. But this time he didn't.

"Ha, they're not stopping us because you're such a prick, Godasse," Boucher chuckled. He liked his own jokes.

At Sorel, Gagné's pager went off. It was Benoît Cliche, a Hells lawyer. He immediately called Cliche back.

"I'm on a cellphone," Cliche said, not wanting to talk. "I'll call you back soon."

But Cliche didn't call, and Gagné grew anxious. He knew that when a Hells lawyer suddenly calls it's important. For now, though, all he could do was wait. Did Boucher know Cliche had called, he wondered. If he did, he wasn't saying. On the way back to Contrecoeur, they passed another police barricade without incident and Mom kidded Gagné again. Then he added, "I've got some dirty work prepared for them."

Godasse told Boucher to be careful about what he said in the truck.

"Oh, to err is human," Mom said.

Gagné replied that he hoped he could say the same thing if he made a mistake.

Boucher laughed. "Be careful, because if the police ever arrest you they'll try to kill you."

Back at Mom's farm, Gagné was eager to get home and call Cliche. He took Tousignant's car and on the way stopped at a telephone booth. Cliche answered and gave him the bad news: there had been some arrests, and Steve Boies had become a police informer. Gagné felt limp. All his cocky, self-assured energy drained away as he thought of Boies helping him attach the fake licence plate to the van used in the Rondeau killing. Even Boies could see the connection, especially with the van pictured all over the papers the day after the murder. And what about Boucher? It was just a matter of time until he'd find out he had been lied to.

Godasse decided it was time to lie low, go into hiding. With his wife, he headed to a motel in St-Ignace, pulling into the parking lot about 11 p.m. But it was too late. Police had been tailing him all along. Several squad cars suddenly surrounded him. The cops cuffed him and took him to SQ headquarters in Montreal.

At two-forty in the morning, an overhead video camera picked him up entering a small, sparse interrogation room with two chairs, a table and a black ashtray. Gagné sat down in the corner chair. Det. Sgt. Robert Pigeon, the undercover officer who had arrested him three years earlier for selling cocaine, followed him into the room. Pigeon, part of the Wolverine squad, had kept an eye out for Gagné ever since that arrest. The word was out that if Gagné ever got nabbed, Pigeon should be called in for the interrogation.

Pigeon began by informing Gagné that he was accused of the attempted murder of Christian Bellemare, the drug dealer. He let Gagné call his lawyer; Gagné left messages with Cliche, but the Hells' lawyer did not call him back. At 3:25 a.m. Pigeon returned, took a seat in the middle of the room and began the interrogation. Gagné sat up, folded his arms across his chest. He grinned as if to say he knew what was coming. He knew the routine and he could handle it.

"Look, I have nothing to say. I am not going to answer questions. You are speaking to an empty room."

Pigeon ignored him. He didn't really care whether Gagné had anything to say about all this. Not right now, anyway. The fact that Gagné's lawyer had not called back gave him time. At three-thirty in the morning, the likelihood of Cliche's calling any time soon was small. Pigeon figured he had Gagné to himself at least for the next four or five hours.

"Okay. Do you remember me?" he started.

"I have nothing to say."

"No, no, I'm asking you that. Do you remember me?"

Gagné stared at Pigeon, searching his mind, but nothing clicked. He shook his head. No, he didn't remember him. But he soon would. In fact, Robert Pigeon was one guy Gagné was going to remember for the rest of his life.

Detective Sergeant Pigeon is a hard guy to read. He is medium height and build. His face is round. His eyes are brown and watchful. His voice is soft but steady. He has an aura of intensity, but at the same time seems to lack all flair or style. Which is probably why he's good at what he does. There's nothing distracting about his physical presence. You tend to listen to him, not see him. And what you hear is the voice that explains your life to you, lays out the choices and then quietly leads you to the right one, making you think you're the one who made that choice. That you're still in control.

Pigeon had been down this road before with many other criminals. Still, Gagné was his most important challenge. Pressure on the police to solve the prison guard murders was enormous. The Hells Angels clearly thought they were bigger than the government. Quebec feared it could become North America's Sicily, where assassins killed judges and policemen with impunity. Hells terror had indeed achieved its goal: Prison guards across Quebec were terrified for their safety and that of their families. About one-third of the guards regularly booked off sick. Police sources claimed the Hells Angels were targeting more guards and possibly police, prosecutors and judges in a determined bid to paralyze the justice system.

Sitting in the interrogation room, Pigeon knew he was staring not at the architect but at the perpetrator of this terror. But Gagné was the best chance—no, the only chance right now—the police had to get to the architect: Mom Boucher. Pigeon had to connect with this man. He had to be at the top of his game.

It was his luck that he knew Gagné's background better than anybody. Since he'd arrested him in 1994, Gagné had periodically shown up on his radar screen. Gagné the wannabe Hells Angel, whose only self-esteem derived from wearing the biker colours and watching the crowds part. Pigeon believed he had a clear profile of the guy, and now he would use it to gain his trust and get him to appreciate that the life he had known was over. He had to get him to understand that if he wanted to save any remnant of his miserable existence, he would have to begin with total confession. Pigeon would be his priest.

"I know what's been going on in your life," he said, his voice soft but full of confidence. "Up to now you've had a promising career. But that's all over now. Everything will change. You can be absolutely sure of that. Everything. All the great dreams you had—and I know how hard you worked for them—they're all gone, they're all in the past. Finished."

Pigeon talked on and, as the seconds, minutes and then hours ticked by, the interrogation became more like a lengthy monologue with Pigeon reciting chapter and verse of Gagné's life—where he had excelled and where he had gone wrong. Never taking his eyes off Gagné, Pigeon kept tightening and then loosening the screw. He talked about

Gagné's wife, Marie-Claude—"a good girl"—his little boy, the "nice house" in St-Hubert.

"You made something of yourself, you've done well," Pigeon praised him. "You chose the path of the Hells. I respect you for that. I'm not here to judge anybody. But somewhere along the way, you made mistakes. You were in a hurry. . . . You trusted people. . . . You understand what I mean? Is what I'm telling you the truth?"

"I have nothing to say," Gagné repeated.

"I understand," Pigeon said, "but is what I'm telling you the truth? You know that at some point you're going to have to be straight with yourself, you're going to have to be true to yourself." Pigeon pointed out that few guys at Gagné's level had managed to save themselves. Gagné shrugged.

"You trust them a hundred percent—one hundred percent—do you? You want to be loyal to them right to the end?"

Gagné perked up and nodded. "All the way, forever," he said. "If you could have waited until the weekend, I would have had my full patch."

Pigeon scoffed. "They get people like you to believe in that world like it's a religion. . . . They have to keep your enthusiasm up. Then they ask you, to ensure your loyalty, to do things that cannot be undone."

"But there's a difference," Gagné interjected. "I'm no informer. That's for sure."

"But it's a matter of choice," Pigeon suggested—his first direct reference to Gagné's turning.

Pigeon then listed names of other low-level bikers. He didn't say they ended up dead. He didn't have to. He knew Gagné knew. "You've seen a lot of people who've been silenced. You think it will never be your turn? I'm telling you, it's finished. Trust my experience with bikers. Your career is finished."

Slouched in his chair, his arms folded across his chest, the accused man remained silent but attentive as Pigeon continued to tell Gagné how he fitted into the Hells history book in Quebec. "The big bosses in Montreal are in danger because of a mistake that was made. They won't forgive you for that—no way."

Pigeon's grilling had lasted more than an hour and a half. But he was in full flight and didn't want to stop. He kept talking about the Bellemare murder but hinted at something bigger, the guards:

"I think you went too far in your power trip when you decided to attack the system," he said. "The system is fucking huge. You can't attack the system. It's never done. You think you can force the police to their knees, force prison guards to their knees and then force everybody to their knees before the Hells . . . that's unthinkable. There was someone who made a bad decision, and it has come back to haunt you."

He wanted to keep Gagné guessing. Was this about Bellemare or the guards? He repeatedly sowed doubts about how loyal the bikers would be to Gagné:

"Do you think your career with them is over?"

"No."

"Do you think they'll be there for you tomorrow morning?"

"Yes."

Pigeon switched tempo, chatting with Gagné about his motorcycle, his family, whether he worked out or not. He was easing the pressure a bit. It's not good to keep tightening the screw. The accused is liable to strengthen his mental defences. You have to tighten and then let up. Pigeon was then two hours into it. His colleague watching the interview on a video screen wondered if he wasn't staying too long. But Pigeon had no intention of taking a break.

"Do you want a coffee? Or something to drink?" he asked.

"No, I want a bed."

"No, not right away."

"When will I get a bed?"

"When we're finished talking."

"I have nothing more to say."

"Yeah, I know, but I want you to think about what I've told you. Because today you are at a crossroads. There's no going back." It was Pigeon's second oblique reference to the possibility of Gagné's turning. "The decisions you'll have to make will be painful. That's for sure."

"I can guarantee I won't make the decision you want me to make," Gagné said, still cocky. "You can take that to the bank."

Pigeon stepped out at 5:31 a.m. Gagné immediately folded his arms on the table and buried his face. He tried to sleep but was beyond tired.

Pigeon had no idea whether his words were having an effect. But he decided that it was time to confront Gagné head-on about the guards. When Pigeon walked back into the interrogation room, he had a different demeanour. He removed his suit jacket and slipped it over the back of his chair. He pushed the chair toward Gagné and took his seat, leaning forward, about a foot from Gagné's face.

Gagné recoiled, but his weasel face stared straight at Pigeon. His eyes narrowed, trying to avoid the headlights of Pigeon's glare. He crossed his arms tightly as if to protect himself. But Pigeon just kept getting closer, his voice calm but a little harsher, a little more threatening, a little more like a knife to his throat. Then Pigeon dropped the bomb. There was no more friendly talk, no easy banter. Just a gritty cop in his white shirt and dark tie peering into him.

"Now I am obliged to tell you also that you are under arrest for the murder of the prison guard Pierre Rondeau. You have the right to the help of a lawyer of your choice."

Gagné was stunned. He blurted out the name of his lawyer as if he was begging for a life raft: "Cliche." The man he had hoped all along would call and save him from all this. Then, Pigeon dropped the second bomb.

"I also arrest you for the murder of the prison guard Diane Lavigne. That's serious, that! You know how serious! But it's over. We have the whole chain, every single link."

Pigeon rose out of his seat and, standing over Gagné, mimicked the firing of a gun with his trigger finger pointed at Gagné's head.

"I know where you parked the little van. I can even tell you that when you set fire to the van you scorched yourself a little. You went to the Dominican Republic with Marie-Claude to let the heat die down. Why? Why did you kill them? Because you wanted to become a Hells Angel!

"Why did you choose Diane Lavigne? Why did you choose that poor woman?" Pigeon raised his voice. He was angry but in control. "Killing prison guards, what were you thinking when you did that? Be enough of a man at least to answer me today!"

"I have nothing to say." Gagné repeated his only refrain, but by then he was mumbling.

Sensing Gagné was cracking, Pigeon tried a one-two punch. He softened him with a suggestion that once again he was used by the Angels: "They made sure you were covered in blood. They injected you with it."

Then he slammed him with the violent details of his slaying of Rondeau in the prison bus. "Be man enough to tell me what you thought when you climbed up on the bumper and shot him." The cop barrelled on, leaning forward and pointing his finger at Gagné's chest. "Christ, a family man, a father. He's not a drug trafficker. He's an honest citizen, that guy. What did you think about, what feeling did you have deep inside yourself? You'll have to live with that all your life. . . . You shot prison guards. Why did you do that? Tell me why you did it. Give me one good reason!"

Suddenly, Gagné rose up out of his chair, his fists clenched. Pigeon stood his ground. The two men were nose to nose.

"Hey! I have nothing to say, you understand? And I want to see a lawyer!"

Pigeon put his hand on Gagné's chest and gently pushed him back into the chair. Gagné's eyes were watering. "Look how aggressive you are," he said. "That's your aggressive side, Stéphane."

"I have nothing to say, I have nothing to say, I have nothing to say!" Gagné screamed, defiant. "And I want my lawyer and I want you to put me the fuck in my cell!"

"Great! You're going to be spending a long time in your cell, Stéphane."

"I don't give a fuck and I'm going to get out of here in two years and then I'm going to say yahoo! Yahoo! They made a mistake—it's not me."

Pigeon struck back: "Yahoo! I killed the prison guards. Yahoo! Me, Stéphane 'Godasse' Gagné, I wanted a Hells Angels patch, and I went as far as killing prison guards to get it. And if you think you're going to get out of here in two years, forget that, Stéphane, my boy. It's all over for you."

Gagné reached across the table to take a cigarette from the pack Pigeon had left behind. The pack was empty. He pushed it aside.

He was allowed to leave the interrogation room to call Cliche at 6:14 a.m. There was still no reply; he left a message on his telephone answering machine and on his pager. He and Pigeon waited together for the lawyer to call back. Gagné was silent, and Pigeon noticed the man's lips were trembling and his eyes were watery. They waited several more minutes. No word from Cliche. Gagné was fidgety. Nervous.

He must have been wondering if the Hells had abandoned him. He had waited all night long for Cliche or somebody else to call back, but nothing. Not a word. The thought of him not telling Mom Boucher about Boies kept racing through his mind. The fact that Gagné had paged Boies after the murder; the fact that the page was on

Gagné's pager records and the police would have seen that and Mom would find out. The pager records alone might get him killed by the Angels if he was lucky enough to beat the murder charges. He worried about the safety of his wife and son. And he calculated he could make good money as a *délateur*: one previous informant got a cool $390,000—at least that's what he had read in the papers. Maybe he could even get some of the $100,000 reward money the SQ had offered for information leading to the arrest and conviction of the guards' murderers. After all, he was about to hand over Fontaine, Tousignant and Boucher. Maybe he should get all of it.

Gagné turned to the cop who had been part interrogator, part father confessor. "I'd like to talk to you confidentially, without the video."

Pigeon took him into another room. Then the biker who killed two guards on the orders of Maurice "Mom" Boucher looked at the police officer and asked a single question:

"If I talk, how many years could I expect to get?"

Pigeon recited the deals made by past informants but cautioned that Gagné's case was different—he had killed two prison guards.

Gagné didn't reply. He stood there, staring at the floor. Dreamy. Finally, he asked to see his wife. "I want to see what she thinks about me becoming an informant."

Two agents brought Marie-Claude Nantais. Gagné's wife was no shrinking violet. She had played an active role in his criminal life. She was his personal confidante. Police had charged her with complicity after the fact in the murders, and she was waiting in a separate cell. The two met alone for seventeen minutes. Gagné wanted her approval, which she quickly gave.

Still, Gagné did not commit himself. He now wanted to see the video of Steve Boies's confession. He wanted to confirm that Boies really had become an informant. So Pigeon ordered up the cassette. Gagné slipped off his running shoes and sat back for the viewing.

About 75 percent of what Boies told police were lies, exaggerations and conjectures made up to try to wring a better deal from the cops. The only true story he told was about helping Gagné clean up the garage and get rid of some clothes. Gagné, however, didn't bother to watch the whole tape. After five minutes, he thought he had seen enough. He saw a scared man eager to give him up and figured Boies probably knew more about his role in the murders than Gagné had realized. So he never heard Boies' lies—lies that could have set Gagné free.

Pigeon's words had sunk in. His career with the Hells Angels was finished. So he told Pigeon to turn off the video.

Pigeon was startled. Why this change of heart? Why didn't Gagné want to see the whole thing? Had Gagné decided not to confess, not to become an informant? Pigeon turned off the tape and told Gagné they were going to continue the interrogation. Gagné said nothing. He slipped his running shoes back on and returned with Pigeon to the interrogation room.

Pigeon wasn't sure where he stood. But he made the quick decision to proceed as if Gagné had already decided to become an informant. He figured that if Gagné was still undecided, he might push him over the edge. He asked an SQ technician to slip a fresh tape into the recorder.

"You have shown an interest to become an informant for the government. . . . Is that right?"

"Yes."

It was 8:10 a.m. Pigeon breathed a sigh of relief. It had been five and a half hours since he'd first put Gagné in the interrogation room. He had done it—broken the killer who could lead the cops to Mom.

Gagné opened up like a river to the sea. Tousignant,

Fontaine and Boucher, what they did and what they said. He held nothing back, constrained only by the limits of an exhausted memory. When he finished, he asked Pigeon to make sure his wife and family were safe because his former biker friends had threatened to kill the family of any future informants. Over the next few days, Gagné gave police two more recorded statements. When police learned from Gagné that Boucher planned to kill policemen, prosecutors and judges, they immediately jacked up surveillance of Boucher and his bikers.

His squealing done, Gagné turned to dealing. He began dreaming of the money he could make by turning informant. He submitted to two lie detector tests and passed them both with flying colours. Two weeks later he went before a special committee to negotiate his informant's contract. The principal negotiator was André Vincent, Montreal's chief Crown prosecutor. Vincent quickly dispelled any hope of a light sentence.

"It's twenty-five years. As far as money is concerned, you won't get one cent," he told him. The only "favour" he gave him was to withdraw the murder charge in the killing of Rondeau. It was, in fact, quite a large concession. If Gagné had been forced to plead guilty to both murders, he would have received the mandatory sentence of twenty-five years with no hope of parole. With only one murder charge, he could apply for parole after fifteen years—under the so-called faint-hope clause.

Gagné signed the contract promising to testify when and wherever justice officials demanded. He succeeded in extracting a bit more cash than the standard $140 a month to pay for cigarettes and candy in prison. The Crown dropped the charges against his wife, and the state agreed to pay her $400 a week for three years to help care for his boy. (The government later revised the payments to $400 a month after Gagné's wife left him in 2000.) When he gets out of prison, the state will pay him $400 a week for two years as he re-establishes himself in an undisclosed location with a new identity.

A life once in the firm grasp of Mom Boucher was now in the hands of the state.

The weekend of December 6 was supposed to be party time for Mom Boucher. But the twentieth-anniversary celebrations turned into a nightmare as the Hells leader grew increasingly paranoid over events that were spinning out of control.

The police had charged Serge Boutin, Boucher's drug lord in the gay village, with trafficking three kilos of cocaine. Boutin was out on $10,000 bail by December 6, but he was certain that one of his people—Boies—had already turned informant and that a second —Gagné— was about to do the same. Boutin immediately drove to meet Boucher, seeking some kind of solace and reassurance. He got neither.

"Yeah, Boies is talking," Boucher said, looking accusingly at Boutin. "It's not good."

It was Boutin who had brought Boies into the Hells organization, so he was ultimately responsible. He could rebuild his organization, but everybody in his network was taking cover. Rumours of mass arrests were rampant.

Police recorded a sequence of cellphone conversations between Boucher and his fellow Angels. The cops were listening for anything that might link Mom to the murder of the guards. What they got was a rising tide of panic about Gagné.

The tapes show that the Hells discussed the whereabouts of Gagné's wife. They knew only that she was with him when he was arrested. They discussed his pending court appearance—slated for Monday, December 8—in St-Jérôme. But mostly they wanted reassurance that Gagné had not turned informant.

On Sunday, Boucher had several phone conversations with Tousignant. Toots didn't know it yet, but he was signing his own death warrant. The first call from Mom came at 7:49 in the morning.

"They arrested Godasse last night," Tousignant told the boss.

"Yeah," Boucher acknowledged.

"There's one charge we know about: attempted murder."

"They didn't want to arrest him with me," Boucher said and hung up.

Just over four hours later, at 11:55 a.m., Boucher phoned again.

"I called all the lawyers," Tousignant said. "There's one charge of murder plus an attempted murder. There wasn't a single lawyer who could get in to see him. The lawyers are asleep at the switch. There wasn't a single fucking one of them who called to tell us that Gagné was arrested."

"Check it out," Boucher ordered. "Stay in town until you've learned everything and then bring us the news."

Boucher wanted Tousignant to stay in town for more than just news gathering. He knew Tousignant and Paul Fontaine were the only people who could link him directly to the murders. And he knew Gagné could finger both men. One of the main reasons behind Boucher's plan to kill the guards was about to be tested. Would the government make deals with a man who killed prison guards? Boucher still didn't believe it could happen. Twenty minutes after chatting with Toots, Boucher called fellow Nomad Normand Robitaille.

"It looks like Godasse has turned informer," Robitaille said.

"What do you mean?"

"Well, that's the news we're getting," Robitaille said, finding it hard to believe it himself. "The lawyers are trying to contact him. They're told they can't talk to him because he's gone over to their side."

"No, it's not true," Boucher insisted.

"No, I understand," said Robitaille, "but that's what I'm hearing so far."

At 1:20 p.m., one hour later, the last recorded words of Tousignant were heard. Boucher called Robitaille, who was with Tousignant. Mom but still refused to accept that Gagné had become an informant.

"The pigs are playing a game with the lawyers. They're telling them a pack of lies," Robitaille said.

"Yeah, I know," Boucher said.

"So I'm going over later."

"Good, okay. Toots, where's he?"

"He's around," Robitaille said and passed the phone to Tousignant.

"That's it, fuck. I've had it with the lawyers," Tousignant complained. "One lawyer calls and says it's this lawyer who's looking after the file. You see that lawyer seven, eight hours later and he says, no, it's not me who's looking after the file."

Tousignant said he was coming to see Mom and wouldn't be long. Mom told him he was at home. This was the last police ever heard from Tousignant. Immediately after hanging up, Boucher called the Hells Angels bunker in Sorel and asked them to send two or three men over to his house from the Death Riders, Evil Ones or Rowdy Crew. Toots failed to show at a court appearance three days later on a weapons charge; he fell off the radar screen.

By Monday, December 8, Boucher was desperate for information about Gagné's scheduled court appearance. There were frantic phone calls between Boucher and other bikers but still no news. Finally, Gagné entered the courtroom in St-Jérôme at three-thirty in the afternoon. Hells lawyer Benoît Cliche approached him, but Gagné ignored him. Cliche asked the judge for permission to speak to Gagné. But Gagné said he didn't want to speak to Cliche.

Cliche left the court and immediately called Robitaille, reaching him at an east-end restaurant. Robitaille was so furious he violently kicked the table. Boutin, who watched Robitaille vent his anger, summed up what every biker was probably thinking: "It's over. That's for sure."

Finally, at 4:11—less than forty-five minutes after Gagné's court appearance—Robitaille placed the call he did not want to make to the boss.

"Well, it's bad," he began.

"Yeah?"

"He refused to speak to the lawyer," Robitaille explained. "He was right in front of him. He didn't say a word. Then the pigs told [Cliche] that [Gagné] no longer needed a lawyer."

"Damn." Boucher paused and then laughed nervously. "Nothing good is going to come of this."

SIX

Biker Justice

"A witness who is not credible may occasionally tell the truth; but the problem is that you never know when he is telling the truth."
JUDGE JEAN-GUY BOILARD

Immediately after Gagné signed his informant's contract, at 8 p.m., Thursday, December 18, 1997, police arrested Maurice "Mom" Boucher. They nabbed him at the entrance to Notre-Dame Hospital in downtown Montreal, where he was taking treatment for cancer of the throat.

The feared Nomad leader was now stewing in a Montreal prison. In Halifax, the one informant Boucher never knew about, Dany Kane, languished in a jail cell, cut off from friends and his former RCMP handlers.

But in less than twelve months, both men would walk away free. The courts, the police and the prosecutors would be made to look like fools. Biker justice would triumph and Mom Boucher would literally laugh his way out of court.

Inside the Halifax Detention Centre in May 1997, Kane endured sixteen hours of questioning about his role in the killing of Robert MacFarlane. But he never broke under the pressure, perhaps hoping his Montreal handlers would protect him. RCMP Const. Tom Townsend wanted to know who hired him, whom he worked for. Kane said nothing. When Townsend offered him protection, he refused it and was put into the normal prison population. When prison guards overheard two prisoners talking about a $14,000 contract to kill him, he still refused protection.

Townsend then played the strongest card he had: he wrote to Kane to warn him that the rules of disclosure— the obligation of the Crown to divulge all its evidence and much of the police investigation to the defence—would reveal at trial that he was a police informant. In other words, the RCMP was telling Kane: You're a dead man if the Angels find out, so we're your only hope of survival.

It made sense; it would have been enough to scare most police spies inside the biker world. But not Kane. Instead, he pulled off the most stunning ploy of his career. He took a gamble with his life and it paid off. He immediately phoned Wolf Carroll and read him the letter.

Then, when another police officer verbally warned him that document disclosure would prove he'd been a source, Kane told his lawyer—knowing full well he would pass it on to the Angels.

"He was very smart," Kane's former handler, Gaetan St. Onge, says. "He knew Carroll had been accused of murder in Halifax and that the police had tried a similar ploy with him. And so he also knew that Carroll would understand and pass the word to the others that Kane was not talking."

However bold his strategy, Kane was nevertheless stressed out. On August 18, 1997, three months after his arrest, he phoned Cpl. Pierre Verdon, his other handler, on his secure line and asked to see him. The RCMP approved the meeting, which was held the next day in an interview room at the Halifax Detention Centre. It was clear to Verdon that Kane was a confused man. He said he believed the Hells knew he was a source for the RCMP because the SQ had told Simard, who then got word to the Angels. He said Wolf Carroll, who had been paying his legal bills and giving money to his wife, was suddenly "treating him differently."

But despite his fears, Kane continued to refuse protection from the police, even signing a statement to that effect. He even asked if he could go back to work for the RCMP. An astonished Verdon decided to lay out Kane's options: he could cooperate with the Halifax investigators; he could plead guilty and accept the consequences; or he could plead not guilty and take his chances. Then he added one last option: Kane could "cooperate with Wolverine investigators." Kane said he would think it over and speak to Townsend.

Verdon was worried: "The situation is very delicate and should be treated with great caution because the repercussions could be disastrous." Disastrous, of course, not just for Kane but also for the RCMP.

Disaster was exactly what RCMP Staff Sergeant Bolduc, Kane's biggest doubter, predicted back in Montreal. The supervisor of St. Onge and Verdon was interpreting Kane's conduct differently than his own men were. Bolduc was convinced his enduring suspicions that Kane was in fact a double agent for the bikers were justified by Kane's refusal to accept any protection. He figured Kane had to be stupid, suicidal or a biker plant—and he placed his bets on the last.

So in September Bolduc outlined his concerns in a thirteen-page report full of uncomfortable questions and analysis of Kane's performance as a source. Why did Kane not seek protection when he knew that even the "slightest suspicion that a biker is an informant could lead to his immediate death?" Bolduc asked. Why was so much of Kane's information lacking in detail or too late for the RCMP to take action? "Perhaps his handlers were unwittingly giving [the source] information that was ending up in the hands of

Mom Boucher," he suggested. He questioned whether successful seizures of explosives hadn't been "orchestrated" by the bikers to give Kane credibility. He referred sarcastically to Kane as the "source of the century" and noted that his information had not resulted in a single drug bust. He claimed the handlers were "dazzled" by Kane and added that while he did not believe they were corrupt, their "lack of experience" allowed Kane to manipulate them.

He ended the report with this high-minded statement of intent: "I am presenting this to you so that competent authorities might be aware of the facts and that the appropriate actions might be taken."

Bolduc did not show his report to St. Onge or Verdon. It ended up on the desk of Superintendent Sugrue. St. Onge would later claim that Bolduc was simply "covering his ass" after the fact of Kane's arrest, that he didn't really care what happened to the report; he just wanted to be on record as not being part of the Kane fan club.

The Bolduc report languished in a sort of bureaucratic no-man's land for more than a year. Then St. Onge accidentally discovered it sitting on the desk of a fellow officer. "What's this?" he asked. The officer blushed with embarrassment. St. Onge took it back to his office, and as he read over Bolduc's slightly mocking and biting phrases, he tried to contain his fury. Bolduc was not just calling St. Onge inexperienced, which was galling enough for a veteran with more than twenty-five years in the force, he was also suggesting indirectly that he might be corrupt.

St. Onge immediately fired off a twenty-three-page point-by-point rebuttal and sent it up the chain of command. The move forced the hand of Sugrue, who six months later wrote his reply. He concluded that St. Onge and Verdon were blameless and had at all times conducted themselves professionally. But he also concluded that Bolduc had raised important questions about Kane's true intentions—including the biggest one of all: "was C-2994 sent to infiltrate the police?"

The RCMP shied away from ever answering that question. Ultimately everybody walked away a winner. Sugrue didn't call for any further investigations. He ordered his report be distributed to the interested parties and then destroyed, with the exception of the copy placed in the file of C-2994. As far as Sugrue—and the RCMP—was concerned, the matter of Dany Kane was over.

But for Dany Kane it wasn't. His trial was held in a specially converted schoolhouse surrounded by a maze of concrete barriers designed to stop car bombers from ramming the building. Plainclothes RCMP officers patrolled the perimeter. Clearly, Halifax regarded Kane as a dangerous defendant and top security risk.

Kane asked for a trial in French, so the Nova Scotia Supreme Court assigned the case to a Montreal-born, French-speaking judge named Félix Cacchione. A streetwise lawyer, Cacchione had made his mark as a defender of civil rights and a harsh critic of illegal police tactics. In the mid-1980s he helped Donald Marshall Jr. before his client became a household name synonymous with the wrongfully convicted. One of the few non-Tories or non-Liberals to get a federal judgeship in Nova Scotia, Cacchione—resplendent with long hair and a thick beard—owed favours to no one. That made him just the kind of judge a defendant like Dany Kane needed—a hard-nosed umpire who could be relied on to make sure the rules of the game were enforced.

Kane's trial didn't get started until October 1998, more than a year and a half after he had been arrested. In that time, he lost weight and muscle structure because he was no longer taking steroids. He let his hair and beard grow longer. Crown prosecutor Pierre Lapointe suspected Kane was trying to change his appearance so witnesses might have a hard time identifying him. (Do you see Dany Kane in the courtroom? Gee, not really your honour, unless he's the guy hiding behind the beard.) But it didn't really matter because the debacle that was to follow had nothing to do with Kane's appearance in the courtroom.

Nor would his former lover Simard play a role. He had pleaded guilty to a reduced charge of second-degree murder with parole eligibility after twelve years; Simard could be back on the street by the time he's forty-three years old. Not bad for three murders, two attempted murders and drug trafficking. Simard even asked the government to pay for liposuction. The government declined. In return, the somewhat corpulent biker agreed to testify against bikers in Quebec and Dany Kane in Halifax. As it turned out, however, no jury would believe him. Discredited by past crimes, which included bearing false witness, Simard was such a terrible *délateur* that not a single biker has gone to prison based on his testimony. Cacchione would later state that Simard "displayed a cold-blooded remorseless and manipulative personality while testifying."

Cacchione quickly lived up to his reputation for toughness when he ruled inadmissible the RCMP computer records showing that Blinn had pulled over the white Buick and checked out Dany Kane. Cacchione claimed Blinn had no cause to stop Kane and therefore had violated his constitutional rights. Evidence arising from the incident was therefore illegal. This included Blinn's CPIC search of Kane, which in and of itself was the single most objective piece of evidence that confirmed Simard's story.

That left the photo lineup evidence the only solid thread that tied Kane to the shooting. Tom Townsend, one of the RCMP investigators on the MacFarlane murder, and Const. Mark MacPherson, an expert in photo lineups, had travelled to Oromocto on May 6, 1997, to question Constable Blinn and his partner, Dale Hutley, about the day, nine weeks earlier, when they'd stopped two males in a white Buick LeSabre. Townsend, a nineteen-year RCMP veteran, wanted to see if Blinn and Hutley could identify Kane and Simard, confirming Simard's story that he was with Kane. A simple enough task, but crucial to the prosecution. Simard had confessed to the murder; all police had to do was confirm that Kane was with Simard, and source C-2994 was without a doubt going to prison for life.

So, the RCMP should have handled the procedure with special care, but that's not what happened. To this day it is not clear what actually occurred. Documents that should exist don't, and stories have changed so many times that it's impossible to say whether it was deception, lies or just plain incompetence and confusion that resulted from the Oromocto visit.

Right from the beginning, it appears the officers did not follow basic police procedures. Normally, investigators have the witness fill out photo lineup sheets that indicate which photos, if any, were identified; the witness then signs the sheet with the time and date. No such sheets were given to Blinn or signed by him in relation to Kane. What's more, Townsend and MacPherson could not get their notes straight. Townsend wrote in his notebook that neither Blinn nor Hutley had identified Kane in the lineup. On the other hand, MacPherson wrote that Hutley had positively identified Simard and recognized Kane. Furthermore, a top-secret RCMP report two months later stated unequivocally that Blinn and his partner "have both identified Dany Kane from a photograph lineup." And a second secret report by Sergeant Barnett, who was the officer in charge of the investigation, stated: "[Blinn and Hutley] have positively identified both Simard and Kane from photo lineups."

By the time the case went before a jury on October 13, 1997, Blinn had testified at two previous hearings that he had positively identified Kane as the man he stopped back in February, two days before the murder. Now before the jury, he again said he picked Kane out of a photo lineup. Furthermore, Blinn identified Kane in the courtroom as the man he stopped in the white Buick. "It's the same guy, definitely, 100 percent the same guy."

Crown prosecutor Pierre Lapointe immediately asked for an adjournment because during the recess he had learned something new. One of his police officers had told him, within earshot of the defence, that Blinn had *not* identified Kane in a photo lineup. Lapointe and defence lawyer Daniele Roy met with the judge in chambers and said they believed Blinn was either mistaken or had perjured himself. The judge sent the jury home for the day and called Constables Townsend and MacPherson to testify.

Both men testified that Blinn had not picked Kane out of a lineup. MacPherson said that when he asked Blinn about the passenger, Blinn told him to ask Hutley, since Hutley had dealt with him. MacPherson added that Blinn hadn't even been able to identify Simard, the person with whom he had had the closest dealings. MacPherson also recalled that after the lineups, Blinn asked to see a picture of the suspect, and MacPherson obliged, but only for Blinn's personal interest. The trouble was, this did not exactly square with MacPherson's notes. But MacPherson then testified that his notes were wrong.

Then Townsend took the stand. He had already changed his testimony twice during previous hearings. He testified during one voir dire hearing that Blinn could not identify either suspect. In the second hearing, he said he had been mistaken and Blinn had clearly identified Kane and even given a statement to that effect. Now, before Cacchione, he changed his story yet again. He claimed Blinn had not identified Kane.

Cacchione, doubtless losing patience, called Blinn back on the stand. He was the only person who stuck to his original story. Blinn told Cacchione that not only did he identify Kane in the photo lineup, but he also identified him in two pictures that were "close or familiar" and gave an audiotaped statement to Townsend and MacPherson to that effect. When the audiotape was played, Blinn was heard identifying photograph number 5 from lineup K—although his answer came after MacPherson appeared to lead him toward the right answer: "You identified him over here on this picture here."

Desperately trying to save a sinking case, the Crown tried to argue that both Townsend and MacPherson were mistaken, and in fact Blinn had picked Kane out of the photo lineups—just as the audiotape proved.

But Cacchione was having none of it. He decided it would be impossible to unravel this Gordian knot of falsehoods. "The misconduct in this case is so egregious that the mere fact of going forward in light of it will be offensive," he concluded. He declared a mistrial and on December 18, 1998, handed Kane a Christmas present—his freedom.

The defence made an application to stay the charges—in effect, to permanently shelve them and block any new trial; in the meantime, Dany Kane was out on bail. He had dodged not just a life sentence from the Canadian courts but also a death sentence from the Angels. His secret life as a police spy remained just that—a secret never exposed in open court.

If the RCMP had wanted to sabotage the case and protect their man, they could not have done a better job. Investigators at Wolverine were jubilant. There were some officers who suspected the RCMP cleverly orchestrated the entire thing so police could put Kane back into circulation. It seemed far-fetched: it would have been a deliberate obstruction of justice that would have not only destroyed the careers of police officers—many of whom would end up in jail—but also undermined the credibility of the entire force.

But whether by design or dumb luck, the police in Quebec ended up with an ideal situation. The Hells Angels considered anybody who could beat a murder trial to be a hero. Kane had cleverly squashed any suspicions and rumours about his being an informant simply by laying them out on the table. It fooled Wolf Carroll. It fooled all of them. Kane had proved that he was a standup guy. The Angels were eager to welcome him back. And Kane was glad to be back with his biker buddies.

Back in Montreal, Mom Boucher was probably not losing much sleep in his jail cell. Quebec has one of the highest crime rates in Canada and was the centre of the Hells Angels hurricane. Yet at the height of the biker war, the province was spending less on justice than any other province. Prince Edward Island pumped in a third more per capita than Quebec: $29 compared with $21. And for prosecutions, British Columbia's figure is more than double: $13 for every $5 Quebec spent.

The Hells in Quebec had plenty to be happy about. Not only were they winning the war against their Rock Machine rivals in the streets, but they were also triumphant against a justice system that seemed over-burdened to the point of collapse. Provincial cabinet ministers spoke with fury and fire against the bikers in the wake of public outrage after the killing of eleven-year-old Daniel Desrochers. They threw money at Wolverine, but the courts and prison system remained woefully underfunded.

When they took on biker cases, the prosecutors received no security protection. One prosecutor says the only protection the government offered her was an automatic car starter. What's more, they were—and still are—among the worst-paid prosecutors in the country, earning about half what their Ontario colleagues are paid.

Prosecutors were expected to work important cases alone. And if they couldn't handle it, their bosses viewed them as failures. Alone and with little support, overworked prosecutors often went up against well-financed biker defence teams—and lost. Crushed by heavy workloads and mounting political and public pressure to jail the bikers and stop the killings, prosecutors laboured long hours, only to suffer burnout and mental collapse.

René Domingue, the veteran prosecutor who successfully took on the Hells Angels in the Sherbrooke trials of the 1980s, was asked in 1996 to be head legal counsel to Wolverine. He says the government granted $5 million for the Wolverine squad but not a cent for the prosecution. "I was alone on a part-time basis. I was running around like mad and unable to do any decent work." So he quit.

In 1997, François Legault prosecuted Hells Angels Nomad Richard Vallée, using the informant Serge Quesnel as his main witness. He found himself handling the murder case alone and also had to do some of his own police work—such as tracing cellphone numbers. "The police were totally disorganized. They didn't know how to do a case like this. They didn't have the structure to properly organize the evidence."

Twice Legault asked for help and was refused. After working seventy-five-hour weeks for almost a year, Legault lost the case and had a breakdown. "I was exhausted and I haven't pleaded a case since. I feel that people think I'm no longer capable. There's a stigma attached to it."

Then in 1998 it was the turn of his colleague Lucie Dufresne. She stood alone against five Hells lawyers when she took on the case against five Rockers accused of conspiring to murder Jean-Marc Caissy, the floor hockey player gunned down by Kane's lover Aimé Simard. Dufresne worked twelve-hour days on the case for almost a year.

"I asked for help and I was refused," she says. "This was a huge case with all sorts of proof, electronic wiretaps, an informant. And I was told, 'There's nobody available.'"

Late one Friday night in April, midway through the trial, she was working in her office when she too suffered a "humiliating" breakdown. "I became ill physically and psychologically." She had to withdraw from the case and take two months' sick leave. She has not tried a case since. "I adore it but I am no longer capable," she says. "You push and push and push until the machine breaks. The vision here is always short term."

The justice department sent in two last-minute replacements. But despite thousands of pages of wiretaps and Simard's testimony, it was too late. They lost the case and the five bikers walked.

"If you look at the rate or percentages of success in cases solved against the Hells Angels, I would say they kill with impunity," says René Domingue. "They have reasons to laugh at the law because they could do what they wanted but for the odd arrest here and there. We ended up being their best place to prosper. We didn't take them seriously enough."

Even when the bikers got convicted, Mom Boucher and his gang seemed to see jails as having revolving doors rather than bars. Boucher himself racked up forty-three charges in just two decades before his arrest on murder charges, but he didn't spend, in total, more than two years in jail. He often pleaded guilty, sometimes to a lesser charge. In 1989, he served five months behind bars for hijacking a tractor-trailer; in 1993, he paid a $500 fine for carrying a prohibited weapon; in 1995, he served four months of a six-month sentence for possession of a semi-automatic pistol. He was consistently violating the terms of his probation. In spite of it all, Mom Boucher seemed to be unstoppable.

So in 1998, even as he faced the most serious charges of his criminal career—murder—Boucher had no reason to believe he couldn't get out of that mess as well.

The unenviable task of trying to put away Quebec's most notorious biker fell to Jacques Dagenais, a respected, soft-spoken Crown attorney who had laboured for years in the smoke-filled corridors of the Palais de Justice. Studying the case file, however, he almost abandoned hope.

He first set eyes on Stéphane Gagné when he viewed his videotaped confession. Dagenais was shocked. The impression Gagné left was completely negative. He came off as the cold-blooded killer he was. He looked dreary, haggard, and his eyes were dead. He spoke in barely audible monotones, his voice cold and without emotion.

This is going to be my witness, Dagenais thought, convinced that no jury would believe him. Dagenais wondered briefly if he shouldn't file a motion to stop the case right then and there. The Crown wasn't being chicken-hearted; he knew the government's track record with informants was miserable.

With Gagné, police assured Dagenais, it would be different: Gagné, they promised, would prove to be a reliable and spirited witness. The police knew he needed polishing. So they gave him a book of instructions on how to testify in court. The book advises people to tell the truth, dress conservatively, avoid jewellery, act respectfully toward the court, remain self-assured and dignified, vary vocal intonation so as not to appear impassive and avoid being dull. Gagné read it twice.

Indeed, when Dagenais finally did meet the informant in person, he was pleased. He discovered that Gagné's uncle had been Chapeau Gagné, a gangster of some repute whom Dagenais happened to know of from his days as a legal counsel to the Organized Crime Commission.

"Gagné struck me as a lively, energetic man, a serious person who was eager to please," Dagenais says. Gagné seemed ready to give the same energy and commitment to the justice department as he had given to the Hells Angels.

Still, Dagenais remained skeptical. He knew the Hells Angels would mass their considerable financial and human resources to fight the case. While he couldn't get a computer, the Hells Angels were overburdened with data. Computers tracked every aspect of their empire: drug dealing, money laundering, surveillance and intelligence gathering. Boucher could afford the best team of lawyers and supply them with the best intelligence. A province with a multi-billion-dollar annual budget couldn't even supply the chief prosecutor going up against a Hells Angels leader with a secretary. In the coming trial, he faced three additional hurdles—little direct evidence, a formidable defence lawyer and a mercurial judge.

For starters, Dagenais had no witness who could testify with first-hand knowledge that Boucher had ordered the guards' murders. By racing to arrest Gagné, police had allowed Paul Fontaine and Toots Tousignant to slip through their fingers. In fact, even after Gagné's confession on Sunday, December 6, in which he implicated both men, they still did not move immediately to arrest the two men. That same day police overheard Tousignant tell Boucher he was coming over to his house, but that was the last anybody heard of Toots. Two months later, on February 27, 1998, police found his burned body in a wood near the resort town of Bromont, about an hour's drive south of Montreal. He had been shot twice, in the head and chest, execution-style.

Police believed Fontaine likely was dead too. They were wrong. The Trois-Rivières Hells chapter was hiding him in various places around Quebec, including, at one point, a suite at the Château Frontenac Hotel in Quebec City and a ski chalet in the nearby resort town of Stoneham. Fontaine would remain alive throughout the entire Boucher trial—but never found.

So Gagné was the prosecution's one and only ticket. On the bright side, in Gagné, Dagenais had a witness whose detailed recounting of the two murders could, to a large degree, be corroborated. When Gagné talked about the clutch slipping on the stolen motorcycle, Dagenais could summon the owner to testify to that fact. He could summon Nancy Dubé to describe having seen a man running from a burning car at exactly the same time and place Gagné claimed to have burned the Mazda after killing Rondeau. Prison guard Danielle Leclair could testify to seeing the motorcycle race by, hearing a loud crack and watching Lavigne pull off the road. Forensics could verify the path of the bullets exactly as described by Gagné. Police had the guns used in the murders, and they matched Gagné's descriptions. Steve Boies could testify to helping Gagné dispose of the evidence. This detailed corroboration could boost Gagné's overall credibility. Still, none of this would amount to a hill of beans when it came to Boucher's involvement. It would prove Gagné, Fontaine and Tousignant were the killers. But what about Mom?

The only proof Dagenais had was Gagné's claim that Boucher had given the order. Even that was conjecture on Gagné's part. His direct orders to carry out the assassinations came from Tousignant and Fontaine, not Mom. The Nomad leader had been careful. The fact that he had made often vague and cryptic references to killing guards to discourage informants was not in itself proof of Boucher's involvement. Furthermore, most of his statements were made *after* the murders. They indicated Boucher's approval, but it would be an uphill battle to prove they showed that he ordered them or counselled the killers.

Statements made prior to the murders—such as Boucher's telling Gagné he had "important work" for him—could not be linked directly to the guards' murders. In fact, Mom's "important work" statement was directly followed by the conspiracy to murder rival gang members in Verdun, for which Boucher personally enlisted Gagné's help. Boucher's most damning statement came when he told Gagné he wanted to "do another screw" as well as kill Crown prosecutors and judges. But this came six weeks after the second guard was killed.

So Dagenais was indeed in a tight spot. Once again, faced with enormous public and political pressure to clean up the bikers, the police, it seemed, had recklessly jumped the gun, leaving the Crown with the job of cleaning up their mess. There was one way Dagenais could pull it off. He could, in effect, put not just Mom on trial but the Hells Angels. He had to convince the jury that Boucher ran the Quebec Angels as a rigidly authoritarian organization that members remained loyal to on pain of death. Rewards came to those who obeyed orders and served the corporation. If he could show that no biker would dare murder a guard without the approval of the leadership, he could build a strong circumstantial case against Boucher, who, as president of the Nomads, was the boss of the killers Fontaine and Tousignant.

In other words, he had to use the Hells' own organization against their leader. Gagné, Tousignant and Fontaine would never have killed the guards on their own. Gagné was a low-level biker in a low-level feeder club, the Rockers. Tousignant and Fontaine were still fighting their way up the Hells' Nomads ladder. None of them would dream of murdering a prison guard, never mind two —bringing the wrath of the entire justice system on the bikers—without Boucher's orders. Bikers don't go solo, at least not in such an important murder. They kill for the organization. And when they do it, they get promoted, as did Gagné, Fontaine and Tousignant. These arguments made perfect sense. But could Dagenais prove them?

Dagenais's second major problem was his opponent. He was up against a powerful adversary in Jacques Larochelle. In many ways, the two are similar. They are tall, lean men in their late fifties, and both look younger than their years. They share a gentlemanly, almost courtly, manner. But while Dagenais is approachable and courteous, Larochelle often seems aloof and, when the occasion demands, displays a much harder edge. A Quebec City lawyer with a reputation as a determined, probing litigator, Larochelle was part of the legal team representing Theoneste Bagosora, a retired army colonel charged with masterminding the 1994 genocide in Rwanda. Compared with Bagosora, Boucher seemed like a walk in the park.

Larochelle believed the Crown's case—built on the word of a thief, drug dealer and murderer who couldn't even testify as to Boucher's direct involvement in the guards' murders—was weak. But he worried that the reputation of the Hells Angels, and Mom Boucher in particular, coupled with the public thirst for justice, could result in a conviction. Larochelle's specialty was in slowly and painfully peeling the layers of lies off the hides of Crown witnesses. Now he prepared for the total destruction of Stéphane Gagné.

The Hells lawyers went to work gathering evidence that would make Gagné seem psychotic and capable of just about anything—including killing prison guards on his own. They got Serge Boutin to canvas his drug network for any dirt on Gagné. Boutin himself signed a sworn statement that Gagné had often talked about his hatred of prison guards and wanted to kill them. Boutin claimed that Gagné sought revenge for two painful rectal searches the guards had performed on him in prison. Boutin also said Gagné had tried to kill the petty drug dealer Christian Bellemare without anybody's permission. So why not the guards?

The defence team also elicited evidence indicating that Gagné was a deviant. In jail, he invented what he called the *pen-merde* or "shitpen." It consisted of a mixture of excrement and urine, which he allowed to ferment for ten days in a shampoo bottle. The stench was so strong that it made Gagné vomit. He sprayed the concoction on guards or rival gang members when they walked by his cell. It was another bit of evidence to show the lengths he would go to show his contempt. Armed with such damning information, Larochelle was confident he could convince a jury that Gagné was simply too crazy to be believed.

Both Larochelle and Dagenais would fight it out in front of Superior Court Justice Jean-Guy Boilard—and therein lay Dagenais's third problem. Boilard is about five feet ten inches and wears his thinning brown hair carefully parted and neatly combed. At sixty-seven years old, he has remained fit and is a powerful presence in any courtroom. The only distinguishing habit he has is sucking on his lips as he enunciates each syllable of every word he speaks. Other than that, there is nothing in the body or manner that would indicate he is without a doubt the most widely feared judge in Quebec's criminal courts.

In 1987, thirty Montreal prosecutors signed an unprecedented petition refusing to plead before him. Many lawyers find him an abusive, contemptuous judge who appears to take pleasure in humiliating and bullying practically anybody in his courtroom—be they lawyers, police officers or even witnesses. When close to two dozen bikers went on trial in 1985 for the massacre of the members of the Hells Angels' Laval chapter, Boilard frequently referred to the lawyers and investigators as incompetent— even though their "incompetence" eventually led to the convictions of almost all of the bikers.

Boilard's aggressive attitude has reduced already traumatized witnesses, often victims of crime, to tears and once caused a female witness to faint. He haughtily upbraids witnesses for using bad grammar or not speaking loudly enough, and goes into fits of impatience when he claims he doesn't understand their answers. His supporters say his tyrannical courtroom behaviour reflects a desire for perfection, sparked by a steel-trap legal mind. And few legal professionals would dispute his knowledge of the law. But his irascible conduct in court often appears to override the interests of justice by personalizing debate and turning cases into little more than the Judge Boilard Show.

Now it was Dagenais's turn to face the judge who was every prosecutor's nightmare. Although Dagenais always considered Boilard a great jurist, he would eventually regard him as his biggest liability.

During the ten months leading up to his trial, Mom Boucher received special treatment. Worried both for his personal safety and his potential as a trouble-maker if he was placed in the general population at Rivière-des-Prairies Prison, the government spent $1 million building a special private cell for him in, irony of ironies, a women's jail. The macho biker's new home was an isolated block in Tanguay Prison, located several hundred yards behind Bordeaux. He had his own phone, exercise equipment and access to the prison yard. He also had his own sound system with music library and was offered self-improvement courses. His defence team was allowed to visit on four hours' notice between 1 and 6 p.m. every day. Nevertheless, he petitioned the court to be moved into the general prison population at Rivière-des-Prairies— arguing that his prison conditions violated his civil rights. The Quebec Court of Appeals denied his request.

Dagenais was basically alone to prepare what was one of the most important criminal cases in Quebec's history.

Two weeks before the trial began, prosecutor France Charbonneau, an experienced trial lawyer with a combative reputation and an impressive track record, agreed to help Dagenais. He wanted her to be his sounding board, give him moral support and monitor the jurors' reactions to the proof. Even though her role was minor, it laid the groundwork for what would become her greatest challenge—and Boucher's greatest defeat—four years later.

As soon as the much anticipated trial began on November 2, 1998, defence lawyer Jacques Larochelle demanded that the case be thrown out for lack of evidence—or at the very least, that Gagné's testimony be excluded. Boilard quickly denied both motions. The sides bickered over procedural issues, so jury selection didn't begin until two and a half weeks later. The Crown expected it to be a long drawn-out process. But they underestimated Judge Boilard and Larochelle, both of whom charged ahead. Within three hours the lawyers had selected a jury of six men and six women. Boilard sequestered them for the length of the trial and ordered their addresses and workplaces kept secret—making sure there would be no repetition of juror bribing as had occurred in the 1986 Hells trial.

The jurors looked glum as they entered the courtroom the next day for the opening arguments. Their sightline gave them a full view of the bull-necked Boucher, clothed in a brown jacket over a black shirt buttoned to the neck. His legs shackled, he sat behind bulletproof glass flanked by three guards. Jurors also had a clear view of the audience, where Boucher's Hells Angel and Rocker comrades had packed into the front-row seats, wearing their leathers and Hells crests. They were an intimidating presence— and that was precisely the idea. Despite the crowds, the Hells' defence team always made sure there were seats for the bikers.

The trial was expected to last almost two months; in fact, it was over in three weeks. Larochelle was fast, and he knew what he wanted done. He persuaded Boilard to exclude five of Boucher's telephone conversations on the basis that police had illegally obtained them. In their warrant, police claimed they were investigating a fire two years earlier at the home of prison warden Nicole Quesnel. Boilard called that subterfuge and ruled the tapes inadmissible. One of those tapes was crucial in helping to establish Gagné's credibility. Police had intercepted Gagné's telephone call from Boucher's home to a restaurant when he'd ordered a club sandwich. The tape confirmed his claim that he was indeed at the house of the Nomad leader. Two other taped conversations proved that in June 1997 Boucher had spoken to Daniel Foster, his automobile dealer friend, about obtaining cars—including the Mazda that would be used as the getaway car for one of the murders. Boilard's exclusion of the tapes seemed like a minor victory for the defence. But for Larochelle it was another important step in keeping any evidence that might confirm Gagné's story away from the jury.

Gagné was the second witness to testify. As Boucher watched from his glass cage, Dagenais took his time carefully eliciting details of Gagné's criminal history, how he came to join the HA organization and how he murdered the two guards. He wanted everything out on the table. He wanted to show that Gagné had nothing to hide. In a grating, guttural monotone, Gagné impassively related the entire story. Two days later, Larochelle began his cross-examination.

He meticulously picked apart Gagné's credibility and highlighted his criminal past: "All the company you kept, your whole life, was spent with criminals like yourself, is that correct?" he asked.

"Yes."

"You shared their values, you adhered to their lifestyle and you were satisfied with being a criminal?"

"Yes," Gagné replied.

"During this entire time, you evidently had no respect for authority?"

"No."

"No respect for other people's property?"

"No."

"No respect for the truth?"

"No."

Larochelle then tried to show Gagné's readiness to do anything he thought would please the Hells Angels. He recalled a hunger strike at Sorel prison that Mom ordered because he was sick of eating shepherd's pie. One inmate broke ranks and ate the meal.

"And without anyone asking you to do it," Larochelle asked, "you went over to beat him up?"

"Yes."

"In fact, you courageously waited until he was asleep and you went to attack him in his bed, is that correct?"

"Yes."

"You hit him so hard with your fist that the bone came out of his nose—all so that you would be noticed, is that correct?"

"Yes."

Larochelle also elicited the sordid details of Gagné's attempted murder of the drug dealer Christian Bellemare. He showed how Gagné acted alone, deciding to kill him because he owed him money.

"The first two bullets hit Bellemare in the throat or in that area. But the other bullets didn't fire, and Bellemare was still alive?" Larochelle said, taking the jurors back to the scene of the crime.

"Yes," Gagné agreed.

"You went running up to Bellemare and you put your fingers around his neck, your two hands around his neck, and squeezed?"

"Yes."

"He tries to talk, is that correct?" Larochelle pushed. "You have a good idea of what he is trying to tell you, I imagine?"

"Yes."

" 'Don't kill me,' or something like that?" the lawyer suggested.

"Something like that, yes," said Gagné.

"That didn't impress you?"

"I had a job to do," he admitted.

Finally, Larochelle dug into the real reason Gagné had turned informant. "In your mind, if you didn't talk, you would be killed?" Boucher's lawyer asked.

"Well, look, Toots is dead," Gagné replied, referring to the biker who was last heard telling Mom he was heading over to his house.

"Agreed? If you didn't talk, you would be killed?"

"Yes."

"Therefore, not only did you talk to avoid twenty-five years in prison, you also wanted to talk so that you would not be killed?"

"Yes."

"Which of the two was more important in your mind?" Larochelle asked.

"Staying alive," came the simple reply.

Gagné's undressing lasted two days. It was not pretty. Stripped clean, he was, however, still standing, straight and confident, giving the impression he was making no attempt at a cover-up. He hadn't been caught out on a lie. The jury already knew he was a bad guy. The question was whether he was telling the truth about Boucher, whether he plotted to kill the guards hoping to please Mom, just as he had beaten a sleeping man senseless because he had violated Boucher's food strike.

By November 25, the two sides were ready to give their final arguments. Dagenais called the murders "strategic . . .

committed by an organization which is pursuing a goal." He stressed the Hells Angels' disciplined hierarchy and Gagné's loyalty to the organization. To argue that Gagné, Tousignant and Fontaine acted alone didn't make sense. Why would Gagné, who had always acted with purpose and in his own interests, suddenly commit such a rash, solo killing that could easily bring the wrath of the entire Hells Angels on his head? Even if his orders came only from Tousignant and Fontaine, he would have made sure that they had Boucher's permission.

"Given this hierarchy, can you imagine a decision that would have more impact on the Hells Angels than killing prison guards? A move that brought the police on their backs?" Dagenais said. "Do you think that a little hangaround would do that without authorization?"

Dagenais made no attempt to hide the fact that his entire case against Boucher rested on whether the jury believed Gagné. Indeed, he emphasized the fact. "If you do not believe Mr. Gagné, well then, you should acquit him." The jury listened carefully and frequently nodded in apparent agreement. When Dagenais sat down, he was confident he had them on his side.

Then it was Larochelle's turn. He painted Gagné as a tainted witness who simply could not be trusted. As he spoke, Dagenais watched the jurors. They weren't nodding. Some sat stone-faced and appeared barely patient enough to listen as Larochelle laid out his arguments. When Larochelle had finished, Dagenais was certain he had won.

But then it was Judge Boilard's turn.

Until then, Boilard had been relatively restrained. He couldn't hold himself in for long. As he began delivering his instructions to the jury, Dagenais realized his case was in serious trouble.

Boilard told the jury that they should discount much of what Gagné said about Boucher's part in the murder. He insisted there was no direct corroborating evidence to support the contention that Boucher ordered the murders. He told the jurors that the fact Boucher was president of the Hells Angels was immaterial.

Then, in a roller-coaster speech, he buried the Crown's case in the deepest of graves by essentially warning the jurors that to convict on the basis of such an untrustworthy witness as Gagné was dangerous. "A witness who is not credible, a witness who is not prompted by a desire to tell the truth, a witness who recognizes that he is a liar, a witness who is not credible is never a trustworthy witness because a witness who is not credible may occasionally tell the truth," he cautioned. "But the problem is that you never know when he is telling the truth."

Boilard then hammered the final nail into Dagenais's case. Gagné, he noted with his customary lip-smacking emphasis, had ample motive to lie. He was facing two convictions for first-degree murder: "Life in prison," he said, "but not in a hotel. It's not a particularly appealing prospect."

Finally, Boilard sent the jurors on their way with one cautionary note: "Don't be pigheaded."

Dagenais was furious. Straining to maintain his usual courtly manner, as soon as the jury left, he rose to object to Boilard's instructions. He argued that Boilard had misled the jury with his claim that there was no evidence confirming Gagné's credibility. He also noted that the judge had erred in law by dismissing the entire body of proof that supported Gagné's testimony and the Crown's case as immaterial. He noted that the rule of confirmation, established by the Supreme Court of Canada, allows the jury to assess the credibility of a witness based on a broad spectrum of evidence, circumstantial or not. He urged Boilard to recall the jury and correct these potentially crippling errors. Boilard refused. Dagenais didn't press the point any further. He was still hopeful that the jury would convict.

The jury began deliberations the next morning, November 27. A tactical force of fifteen uniformed police officers secretly waited in a nearby courtroom in case the bikers, who crowded into the corridors dressed in their colours, got out of hand.

André Bouchard, the Montreal officer who had worked so hard to get Boucher to court, had also been ordered to take a few of his men down to the courthouse just in case the bikers made trouble if their leader was convicted: "I want you to supervise them. Don't fuck around."

Bouchard said okay and took twenty of his biggest guys.

The Commander found the corridor full of the bikers, playing muscle and trying to intimidate everybody, including the cops. Tensions ran high. One biker started snapping pictures of the cops. Bouchard didn't like that. He grabbed one of the biker lawyers and barked, "Tell that little prick, if he takes another picture, I'm going to shove that camera so far up his ass, *hostie*, he's not going to be able to take it out. Do you understand me?"

When the lawyer took no action, Bouchard made his point again: "Stop being a fucking asshole, okay. I'm telling you right now if he takes another picture, I'm throwing him in the can and you can defend him afterwards. But he's going to be inside, do you understand me?" The picture taking stopped. But it was to be Bouchard's only victory that day.

Inside the courtroom, the jury returned once to ask Boilard if his directives were simply guidelines or had to be followed to the letter.

"Absolutely to the letter," Boilard responded.

Dagenais waited stoically. He still clung to a glimmer of hope, which he later admitted was probably an indication that he had lost touch with reality. And indeed, soon after Boilard's final "to the letter" instruction, the six men and six women returned with their verdict:

"Not Guilty."

Boucher immediately jumped up and asked the judge if he was free.

Boilard nodded. "You're free to go."

The guards removed the chains from Boucher's ankles. He gingerly stepped over the barrier that separated him from the rest of the courtroom and into the arms of his fellow bikers, who hoisted him onto their shoulders. Cmdr. André Bouchard, the man who had fought bikers on the streets in the 1970s, struggled through the troubles of Wolverine and then pushed hard to find the killers of the guards, couldn't believe it. He sat in the audience, his head bent forward, staring down at nothing.

Boucher was a free man, and Montreal was about to become his Gotham City. As he left the courtroom and entered the crowded corridor, he hesitated briefly, as if momentarily startled by his sudden freedom. Then, his massive chest heaving through a green golf shirt and dark tweed sports jacket, he barged through the crowd of reporters and photographers, knocking several to the ground. Bikers greeted their victorious hero with kisses and hugs, eagerly reaching out to touch him as if he were a living icon, the pope himself.

Dany Kane would later tell police they had no idea how powerful Boucher had become. "Boucher is considered a god," Kane warned. "The prison guard thing, that's nothing compared to what's coming."

Lined up along each wall of the corridor were the police detectives from Wolverine and Montreal homicide: the SQ officers on one side of the corridor, the Montreal police on the other, silently eyeing each other. Since the Montreal police had walked out of Wolverine, refusing to work with the SQ, whatever personal friendships and mutual respect existed between individual officers had evaporated.

"There was a coldness," Detective Sergeant Roberge

recalls. "We watched each other, just like that. We were no longer working together. We were split. Then the bikers left the courtroom triumphant and walked right through the middle of us, united more than ever. And at that point you could say that the bikers had beat the police and the entire system. The Hells are stronger, and Mom Boucher is the strongest of them all. And we were divided."

While the cops glared at each other, the bikers partied. Wild, celebratory scenes of laughing bikers were replayed over and over on TV screens across the province. Boucher's huge toothy smile, so wide that you could see his tonsils, was splashed across the front pages of local newspapers. Montrealers watched as the Hells Angels seemed to turn the city's courthouse into their own personal playground. When Boucher finally emerged into the fresh autumn afternoon, a waiting SUV whisked him away amid a cavalcade of cars, as if the bikers had known all along that he would win. As uniformed cops watched from their cruisers, the bikers drove through a red light. Nobody bothered to stop them. Mom was free. Gagné's testimony that Boucher had planned to kill policemen, prosecutors and judges seemed forgotten in the giddy excitement, shock and confusion surrounding his sudden resurrection.

Crushed, André Bouchard and his men withdrew to a little bar on St-Hubert Street. "We got this son of a bitch to give it up," he said, referring to Gagné. "Hey, guys, we did our job, we did *our* job!" But his words rang hollow, and he knew it. Over the last four years, there had been 424 acts of violence linked to the Hells and their war with the Rock Machine. That tally included 94 murders, 103 attempted murders, 85 explosions and 142 fire bombings.

The pain of defeat didn't end there. That night he was due to work as an official at the Canadian middleweight boxing championship between Dave Hilton and Stéphane

Ouellet. As usual, he arrived early and took his seat at ringside. His job was to start the count as soon as a boxer went down. Bouchard loved boxing, and he hoped a good match on the mat would help take his mind off the humiliating defeat in court. But it wasn't to be.

A roar suddenly filled the sold-out Molson Centre. He thought the fighters were coming in. He was wrong. "We heard an uproar, and as I turned to my left it was like Moses had parted the water, and who did we see coming through the crowd—Mom Boucher in full colours, escorted by his henchmen," Bouchard recalls.

Boucher and his leather-jacketed pals settled into their front-row seats, laughing and joking, patting one another on the back. And many in the crowd loved it.

"What broke my heart was seeing hundreds of people actually give him a standing ovation as if he was a rock star," Bouchard says.

The homicide detective was almost sick to his stomach. It was the worst day of his career.

Mom Boucher was not the only biker celebrating his new-found freedom at the end of 1998. Three weeks after the Nomad leader was treated like royalty at the boxing match, Dany Kane walked out of a Halifax courtroom.

He partied hard over Christmas and New Year's, glad to be back among his biker brethren. But he wanted to complete the circle. There was one more friendship to renew. So at 11:05 a.m. on January 5, 1999, soon after the partying died down, Kane called Sgt. Gaetan St. Onge. Dany Kane had a simple message for his favourite police handler: he was ready to go back to work.

PART II

THE ANGELS SPREAD THEIR WINGS

across the country. Out east, Nomad Wolf Carroll, according to the Kane intelligence reports, sent in hitmen to Halifax to make sure Nova Scotia stayed in the Angels' grasp. In the rich drug market of Central Canada, fellow Nomad Walter "Nurget" Stadnick continued to woo Ontario bikers in preparation for the Hells Angels' takeover of that province.

And in Manitoba—Stadnick's second home—the Angels were blessed: politicians and police leaders had done little to put up roadblocks against the incursions the bikers had been making in the province throughout the 1990s.

Now the citizens of Winnipeg were going to pay the price.

Events had moved quickly in Manitoba since October 1997, when Dew and the Brovos had accepted Walter Stadnick's entreaties and begun their probationary journey to full Angels status. The HA had wisely chosen the most powerful bikers in the province. Within months, their only serious rivals—the Spartans—were in tatters.

In May 1998, Darwin Sylvester, the hulking, fearsome leader of the Spartans, went to a meeting and disappeared. Police never found his body but never doubted he was murdered. A few months later, Robert Glen Rosmus, a close associate of Sylvester's and an executive member of the Spartans, was executed with multiple gunshots to the head. He had driven Sylvester to the meeting on the day he vanished.

Neither case has ever been solved. But Darwin's brother Kevin convinced himself without any solid evidence that Rod Sweeney, a Brovos biker on his way to becoming a Hells Angel, had played a direct role in the disappearance of the Spartan leader. The seeds were sown for a blood feud between the Sweeneys and the Sylvesters that would soon spill out onto the streets of the city.

The Brovos, now ruling supreme, were poised to take the next step as the Angels' anointed followers. On

Saturday, July 21, 2000, came the big event—the formal induction. About seventy Angels rode in from across the country to join in the celebrations. Police kept close watch on all the bikers, pulling them over for spot checks, checking for outstanding warrants. In one incident, a female member of the police gang unit confronted a young Hells Angels wannabe from Winnipeg named Ian Matthew Grant. According to police, Grant was furious with the humiliation; bikers have little respect for women, even less for female officers. Grant allegedly slapped Const. Esther Schmieder and was immediately charged with assaulting a police officer, but the charges were stayed a year later because of delays in bringing the case to trial.

At 6 p.m., the police heard a loud cheer from the clubhouse, which was located right across the street from an elementary school in the Elmwood section of the city. A few minutes later, Ernie Dew and his friends strutted onto the street, beaming with their new Hells Angels vests. The single word "Manitoba" was emblazoned in red on a white panel—called a rocker—across the bottom. They were now prospects; by the rules only after a full year of probation could they add the words "Hells Angels" as the top rocker and the winged Death Head on the jacket's back.

"When you put on a piece of that patch, it's a good feeling," Dew recalls. "You haven't made it yet by no means, a lot of things can happen, things can get screwed up. But there was a sense of pride."

A dozen Brovos had officially signed up with the HA that night. But it was symptomatic of the criminal nature of the gang—despite their protestations that they were just another bike club—that five of the new members couldn't make the party. Jeff Peck was still in jail on drug charges; Darren Hunter out on bail and his stipulations forbade contact with fellow Angels; another biker, Ricardo Oliviera, originally from Portugal, was facing deportation hearings; and two other Brovos—Rod Sweeney and Shane Kirton—were on the run.

The newly minted Angels rode to a fancy restaurant to celebrate. Ray Parry remembers chatting with biker Bernie Dubois as he drove by in a car. Dubois rolled down his window.

"Looks good," Parry said, pointing to the new vest. "Good luck." Parry understood the big leap that his biker opponents had taken. "They were proud to be where they were. They had taken their first steps into the big leagues."

The Hells Angels are the corporate monopolists of the biker underworld—they don't like competition, and they'll stop at nothing to crush anything and anyone who stands in the way of their hegemony.

It's not that the drug trade in Winnipeg wasn't big enough for all the gangs to share. The crack cocaine trade itself was so lucrative that the dealers were having a hard time keeping up with demand. They had set up a "dial-a-dope" delivery network no less efficient than Pizza Hut's. You need a hit? You dial one of the cellphone numbers given out on the street, name your street corner and in no time a car pulls up with your order.

There was plenty of profit to go around—and traditionally, the various gangs in Winnipeg shared the loot. But not once the Brovos became the Hells Angels. "They took a lot of steps in a short period to take control of the situation by knocking out any rival groups," Rick Lobban explains. "They start with verbal persuasion. 'You can sell drugs, but you have to sell our drugs.'"

But those who refuse to negotiate with the new monopolists pay the price. At thirty-one, Bradley Russell Anderson was a former member of the Redliners running a small but flourishing independent coke network. He got some of his drugs from the Hells Angels but also from a number of other suppliers. In a dispute, he stabbed a Hells Angels member. A week later, someone gunned down Anderson and dumped his body outside city limits.

Anderson was easy to eliminate—he was just one guy.

The Angels faced stiffer competition from the Mir gang. Twin brothers named Husan and Husain Mir ran a non-stop drug trade, supplied in part by their Asian connections. To counter the Mirs, the Hells Angels had a support group called the Zig Zags. Traditionally, gang members in Winnipeg came from the tougher North End. The Zig Zags were different—they were richer kids from the more affluent suburbs in the South End. "These guys are clean-cut, trendy," says Rick Lobban. "Most of the guys if they pulled up to my house—I have three teenage daughters—I wouldn't blink. I wouldn't say, 'Look at who she's going out with.' They come from middle-class, upper-class backgrounds."

"They're the next wave of HA coming through," adds Ray Parry. "Very businesslike, very professional. This is their life."

The young Zig Zags were eager to prove their worth to the senior Hells Angels. They ran smack into the other young punks working for the Mirs. A drive-by shooting on November 20, 2000, of two drug dealers in the trendy Osborne Village section of the city was the opening salvo of the new war. There were more than a dozen more shootings in the next six weeks: a shattered window in a house, blown out by a shotgun blast; a minivan riddled with bullet holes. Parry saw dealers wearing body armour, taping it to their bellies so it would stick. It got so bad that they sometimes ended up shooting not enemies but potential clients.

That's what happened to one Zig Zag, a boxer named Ralph Moar Jr. who bought a 9 mm handgun for $400. On Wednesday, December 13, he was driving in the North End. He spotted a car he thought had been following him and fired five bullets. Moar hit a fifteen-year-old passenger in the head; the boy survived, needing only a few stitches. The irony was that his targets were not rivals but young people looking to score some drugs. The police charged Moar with attempted murder; he would eventually plead guilty to a lesser charge and get a four-year sentence.

The unprecedented wave of violence sparked outcries from a worried public and a besieged police brass. Under the gun for a quick fix, the police did what they often have to do in gang warfare: they made a Hobbesian choice and went after the weaker side. "To eliminate the problem, you choose the path of least resistance," says Ray Parry.

Just as Quebec police went after the Rock Machine to the benefit of the Hells Angels, it was easier and quicker for the Winnipeg cops to take out the Mirs—they were much smaller and less organized than the Hells Angels. In cracking down on the Mir gang, the police fulfilled their first duty to public safety and curbed the violence in the short term—but they also helped the Angels by eliminating their competition.

Even jaded cops like Lobban and Parry were surprised by how quickly the violence escalated in their town. It was more than a decade after the Hells Angels first set foot in Quebec before the open biker warfare erupted. In Winnipeg, it took less than two years.

"Gone are the days of taking the guy out to the parking lot and thrashing him. Old-style guys would duke it out," explains Lobban. "Now we're seizing weaponry and explosives that far outweighs that stuff. The fear and intimidation factor has become a method, and it's escalated tenfold, a hundredfold."

The same violence hit Halifax like an Atlantic storm. In four weeks at the end of 1998 there were three gang-related murders—in a city that sees only a handful of homicides in a year. By the time the biker gale petered out, the police had eight murders or disappearances on their hands.

More than any other chapter in Canada, the Halifax Angels were dependent on Quebec—for leadership and drugs. Almost all the cocaine sold on the East Coast came from Montreal, even if the raw narcotics first arrived in the country along the Nova Scotia shoreline. The bikers had it transported to Quebec, where it was cut and packaged and then sent back to Halifax for the boys to distribute.

The Nova Scotia bikers had never been shy about showing their fealty to Central Canada. The Thirteenth Tribe, the precursor to the Halifax Hells, earned their spurs by babysitting Walter Stadnick while he recuperated in a Hamilton hospital in 1984. They got their full HA patch on December 5, 1984, and by early in the next year, most of the new Halifax Hells rode up to Quebec for some action.

They were there to help the Sherbrooke chapter confront the wayward Laval club, whose members were accused of stealing drugs and money from their Halifax brothers. That confrontation led to the bloody massacre of the Laval chapter, and most of the visiting Halifax Hells ended up in jail on one charge or another. Those events changed the lives of three bikers—Wolf Carroll, Mike McCrea and Randy Mersereau—and shaped the contours of the Halifax gang wars for years to come.

Unlike most of the Halifax boys, Carroll came away with something positive from his time in Quebec: he learned French while in a Montreal jail. He got a taste of big-city life—and big-city crime. When Carroll returned to Halifax in 1986, he was so poor that he had to steal groceries.

Carroll found himself in Quebec just as the biker war was heating up, and his ruthlessness quickly catapulted him to the top ranks; along with Stadnick and Donald Stockford, he became one of the few anglos in the inner circle of

Nomads—and one of Dany Kane's bosses. A good-looking man with a wry smile, curly hair and a neatly trimmed beard, Carroll took up with a French-speaking woman; they had a son and lived in a comfortable cottage in Morin Heights, a picturesque village in the Laurentian mountains about an hour's drive north of Montreal.

Kane would frequently drive up from Montreal to visit Carroll and discovered the Nomad didn't find it difficult to mix family and business. He could talk drugs with Kane at his home—asking him to pay up on a $55,000 debt for two kilos of coke—then play ball hockey with his ten-year-old boy and take his son and his biker pals to a Vietnamese restaurant.

Kane told police that Carroll had partnered up with a member of the Rizzuto Mafia clan to run a popular bar in the nearby tourist town of St-Sauveur. "No drug sales were allowed at first," Kane said. "Maybe because they wanted to attract a clean clientele to give the establishment a certain credibility." Discreet drug sales did eventually start up, according to Kane, and it wasn't long before Carroll controlled a flourishing drug trade in the nearby tourist villages as well. By 1997, things were going well enough for Wolf that he bought some land at the foot of the busy ski mountain in St-Sauveur to build condos. "A great chance to launder a bit of money," Kane remarked. Carroll also ran several nightclubs in downtown Montreal.

Carroll often demonstrated an explosive anger to which Kane, as one of Wolf's boys, got a ringside seat. Carroll "seemed to take the [biker] war personally," Kane said, convinced that "there did not exist any peaceful means to end the conflict." Carroll was a man of his word: at one point Kane reported that he went out and bought a Cobray machine gun. In early February 1995, Wolf, according to Kane, was responsible for a bomb blast in Quebec City that cost the victim a leg; by mid-year, he and his associates were experimenting with new ways to set off car bombs with pagers and car alarms; by October, he was planning to set a rival poolroom on fire but didn't want to use any dynamite so "it would not be blamed on the bikers."

Still, for all his bars and bombs, Carroll—the hard-drinking party boy from Halifax—missed the good ol' days of booze and bikes. "He's a little bit disappointed in the way things turned out," says Tom O'Neill, an RCMP constable in Montreal's Wolverine squad.

And they didn't slow down. As if he didn't have his hands full running the biker war in Montreal, Carroll also had to keep an eye on his hometown of Halifax. He knew everything that was going on there; he was the glue. Carroll supplied his Halifax pals with cocaine; the club did most of its drug business through him. In one eight-month period from April to November in 1996, Kane told police that Carroll had shipped thirty kilos of coke to Halifax.

But he was more than their pipeline; he was also their god. David "Wolf" Carroll was the Dartmouth boy who'd made it big among the Nomads in Quebec. "Everybody bowed down to him," says Tom O'Neill. O'Neill recalls what happened when he went down to Halifax on a sur-veillance mission: "It was like the general is coming down; they've got to snap to attention and salute the flag: 'Wolf's in town—everybody's got to go to the clubhouse. Get your bikes out, get your colours out—Wolf is here.'"

Despite their obsequiousness, Carroll didn't think much of his Halifax crew, dismissing them as "a bunch of Boy Scouts." He put much more faith in a business acquaintance and good friend named Paul Wilson, another Dartmouth boy. "Wolf relied on him much more than on others," says one local biker cop. "I think Wilson was a better bang for the buck for Dave." At six foot two and 286 pounds, Wilson could take care of himself. He managed the Reflections bar in downtown Halifax. It was a gay bar, but that did not stop the local Angels from frequenting it—it was one of the few bars in town where the bikers could wear their colours. Wilson was also the brother-in-law of one of the local Angels.

Wilson made several trips to see Wolf in Montreal; he spent four days in his home in April 1996 and returned from February 3 to 9 in 1997. Kane, who would pick Wilson up at the airport and drop him off, described him as Carroll's "confidant." Their business relationship was unclear, but according to Kane, "Wilson regularly sends an envelope containing cash to Carroll." Wilson certainly at times had large amounts of cash on hand. In February 1998, Quebec police stopped Wilson in a car in Montreal and found $294,010 in cash. They seized the money, locked it away in National Bank of Canada—account number 04-534-29—and Wilson would eventually be charged with money laundering.

Aside from Wilson, the one local Angel Carroll did respect was a good friend of his, the chapter president Mike McCrea. McCrea made regular trips to Montreal, and when Wolf was down east, the two men and their wives would sometimes go on vacations together. Like Carroll's, McCrea's life was changed by the 1985 arrest of most Halifax gang members. A young prospect at the time, McCrea found himself one of the few soldiers still standing in the East Coast organization. To shore up the Halifax chapter—depleted well below the minimum six active members needed for full status—the Angels temporarily brought in some reinforcements from B.C. But McCrea was emerging as an able leader; by 1987, he became a full-patch member.

McCrea lived comfortably, renting a large home on Old Sambro Road in Williams Wood, overlooking Moody Park Lake. At various points, he ran a fishing supply firm, a real estate business and a computer company. "He's smart as a whip," says Keltie Jones, a constable with the Halifax Regional Police. "If he took his knowledge and put it to legal use, he'd probably do very well."

McCrea's handsome, almost boyish face—not to mention the absence of any criminal record—made him the perfect public face for the Halifax Angels. He became not only chapter president but also the East Coast secretary-treasurer for the Canadian Angels—in effect, the club's official spokesman. McCrea's talents led him to international biker fame. He befriended Sonny Barger, the California biker legend, and eventually became the world secretary for the Hells Angels. It was more a coordinating job than anything else, but it gave the local boy a chance to travel to biker events around the globe.

As talented as McCrea was, though, he didn't have much to work with. He was one of the few bright lights in a club that was always a few watts short of brilliance. Many of them hardly lived high on the hog. "Some of them don't have a pot to piss in," says Bruce Macdonald, the local RCMP biker specialist.

It was not an impressive crew. Mike "Speedy" Christiansen, the only remaining member of the Thirteenth Tribe, spent ten years in jail for his part in the 1971 gang rape of a sixteen-year-old girl. The sergeant-at-arms for the club was the bearded and beefy Danny Fitzsimmons, known for his short fuse. He once attacked a CBC journalist at a public biker celebration, breaking his camera. "I told you to get that out of my fuckin' face!" he said. Rounding out the crew were Neil "Nasty" Smith and Clay McCrea, Mike's brother and a low-level drug dealer who would never have made it into the club without family patronage.

By 1998, the Halifax operation was a shambles—plagued by internal weaknesses and external threats. Police had run an undercover operation that led to the arrest of the full-patch member Gregory Brushett. The bust sowed more dissension in the ranks. Brushett was kicked out. He didn't show up for his court date to plead guilty on three cocaine trafficking charges. Police were sure he hadn't skipped town; they concluded Angels simply disposed of him.

Sensing the Angels were teetering, their local rivals were moving in. Chief among those was an ex-Angel named Randy Mersereau. As one of the Thirteenth Tribe bikers charged with the gang rape of 1971, Randy had already done time. Like Carroll, he'd been one of the founding members of the Halifax chapter and was also caught up in the 1985 arrests after the Lennoxville massacre. But unlike his former buddy, Mersereau found life as an Angel miserable. He didn't much enjoy the return visit behind bars that his new Angel colours had brought him. Once back on the streets in Halifax, he liked what he saw even less. "I'm here to make money," he told his friends, according to police. "I'm not making money as a Hells Angel."

So Mersereau did what few bikers have the guts to do—he gave up his Angel colours. He set up his own organization just outside Annapolis Royal, figuring without the Angel patch on his back he could make more money pushing drugs in the outlying regions with less attention. The Angels don't take kindly to quitters; they were even more upset when Mersereau started moving his product into their domain in Halifax. Randy Mersereau—and eventually other members of his family—would soon face the wrath of the Hells Angels.

On a second front, the Angels faced headaches from a feisty clan who were not so much enemies as uppity competitors and sometime allies. In the suburb of Spryfield, the Marriott clan ruled supreme. Led by a tough father, Terry, and even meaner brothers, Ricky and Billy, the Marriotts controlled their drug turf with a vengeance—

hash, coke, whatever they could get their hands on. A road accident put Ricky in a wheelchair, but that didn't stop him from getting into a good fight: he'd go to a bar, somebody would knock an opponent down and he'd roll over him in his wheelchair. Billy was closer to the Angels; while doing some jail time he became "very, very tight" with Angel Neil Smith, according to police. His brother, Ricky, was not as friendly.

Back in Quebec, Wolf Carroll was angry. "Carroll is very disappointed by the leadership exercised by the Hells Angels in Halifax," Dany Kane reported. His Angels were losing face—and business. "Carroll wanted to take control of the drug trade in that city but feared that the HA in Halifax didn't have what it takes to do the job. It was time," as he told Kane, to "shake things up."

Over the next two years, eight bodies would fall—including two women, whose only crime was that they happened to be home when someone executed their husbands. All were drug- or gang-related deaths or disappearances. Seven of the murders remain unsolved.

It began in October 1998 along a dirt road in the Harrietfield area outside Halifax. A hunter found the twisted body of William Wendelborg, a Hells Angels associate, wrapped in a blanket. According to later trial testimony, Billy Marriott and his partner Larry Pace killed Wendelborg in a contract hit—a hit ordered and paid for by Wolf Carroll's local associate, Paul Wilson. The killers lured Wendelborg to Marriott's home on St. Margaret's Bay Road with the excuse they wanted to buy drugs. They clubbed him with a baseball bat, gagged him and bound his hands with duct tape. Then they injected him with a lethal overdose of cocaine, jammed the corpse into the trunk of his own car and drove to an isolated dirt road, where they dumped the body.

Four weeks later, police found Billy Marriott at the scene of another murder—this time at the home of his own brother, Ricky. On November 20 at nine-thirty in the evening, the white house with the wooden porch and ten cedars lined up along the front lawn looked peaceful. But inside, Ricky was sitting slumped over his kitchen table, a newspaper in front of him, a bullet in his left temple. His wife, Gail, had been shot on the couch nearby. Clearly the killer was someone they knew and trusted, probably sitting across from Ricky at the kitchen table.

Billy said he'd rushed over after receiving a panicked call from Gail and found the bodies. Police doubted his story. They suspected Billy killed his brother and sister-in-law, perhaps in a rage over being left out of a business deal. Without a murder weapon, though, the police had little to go on, and Billy stayed free.

But not for long. A friend of his, Rodney McDonald, knew of Billy's execution of William Wendelborg and turned snitch, becoming a protected witness. Larry Pace pleaded guilty to being an accessory to the murder and received ten years in jail. Wanda Lynn Campbell, Billy Marriott's common-law wife, who helped clean up the blood at her home, elected for a trial and was also found guilty as an accessory.

Billy Marriott didn't make it to court. He hanged himself while awaiting trial on Monday, August 7, 2000, at the Halifax Correctional Centre.

Key members of the Marriott clan were dead and David "Wolf" Carroll was plotting against the Mersereaus. He was confident that his Hells Angels in his old hometown had a much brighter future ahead of them. In the space of a couple of years, Carroll as mentor and kingpin had transformed a beleaguered and broken bike gang into the cocky kings of Citadel Hill. Their fancy new clubhouse was a symbol of their power. Nestled among a restaurant, a convenience store, a tailor's shop and a denture clinic in the

Fairview district of town, it sat right across the street from the Halifax West High School on Dutch Village Road (although the school eventually closed down). The brown brick three-storey building used to be a pizza shop. Now it was a biker bunker with all the trimmings. A bright red-and-white neon sign in front and a splashy Death Head mural on the side greeted visitors openly. A camera atop the door, one on the roof and another out back spied on them more discreetly.

While Mom Boucher and his circle of killers were bombing and shooting their way to the top of the streets in Montreal, his fellow Nomad Wolf Carroll had done an impressive job of regaining control of his hometown of Halifax. Now it remained to be seen what another anglo Nomad, Walter Stadnick, could do in the town he called home: Hamilton.

EIGHT

The Battle for Ontario

———

"They don't get up in the morning and go to work at
Stelco or the local manufacturing industry. They go
out and generate crime. Their industry is drug
trafficking, peddling fear and extortion."
KEN ROBERTSON, HAMILTON POLICE CHIEF

The smokestacks of Stelco and Dofasco dominate the sky-
line of the Steel City. Down on the streets, it's the crime
bosses who rule with an iron grip. This was the home of
powerful—and feuding—Italian crimelords. For years,
Johnny "Pops" Papalia ran Hamilton and other parts of
southern Ontario; he was tied to the Buffalo Mafia and in
Montreal to the Cotroni family. Papalia controlled much of
the drug business in the region, working with Niagara area
criminals who would eventually become Hells Angels. In
May 1997, he was gunned down by a hitman working for
rival Mafia bosses. Papalia's right-hand man, Carmen
Barillaro, became the boss of the Hamilton area—but not
for long. He was killed just a couple of months later.
Prominent bikers such as the Para-Dice Riders John Neal
and John Gray—both of whom would become Angels—
attended the Mafia funerals.

Hamilton is also home to the two most powerful biker
leaders in the province—the Angels' Walter "Nurget"

Stadnick and his arch-enemy, Outlaws leader Mario Parente. Stadnick, at least, could count on one important ally in the neighbourhood: his close friend Donald "Pup" Stockford lived just outside the city, in Ancaster. When he wasn't acting as the vice-president of the Quebec Nomads, Stockford was acting in movies. He was a professional movie stuntman. Dany Kane told police that Stockford travelled out to B.C. in January 1996 to do some film work; Kane also mentioned that Stockford was friends with Chuck Zito, a prominent member of the Hells Angels in the United States since 1979 and a star in his own right. (Zito's rap sheet includes weapons possession and a seven-year drug sentence. But that has not stopped stars such as Sylvester Stallone and Liza Minnelli from hiring the Hells Angel as a bodyguard. Zito would go on to fame in the TV prison drama Oz and the USA Network would eventually give him his own series, called *Street Justice*.)

Back in the real world, Stadnick and Stockford took a cold, hard look at the scene in Hamilton and decided not to form a chapter there—even when, over the next few years, the number of Angels who lived in the city would grow to eleven. Stadnick, as the saying goes, did not want to piss in his own backyard: it was fine being an Angels leader in Quebec and Manitoba, but Stadnick did not want the police attention and harassment that would come from setting up a chapter right in his hometown. He also could not ignore his history with the man who was now chief of police in Hamilton, Ken Robertson.

As a sergeant back in the 1970s, Robertson had first run into Stadnick's Wild Ones when the bikers were setting off bombs for the Mafia; he'd then helped put together a joint forces unit to tackle organized crime in his city. "We have to accept the fact that the bikers are criminal organizations," he says. "They don't get up in the morning and go to work at Stelco or the local manufacturing industry.

They go out and generate crime. Their industry is drug trafficking, peddling fear and extortion." Today, Robertson chairs the organized crime committee of the Ontario Association of Chiefs of Police. Not a man in front of whom Stadnick needed to wave a red flag, especially a flag with the Angels' colours.

"Stadnick did not want a chapter here because it would result in more heat," explains one of Robertson's men on the frontlines, Det. Steve Pacey. "Walter has been able to carry out his business for a long time. Why would he want a chapter? He doesn't need it. I think he gets more of a rush by being the only dog in town."

It would be easy for a citizen to mistake Steve Pacey for the bikers he's watching. It's not just the shaved head and goatee, the gold earring and diamond stud in his left ear. Or even his imposing bulk—standing six foot two and weighing 265 pounds. It's the tattoos that cover his arms: H-D on his right arm for his favourite Harley-Davidson bike (even though a bike accident left him witha serious neck and back injury); on his left arm is a menacing panther and a design of a Native headband—"for courage," Pacey says.

He needed all the courage he could get because in Ontario the Hells Angels were on the verge of becoming the pre-eminent gang, thanks in large part to the tireless work of Walter Stadnick.

"There are traditional organized crime members in this city who are very active," says Pacey. "But in terms of sheer volume, Walter's influence spreads way beyond Hamilton."

Business for Stadnick must have been booming. For a man who had no job—at one point he ran something called the Wild Ones Investment Corporation—he enjoyed an enviable life. He vacationed in the Caribbean. One family photo shows him in an elegant Armani suit. At various times, he owned several motorcycles, a white Chrysler and a four-by-four Bronco and—when he was national president—a Jaguar, courtesy of the Quebec Angels. Says John Harris, the Hamilton police sergeant who tracked Stadnick in the late seventies and eighties: "He was a little guy you wouldn't even notice; now he's become a guy that people pay attention to."

Stadnick lived with his wife in a two-storey home on Cloverhill Road. Though it was nominally valued at $156,000, Stadnick had poured tens of thousands into his residence, making it the finest on the block. A Canadian flag and a red mailbox grace the front porch. A newly finished second-floor balcony looks out over the backyard. On the side, work has begun on a swimming pool. Inside, on the first floor, gold-coloured plates and candles adorn a glass table in the dining room. A black marble counter dominates a tastefully done kitchen. Upstairs in his second-floor office, lined with books on seven shelves, Stadnick has all the conveniences a modern businessman needs: a computer, fax, scanner and, of course, the shredder. The bathroom sports a Jacuzzi and a built-in TV. The master bedroom—done in the Angel colours of red and white—has a four-poster bed, hardwood floors and a large walk-in closet with piles of shoeboxes.

"How can you have a guy like Stadnick who has never held a job in his life living in a gorgeous little house, with a place in Quebec, a place in Winnipeg, travelling all over the world, wearing Armani suits?" asks one Ontario police officer.

Good question. Stephan Frankel is the affable lawyer on Main Street in downtown Hamilton who has handled Stadnick's legal affairs since 1979—not any criminal matters, just in a "real estate and corporate capacity," as he puts it. "I've always liked my dealings with Walter, no question about it. He's been a very intelligent, understanding, cooperative type of client to have. Always understood the bigger picture," he says.

What exactly does his client do? a journalist asks. Frankel pauses for a moment. "What does Walter do for a living? I don't know. I really don't know," he says. "It wasn't something that would generally come up. It wasn't a fact that I needed to know. I don't know if it's strange, necessarily. Walter also is a very private person."

Well, not that private. When in town and not in his well-furnished digs, Stadnick could almost always be found at the Rebel Roadhouse, a bar at the corner of Upper Ottawa Street and Fennel Avenue. Stadnick's name never appeared on the ownership papers, but he basically ran it. "He had an office in back, through the kitchen," says one Hamilton police officer. "It was a good place to entertain visiting Angels."

"He was a hard guy to nail," admits Hamilton police sergeant John Harris. "You start to realize this guy is smart. He does know his way around the system, and he's got the money to afford decent lawyers. It would take a bigger organization, more than just one police force. And we had to make sure we dotted all our *i*'s and crossed all our *t*'s and did it properly."

Stadnick wasn't going to wait around for the police to get their spelling or their act together. When he was not taking care of his business as a Nomad in Montreal or flying to Winnipeg to keep an eye on his protégés, Stadnick—along with fellow anglos Pup Stockford and Wolf Carroll—was concentrating on winning the big prize: Ontario.

Police debriefing notes from Dany Kane during this period and eventually entered into court records offer a glimpse at how determined the Nomads were to get a piece of the Ontario action. On February 20, 1996, Stockford and Carroll met in St-Sauveur, the Laurentian village not far from Carroll's cottage. "Their goal was to take a big part of the Toronto drug market," Kane reported. On the weekend of May 3, Kane told his handlers that Stockford had sent a shipment of drugs to Toronto. The courier simply had to call pager number 416-554-0177 and punch in either 1 for a pickup at the Holiday Inn on the Queensway or 2 for the nearby Ramada, and someone would arrive to pick up four kilos of hash. Then, with one kilo of cocaine and a thousand ecstasy pills, the courier was to head to the Tim Hortons near the Bronte Road exit, dial pager number 416-376-6118 and punch in code 17; a cousin of Stockford's would show up for the goods.

Toronto was just one of the targets. On November 29, Stockford had another three hundred kilos of hash destined for the Hamilton region, Kane said. Two months later, Stockford and Stadnick sent four kilos of coke to Oshawa.

Naturally, this push into Ontario raised the ire of the indigenous bikers—and the anger was directed at Hamilton's best-known Angels, Stockford and Stadnick. "The Hells Angels who lived in Ontario are more and more careful," Kane reported. Pup Stockford, according to Kane, said the doorbell rang at his Ancaster home for a supposed pizza delivery—except he had not ordered any; he didn't answer. In mid-November 1996, Stadnick told his Quebec buddies that he narrowly escaped an attack. He was driving in Hamilton and stopped at a light. "All of a sudden, a big member of the Outlaws got out of a pickup [truck] and tried to grab him," Kane said. Stadnick pushed him away and made a dash for it—catching sight of a revolver in the hand of the passenger in the truck giving chase.

Stadnick knew he faced his most serious rivalry from the Outlaws and from another long-time resident of Hamilton, Mario "The Wop" Parente, their seemingly invincible leader. Established in Canada since 1977, the Outlaws had fought long and hard to keep the Angels out of Ontario. Unlike the Angels, the Outlaws had succeeded in creating chapters throughout the province—about ten.

It was the Outlaws who had tried to fire a rocket launcher at Stadnick's Roadhouse bar. It was Parente in 1983 who shot up a bus in Wawa in an attempt to murder some Hells Angels passengers—prompting Stadnick to seek police protection while he was hospitalized after his accident.

Stadnick tried to keep up decent relations with Mario Parente, but an alliance with the feisty and independent Outlaws looked out of the question. To outflank the Outlaws, Stadnick focused on two groups that had a long history in the province, healthy numbers and at least some openness to the Hells Angels: the Satan's Choice and the Para-Dice Riders.

The Choice had about eighty members in key urban areas such as Toronto and Kitchener-Waterloo but also in more northern locales where the drug trade was flourishing, like Sudbury and Thunder Bay. Members of the gang were charged with bombing a Sudbury police station in 1996, causing more than $130,000 in damage. Their leaders were also of the calibre the Angels wanted—men like Andre Watteel, president of the Kitchener chapter of the Satan's Choice who owned a successful restaurant and hobnobbed with local businessmen and politicians.

Meanwhile in Toronto, Stadnick and the Hells Angels had their eyes on another promising biker group with its own coterie of talented and wealthy leaders: the Para-Dice Riders. "They were well thought of in the biker world, along with the Satan's Choice," says George Coussens, the Toronto cop in charge of keeping an eye on the PDRs.

With deep roots in the city going back to the early 1960s, the PDRs at one point grew to as many as seventy-five members, enough to split into two chapters in Woodbridge and Toronto. They were an eclectic mix of old-time bikers out for the booze and the babes, along with more serious, up-and-coming criminals. One gang member—Michael Elkins—was in jail for manslaughter.

Steven "Tiger" Lindsay, a thirteen-year veteran of the PDRs, was typical of their tougher edge. "He's a big, intimidating person, well respected by all the bikers," says Coussens. Over six feet and weighing about 230 pounds, Lindsay looked almost like a Viking. He shaved his reddish blond hair on the side of his head almost down to the skin—like a Marine Corps brush cut. In the front he sported a pointed beard down to the middle of his chest; in the back a full ponytail to his waist. Lindsay and his girlfriend were co-owners of a bar in Woodbridge; he also worked at Red Pepper, a trendy downtown bar popular with the PDRs.

"He'd kick your ass as soon as look at you. He was tough, he talked tough," says one man who befriended Lindsay at the time. Indeed, the Tiger's tough talk would eventually land him—and the Angels—in court in a precedent-setting case that could determine the criminal nature of the HA in the eyes of the courts and the legitimacy of Canada's anti-gang laws.

The most promising PDR member was Donny Petersen, a smart, smooth-talking businessman who would eventually rise to the top of the Hells Angels hierarchy in Ontario. Petersen is now neat and proper, his trim, light-coloured hair belying his fifty-four years. For more than half his life, Petersen had been a proud Para-Dice Rider, serving as vicepresident and in other positions. At one point, he wore his hair long and carried the nickname "Sleaze." He didn't think twice about getting into scuffles with police. In 1996, the Para-Dice Riders found themselves in a heated dispute with police when one of their members was arrested. "Donny got right in the middle—he was at the forefront," recalls one cop. "He's got that streak. But these days you don't see it. It's well hidden right now."

Petersen doesn't smoke or drink. He has no criminal record. According to his biography posted on his Web site, he was a social worker in Toronto's housing projects and "then began working with drug induced problems in the early seventies hippie era"—although the site is vague on whose drug-induced problems he solved or where.

Petersen found his business niche when he became a licensed mechanic in 1977. He opened a successful bike store in east-end Toronto called Heavy Duty Cycles and has gained international stature as a tech writer and teacher. In the spring of 1997, Ottawa even invited Petersen to teach the Havana Harley Riders Club at the Canadian embassy in Cuba. That fall, he also had the distinction of being the only biker ever to address the Empire Club in Toronto—whose roster of previous speakers, the Para-Dice Riders' Web site was quick to point out, included the likes of Ronald Reagan, the Dalai Lama and Billy Graham.

Petersen's sermon to the illustrious crowd came about because at the time he and two other Para-Dice Riders were challenging routine police road checks of bikers before the Ontario Court of Appeal. The invitation to speak came straight from the Empire Club president himself, Gareth Seltzer, a prominent Bay Street investor who had also faced annoying police stops while he cruised on his Harley Dyna Super Glide.

At the head table joining Petersen were such luminaries as Charles Dubin, former chief justice of the Ontario Court of Appeal, and Alan Borovoy, head of the Canadian Civil Liberties Association. The well-heeled crowd gave Petersen a warm welcome, but the high court was less sympathetic. The Para-Dice Riders lost the case, but Petersen's career—and credibility—continued to soar. In February 2000, the Ontario minister of Training, Colleges and Universities in the Conservative government of Mike Harris—citing Petersen's "expertise and experience"—appointed him to a government committee to assess apprenticeship training programs for mechanics.

THE MANY FACES OF DANY KANE

Dany Kane, second from left in sunglasses, among his fellow bikers. For years, he spied for the RCMP and later the organized crime task force called Wolverine, burrowing deep into the Hells Angels hierarchy.
(John Mahoney, *The Gazette*, Montreal)

Dany Kane wasn't cut from the same rough cloth as other bikers. No matter how tough he dressed, police said he always looked too boyish to be a Hells Angel.
(*Allô Police*)

The Rockers did the dirty work for the Hells Angels Nomads. Evidence shows they carried out many of the bombings, beatings and killings ordered by the Hells. Dany Kane is kneeling, second from left. (Photo entered as evidence in mega-trial)

Dany Kane in front of his VW Bug—caught by surveillance camera. (Police photo)

THE KANE FILE

VERS FEVRIER 1997 A LA DEMANDE DE
PAUL NILSON D'HALIFAX, MOI ET AIME
SIMARD NOUS AVONS COMPLETE L'EXECUTION
DE ROBERT MC FERLAND. APRES AVOIR
LOCALISE MC FERLAND, AIME SIMARD A
L'AIDE DE 2 ARMES PONG A
EXECUTE MC FERLAND DANS UN STATIONNEMENT
D'UNE ENTRE POT. A MA PRESENCE. L'EVENEMENT
EST SEVENU DANS LA REGION D'HALIFAX.
J'AI RECU 25 000.00 DOLLARS POUR CE
CONTRAT.

et je fais cette déclaration solennelle, la croyant consciencieusement vraie et sachant qu'elle a la même
force et le même effet que si elle était sous serment, aux termes de la Loi sur la preuve au Canada

Signature du déclarant

Déclaré devant moi

à   MONTREAL   ce   10

Jour de   MARS   19   2000

Kane confesses to murdering Robert MacFarlane, whose name he misspelled,
in this signed confession when he officially became a Wolverine squad source in
March 2000.

Kane tells his RCMP handlers that Maurice "Mom" Boucher orchestrates the biker war.

Kane says Mom Boucher was tipped off that the Sûreté du Québec had a source inside the bikers. Boucher's desire for payback led to the murder of two prison guards.

Thanks to Kane, the police knew about the creation of the powerful Nomads and their identities even before the HA announced the creation of the elite chapter.

96 03-19	4000. 00	96-03-19 au 96-3-31
96.04-07	4000. 00	96-04-01 au 96 04-15
96 04-15	4000. 00	96 04-16 au 96-04-29
96 04-29	4000. 00	96-04-29 au 96-05-13
96 05-13	4000	96-5-14 au 96-5-27
96 5-26	4000	96-5-28 au 96-6-6
96-6-6	→ 1000	avance sur le 96-6-10
96-6-10	3000	96-6-11 au 96 6 24

An excerpt from the pay sheets showing the RCMP's payments to Kane.

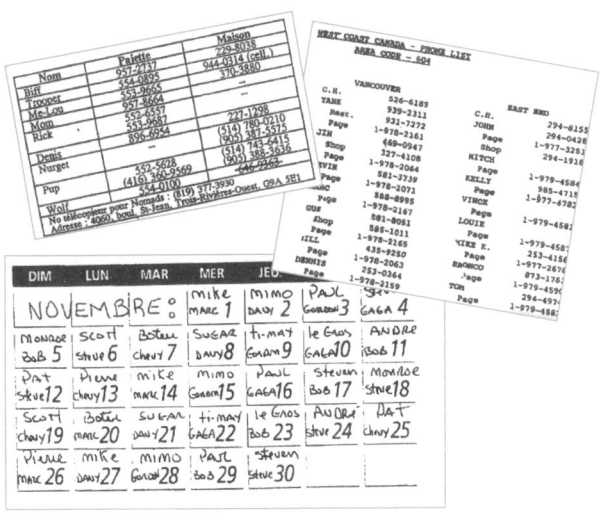

Kane gave the police regular updates, the Nomads' contact sheet, the phone list for the B.C. Hells Angels and even the guard duty roster at a Montreal bunker.

THE NOMADS

The ever-smiling Mom Boucher was jovial, even at a Hells funeral. Standing next to Boucher is David "Gyrator" Giles, a member of the East End Hells Angels chapter in British Columbia. (*Journal de Montréal*)

Hamilton native Walter "Nurget" Stadnick, who was badly burned in a motorcycle accident, became one of the most powerful Nomads, with influence in Ontario, Manitoba and Quebec. (*Allô Police*)

Walter Stadnick, left, meeting with other Angels on one of his many trips to Winnipeg. (*Winnipeg Free Press*)

One of Dany Kane's bosses was David "Wolf" Carroll. A Nova Scotian who became a Quebec Nomad, he ruled the Maritimes until he became a fugitive in 2001. (*Allô Police*)

THE KILLER

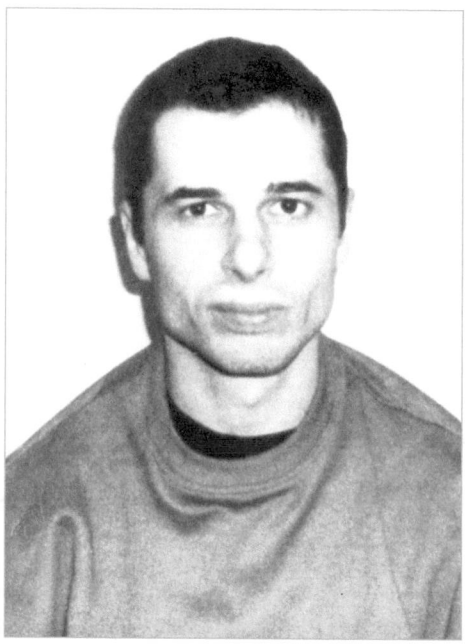

Hoping to scale the Hells hierarchy, Stéphane "Godasse" Gagné murdered two prison guards for Mom Boucher. He ended up testifying against his boss. (Police photo)

AND HIS VICTIMS

Mom Boucher's assassins waited outside Bordeaux Prison in June 1997, plotting to kill a prison guard. They chose Diane Lavigne as she drove out through the gates. (William Marsden)

Diane Lavigne, a 42-year-old mother of two, was shot dead—four bullets in her chest—on June 26, 1997. (Police photo)

Fonfon Fontaine climbed onto the hood of this prison bus and shot the driver, Pierre Rondeau, point blank through the windshield. (Police photo)

Pierre Rondeau, a 49-year-old father of a teenage boy, was murdered on September 8, 1997. (Police photo)

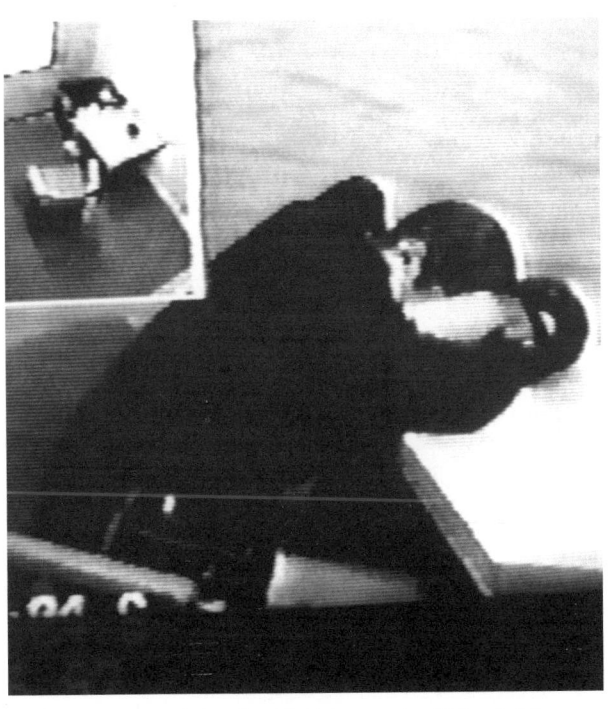

A tired Godasse Gagné during a break in his interrogation. (Police photo)

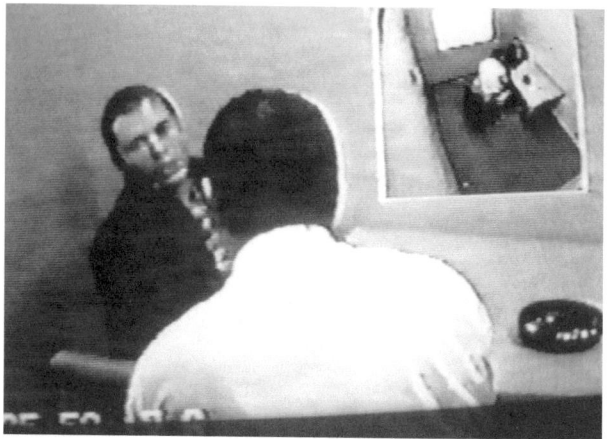

Three hours after he began the interrogation, Sgt. Robert Pigeon begins to confront him about the murders of the guards.

Gagné taunts Pigeon, saying, "Yahoo! Yahoo! They made a mistake—it's not me."

Gagné finally confesses to killing the guards and is ready to testify against the Hells.

For homicide Commander André Bouchard there's only one colour in Montreal and that's police blue. Arguably one of the toughest cops in the country, he targeted Mom Boucher for the prison guard killings. (William Marsden)

(below left) RCMP Sergeant Tom O'Neill was one of the leaders of projects RUSH and Ocean that led to the arrests of more than 120 Hells Angels, Rockers and their associates in Quebec. (William Marsden)

(below right) Sûreté du Québec Sgt. Robert Pigeon, a leading member of Wolverine and the SQ's best interrogator, turned Stéphane Gagné into the chief witness against Mom Boucher. (William Marsden)

Montreal Det. Sgt. Benoît Roberge, who has spent his career tracking bikers, resurrected Dany Kane as a police agent and became his main handler. (William Marsden)

AND ORDER

Prosecutor France Charbonneau fought hard to win an appeal of Boucher's acquittal. She then successfully prosecuted him in 2002, sending the HA leader to prison for life. (William Marsden)

FROM SEA TO SEA

In Vancouver, Ronaldo Lising and another full patch HA member were arrested in 1998 and convicted in 2001 on charges of trafficking in cocaine—one of the few successes police had against the West Coast Angels.
(*The Vancouver Sun*)

Manitoba biker veteran Ernie Dew, who led the Los Brovos into the arms of the Hells Angels, says, "We've had our share of shit fly here." (*Winnipeg Sun*)

Halifax president Mike McCrea tried to give the local Angels a smooth PR image—until his chapter was battered by arrests for murder and cocaine charges, including the conviction of his own brother on drug offences.
(Reprinted by permission of the *Halifax Herald* Limited)

While all this was going on, Petersen's biker career was about to reach new heights. For some time, the Hells Angels had been actively wooing the PDRs. "They were circling in the summer of '98, and then they came in the spring and summer of '99 and really started to push. They were here all the time, riding around with colours on and shit like that," recalls Cal Broeker, a beefy undercover operative who infiltrated the Toronto biker world for the RCMP. He spent a lot of time around the PDRs in their favourite hangouts like the Red Pepper.

"There was a lot of excitement about the Hells Angels from most of the guys: they were small bit players who got a big ticket," Broeker says. "They saw this as their solution to all the fragmented little gangs. It was an opportunity of a lifetime."

The PDRs assumed they would become a puppet club or maybe remain loosely affiliated with the Angels. No one was quite sure how—or when—it would happen. But it had to come soon.

Stadnick had been active for more than a decade in the province. His courtship of the Satan's Choice and the Para-Dice Riders was going well, but he still had no formal presence in the province. And as if competition from the well-entrenched Outlaws was not enough, the Angels suddenly had to face a new interloper in the race for Ontario's riches from the Angels' home province of Quebec: the Rock Machine.

In mid-June 2000, the Rock Machine took many people by surprise when they set up two new chapters in Ontario. One was in Kingston, where the gang had been busy for more than a year. But the real shocker was in Toronto, where the Rock Machine persuaded nine bikers from the Outlaws to switch sides. This gave the Rock Machine something the Angels had never had but always lusted after: a chapter in Canada's biggest city.

NINE

Porous Ports

———

Gary Fotia grew up on the waterfront. From his bedroom window, he could see the towering orange cranes stretching up to the Vancouver skies. Closer to the ground, he could also see the dockside brawls, gambling and prostitution. "In the schools I went to, you either ended up a cop or on the other side." Fotia worked on the docks to put himself through school, "I saw first-hand what was going on—the thefts, the intimidation."

At twenty-five, Fotia, a short, stocky Italian Canadian with jet-black hair and a thick moustache, ended up a cop—a member of the Canada Ports Police. Rising through the ranks, he became a sergeant in charge of intelligence and investigations. Two truths hit him hard: the port was a beehive of drug smuggling; and the port bosses did not seem to care. "They opposed us at every turn," says Fotia. "It was said to me personally, 'You don't interfere with port business.'"

Over a million containers—not to mention a million tourists on cruise ships—move through the Vancouver port every year. It is Canada's largest port, trading over $29 billion in goods with more than ninety nations. The ships from around the globe bring in cars, electronic goods, food—and drugs. In the decade before their department was disbanded in 1997, the ports police and other agencies in Vancouver seized over $1.25 billion in drugs, and barely scratched the surface.

Orchestrating the importation of a lot of those drugs are the Hells Angels, according to confidential police reports going back at least a decade. From the early 1980s and throughout the 1990s, they created a network of full-patch members and associates to infiltrate the ports of Vancouver, Montreal and Halifax. It's a network that flourishes to this day, while the corporate chiefs who run the ports and the politicians in Ottawa turn a blind eye.

The Angels had set down solid roots on Canada's West Coast with four chapters in the early 1980s. They dominated the cocaine trade and controlled much of the booming export of "B.C. Bud"—a potent grade of homegrown marijuana. By 2000, the Angels had almost doubled their size, expanding to seven chapters in the lower mainland, with over seventy members and another thirty or so prospects and hangarounds.

Walter Stadnick made a few trips to the coast, but unlike their counterparts in Halifax, Manitoba and Ontario, the Angels expanded in B.C. without much help from Quebec. There was no mistaking the pedigree, however: the West Coast Angels used the same ruthless tactics their Quebec brethren had employed to wipe out any threats to their B.C. bonanza. You can always tell how valuable someone's treasure is by how far he's willing to go to protect it. "Our guys out here have proven they are prepared to do the exact same thing as the boys back east—car bombs on city streets—with total disregard for the public safety, just to take care of business," says Sgt. Larry Butler of the Vancouver police's small Outlaw Motorcycle Gang unit.

Butler should know. For several days back in the fall of 1993 he did surveillance on a hit man hired by the Angels to take out a rival group called the Russians. "We'd watch him load his guns every day and go hunting," Butler says. The police could not arrest the man, though, without burning an important source; in the end, they seized the weapons but did not charge him.

The Russians were in a war with the Hells Angels to control Vancouver's cocaine trade. They lost after a series of car bombings and executions.

The Angels' position was secure, and it was in no small measure because they had control of the West Coast ports. In Vancouver, the top cop at the ports was Mike Toddington, a fastidious Englishman who, when he joined the harbour police in 1969, brought with him a small-town English obsession with order, detail and "the proper way things get done."

Toddington and Fotia began compiling a mountain of intelligence dossiers and briefing notes. In August 1994, their first major report unveiled "a massive billion-dollar-plus drug import industry." At its centre was one group: "The Hells Angels have extensively infiltrated the operations of the port. Angels are among the first to board arriving ships. They unload the goods, place them for storage, load them onto trucks and prepare the necessary documents for shipping." The ranks of the biggest union on the waterfront, the International Longshore and Warehouse Union (ILWU), were "littered with members and associates of the Angels. They are placed in key positions that enable them to commit crimes."

The police found ten full-patch HA members plus thirty associates with ILWU accreditation.

The East End chapter had the largest contingent of port workers in its ranks—hardly surprising, given the chapter's physical proximity to the harbour and its historical affinity with drug smuggling. In 1994, police files indicated no fewer than sixteen East End members or associates had an ILWU number, including John Bryce, the chapter president. Ernie Ozolins, the leader of the Haney chapter, held a union number, though he was listed as inactive.

But many other Angels still worked the port and were long-standing members of the union, some with over twenty years' experience. White Rock Angel Robert Robinson was a foreman at the Roberts Bank Superport in Delta, south of Vancouver. Another foreman there was Al Debruyn, who wore his full colours during the groundbreaking ceremony for the new facility. One of Debruyn's brothers was a crane operator at the Surrey docks. Another was a business agent for the union, allowing him to travel free and unfettered to any port in the province.

"They're in key positions to have anything moved to where they want it to be moved," says Gary Fotia. Some worked in offices and, according to police reports, "held key positions that allowed access to sensitive shipping information." Others were forklift drivers or dispatchers who control the movement of cargo; still others, like Debruyn, were promoted to positions of managers and foremen and could control the movement of people. "You could have people putting the containers anywhere they want," says Toddington.

Customs inspectors check only 3 percent of all the containers coming into the country. So on the docks in Vancouver and across the country, smuggling has become a sophisticated, well-orchestrated operation. The bikers put people in key positions to facilitate a "tailgate operation," so called because the bikers can organize the movement of drugs from a container right onto one of their waiting vehicles with exquisite precision.

Here is how it sometimes works: The bikers on the waterfront know exactly what container to look for on what vessel. Once the ship docks, a Hells foreman or sympathizer arranges a work crew—the crane operator, the forklift driver, the flatbed driver all have to be in on it. The targeted container is set apart from the others, perhaps in the corner of a warehouse or somewhere else out of sight. The bikers then back the container right up into one of their trucks—tailgate to tailgate—that is parked on the dock. They break the seal on the container and remove the drugs.

Inside one of the drug bags or sometimes taped inside the door of the container itself are a duplicate set of seals. The smugglers then simply close the container, reseal it, put it back on the truck and ship it off with the rest of the consignment. No one is ever the wiser. "Everything looks normal," says Gary Fotia. "It's what's happening behind the scenes that's important."

Keeping tabs on all this illegal activity along 138 miles of port coastline was a daunting task for Toddington and his team. By 1996 they numbered only twenty-nine officers, down from forty-two a decade earlier. They faced constant intimidation and threats. "Cargo can fall, people can fall in ships' holds. 'Accidents' on the waterfront just written off as accidents," Toddington says. "Certain things have happened to people who don't play ball."

The ports cops knew that harassment from the criminal element went with the territory. But it was the negligence by the businessmen who ran the port that most shocked the police officers. Repeatedly over the next few years, Toddington and his men, in written and oral reports, tried to warn the port bosses about criminal activities and the Hells Angels. On June 1, 1995, Toddington personally briefed Bob Wilds, then president of the B.C. Maritime

Employers Association, the group responsible for hiring most of the dockworkers. At a luncheon four months later with the VPC board of directors, Wilds seemed to acknowledge that the Hells Angels were a problem. According to a police memo, this short conversation then ensued between him and another board member:

"Yes, they're a bad group; they're even in the work-force," Wilds admits.

"The Hells Angels?" says an incredulous board member.

"Yep."

"Are they in a position of influence?"

"They sure are," Wilds replies.

Yet publicly, the ports bosses insisted all was quiet on the waterfront. Security was a low priority. Just how low became clear when Ottawa decided it could save $10 million a year by disbanding the national ports police. The plan would force the ports corporations to pay for their own security by farming out the task to the RCMP, local police and other bidders. Ottawa announced its plan to dismantle the ports police in 1995 and succeeded in wiping them out by 1997—despite warnings from major police forces, some of its own advisers and the provinces.

The story of the blind port authorities continued in Montreal, the headquarters of the most powerful Hells Angels drug network. Dominic Taddeo, the president and CEO of the Montreal Port Authority, dismissed as "hearsay" any reports of organized crime there. "There's no question of that in Montreal," he said in early 1998. "Our terminals are secure."

Taddeo's statement was stunning because on the payroll at the port was one of Montreal's most notorious crime kingpins— Gerry Matticks. "Nothing comes out of the harbour until Matticks say it comes out of the harbour," says André Bouchard, Montreal police commander of major crimes. "How the hell can [Taddeo] honestly say on camera that it's the best-run business? What are you, blind?"

Gerry Matticks was born in 1940, the youngest of fourteen children of a poor Irish family that lived where most of the poor Irish did in Montreal—the bleak streets near the Lachine Canal known as Point St-Charles. Matticks became part of the Irish Mafia known as the West End Gang, a loose affiliation of hoods who had enough guts and guns to stay independent of the warring bikers and the Italian mob and yet form alliances with both. He found prosperity in the trucking and meat business; a Quebec government inquiry into organized crime in the seventies fingered Matticks and his brothers as leaders of a truck hijacking-and-robbery ring. But it was his unrelenting control over the port of Montreal that brought Matticks real fame and fortune. Most of the checkers—the men who control the movement of the containers off the ships—came from the Point. And most owed their jobs to Matticks. Gerry's own son Donovan was a checker.

"I know a lot of people who work on the waterfront," says Kevin McGarr, an Irish Montrealer and former detective who spent the better part of his career breaking up the West End Gang. "Most of them got their jobs from Matticks. He had a stranglehold on the checkers."

Like all good crime lords, Matticks never forgot his roots—and he knew how to buy loyalty. "There's a bit of Robin Hood in him. It was a legend down in the Point," says McGarr. "If a truck of hams went missing, you'd be sure everyone in the Point was having ham that week." When he was not playing Robin Hood, it was Santa Claus. "If one of these checkers had a fire in their house the week before Christmas, don't worry—they're still going to have Christmas dinner and the kids are all going to have gifts," says McGarr. "Matticks would take care of them. Which is why these people are not going to rat on him. It's not going to happen."

Matticks himself was honest enough to confess that he had more hell than holiness in him. "I inherited who I am from my family. We're not saints," he once told a reporter as he sat drinking on a Thursday night in the country-and-western bar called Mickey's that he owned.

"You'll notice there are no drugs here," he said. "I don't like drugs." Maybe not to consume, but Matticks had no problem growing fabulously wealthy by importing them. On the wall of his bar was a photo of Marlon Brando from the movie *On the Waterfront*. In the Hollywood version, Brando defeats the criminals who control the dock union; in real-life Montreal, Matticks had no Brando—or any other opponents—to worry about.

Containerized cargo traffic is the fastest-growing business at the Montreal port, accounting for half of the shipments. Matticks had his people at all four of the container-handling facilities, though the Termont terminal along an eastern stretch of Notre-Dame Boulevard was his power base. To control the smuggling, Matticks needed only a small group of workers at a time: someone who has access to the shipping plans and the checker who knows the container number. Even if you didn't have the seal number for the container that held your dirty cargo, Matticks could help you. You order dope from Pakistan via Asia and the Netherlands. It leaves Peshawar to Singapore. Someone there snaps a Polaroid of your container. You get the picture and you give it to Matticks, explains Kevin McGarr, the former Montreal police detective. "And you say, 'When this one comes off the boat—there's no paperwork for it—just have it put somewhere.' No problem."

Even when nothing moved on the port, Matticks could get things moving. During a truckers' strike in the fall of 2000, pickets blocked access to the docks. One truck got through the lines to pick up a container, supposedly packed with chocolate from Belgium. When police followed it to a factory, they also found a tonne of hashish.

Matticks dealt with everyone—the Italians, the Russians, the Asians and all the rival biker gangs. In 1997, his brother Richard got three years in jail for his part in a $39,000-a-kilo coke deal with Giovanni Cazzetta, the head of the Rock Machine. At one point during the biker war, the Rock Machine boys sent Gerry Matticks a letter asking him to attempt peace talks with the HA. Friend to all, Matticks became friendliest with Mom Boucher as the Hells Angels became the biggest players in town. Court records show that Matticks guaranteed the mortgage on Boucher's estate in Contrecoeur. Police surveillance caught Mom and Matticks at frequent meetings. Boucher's nickname for his man at the ports was "Boeuf"—a reference to Matticks's meat business; Boeuf was the code name the Nomads used on their computer banking records to identify Matticks's account.

Cocaine, as in Vancouver, was a big staple in Montreal, but the city also is one of the world's biggest hash markets. Of the 200 to 250 tonnes of illegal hash that move around the globe every year, about 75 tonnes make their way to Quebec. Matticks was an important supplier of the brown gold to the Angels. And gold it was. Hash that cost $200 a kilo in Afghanistan could sell in Montreal for $4,500 to $5,000 a kilo. Matticks rarely took his fee completely in cash; he often wanted to be paid in product. Even his best customers had to fork over a 25 to 30 percent cut. When Matticks got his huge share in drugs, he would sometimes sell it back to the Hells Angels. At times, prosecutors would later contend, the Hells Angels owed him as much as $7 million.

Despite—or perhaps because of—his legendary crime wealth and clout, Matticks always managed to stay one step ahead of the law. His sole conviction in 1989 was for truck hijacking; he paid a $10,000 fine and spent ninety days behind bars. Matticks and his brother John were put on trial in 1972 when a man said the brothers tried to murder him because they suspected he was squealing to the ports police. Three witnesses who insisted that Matticks was at a bar at the time of the shooting convinced the jury to acquit him; one witness was a member of Matticks's gang. In 1994, evidence planted by the Sûreté du Québec allowed Matticks to walk away from charges of smuggling tonnes of hashish through the port. So Matticks's activities were hardly a secret to the ports police. "We knew about him, and we knew about the people he controlled," says Sidney Peckford, the national director of the ports police. "I had intelligence reports coming out of my ass."

The only person who continued to profess ignorance about what Matticks and his pal Mom were up to at the waterfront was ports boss Dominic Taddeo. "We don't control who the unions hire. We're not washing our hands of responsibility," he said, doing, of course, just that.

Halifax completed the trio of Canada's blind port mice. Only 620 miles from Montreal, the port and the rest of the Nova Scotian shoreline was one of several key landing zones for the tonnes of coke needed to feed the drug distribution machine of Mom Boucher and his powerful Quebec Nomads. Every year, more than 500,000 containers move through two Halifax terminals, Cerescorp and Halterm. Since 1991, customs and police have seized about $2.5 billion in drugs hidden in just about anything: a shipment of wine, factory-sealed tins of pineapple, motor oil and once in pickles from Iran.

The Halifax chapter of the HA was small and relatively weak. It was Wolf Carroll and the Montreal Nomads who controlled the drug importation, not the local boys. So unlike on the West Coast, there was no need here for local

Hells Angels members to be working directly on the docks. Instead, relatives, friends and associates—including some with direct ties to the top men in Montreal—were peppered throughout the docks. "I knew them all—I knew their faces, I knew what they were involved in," says Peckford, who had headed the Halifax ports police detachment for eight years before he became national chief in Ottawa. "Nobody was prepared to muscle them around because they didn't know what repercussions were going to occur off the docks."

Peckford's replacement in 1993 was a six-foot barrel of a man with a bald head, bushy eyebrows and a wide grin named Bruce Brine. With twenty-two years of ports policing behind him, Brine was a stickler for detail who had little patience with playing politics with the port bosses. "I was naive politically. I thought an honest cop could survive," he says. "Within about two months, I knew I was in the fight of my life."

His troubles began when he sat down with Eric Mott, a determined constable who had been trying to keep tabs on certain individuals on the dock. Mott showed his new boss some of the "links analysis" he had drawn up on his computer, based on intelligence files and surveillance. They revealed circles of influence and connections. One was centred on Paul Arthur, a crane operator. Tied to Arthur on Mott's charts were several other port workers, including Robert Langille. Almost a decade later, police would arrest Arthur and Langille in one of the biggest East Coast drug busts in history—but for now, nobody paid attention to the ports police warnings.

Other names on Mott's charts included Brian Dempsey, a Hells Angels associate who would later be convicted on drug charges; Patty Holmes, a stevedore at Halterm and later a crane operator who was a good friend of Randy Mersereau, the former Angel who became an independent drug lord; Gary Novelli, who had no criminal record but was an uncle of the wife of the Halifax Hells Angels leader, Mike McCrea; and Derrick Paul Slaunwhite, a stevedore who was convicted of possession of stolen goods and later killed in a car wash in a drug-related murder.

The criminal connections worried Mott and Brine, but their bosses apparently did not share their concerns. Mott remembers a conversation he had in the summer of 1994 with David Bellefontaine, then president of the Halifax Port Authority. "Bruce [Brine] wants to do police work. He really thinks he's a policeman," Bellefontaine said.

"Well, we are policemen," answered Mott.

"I know you are, but we don't need you to do all that extra work. We really don't need policemen. We just need some guys around the port. That's not what we're about."

Brine's first major run-in with his superiors occurred over a cleaning company that had a service contract with the port—including after-hours access to corporate and police offices. The woman had no criminal record, but the ports police believed that over the years she had been too friendly with the biker community. "She grew up with these guys," Mott says. "She's been long-time friends with them." A girlfriend who worked with her also lived with Clay McRea, the brother of the HA chapter president.

Brine raised his security concerns with the port directors; they dithered, but the police at least barred the cleaning company from their offices. When the company's contract came up for renewal, the port told the owner she could not get security clearance and put the contract out to re-tender. She sued and won an out-of-court settlement with the ports corporation. Today, she says she cannot discuss the details.

The incident helped to poison relations between Brine and the port authorities. Even Sid Peckford, Brine's own boss as national head of the ports police, thought Brine was pushing it. "He made it almost a personal vendetta. It's the real world—you can't dwell on these things forever."

Brine and Mott's next target made port officials—and Peckford—even less happy. Debbie Milton worked at Protos Shipping, one of the busy commercial lines at the port (a job she continued to hold until the late 1990s). Her husband was Robbie Milton, one of the founding members of the Halifax Hells Angels. A heavy cocaine user, Milton had his colours pulled in 1988, but police say he has not cut off all ties with his buddies. Debbie split up with her Hells husband, but ports police intelligence indicated that one of her close friends was the wife of Wolf Carroll, the Quebec Nomad who ran the Halifax biker scene.

After her breakup with Robbie Milton, Debbie took up with Laurence Coady, a small-time shipping agent who would eventually figure in a big-time drug bust. Constable Mott, who knew Coady, tried to warn him.

"I hear you're with Debbie," Mott remembers telling Coady on the docks one day in 1995.

"Yeah—she's giving up her past," the young man insisted.

"She'll never give up her past," Mott said. "You don't want to go down that road. Just take it from me."

Sure enough, a few months later, Coady told Mott that Wolf Carroll came by for a visit and stayed for a week at Milton's home.

"Jesus Christ, I almost shit myself!" Coady recounted to Mott. "I'm home, there's a knock on the door, and who shows up—Wolf Carroll."

Coady's house guests were his own problem. What disturbed Mott and Brine were reports about Debbie Milton's friendliness with ports corporation officials—and their own boss, Sid Peckford. At least two different ports police officers had told them they had seen Peckford on friendly terms with Milton, dating back several years.

Peckford, for his part, adamantly denies there was a problem. "I've heard the name before" is what he first says when asked about Debbie Milton in an interview for this book. But later in the conversation he said, "I might have met her at a cocktail party or something—I don't know. These people have an overdeveloped imagination. . . . I might have met her briefly in a function somewhere—she could have been there. I remember the name, but I wouldn't be able to tell you what she looks like." When asked about Milton's ties to Angels leader Wolf Carroll, the former director of Canada's ports police had this to say: "So she entertains someone in her private home? But beyond that what do you do? Does that mean she is not supposed to be employed by a shipping company?"

What Bruce Brine saw as methodical police work, others saw as meddling insubordination. In 1994, he won a governor general's award for exemplary service, but that service was taking its toll. He was seeing a stress counsellor as early as September 1993, and by January 1995 he had taken sick leave, hospitalized for what doctors diagnosed as heart problems brought on by stress; later he had a complete nervous breakdown. While Brine was stricken, he received another blow: Ports Canada notified him that he was fired for "serious misconduct." Originally, the port said the dismissal was "for cause," which meant a loss of pension and medical benefits. The port later changed that to more neutral wording, but it took Brine two years to get his full benefits back.

In September 1997, Brine asked the RCMP to investigate his dismissal as an obstruction of justice, arguing that the port authorities fired him because he was investigating illegal conduct. After a year-long yet surprisingly incomplete inquiry, the RCMP dismissed all of Brine's allegations.

A Mountie investigator did speak three times to Eric Mott, the ports constable who headed criminal intelligence for the Halifax detachment and worked for Brine. "There was no question in my mind that there were investigations going on—I did them!" Mott says, referring to the many reports he filed.

On his own, Brine was able to gather impressive documentation that his firing was indeed prompted by his dogged pursuit of organized crime connections. From Ottawa came testimony by Richard Godin, a former senior officer at staff headquarters. He said national ports police boss Sid Peckford told him that "Brine did not know when to quit" and Brine's investigations of biker ties to port workers "were causing him a lot of grief because of the complaints being raised by port and other powerful officials."

Nevertheless, the Mounties insisted there was "no independent evidence" that Brine and his ports police ever carried out the investigations he asserted got him fired in the first place.

Brine also complained that Peckford, his boss as the director of the ports police, got a $10,000 payment from the ports corporation just as the police were being disbanded. Internal ports documents show Peckford was approved as one of the "bonus candidates." The RCMP concluded the "monies were properly authorized." Peckford calls it a salary increase and says Brine was wrong to conclude it was the money that kept him silent about the abolition of the ports police. "I didn't publicly say anything at the time because I couldn't," he says today from his home in Orleans, Ontario, where he retired. "I could very well have committed suicide and tomorrow I'd have no job. I'm not saying I'm happy about this whole experience. That's not a chapter I'm very proud of."

With Bruce Brine gone in Halifax, it was only a matter of time before the other outspoken ports police commander at the other end of the country got the chop. And in Mike

Toddington's case too, his fate was sealed in a security battle over a woman.

A low-level employee at the Vancouver Ports Corporation (VPC) for almost eighteen years was also a cousin of a Hells Angels member according to a background check by the ports police. That was hardly a firing offence. But Toddington grew concerned when the woman got a job as a receptionist in the office of VPC chairman Ron Longstaffe in 1994. He felt she might now be privy to sensitive and confidential information and at a minimum should be subject to a standard security screening. The VPC refused.

The police decided to open their own investigation anyway, naming it Project "Eh." They followed her on at least two occasions to a Burnaby home they believed was a crack house—even though the RCMP drug section "was unable to find any conclusive evidence that there was drug trafficking taking place there." Still, the ports police took swabs of the door handle of her Volkswagen beetle. "The resulting reading . . . was described as a high, positive reading for cocaine," a police report notes. A subsequent test for traces of drugs on her driver's licence turned up similar results.

"That was enough for us," Toddington says. On January 17, 1997, at 3:20 p.m., he went to see Norman Stark, a former ports police chief himself who was now port manager. "We know she has relatives who are organized crime," Toddington said. "You've got a problem. . . . She is a serious risk."

Stark insisted it was a matter for the personnel office and expressed concern that the receptionist could file a complaint of harassment. On March 4, at 3 p.m., Toddington got a call from his boss in Ottawa—Sid Peckford. Peckford pressed him to close the file.

"Just write it off and leave it at that," Toddington recalls Peckford telling him.

"All right," Toddington said. He put the phone down, but then said to himself, No, this is wrong.

He called in Gary Fotia, the sergeant in charge of intelligence whom he had grown to trust. He handed the file to Fotia, who put it in his desk. "This investigation is continuing, as far as we're concerned," Toddington said.

It was the last decision he ever made as ports security chief. Fifteen days later, the ports corporation fired him. The port said it was part of the dismantling of the police force that was scheduled for July. Toddington did not buy that for a moment—and he sued for wrongful dismissal.

"We were racing against time," Gary Fotia says. With his boss gone, he knew it would be only months before the entire ports police force would be disbanded and he would be out of a job. "We never finished what we started, so we don't know how deep organized crime is on the waterfront."

Fotia and his colleagues were not opposed in principle to the idea of abolishing the ports police as an organization—as long as their accumulated knowledge and experience was absorbed into a new policing effort. Fotia suggested that they keep the veteran ports police officers on in an intelligence section, feeding the RCMP and other police forces scheduled to take over port security.

Instead, in July 1997, when the ports police were formally disbanded, not only did the government fire all the officers, but all their intelligence files also disappeared. The new supervisor who had come in to replace Toddington had shredded many of the police files. At national headquarters, it was the same story: "I have colleagues in Ottawa who told me they were destroying material they knew they shouldn't be destroying," Mike Toddington says.

In Halifax, Superintendent Bruce Brine was already out the door, and his investigator Eric Mott was close behind. Mott was suspended a month before the official elimination

of the ports police for talking to the media. "All of our intelligence records disappeared—three drawers full," he says.
His top drawer was packed with active files; a second drawer
had intelligence files and a third had other police files. Mott
had done a check on more than seven thousand people who
had ever worked at the port going back ten years—and
found that 75 percent had criminal records, from rape to
manslaughter, theft and fraud. Now those records—and all
his investigations into organized crime—were gone. Ten
years later, three of the people in his files would finally come
to public attention in a multi-million-dollar drug bust.

It was a curious way to fight organized crime: the Hells
Angels keep their jobs on the docks, but the cops policing
the ports get fired—and the two police superintendents in
the Halifax and Vancouver ports most diligent in pursuing
organized crime are singled out for the harshest dismissals.

Mom Boucher and the rest of the Hells Angels could
only laugh. Just as Boucher and his biker allies across the
country were reaching the pinnacle of their power, the
government handed them an end-of-millennium gift.

PART III

TAKEDOWN

TEN

The Kane Mutiny

"It's been ten years, ten years that I've been with the Hells Angels. . . . Fuck, that's a long time. But it changes nothing. It counts for nothing . . . nothing you do counts."
DANY KANE

Once Maurice "Mom" Boucher was acquitted of murder charges, it wasn't long before he began plotting his revenge against a justice system that had dared to challenge his supremacy. Since the killing of the prison guards, there had been fears that the Angels planned to target police, Crown prosecutors and judges. Dany Kane's words of warning still rang in Gaetan St. Onge's ears: "The prison guards murders, that's nothing compared to what is to come." Those fears became reality in the spring of 1999.

In April, Montreal police discovered first one, then two, then five bombs packed with dynamite hidden just outside five different police stations in the city. Luckily, the bombs never exploded. The detonators, all from the same package, were faulty. What mattered was that the emboldened bikers appeared determined to snap at the heels of what they thought was a retreating army of discouraged and powerless police officers.

Police discovered two years later that a satellite group of the Hells Angels called the Scorpions, led by the Gay Village drug dealer Serge Boutin, had set the bombs. A Scorpion testified that the orders came from "Les Lunettes" ("Glasses"), a nickname the bikers used for the bespectacled Mom Boucher.

"There were rumours that the Hells were going to go after police, prosecutors, judges," Det. Sgt. Benoît Roberge says. "So now it seemed it had started."

The police station bombs seemed to shake the police out of a stupor caused by the previous year's string of court defeats. The bombs had the effect of galvanizing the forces into a single unit. There was fresh emphasis on cooperation, and within a month of their discovery, Roberge found himself back at Wolverine along with other top Montreal investigators. It was a new squad with new bosses and a fresh attitude. It also had a new name: Regional Task Force—Montreal, known by its French acronym ERM. But investigators still preferred to call it by its familiar title, Wolverine.

Police also decided they had to shift their focus away from individual gang members and target the entire organization, taking advantage of Canada's new anti-gang law. Chasing down individual bikers had failed to weaken the Hells. There seemed to be an endless supply of recruits willing to take their place. "Everybody was saying we have to try and go after the criminal organization," RCMP Sgt. Tom O'Neill, a senior investigator at Wolverine, recalls. "We have to investigate them as an organization and not as we traditionally investigated them by individuals or com-modities, by incident or by event."

But the new law, passed in 1997 and known as C-95, had never really been tested. The law made it illegal to be part of a criminal organization, but the burden was heavy. Some prosecutors feared it was unconstitutional and the

Supreme Court would likely reverse any convictions. Others argued it would be too expensive to enforce because the investigations would require enormous police and justice department resources. "Bombs are going off in Montreal, and people are dying," O'Neill recalls. "The public is in an uproar over how the Angels and the Rockers control the city of Montreal. And I thought that has to be included in part of the equation. You can't just put a dollar figure on it."

A handful of prosecutors, including veterans André Vincent and Pierre Paradis, agreed with O'Neill, and the anti-gang law advocates won out. For the first time—years after the biker wars had started—the Quebec government finally formed a special team of prosecutors called the Organized Crime Office (Bureau de Lutte au Crime Organisé). They were given their own suite of offices in a commercial highrise in downtown Montreal, computers and a decent budget. Their job was to advise the Wolverine investigators, prosecute the anti-gang cases and confiscate the bikers' criminal assets. The overall investigation was called Project RUSH. The target was the entire Hells Angels organization in Montreal, including the Rockers and other satellite clubs. The investigation and prosecution would cost tens of millions of dollars—and nobody had any idea if it would ever pay off.

The police needed snitches, informants and spies. "There were some active sources that were providing us with some information, but nothing big. Old sources. We had to actively recruit new ones," O'Neill says. "Just tapping a phone and doing surveillance you are going to get only part of the picture. You have to have somebody inside to be able to tell you exactly what's going on."

Trouble was, O'Neill had nobody in mind. Nor did any other cop. Except Benoît Roberge.

Roberge is a tall, well-built Montreal detective who had spent most of his fourteen-year career gathering intelligence on biker gangs and trying to convince his bosses that the Hells should be taken more seriously. He was the policeman who had sat across the desk from Gaetan St. Onge at Wolverine working closely with the RCMP veteran who controlled the best biker source police had ever had—Dany Kane. But until the MacFarlane murder investigation, Roberge had not known the true identity of C-2994. In fact, Roberge was one of the officers who had helped end Kane's undercover career. It was Roberge who had phoned the RCMP in Halifax to tell them that Montreal had caught Aimé Simard.

Now, two years later, Roberge was back at Wolverine with a promotion to detective-sergeant. His job was twofold: gather intelligence and do the investigations. Roberge soon realized, however, that the intelligence he was getting was of little value for an anti-gang prosecution. It amounted to bits and pieces. He needed a more global picture. Something like what Dany Kane had supplied. And since that was the case, why not corral the real thing—Dany Kane himself?

The MacFarlane case had dropped the veil on Kane. Everybody thought the man was blown. But not Roberge. Roberge thought he could pick the veil up again and revive Kane as a police informant. He talked it over with Sgt. Robert Pigeon, the SQ officer who had so successfully turned Stéphane Gagné into a weapon against Mom Boucher. Both officers doubted Kane would bite, especially after his experience with the RCMP and his hatred of the SQ. The MacFarlane affair had badly exposed him. Too many cops now probably knew about Kane's secret life as a spy. In fact, given all the leaks inside the force, Roberge thought it was a miracle Kane was still alive. Yet Kane was still alive. The Angels obviously still trusted him. So, the two officers thought, perhaps Kane's exposed position could be turned to their advantage. Few people would expect that the police would even consider hiring Kane as an informant. And fewer still would suspect that Kane would have the balls to return to his former undercover life. The audacious irony of it all made Roberge smile. It also made him even more eager to try to make it work.

There was the messy fact, however, that Kane was a known murderer. Roberge had to get the support of his bosses and the prosecutors. "I wanted to be sure management was behind it. Can we live with him? Are you ready to work with this guy who has killed people?" They agreed but warned Roberge that Kane would have to be kept on a very tight leash. "They didn't want any surprises," Roberge says. "You invest a lot in a person like that, an informer, an agent, it's big." So Roberge made his move. It was a gamble, but these were desperate times. "The murders, bombings continued and it was an accumulation of things that made us decide to approach Dany Kane," Roberge says.

On August 18, 1999, Roberge phoned Kane's mother and, without disclosing his identity, left a message that he was trying to find Dany. She phoned back and to Roberge's surprise left Kane's number. Roberge immediately phoned Kane, who agreed to meet five days later on August 23. Roberge gazed around him in amazement. It was that easy. Two days later, Kane called back—another surprise. Roberge logged the call into his notebook at 8:30 a.m. Kane informed him that the Rockers had just tried to kill one of their own members, Stephen Falls, a biker in debt to the Rockers whom they also suspected of being an informant. Kane then confirmed the August 23 meeting. The unflappable Dany Kane, it seemed, was eager to get back into the spy business.

Kane's meeting with his new handlers was a carbon copy of his first encounter with the RCMP five years earlier. The meeting began at noon in a west-end Montreal hotel room. Present were Kane, Roberge and Pigeon. Kane talked, Roberge listened and Pigeon took notes. Just as he had done with the RCMP, Kane took control and started rattling off the latest information about the Hells and the Rockers. He told them Wolf Carroll had paid $350,000 in legal fees for the Halifax murder trial. He said the Rockers were about to split into two groups. One would control the east end of Montreal and the other the west end. He gave them the name of the Hells' real estate agent who "makes false documents with phony names and pays a contact at the banks to obtain loans," which allowed the bikers to hide ownership so their properties couldn't be seized by tax auditors or by police under proceeds-of-crime laws. He outlined who controlled what territory in Nova Scotia, Quebec and Ontario.

But most important, he described the Rockers' club meetings. A member of the Nomads usually presided at the meetings, where each Rocker had to pay monthly fees of 10 percent of his earnings to the club. "The money comes from crime and the most profitable is drug trafficking," Kane said. The Rockers jokingly called these meetings la messe, the French word for "mass," but they were referred to by English bikers as "church meetings." They held the church meetings in different hotels. Kane described how members never knew when or where the next meeting would take place until the evening before, when a striker, a first-level Rocker recruit, would distribute hotel business cards with the time written on the back. The Rockers thought their system made it impossible for the police to learn about the meetings soon enough to get a warrant and bug them.

To date, the system had worked. Police had never infiltrated the Rockers' church meetings. In fact, they hadn't even tried. Roberge and Pigeon decided it was time to change that. If they could prove the connection between the financing of the club and the crimes committed in the name of the club, they could send most of the members away for a long time on charges of gangsterism. The two detectives decided they had to get inside these meetings.

First, however, they had to settle up with Dany Kane. Kane had talked for four hours, and Pigeon had filled fourteen pages with handwritten notes. Kane was back in action. This time, however, he wanted to go much further than he had gone with the RCMP. He told Roberge and Pigeon he was ready to become what in Quebec is called an *agent-source*—a category of informant who not only works full time under contract gathering evidence for the police but also commits to wearing body packs and testifying in court on the evidence he or she has collected. Dany Kane was ready to do all that. But it would come at a hefty price. He wanted $10 million. "It was crazy," Roberge says. "There was no chance we would pay that." Negotiations would last six months. Still, Kane was ready to start work with or without a contract. Police agreed to pay him $750 a week plus expenses—a major pay cut compared with the $2,000 he was making with the RCMP. But Kane didn't seem to care. He must have assumed that sooner or later the police would need him so badly that they would surrender to his demands. Meanwhile, the $750 would have to do. Police also gave him a new number. The former RCMP source C-2994 became, in his second life as a spy, police agent number 3683.

Roberge and Pigeon were far more focused in their use of Kane than his former RCMP handlers had been. Both men wanted Kane's work to lead as quickly as possible to mass arrests. With Kane on board, the immediate focus of Project RUSH became the accumulation of enough evidence to secure a warrant so police could bug and film

Hells Angels' and Rockers' church meetings wherever they were held in Canada.

Kane contacted Roberge two or three times a week, filing a steady stream of reports with updates about Hells' and Rockers' criminal activities and meetings. Much of it was like the intelligence he supplied the RCMP—a mixture of hard-core criminal information, gossip, rumours, opinion and trivia.

But within three weeks, Roberge ran up against his first Kane-related crisis. It struck like a recurring nightmare because once again it was triggered by a murder plot in Halifax.

Just over two years previously, Kane had carried out the contract killing of Robert MacFarlane, and now, according to police intelligence reports, David "Wolf" Carroll had new targets for elimination in Nova Scotia: Randy Mersereau, his brother Kirk and their entire gang. Randy Mersereau, a former Angel, had ditched his colours to become an independent drug trafficker. Not only was Carroll's former friend cutting into his drug sales in Halifax, but now there were rumours he was allying with the Hells Angels' hated foe, the Bandidos, travelling to New Mexico for meetings at the club's headquarters. Kane told Roberge the Hells had learned from a friend of Mersereau's that he had put out a contract on the heads of Carroll, Boucher and Mike McCrea, the president of the Halifax chapter. So there was ample reason for Carroll to decide that Randy Mersereau had to go.

Roberge learned about it almost by accident. During a meeting in a Montreal hotel room on Wednesday, September 22, Kane mentioned that he was going to Halifax with Carroll. "Whoa! Whoa! What's this about?" All Roberge's alarm bells rang. He dragged the whole story out of Kane, who told him that a month earlier he and

Carroll had been in Halifax staking out Mersereau and planning the murder. He mentioned that after they wiped out Mersereau and his gang, the Angels intended to send the Rockers and Scorpions to Halifax to trash Mersereau's bars and take over the city.

The next day, Thursday, September 23, a huge blast blew out the windows of Mersereau's office at his car dealership in Truro. The bombing injured seven people, including Mersereau. Kane told his handlers, according to documents in the court record, that McCrea "organized the bomb attack." No charges were ever laid. Mersereau survived, but the Angels kept coming after him. Kane and Carroll were due to drive to Halifax the next day in a rented car. "He told me to get a gun," Kane said. " 'We're going there, I don't know when we're coming back, but bring a gun.' "

Roberge was in a squeeze. If he stopped Kane from going, he risked raising Carroll's suspicions: Carroll had already entertained some doubts about Kane after the MacFarlane murder. So Roberge and his informant worked out a plan. Kane set off for Halifax with Carroll, but when the two bikers reached Rivière-du-Loup near the New Brunswick border, an SQ patrol car pulled them over for speeding. Unknown to Carroll, the officer was in fact a member of Wolverine. When he inspected the trunk, he discovered Kane's .38 revolver and Carroll's machine gun and silencer. Both men were arrested and interrogated by Wolverine detectives, then released on bail.

The ruse protected Kane's cover, but it did little to save Mersereau's life. The last time anyone saw forty-eight-year-old Randy Mersereau alive was October 31, 1999. Police found his abandoned car along Highway 102, between Halifax and Truro. He had vanished like a ghost on Halloween. The case remains unsolved and there are no official suspects.

In fact Kane had informed Roberge that Carroll had set up a new hit squad to take out Mersereau. On November 3, Kane reported that the bikers had executed Mersereau with a 9 mm machine gun equipped with a silencer—the same type of weapon seized from Carroll at Rivière-du-Loup. Kane said the killers had buried Mersereau with the gun that killed him. The body has never been found.

Back in Quebec, Roberge's main focus continued to be the infiltration of the Rockers' church meetings. By November he had secured a warrant allowing police to bug and film the meetings anywhere in Canada for a period of one year. It gave police plenty of time to let the bikers hang themselves with their own words. The first opportunity came on November 30. At 8:10 in the evening, Kane phoned Roberge to tell him the Rockers were holding mass the next afternoon, giving him the precise time and the place. Police sent in a technical team to wire the room. They hid a camera in a corner of the ceiling to give them an overhead, fish-eye view of the proceedings. The meeting began at twelve-thirty with the tinkling of a water glass as one of the Rockers brought his sixteen fellow bikers to order. When the meeting ended three hours later and the Rockers left, the police retrieved their equipment and that evening held what amounted to a premiere of their first Rocker film.

"It was like a village party," O'Neill says. Roberge recalls, "Everybody was there, about fifteen to twenty cops. Everybody was in a hurry to see it. All the top guys. It was a party. We all sat down in front of a big-screen TV with popcorn and orange juice."

The occasion marked the first time police in Canada had seen footage detailing the inner workings of Canada's largest crime syndicate. What they saw was a grainy black-and-white film of seventeen Rockers sitting around tables arranged in a square and covered with white tablecloths.

Over soft drinks, bottled water and sandwiches, the bikers talked about arrangements for the Hells' annual anniversary party; about welcoming new members and suspending others. It could have been a meeting of the local minor hockey association trying to work out a schedule for an upcoming tournament or the ladies' auxiliary organizing a fundraiser. Over the next three months, police bugged and videotaped four more meetings in various hotels around Montreal. The video quality progressed from black-and-white to colour and stereo sound.

Overall, it was tame stuff filled with everyday banalities: bikers complaining about psoriasis during the dry winter months, about tax problems and alimony and hair transplants. They argued over a $114 bill for sandwiches and whether the hotel was cheating them. They discussed the problems one biker had with the Child Protection Department; it threatened to remove his ten children unless he bought them beds and sheets and cleaned up his filthy farmhouse. "Fuck, it *is* dirty," one biker said. The bikers decided to send their wives over with new mattresses and sheets, complaining that they too were having similar problems with government agencies. Some of the men grumbled about having to work weekends for the Hells when they would rather be with their families. Others actually complained that they hated driving motorcycles. Some muttered that they were too often passed over for promotion to the Nomads while younger bikers moved up the ranks. Another biker quit because he disliked the violent lifestyle. "My heart will always be with you," he told the meeting. "I really love you guys, but I didn't feel good about what I was doing. I would rather work with people who aren't fighting. I want to be with regular people, okay, that's it."

The bikers understood. "That's okay, at least you're honest," one replied.

"Well, you tried," another biker commented.

After the ex-biker had left the room, one of the Rockers said, "It's his wife. The problem is his wife."

"It's always like that," another biker lamented, to which the others nodded and mumbled in general agreement.

Although gang members were forbidden to discuss their criminal activity, the meetings gave police ample proof that the Rockers were a rigid organization that grows through intimidation and takes its orders from the Hells Angels Nomads, whom they referred to as "les Mon Oncles"—the Uncles. When the Rockers discussed a proposal to divide the Montreal club into east and west chapters, one Rocker argued it would give them a more menacing presence in the city: "They'll see us as even bigger and that we truly control Montreal. They'll say, 'Shit, they've grown bigger and bigger.' And we'll truly control Montreal. Because we have control, but not all of it, not all of it." It was confirmation of what Kane told police was at the core of a biker's image: intimidation through random violence. "A biker can at no time allow himself to be pushed around or insulted without immediately fighting and avenging the insult, never losing his honour. [Any insult] must be immediately punished with violence so that everybody is constantly afraid of the bikers."

The most important proof of crime the police obtained was the 10 percent each member had to pay out of his illicit earnings to the club. Together with other evidence obtained during the overall investigation, the meetings showed that "everybody did crimes, everybody went to the meetings, everybody participated, everybody is implicated," Roberge says. The videos showed that the meetings were often preceded by a ritualistic handing-over of cash-filled envelopes. At one meeting, the video camera picked up Dany Kane counting out $1,000 and handing it to the club treasurer. That same day another biker asked if he had to pay the 10 percent when he was in prison.

"If your business is still going, then yes," one biker said. "Look at the other guys who were inside—they still paid up."

Police never told Kane they were videotaping the meetings, although he probably suspected it. It's likely he didn't really care, because during this time he began sinking into a deepening depression.

Although Kane disguised his personal feelings, Roberge spotted the growing problem by January 2000: "The source is going through a phase where he is not motivated and he's rethinking his personal life." Roberge later said he never thought Kane's depression was serious. But given Kane's guarded personality, the fact that Roberge spotted it at all was probably an indication of its depth. The entry in Roberge's intelligence report is the first and only official sign there was something wrong with Dany Kane.

Other signs can be gleaned from the reports themselves. They lack the colour and spark evident during his RCMP days. Kane no longer demonstrates a careful eye for detail. His handwritten diaries describing his daily activities seem routine and uninspired. His reports to Roberge are often skeletal. His fellow bikers also appeared to notice a change. In February 2000, the Rockers suspended him from the club because he owed about $3,000 in dues and wasn't taking part in club activities. Kane also had crippling debts outside the club. He had foolishly backed a loan from a Sherbrooke Hells Angel to Nomad Denis Houle that climbed to $130,000. When Houle didn't repay it, the debt fell to Dany. His status within the Hells Angels remained secure only because he was backed by heavyweights like Normand Robitaille and Wolf Carroll.

Still, the bitterness at being rejected gnawed at him. "It's been ten years, ten years that I've been around the Hells Angels," he told Carroll. "Fuck, that's a long time. But it changes nothing. It counts for nothing. Wolf, nothing you

do counts." Yet his current problems and increasingly con-
flicted state of mind over his personal life and bisexuality
did not seem immediately to affect his willingness to continue undercover work. Even when the Angels stole a police
computer with highly sensitive intelligence information
that could have exposed him, Kane didn't blink an eye.

The theft happened at the Hells' annual Quebec
anniversary party on the weekend of December 4, 1999. As
usual, squads of police showed up to conduct surveillance.
This included Sgt. Guy Ouellette, who was the Sûreté du
Québec's expert on bikers. Ouellette, a media favourite,
was a walking biker *Britannica*. Given a biker's name, he
could recite all the relevant statistics: date of birth, address,
when he became a biker, his various promotions through
the biker ranks and his complete criminal file. With him
that weekend was Rick Perrault, an intelligence officer
from the Ontario Provincial Police. Despite strict rules not
to stay in hotels with bikers, the two officers checked into
a Sherbrooke hotel in full view of several bikers hanging
around the lobby.

The next morning, Perrault joined Ouellette for breakfast in the hotel dining room. "I left my room for just
twenty-five minutes," he later recounted. It was more than
enough time for two of Serge Boutin's Scorpions to break
into his room and grab his laptop. They thought it was
Ouellette's, but it hardly mattered. It was still a gold mine
for the Angels and a disaster for the police.

For starters, a major operation the police were mounting against Walter "Nurget" Stadnick had to be scrapped
because Ontario police were worried information on
Perrault's hard drive might have compromised the investigation. The SQ had also given Perrault much of its database
on the Quebec bikers—not just on the HA but on their
Rock Machine rivals. In later raids, police found a compact
disc under the bed of Nomad Rick Mayrand—with the

contents of Perrault's computer. In the homes of about ten bikers, police also found photo albums neatly divided into eight sections with pictures of the Hells, the Rock Machines, the Outlaws and the Bandidos. Police suspect they came from Perrault's computer. While the theft caused long-term concerns for security breaches, the most immediate danger fell to an unsuspecting police informant.

The Hells analyzed the computer's intelligence reports, searching for clues to help uncover any moles. They struck gold when they found a reference to a meeting between a coded informant and Nomad Normand Robitaille. The report gave the date and place of the meeting. Robitaille recalled that the information fitted the time and place he had met with Claude De Serres, who was a marijuana trafficker for Serge Boutin. So Robitaille called Boutin and asked him to bring De Serres to a chalet in the Laurentians. Boutin, who had only just returned from a vacation in the Dominican Republic with De Serres, drove his friend to the chalet on a cold February day in 2000 on the pretext that the Hells wanted him to run a hydroponics marijuana operation.

Neither Boutin nor the armed bikers waiting at the chalet knew De Serres was wearing a body pack—a tape recorder that would chronicle the last moments of his life. A Wolverine surveillance team followed him, but lost their source by the time Boutin reached the chalet. The bikers took De Serres into the basement. Later, when police found his corpse dumped in a snowbank, the tape recorder was still attached to his body.

"Listen, why do you work for the police and how long have you worked for the police?" an unidentified voice demands.

"I have a problem," De Serres responds.

"You're not going to say anything," another voice says.

Then four gunshots explode over the tape.

The theft of the police computer rattled Roberge. Even before De Serres's murder he worried that Kane could somehow be exposed. "We have advised the source to quit the gang and stop all his [undercover] activities," Roberge states in his intelligence report of January 21, 2000. Kane's exit would have been a major blow to the police investigation. But Kane refused to quit. He later coolly recounted in his diary a conversation he had with Robitaille and several other bikers about De Serres's murder. "[One of the bikers] joked that it's the first time an informant didn't show up to testify. Ha, ha."

Far from backing off, Kane finally made his dealings with the police official on March 10, 2000, agreeing to become an agent-source and testify against the bikers in court. Police contracted to pay him $1.75 million in three instalments: $590,000 when the bikers were arrested, $580,000 after testifying at preliminary hearings and $580,000 after testifying at trials. The contract was far less than the $10 million he originally demanded, but it was enough to provide for his family after they went into the witness protection program. In addition, he got $63,000 in cash as a signing bonus, which he used to settle a debt with Carroll, $2,000 a week for food, car leasing fees and living expenses and $1,649 in monthly mortgage payments. Police also paid $3,000 in legal fees for his court appearance in Rivière-du-Loup; $1,500 to buy a gun from an arms trafficker to impress the Hells Angels when he served as a bodyguard (police rendered it unusable); $1,500 legal costs to have the suspension on his licence lifted; $600 for two new suits because Robitaille had complained that Kane was beginning to dress shabbily; and finally $1,000 as a cash wedding gift for a Hells Angels Nomad. In return, Kane swore out a ten-page handwritten confession of all his crimes since the age of seventeen. They included two murders, numerous bombings, thefts, drug dealings and assaults.

It wasn't long before Kane griped that the money was not enough. He told his controllers that other bikers routinely earned $5,000 to $10,000 cash a week and he needed to show that amount to maintain his cover. He wanted to be allowed to sell more drugs than the police had authorized. He argued that in the biker world image is everything and the only image the Hells respect is cash—lots of it. Primarily, though, Kane needed money to pay his mounting debt, which was beginning to weigh heavily on him as the Hells applied continued pressure to pay up. The police had little sympathy. There would be no more money. Kane would have to make do with what he had.

Soon after Kane signed his contract with the police, he told his handlers that his mentor, Wolf Carroll, contracted him for yet another murder. Again it was in Halifax and again the target was a Mersereau.

On March 31, Kane was driving Wolf to a licence bureau in the Montreal area, when, according to Kane, Carroll talked at length about his Nova Scotia problems. It had been just a few months since Kane had detailed Carroll's plots to eliminate Randy Mersereau, ending in his execution on October 31. Now Wolf told Kane he had recently sat down with Randy's surviving brother Kirk at a meeting in Halifax to straighten things out. It hadn't gone well.

Kirk was not intimidated. He told the Quebec Nomad if he ever found out who killed his brother, he would kill him. Wolf responded that Randy "had done some bad things." He then came out and asked Kirk if he had put out a contract on his head. Kirk denied it. But Carroll suspected he was lying.

"Wolf told me he tried to explain things to that guy but he didn't understand," Kane reported. "He told me that Randy's brother was going to die very soon."

Three months later, on Sunday, June 25, 2000, Kane got a call from Wolf asking him to come to Halifax right away. Kane had little doubt that, like other trips down east, it was for a hit. This time, however, he informed his handlers. The next afternoon Kane rented a van and headed toward Nova Scotia. Roberge and another Wolverine detective drove about a mile ahead. The small cavalcade arrived in Fredericton, New Brunswick, at 11:45 p.m., where the police had rented Kane a hotel room. Around noon the next day Kane called Wolf Carroll in the presence of his handlers and arranged to meet him in Truro, Nova Scotia. They met at a McDonald's. Carroll brought along his young son. After dining on burgers, the two bikers took a long walk. Kane later reported to his handlers that Carroll was "very talkative."

"He told me that Randy's brother had put a contract on his head and he must die for that," Kane wrote in his daily report. What infuriated the Nomad more than anything, apparently, was the discovery that Kirk had sent some friends to case out Carroll's private home in the Laurentians. That was striking too close to family. At 7:14 p.m., Kane placed a quick call to his handler. "He wants to kill Randy's brother," he told Roberge. Kane reported that he was heading back to Halifax with Wolf for a meeting at the Angels clubhouse.

It was dark by the time the two Quebec bikers pulled up to the secured brown brick bunker on Dutch Village Road. They walked by the pool table on the first floor, up to the long green marble bar with a brass foot rail on the second floor. A club photo loomed large behind the bar. The shelves were stocked with plenty of good quality alcohol and glasses adorned with the names of the members. Upstairs on the third floor—secluded by a "Members Only" sign—there was an office with a computer, fax and closed-circuit TV.

Mike McCrea, the amiable Halifax chapter president who tried so hard to put on a sweet face for the media, joined Wolf and Dany for a fateful talk, according to Kane. Wolf and Mike spoke English to each other, but Kane understood enough to know what they were saying. Kane reported they also used hand gestures and wrote on a board (a common practice among bikers to make sure incriminating words are not captured by any audio bugs).

"Mike and Wolf talked about having Kirk killed," Kane wrote. "Wolf said to Mike that he would have to kill Kirk." Mike then told Carroll that Kirk was probably either en route to Montreal or already there. Carroll then turned to Kane. He wanted Kane to help the man the Angels had chosen to kill Kirk Mersereau: Jeff Lynds. Lynds was a former member of the Mersereau gang, and an HA prospect. The problem was that Lynds did not know his way around Montreal, where Kirk was now heading. So Wolf told Kane he would send Lynds to him "so that I could show him places where he could find Kirk . . . and kill him."

Two days later, Kane phoned Roberge to tell him he "had to leave for Montreal tomorrow and bring Jeff [Lynds] . . . who has the mandate to kill Randy's brother." Kane meanwhile picked up $400 his handlers had left him behind the sink in the bathroom at a local Tim Hortons. Roberge was concerned that events were beginning to spin out of control. He wondered how he could stop a murder, extricate Kane and guard his cover, all at the same time.

The next day, on June 30, fate stepped in and solved Roberge's problem. Kirk had had a car accident en route to Montreal and was laid up in hospital in Fredericton. The planned hit was called off. Wolf told Kane to return to Montreal by himself. Kane then drove to Truro, where he met his handler and told him that Wolf no longer wanted him involved in the murder attempt because he wanted him to expand the "business" in Nova Scotia.

It only delayed the inevitable. Ten weeks later, Kirk Mersereau was killed. On September 10, 2000, police found Kirk and his wife, Nancy, executed in the living room of their isolated farmhouse, their eighteen-month-old child left alive but orphaned. To this day, police have not laid charges and have no suspects.

Police never warned the Mersereau brothers of the impending danger. They believed the two bikers already knew their lives were at risk. But more important for police, Roberge had no intention of endangering Kane and, by extension, his investigation. "It wasn't my responsibility," Roberge says about notifying the Mersereaus. In fact, the Quebec police did not even tell police in Nova Scotia about the plot hatched in the Halifax clubhouse to kill Kirk Mersereau. Not when Kane reported it and not after Kirk and his wife were killed.

To this date, the Halifax RCMP have never seen Kane's reports on the murder of Kirk Mersereau—even though the evidence from Dany Kane's handwritten reports and his police handler's phone logs reveal a plot by the Hells Angels to kill Kirk Mersereau going back months before his final demise. Those reports cited above would be entered into the court record in Quebec during the biker trials of 2003, but few people noticed.

Just under a year after the execution of Kirk Mersereau and his wife, the Hells Angels promoted Lynds to full-patch member. He got his colours exactly two years to the day after the bombing at the car dealership in Truro that nearly killed Kirk's brother Randy—the first act in a chain of events that eliminated the Mersereau clan as a problem for David "Wolf" Carroll and his Halifax Hells.

Kane's reports also shed light on other murders—and the frantic activities of Paul Wilson, the Halifax bar manager and one of David Carroll's other acquaintances in Nova Scotia. When Kane signed on as a full-time paid informer for Roberge and the Quebec police in March 2000, he gave a signed confession to the 1997 murder of Robert MacFarlane. "On the demand of Paul Wilson of

Halifax, me and Aimé Simard, we plotted the execution of Robert MacFarlane," Kane wrote. "I received $25,000 for this contract." No other evidence that Wilson did in fact put out the hit on MacFarlane had surfaced, but other members of the Halifax criminal underworld were soon repeating the story.

Wilson vanished from Halifax in June 1999. According to Kane's diaries, he showed up in Montreal on March 14, 2000, when Kane drove him and Carroll to the airport. But by June 2000, Wolf Carroll was beginning to turn sour on his pal Wilson. When Carroll had brought Kane to Halifax on June 27 to discuss the killing of Kirk Mersereau, another murder was also on the agenda. Carroll had obtained a police statement by Okan Arslan, "a guy who was close to Paul Wilson," Carroll told Kane. Carroll handed Arslan's statement—dated November 1999—to Kane at the Halifax clubhouse and Kane read it carefully. It said that Kane was a hitman for Wolf—and it also claimed that Wilson paid Kane for the murder of MacFarlane.

Bad enough that Arslan was squealing to the cops. But Wolf now feared Wilson himself might turn. Arslan "was saying that Paul Wilson was squealing [to the police] on Wolf and me," Kane wrote. "Wolf told me that Paul has to die." When Kane called his handler at 7:14 p.m. and again at 10:45 p.m., he said as much: "Paul Wilson must die. . . . Wolf is afraid Wilson will become an informer."

Wilson, meanwhile, was staying as far away from Halifax as he could. He settled briefly out west where, according to court documents, "he admitted he was involved in the drug trade in British Columbia." He had a business card identifying himself as David Michaud, "Consultant," but he also found living accommodations under the name John MacDougall. "He travelled, opened bank accounts and post office boxes and rented apartments under false names," a judge later ruled.

About a year later, Wilson sought a warmer refuge on the tropical island of Grenada. He arrived there in the final week of June 2000, using a false passport. That wasn't what got him into trouble. It was the two suitcases packed with almost nineteen kilos of cocaine and worth about $1.15 million that police found in his room six weeks later. According to local press accounts, the Grenadian courts imposed a fine of about $300,000. Wilson could not come up with the cash. So they threw him in jail on a three-year sentence. When the Mounties from Halifax finally tracked him down, it took some time to convince authorities there that the inmate they knew as Lawrence David Michaud was really Paul Wilson. By November 27, the RCMP had escorted Wilson back home, where he was arraigned on more than a dozen charges.

For starters, there were drug charges—cocaine trafficking and a large marijuana-growing operation. Police also charged Wilson with money laundering in connection with a seizure two years earlier in 1998 of $294,010 in cash from Wilson during a trip to Montreal, when he was accompanied by Arslan. Wilson also admitted he had $13,794.44 in an offshore account in Antigua and was owed about $134,000 in "drug debts."

Federal prosecutors also went after Wilson on two first-degree murder charges. The first was the 1998 slaying of William Wendelborg. A federally protected witness had testified in open court that Paul Wilson paid Billy Marriott and his partner $10,000 each and two kilos of hashish to knock off Wendelborg because he had been "running his mouth off about another murder that happened." The witness did not say what the other murder was. In February 1997, Robert MacFarlane had been killed by Aimé Simard and Dany Kane; Wendelborg was a good friend of MacFarlane's. Perhaps he'd heard what Dany Kane had already told police—that Wilson was behind the contract killing.

Halifax police slapped a second murder charge against Paul Wilson for the death of Robert MacFarlane. Wilson would eventually plead guilty in April of 2004 to second-degree murder, admitting to "making the arrangement, with Dany Kane, to have Robert MacFarlane murdered." He got life in prison, with eligibility for parole in ten years. He also pleaded guilty to conspiring to murder Wendelborg and to fourteen drug and money-laundering charges.

Halifax was just a sideshow for Kane—albeit a murderous one. His main job in that hectic spring and summer of 2000 was spying on Boucher's Angels. Dutifully, every morning he met his handlers to plan the day and, with increasing frequency, be outfitted with a body pack. Over the next four months, Kane would record fourteen hours of conversations. His tapes captured the Hells Angels, Rockers and Italian Mafia figures plotting to control drug trafficking, loan sharking and even telemarketing fraud in Montreal, Ontario and elsewhere in Canada.

Maurice "Mom" Boucher and his Hells Angels were at the pinnacle of their power. He and his fellow Nomads never suspected their days were numbered. But then, so were Dany Kane's.

ELEVEN

Crime Prince of the City

———

"Jesus hung around with bad people. . . .
Are they killers and criminals twenty-four hours a day?
You can't be rotten from morning till night."
QUEBEC SINGER GINETTE RENO
ON PARTYING WITH THE ANGELS

By the spring of 2000, the warrior cult of Mom Boucher was beginning to take on monstrous proportions as his Hells Angels became unchallenged masters of Canada's underworld. Never before in the history of the Hells had they risen to such commanding heights in a country's criminal hierarchy. Success resulted primarily from Boucher's undisputed triumph in the war against the Rock Machine. Combined with a certain business acumen, ruthless determination and an old-fashioned flair for image building, his vision carried the Hells Angels far beyond the traditions of the hard-drinking, rabble-rousing Harley riders. As Wolf Carroll lamented to Dany Kane, "The Nomads judge you by the size of your portfolio. If you don't have money, you're no good. Our club is no longer really a real biker gang. There are some members who have told me they don't even like biking."

Like any modern business conglomerate, the Hells had their own security department. While the Montreal police were busy using Dany Kane to spy on Mom Boucher, the Angels were doing some impressive surveillance of their own, collecting intelligence on their enemies—rival bikers, journalists and the police.

Dany Kane told his RCMP and later his Wolverine handlers that "Mom Boucher has many contacts inside different police forces and can get pretty much what he needs." To a large degree, Boucher was just trying to show off to his henchmen, to make them think that he was ten steps ahead of the police. For instance, Kane once described to the RCMP handlers how Boucher had stopped to chat with a man and a woman in a new black Mustang. The exchange lasted less than a minute. When it was over, Boucher turned to Kane and two Rockers.

"That's my pig," he said. "He's on surveillance today."

In mid-March, Mom specified that his "very good source" was in the Montreal anti-gang unit. When the RCMP investigated Boucher's "pig," they found he was a former private investigator who had been fired by a security company after police turned up allegations of corruption. They also discovered that the woman in the Mustang with him was the cousin of Boucher's mistress. Police claimed Boucher likely used the man in the black Mustang to buttress his leadership image.

Boucher was not alone in bragging of a pipeline into the police. Fellow Nomad David Carroll said he had "a very good contact in the police." Kane reported that another Nomad, Normand Robitaille, had a girlfriend who worked at the Palais de Justice and passed on information. Scott Steinert also claimed he had a source in the Montreal police anti-gang unit. Even prospect Toots Tousignant boasted he had a police officer in Greenfield Park, a South Shore suburb, who provided data on investigations.

What was undeniably true was that the Angels used a variety of intelligence-gathering techniques—from employing former cops to collect information to buying off government employees.

According to the Union of Canadian Correctional Officers, bikers gathered data on guards working in penitentiaries across Canada. A list of names and addresses was seized from a person "very close to a biker gang," a senior union officer reported. At the home of Quebec Rocker Dany Saint-Pierre, police found nine copies of a group photo of more than fifty police officers and civilians who worked at the Wolverine squad. In a raid of the Quebec City clubhouse, police found a list of the radio frequencies in the area and a list of the names, home addresses and social insurance numbers of several SQ officers. In a raid on Walter Stadnick's home in Hamilton, police would find reports about undercover operatives for the police, witness lists for some trials and photos of a man playing baseball identified as an "RCMP informant."

In Montreal, the Rockers—the HA's enforcers—intercepted police radios and recorded them. They also put together a list of names and addresses of the officers on the police tactical squad. In Sherbrooke, the Angels rented a room that overlooked the employee parking lot of the RCMP. With a zoom lens on a video camera, they recorded the comings and goings of the officers—and the licence plates of their personal cars. The Angels also had spies in key government agencies, notably the licence bureau. Ginette Martineau and Raymond Turgeon both worked at an agency authorized by the Société de l'Assurance Automobile du Québec (SAAQ) to issue drivers' permits and licence plates. Police intercepted Turgeon talking on the phone and meeting Jean-Guy Bourgoin, a member of the Rockers. For a pittance—according to one intercepted phone call they got $200 for the information—they spied on twenty-five confidential files between November 23, 1999, and October 31, 2000. Almost all were biker rivals or enemies; four were eventually killed, and attempts were made on the lives of five others.

Boucher was so cocky by now that he did not even try to hide his arrogance—he decided to move his operations directly into the enemy camp.

The Montreal police department's homicide and anti-gang squad is headquartered deep in the city's east end on the fourth floor of an indoor shopping mall called Place Versailles. Nothing advertises the police officers' presence except the fact that each morning beefy cops sit around the Au Bon Café terrace drinking coffee, smoking and chatting amid circulating shoppers and gushing water fountains. Then one day the comfortable regularity of the detectives' morning ritual was shattered by what they regarded as a home invasion.

It was the spring of 2000. The Quebec Court of Appeals was still reconsidering Boucher's acquittal on the prison guards' murders. Cops coming down to grab a coffee found Mom Boucher and a handful of other Hells sitting in the terrace café where the cops were supposed to sit. Four of their Rocker watchers were on the balcony overhead keeping a lookout. Outside in the parking lot, more Rockers guarded their cars. When Commander Bouchard learned about the unexpected interlopers in a building he regarded as his own, he thought, That's great—we have him under surveillance. He can't do anything here. But when Boucher kept coming back, Bouchard's attitude hardened. Mom Boucher, his fellow bikers and their lawyers were sitting in the cops' seats three or four times a week holding meetings. Boucher would sit there with that ever-present smile of his, silently eyeing the cops. It went on for weeks, then months, with Boucher putting on a show and pushing the cops' buttons. It was as if the bikers had walked into the cops' offices and made themselves at home. The final insult was when they showed up in their colours, their full patches. The way Bouchard saw it, there was only one colour in Montreal and that was police blue. "'Cause I'll tell you something. He wouldn't have done that twenty years ago. Twenty years ago we would have kicked the shit out of him right there in front of everybody. We would have grabbed him; we would have ripped his fucking jacket off, put him on the floor. We would have thumped the son of a bitch. Because you do not intimidate a cop. You've got to show them, 'I'm not afraid of you, you prick.'"

Bouchard's bosses told him to leave it alone. But enough was enough. At first, he thought he'd bug the tables. But Boucher's lawyers frequently showed up, and you can't bug lawyer/client conversations. Finally Commander Bouchard called his bosses and said he wanted to go down there with forty guys, spread Boucher and his pals on the goddamn floor and strip-search them right there in front of the shoppers.

"You can't do that, Butch," they said.

"What do you mean I can't do that? Fuck, the guy's laughing at us. I want to go down there and show them. 'Fuck, you got force. I'll show you how much force we got. You don't come into my building, *hostie*.'"

"Butch, you don't do that."

But Bouchard did it anyway. Not exactly as he would have done twenty years ago. But a variation. He sent twenty guys down to the mall. They took seats around the bikers, eyeballing them and listening to everything they said. This went on for about ten or fifteen minutes until Boucher simply got up and left. A couple of days later he came back. This time, Commander Bouchard sent down thirty guys. Boucher sat there again, smiled, never said a word. As far as the cops were concerned, all he had to do was utter a threat and they would have arrested and stripped him right there. He would have got off, but Bouchard didn't care. He'd have made his point.

On the morning of April 25, Mom Boucher went somewhere else for breakfast. At Shawn's sports bar in the north end, the waitresses wear bikinis while pouring coffee and serving heaps of scrambled eggs and sausages. Sitting across the table from Mom was André "Dédé" Desjardins, a former construction union leader turned loan shark. A friend of Boucher owed the pudgy criminal some money. The Hells leader wanted his breakfast companion to drop the debt.

"You are going to calm down and you are going to forget about it," Boucher ordered. He told the loan shark to return to the Dominican Republic where he had a vacation home. "Get the fuck back there and have some fun, okay?"

"Over my dead fucking body," Dédé retorted, not realizing how prophetic his words would be. "If you think that prick's going to get away with $400,000 . . ."

"I'm telling ya, okay, knock it off."

Unable to resolve their dispute, the two men agreed to meet again the next morning.

Dédé showed up at about nine-fifteen, expecting Mom and a coterie of other Angels shortly after. He sat down at the same table as the day before and had ordered his food when his cellphone chirped. Unknown to Desjardins, the call came from his killer waiting in the parking lot behind the restaurant.

Dédé Desjardins walked out to the parking lot. The shooter pumped eleven bullets into his body, dropped the gun and fled—leaving Desjardins dead on the blacktop, his fried eggs still sizzling on the grill. The police never found the shooter.

What interested the police was that Desjardins and his sidekick, Bob Savard, had made millions financing drug deals and laundering biker money by putting it out on the street. Twenty minutes after his slaying, police wiretaps picked up a call from Montreal to the Dominican Republic.

"Okay, you can go," came the order.

On the sun-drenched island that Dédé would never see again, a man jimmied the door of his condo, walked in and stole the vault filled with cash. André "Dédé" Desjardins had made his last collection; now the Hells Angels were collecting from him.

Homicide detectives were eager to talk to Boucher about the breakfast meeting. Since he was back at the mall drinking coffee at Au Bon Café, Bouchard sent them down to confront him.

"We have to talk to you about the murder of Dédé Desjardins."

"I got nothing to say," said the smiling Mom Boucher.

"We're going to have to speak to you eventually because we're seeing all the witnesses."

"Talk to my lawyer." Again the smile.

So they talked to biker lawyer Gilbert Frigon and set up a meeting. Boucher came up the elevator and into the homicide offices. Very polite. And he answered the questions.

"You had a meeting?"

"No, I had breakfast with him."

"Who were you with?"

"I don't really remember."

"Were you supposed to have breakfast with him the next day?"

"No."

"Could you tell us what you discussed with Mr. Desjardins?"

"Oh, yes, he came from the Dominican Republic and he said it was nice down there and he had come to see his family here. He wanted to say hello to the boys."

And that was it. Boucher left. "My pleasure. If I hear anything I'll call you."

What police didn't realize was that Desjardins's murder was not an isolated killing over a simple debt. It marked the beginning of a new era of consolidation of the Hells' now massive drug empire, which extended throughout Quebec and the Maritimes and was fast spreading into Ontario and Western Canada.

The Hells had contracted with a new money launderer and loan shark with Middle East banking contacts particularly in Israel and Jordan. His name was Joseph Ghaleb, 39, and he was a ruthless gangster with his own network of assorted Arab and Jewish street punks involved in drug trafficking, extortion and illegal telemarketing schemes. Ghaleb also had connections with the Montreal Mafia. Police came to believe that Ghaleb's people had murdered Desjardins. Consolidation also meant that the Rock Machine was no longer a significant competitor.

The only major competition came from the Italian Mafia and large independent importers undercutting the Hells' prices. Traditionally, the Mafia had the closest ties with the Colombian drug lords through Sicilian connections in Venezuela and Brazil. They brought the coke to Canada and expected most everyone else to buy from them. The Angels, with their vast distribution network across Canada, were willing partners. But now Mom wanted to change all that. According to Stéphane "Godasse" Gagné, Boucher's long-term plans were to remove the Italians from the equation. But for the time being, they would be dealt with through diplomacy.

For three years, the Nomads had been organizing a fully integrated vertical business structure, importing their own drugs and selling them through their own sales network. They planned to set the wholesale prices and control distribution right down to the street. Beginning in 1997, Guy Lepage became their chief emissary to the Colombian drug cartels. The tall, stocky Lepage had worked as a Montreal police officer from 1966 to 1974, when he was forced out under suspicion of fraud. He became a member of the Rockers and a driver for Mom Boucher. His first trip to Colombia was in the summer of 1997. He stayed about two months with Miguel Carvajal—a member of the Mejia Twins cartel in Barranquilla—while he negotiated cocaine shipments. The plan was to ship the drugs into the United States by boat, where the Hells would pick them up and truck them to Canada. According to a U.S. investigation in Florida, the Hells transported 200 kilograms of cocaine to Canada in December 1997, 300 kilograms in March 1998, 392 kilos in April 1998, 500 kilos in August 1998 and 300 kilos in September 1998. Lepage visited Colombia every summer from 1997 to 2000 to negotiate the shipments. Police affidavits claim Nomad André Chouinard organized the payments. He shipped the cash via a courier to Miami, Florida, where it was transferred to a representative of the Colombians.

It was over the next month's shipment—in October 1998, the Colombians sent a shipment of 2,400 kilos of cocaine directly to Quebec—that things began to unravel. The drugs were secretly offloaded in the Gaspé, but police seized a small portion of the shipment, sparking a wider investigation that led to Lepage. A suspicious patrolman pulled over a Hells' courier as he drove his brand-new SUV through a small village in the Gaspé. The officer found 480 kilos of cocaine in the back. Police also found two phone numbers for Raymond Craig and two for Guy Lepage. Craig, whose wife, Sandra, was the daughter of a Bolivian drug trafficker, had been importing cocaine for the Hells for years.

The bust sparked a joint investigation by Canadian and U.S. authorities and led to the seizure in a Miami hotel on April 14, 1999, of $2.5 million in U.S. funds from a Hells courier. A trace of the serial numbers revealed that most of the cash had come from two banks: the Bank of America International in Toronto and the Royal Bank in Montreal.

U.S. customs records show that the courier had travelled into the United States fifteen times from 1998 to 1999 before he was caught.

Still, the Hells cocaine continued to flow into Canada from Colombia, some of it via Amsterdam. In the summer of 2000, Lepage informed the Hells' Colombian suppliers that a shipment of about 2,400 kilos had arrived safely in Canada, according to evidence before a U.S. Federal Court in Florida. (Lepage's business would come to a stop only in 2002, when he was arrested and extradited to the U.S., where he pleaded guilty to conspiracy to import drugs. He got ten years in prison.)

With a well-established supply route, the Nomads further consolidated their operations by implementing a price-control mechanism. They created a central committee through which all drugs were sold and prices fixed. It was referred to as "The Company" or "La Table." Police first heard about it in 2000 from Dany Kane.

Police intelligence reports say five Nomads sat at the table: Mom Boucher, Denis Houle, André Chouinard, Michel Rose and Normand Robitaille. La Table paid each member $5,000 a week in addition to the huge profits they made wholesaling cocaine, hash, marijuana and ecstasy. Every Hells Angel in Quebec (except the Sherbrooke chapter, which jealously guarded its autonomy) had to buy his drugs through La Table. The Hells realized, however, that La Table wouldn't work unless they brought in the Italian Mafia, the other major importer.

Historically, Mom Boucher had always had a good, if at times testy, business relationship with the Mafia and top boss Vito Rizzuto. Rizzuto has been called "the godfather of the Italian Mafia in Montreal" in court documents filed by Revenue Canada in a tax evasion case. Faced with allegations that he failed to declare $1.5 million on his taxes, Rizzuto settled out of court. His Sicilian family wields tremendous power in Montreal, but also in Toronto and Hamilton. Yet aside from an arson conviction in 1972, Rizzuto's record is clean. He was acquitted in 1987 and 1988 in two separate drug investigations. (By late 2004, however, the federal justice minister would order his extradition to the United States in connection with the 1981 killing of three renegade Mafia captains in Brooklyn. The order is subject to appeal.)

Rizzuto's underlings have had problems of their own. From 1990 to 1994, the RCMP in Montreal ran a phoney currency-exchange house in downtown Montreal. By the time the Mounties had wrapped up their sting, they'd foiled a conspiracy between the Hells Angels and members of the Rizzuto clan to ship cocaine from Colombia to England. The police laundered $135 million in illicit money. Fifty-seven people were arrested, including lawyer Joseph Lagana, and Rizzuto's right-hand man, Jimmy Di Maulo, who got twelve years for drug conspiracy and eight years each on two money-laundering charges. As late as 2003, police were still trying to track down all the money that had passed through their exchange house.

Di Maulo, a convicted murderer, kept some of his wealth in a Geneva bank. To bank officials there he introduced a good friend and fellow investor, HA Nomad Michel Rose. Police eventually seized about $300,000 in Rose's account. "If Jimmy Di Maulo took the trouble to introduce Rose to his banker, it's because there was a strong link of confidence between the two men," says Pierre Bolduc, the Mountie who ran the sting operation.

Another Mountie sting in the early nineties nailed Jimmy Di Maulo's brother-in-law, Raynald Desjardins. Desjardins worked directly under Vito Rizzuto, meeting the Mafia don almost every Sunday at Buffet Roma or other favourite haunts. Desjardins had another regular meeting partner: Mom Boucher. The men talked business in the Nickels restaurant in Laval and at the office of Desjardins's pinball and poker machine business. "Raynald and Mom were really good friends," says Jean-Pierre Boucher of the RCMP drug squad. He ran Project Jaggy between 1993 and 1994, using wiretaps, an informer and physical surveillance to gain an insider's view at the partnership between Boucher and Rizzuto.

The Mafia-Angel plan was to import massive amounts of cocaine from Colombia by boat through the St. Lawrence. The Quebec City Angels served as the front men to approach people to buy ships in Nova Scotia. But it was clearly Boucher and Desjardins who were calling the shots from Montreal. "Every time Quebec City did something wrong, Raynald called Mom to solve the problem," says the RCMP's Boucher. At one meeting, the RCMP saw the two men studying maps.

Rizzuto, always a nattily attired businessman, tried to avoid any direct contact with someone as notorious as Mom Boucher. "Vito didn't really want to be associated with him," says the RCMP investigator. "He didn't want to be seen with those guys; he knows he's being watched all the time."

Any hope for immediate profits sank when their delivery boat experienced rudder problems off Sable Island. Smugglers had to dump more than a dozen pipes packed with 740 kilos of coke overboard. In the end, police had enough evidence to charge Raynald Desjardins and eighteen other Mafia and biker associates, but not Boucher or Rizzuto. Desjardins pleaded guilty and got a fifteen-year prison sentence.

In the late nineties, the Angels increased their cooperation with the Mafia for moving both drugs and money. The Mafia had experience in money laundering that the bikers, flush with cash, needed badly. Wiretaps in one court case caught Hells Angel supporter Stéphane Sirois asking another Rocker named Jean-Guy Bourgoin for a good accountant. Bourgoin gave him the name of one in Laval.

"He's one hell of a good guy," Bourgoin said. "He worked twenty-five years for the government. And he was Rizzuto's accountant—he's always worked for that Italian clique. You give him cold cash—'Here, wash this for me'— and he will play with your money."

Cal Broeker infiltrated organized crime circles in Montreal as a paid RCMP agent, posing as a money launderer. He met with a top Rizzuto associate who was handling dirty money for the Mafia and, as he boasted to Broeker, for the bikers as well. "We're connected to all the Hells," the Mafia man said during a meeting at Le Moulerie restaurant in downtown Montreal. "I'm meeting with Hells this afternoon in the east end. What we can offer you is all the money laundering for the Hells if you have the right system."

Now, with the Hells at the peak of their power, the Nomads decided to solidify their links to the Mafia, making a deal to fix cocaine prices and monopolize the drug trade. The price fixing was revealed to police in June 2000 in the following conversation between Wolf Carroll and Kane:

"You won't be able to sell a [kilo] for below $50,000 here in Montreal, but that won't work outside the city," Wolf said.

"But there's going to be a big meeting with the Italians; the Italians want to sell for the same price," Kane responded. "They are arranging it with Vito Rizzuto."

"Yes. Everybody will have to sell at the same price."

"In Montreal."

"In Montreal and throughout Quebec, I think."

In a Laval restaurant on June 21, Nomads Normand Robitaille, Michel Rose and André Chouinard met with Vito Rizzuto, Tony Mucci and two other Italians. Kane said that Mom Boucher phoned to say he might come, but he never showed up. With such a high profile, he was probably nervous about drawing attention to an important summit of underworld bosses. Kane reported that the meeting fixed the price of a kilo of cocaine at $50,000 and divided up the greater Montreal territory between the Hells and the Italians. They also decided to divide profits from a $1-million-a-week telemarketing scam with one-third to the Hells, one-third to the Italians and one-third to the operators. (According to Kane, the scam involved calling credulous Americans to tell them they had won a car but first had to send a cheque to cover the sales tax.)

The Hells clearly felt the deal would avoid a costly war. Kane disclosed as much in his diary when he cited a conversation he had with Normand Robitaille: "Norm told me that Vito was very nice and it wasn't a pretence. He told me that the Italians were strong and that if they were at war with them, the Hells Angels would have more trouble with them than they had with the Rock Machine."

Montreal's new drug cartel would be a huge windfall for the Hells and the Italians. Kane said he overheard Vito's son Nick tell Robitaille "250 kilos [of cocaine] were going through Montreal each week." That meant that the cartel was grossing about $12.5 million a week—half of that as clear profit.

Not all the Hells, however, agreed with the new system. Kane noted that members of La Table were pressuring Louis "Melou" Roy, forty-one, one of Mom's oldest friends and a senior Nomad, to join their company. But Roy was making enough money on his own and had been dealing with the Italians for years. He objected to being forced to trade through the new cartel. Wolf Carroll told Kane he hoped the rift wouldn't create problems. But it did. Roy disappeared after a Nomads meeting on June 23, 2000, held just across the street from Boucher's father's duplex in east-end Montreal. Police found Roy's blue-and-mauve Mercedes parked nearby. His body has never been found.

The Craigs were next on the list. As major importers, the Hells didn't need them any more and didn't want their competition. Two men attempted in June to kill Sandra Craig, the daughter of the Bolivian drug lord. The shooters missed, but about two months later, on August 29, two men shot Raymond Craig dead as he and Sandra were driving away from a bar in the Laurentian resort town of Ste-Adèle.

Others who were murdered included Bob Savard, forty-nine, the former partner of Dédé Desjardins, the loan shark who was executed eighteen months earlier after breakfasting with Mom Boucher. It was almost a case of history repeating itself. On July 6, Savard was spotted having breakfast with Mom. The next day he was face down in his fried eggs. With two of Boucher's principal loan sharks and money launderers dead, police said the Hells were consolidating that business by transferring it to a gangster in Laval. Crime reporter Michel Auger of the *Journal de Montréal* picked up on the house-cleaning theme and wrote a series of articles on the murders. His boldness would cost him dearly.

In all, between February and October 2000, eleven Hells and Hells associates either were killed or disappeared. At the time, Carroll declared to Kane that Boucher now "controls all of Montreal—it's his city." Showing up in the morning at the anti-gang headquarters with his in-your-face swagger was Boucher's way of sending that message to the police.

Nothing typified Mom's clout as the crime prince of the city more than the wedding party he threw on August 5, 2000, for René "Balloune" Charlebois, a Hells Angels Nomad. The crime tabloid *Âllo Police* devoted five pages to the reception, held at Mom's estate in Contrecoeur. On hand for the festivities was famed Quebec singer Ginette Reno. A photographer captured Mom hugging and kissing the star—and the resulting storm of publicity forced Reno to make an apology of sorts. "Jesus hung around with bad people," she said, trying to defend her appearance with the bikers. "Are they killers and criminals twenty-four hours a day? You can't be rotten from morning till night."

It seems the star goal tender for the Montreal Canadiens thought along the same lines. José Théodore partied and played golf in 1999 and 2000 with Hells Angels members in Montreal. A photo seized by police shows him drinking beer at an Angels' clubhouse. The National Hockey League warned Théodore to stay away from the Hells, but he ignored them. (Théodore's father and brothers were later charged with running a massive loan-sharking operation at the Montreal Casino.)

While Quebec vedettes were socializing with the bikers, few people paid much attention to the small news reports on August 7 about yet another biker death. A Rocker had been found in his garage, dead in his car—apparently asphyxiated.

Dany Kane was having a rough summer. Command of the drug markets brought enormous wealth to the Nomads. But all Kane could do was stand aside and watch. At a party thrown by Michel Rose in late June 2000, Kane noted that Rose had two new full-chrome Harley Softtails valued at about $80,000 plus two top-of-the-line Mercedes-Benzes at his spacious riverside retreat in Montreal. He also had three racing boats—a thirty-footer, forty-footer and forty-five-footer, which Rose called *El Rapido*. Kane wrote in his report that he was told *El Rapido* was worth "at least $500,000." Kane went for a spin in it and later told Rose:

"Every time you open her up, shit, that's a lot of petro dollars pouring out the back!"

"No, coca; coca dollars."

Kane laughed. "Coca. Ha, ha, ha! Shit, that's sick."

Another biker joked, "Narco dollars."

While the Nomads wallowed in their wealth, Dany Kane sat on the sidelines, still living the mundane though stressful exist-ence of a spy acting as chauffeur, gofer and babysitter to the Hells. His life belonged to others. Between his biker bosses and his police handlers, he worked eighteen-hour days. He would meet his handlers at around 7 a.m. to plan strategy and get outfitted with a body pack. He often met them again to get a fresh tape, or he'd pick one up from a restaurant toilet, where police would sometimes hide it for him. There was always the chance of detection. With practically every biker around him carrying guns, the retribution would have been swift and deadly. He walked a tightrope without a net. He often drove countless miles a day chauffeuring Normand Robitaille from one bar or restaurant or street corner to another. Kane standing by as Robitaille met contacts in parking lots and toilets. Robitaille playing the big-shot Hells Angel with his dark glasses and sleek Corvette, issuing orders, meeting with the Italians and other Hells, discussing high-level club business while Kane, like a servant, sat at the next table or the bar or outside in the parking lot keeping watch. He was always on guard, careful about what he said and did with his fellow bikers. And wherever he went, the police were watching. With his consent, police had electronic and video surveillance on Kane's home, car and telephones. There was no place he could go without their knowledge.

With the Hells' success came creeping paranoia. "I'm starting to deal with a lot of people. I'm afraid of getting picked up," Robitaille confided to Kane. "At some point, a *délateur*, a stoolie or informer is going to give me up." They were prophetic words said to his very own Judas.

Everybody seemed to want a piece of Kane. In July, the Rockers wanted him to help kill members of the Rough Riders, a Montreal gang of drug dealers and extortionists, who had become a bit too independent for the Rockers. The plan was to send them to Nova Scotia on the pretext that they would help expand the Hells' drug territory and then wipe them out in what one biker described as a "trap shoot." Defence lawyers wanted money for Kane's legal costs. The Hells wanted him to pay the debt—then at $80,000—that Nomad Denis Houle owed to the Sherbrooke Hells Angels. By August, Robitaille was putting heavy pressure on him to pay up, claiming he was giving the Nomads a bad name. Yet the Nomads had forgiven a $400,000 debt Wolf owed La Table. It didn't seem fair.

And to top it off, Kane was due to return to Rivière-du-Loup in October 2000 to begin serving his five-month prison sentence for the guns seized on his way down to Halifax with Wolf Carroll. He hated prison. The fact that he was also taking the rap for Wolf must have further galled him. He was again sacrificing himself on the altar of the Hells Angels.

During the first week of August, Kane seemed to run out of energy. His diary entries are sparse. On August 3, he wrote that he'd spent four hours taking notes. Yet there are only six lines of largely useless information. Kane signed the page and, after 190 pages of diaries, never wrote another line in his black Blueline notebook.

The next day—August 4—was a Friday. Roberge was on holiday that week, and Kane had to meet that morning with another detective who gave him $1,000 to be used as a cash wedding gift for Nomad René Charlebois, who was getting married the next day with Ginette Reno as the entertainment. Later that afternoon, detectives called him with the good news that they would pay his $80,000 debt to the Sherbrooke chapter. They told him the money would be available the following Monday or Tuesday.

Roberge returned to work that weekend, and in his notes for August 5, he wrote "no call," meaning Kane hadn't contacted him. He wasn't worried. Although he normally talked to Kane once or twice on the weekend just to keep in touch, he figured Kane wanted to be alone with his girlfriend Patricia, her eight-year-old son, Kevin, and their three-month-old baby.

The next day—Sunday, August 6—at about 6:30 p.m., Roberge paged Kane twice and got no reply. He phoned his two cell numbers, but they were turned off. Roberge found it puzzling. This was the first time Kane had not returned his calls. Still, it was a Sunday evening. "He had his family to look after," Roberge recalls thinking.

For about a year, Kane and Patricia had been renting a brown-trimmed bungalow in the rural town of St-Luc just a few miles from Kane's childhood home in L'Acadie. The house, surrounded by tall pine trees and tidy gardens of cedar bushes, sat on a large lot that sloped down to the L'Acadie River. It had two bedrooms, two bathrooms, a living/dining room, a family room and an attached two-car garage with three faux brass gas lanterns at the end of the driveway.

After spending part of the day inline skating, Kane told Patricia he was expecting a visitor that evening and would be leaving the house earlier than usual the next morning. He asked her to take the children and spend the night at her mother's in Montreal. Patricia wasn't surprised. She and Kane had been living together for five years, and she had grown used to his ways. But while he had on occasion asked her to leave the house while he met with visitors, he had never asked her to stay out all night. Kane then phoned his sister and asked her how to write a letter on his computer, which he had used only to surf the Net.

His parents drove over to his house at about 9 p.m. to take Patricia and the children to her mother's place in the city. Kane gave his father his Dodge Caravan to make the trip and handed him $50 to fill the gas tank. After his parents left, Kane moved the Mercedes-Benz—he'd been leasing it through a third party for two months—from the driveway into the garage.

Later that evening, Kane phoned Patricia to see if his parents had left. He wished her good night and said he loved her. Within a few minutes, his parents returned. Dany was sitting outside waiting for them. When they asked why his Mercedes wasn't in the driveway, he replied that his visitor had taken it and would be back soon. They talked for a few minutes before his parents climbed into their car and drove home.

Monday, August 7, began with a hot and overcast morning. At 7 a.m., Roberge and another detective were waiting for Kane at a safe house in Montreal. As usual, they wanted to fit him with a body pack. When Kane didn't show up by seven-fifteen, Roberge paged him. No reply. Ten minutes later Roberge paged him again, this time using the code indicating the call was "semi-urgent." Still no reply. Roberge was both angry and worried. He wondered what Kane was up to. He was nothing if not punctual. The detectives got in their car and drove to St-Luc, cautiously passing in front of Kane's house. His Dodge Caravan was in the driveway, and they noted that the garage door was closed. Roberge wrote in his report, "We saw no activity."

They then drove to Robitaille's home in nearby Candiac. No sign of Kane. They did a quick tour of Kane's and Robitaille's haunts—the workout gyms, restaurants, bars. "Negative," Roberge wrote. They tried electronic tracing. Was his voice coming up on any surveillance wire? Still nothing. They headed back to headquarters.

Early that morning, Patricia phoned home. There was no answer, but she wasn't worried because Dany had said he was leaving early. She left a message on his pager. He didn't call back. That didn't bother her either, because he often didn't return calls when he was busy.

A friend drove her and Kevin home at about 9 a.m. She had left her baby fast asleep at her mother's. She couldn't open the front door because it was locked from the inside. She retrieved the remote garage-door opener from the Dodge Caravan, but it didn't work. She went around the back and unlocked the door to the garage. Kevin tried to open it, but it was blocked. She and her friend then pushed it ajar enough so her son could squeeze through. Kevin saw Kane "unconscious" in his Mercedes. He unblocked the door, and Patricia immediately smelled the dense odour of carbon monoxide. She saw Kane motionless in the car. She noticed that towels had been placed under all the doors, including the garage door. A rope attached to the door leading into the house kept it shut. Wires leading to the electric garage-door opener had been cut. The Mercedes' sunroof and windows were open. The key was in the On position, but the motor was off. Patricia and her friend desperately tried to open the garage door before realizing it was padlocked. Her friend took Kevin out the back. At 9:22 a.m. Patricia called 911. By then, however, Dany Kane was already dead. He was thirty-one years old.

Roberge arrived back at Wolverine headquarters at 10:50 a.m. and was immediately called into his boss's office for a meeting. When he sat down, his boss told him straight, "Your man committed suicide in his garage."

"It was a huge, huge shock," Roberge recalled. "That guy was a little like a partner. He wasn't my partner. He was a criminal. Except that we worked as a team."

Roberge's last handwritten entry into agent 3683's intelligence file reads, "In the office, we learn of the death by suicide in his garage of the agent-source."

Across town at the RCMP headquarters, St. Onge entered notice of the suicide into the file of C-2994.

Even in death, Dany Kane didn't have a name.

———

Mystery surrounded Kane in life and in death. Some defence lawyers and journalists have hinted that Kane is still alive or that the police killed him to cover up their own possible malfeasance. They suggested police might have wanted to silence Kane so he couldn't disclose their part in his crimes, if indeed they'd ever played any part. Unless the pathologists, coroners and investigators who performed the autopsy and examined his body and the crime scene are all corrupt, there is no evidence to support any of these theories. Any doubt that he is still alive is put to rest by police photos of the naked, lifeless body of Dany Kane stretched out under incandescent lights on a slab at the Montreal city morgue.

His family expressed bewilderment at his death, claiming he was not suicidal and was possibly murdered. Yet there were signs. According to the coroner's report, Kane had recently talked about suicide with Patricia after an attempted suicide by a friend. Kane had mentioned that gas was the best method for a successful death.

The man who seemed to know him best was Roberge. Nine months earlier he had noted in an intelligence report that Kane seemed depressed and lacked motivation. "He no longer had the heart for it; his morale was rock bottom," he later recalled.

Police found two suicide notes in Kane's computer that he had written at nine the night before. Police speculate that he chose not to write them by hand because he wanted to embed them on the hard drive so they could not be easily destroyed. It was typical of Kane's careful planning. The first note was addressed to Patricia and his four children. He told them they probably would never understand his suicide, but he could no longer continue to be "pulled apart from all sides." He said he loved them all equally. He told Patricia that she was the "love of his life" and asked her forgiveness.

In his second letter, Kane addressed his police handlers. The note shows he was a man at war within himself. He told them he could not reconcile his bisexuality and his conflicting loyalties to the Hells and the police—to good and evil: "Who am I? Am I a biker? Am I a policeman? Am I good or evil? Am I heterosexual or gay? Am I loved or feared? Am I exploited or the exploiter?"

Kane, the biker who murdered people for the Angels and risked his life almost every day by spying on Mom Boucher and the Nomads for the police, was completely burned out: "I would love to be able to continue in my role as an informant," he wrote, "but I have been squeezed dry and have nothing left to give." He ended by wishing his handlers good luck. To this day, Kane's mother, Gemma, carries copies of both notes in her purse.

Kane, says Roberge, was a different kind of criminal, full of self-doubt, constantly questioning what he was doing. "Kane expressed himself well; he was polite. That's not the tough guy sort. . . . I don't think he really wanted to be a criminal. It was a bit by accident."

Six years earlier he had methodically positioned himself to begin spying for the RCMP. Now he had planned his suicide with a similar precision. The revenge he had originally claimed as his motivation no longer mattered. Just as he had it in his grasp, he let it go. Kane knew that the time was fast approaching when he would have to testify against his friends and expose his true self to the world. There was no way out of that. So, the suicide reflected the complexity of his situation. "He seemed to be a traitor in all areas of his life," Roberge says. "He knew he would have to go to court. He was troubled by betraying his world."

Left behind was a shattered investigation. Roberge and the rest of the Wolverine team had to figure out how to pick up the pieces.

TWELVE

Spring Cleaning

"Nobody got hurt. The majority of the bikers
were arrested. It was the best day of my
police career. But the work had only begun."
RCMP SGT. TOM O'NEILL

This was Roberge's fear. A year's work down the drain. The thought was on everybody's mind: Had Project RUSH—all their painstaking efforts to target Mom Boucher and the entire Hells Angels network—died with Kane?

In the days following his suicide, detectives and police analysts grappled with the realization that their main witness could no longer testify. They performed what amounted to a series of autopsies on the case. The walls of Wolverine's conference room—the "bunker," as the police called it—became covered with evidence charts. Pictures of all forty-two Hells Angels and Rockers were pinned up around the room. Brainstorming into the late-night hours, arguing about what proof they had and whether it would stand up in court. With Kane out of the equation, who could they arrest tomorrow?

After three days of meetings they realized their situation was grim but not lost. They had enough proof to convict most of them but nothing that would send them away for long enough to meet the original goals of Project RUSH. They were weak on crucial aspects. They had made a few drug seizures but not enough to prove the kind of global conspiracy they had dug up through Kane's undercover work. And they had no money. Not one dollar to show the enormous cash profits the drugs brought into the Hells' coffers. "So we're dope shy, dollar short and a day late," O'Neill says. "But we're still in the game." It was time to go back to work.

Before his death, Kane had left the police with two tantalizing clues. First, on July 25, Normand Robitaille had given Kane his briefcase to guard for the day. Kane slipped it to his handlers, who quickly copied its contents. Among the papers were financial accounting records. They pointed to a sizable drug operation, though in and of themselves their significance was not clear. Second, Kane had told police that the Hells were running hundreds of kilos of cocaine and hashish a week. Police had no idea where they were stashing the drugs. Kane had frequently mentioned in his reports a Rocker named Jean-Richard "Race" Larivière as the Hells' hands-on dope man. He supervised the Nomads' drug distribution system and took his orders directly from La Table. Here was the man who could possibly lead police to a major stash house, the man who could possibly save Project RUSH. Almost every Wolverine surveillance unit now concentrated on Larivière.

The payoff was surprisingly quick. Police surveillance showed that Race frequently went to a modern six-storey apartment building at 7415 Beaubien Street in east-end Montreal. Detectives first thought he was just visiting family, but checks of old surveillance logs revealed the address had come up in previous investigations. So they put four teams of seven to eight surveillance men and women on the building and quickly noticed a parade of drug runners—some known, some not—entering through the front lobby carrying paper bags, plastic bags, hockey bags or gym bags. Police trailed these runners and discovered that they came from all over Quebec and had ties to Hells Angels chapters throughout the province.

Locating the exact apartment unit each biker visited took time. Police had no idea what kind of security the Hells might have slapped on the building. They could have permanent watchers renting various apartments. Anything was possible.

The building had seventy-five units. Through a process of elimination and by watching the elevator rise up through an atrium, they determined the apartment was on the fifth floor. The rest was basic tracking. Hydro-Québec records for electricity consumption in every apartment on that floor showed one apartment—504—had consumed an unusually low amount. Nobody, it seemed, was cooking food, turning up the heat or taking hot showers. "It was as if there was no life there," SQ Sgt. Richard Despatie later told a court. Further checks showed someone who didn't even live in the building rented it. They soon confirmed that 504 was indeed the unit where the runners were leaving their bags. Race Larivière, police hoped, had led them to a major Hells Angels stash house for dope. Despatie, playing on the biker's last name, casually commented to his colleagues, "It seems the river has led us to the ocean." So they code-named the investigation "Project Ocean."

It was mid-September, and they began preparation for a full-court press on apartment 504 when something happened that jolted not only Wolverine but the entire province.

Michel Auger, Quebec's premier crime reporter, had returned from his summer vacation feeling relaxed and contented. He was fifty-six years old and had decided it was time to slow down and prepare for his retirement. For starters, he intended to cut back on his frequent television and radio appearances. As one of Quebec's experts on biker gangs, he was constantly called upon to do commentary for the electronic media. Now he wanted to drift into relative anonymity.

On September 13, 2000, he made one of his regular visits to the anti-gang squad at the Place Versailles mall where Mom Boucher had been holding court. Auger's tabloid, *Le Journal de Montréal*, was preferred reading for the bikers. "Not all my readers are criminals, but all the criminals are my readers," Auger liked to joke. But the bikers were frequently not amused, complaining to Auger that he was too negative. Auger ignored them. On this day he met with several detectives in the anti-gang squad and then drove back to his office. He pulled into the parking lot shortly before 11 a.m., climbed out of his car and opened the trunk to fetch his laptop. As he reached for the computer, he didn't notice a man dressed in black, with a black hat and carrying a large blue umbrella approach him from behind. Auger suddenly felt a stinging pain in his upper-right shoulder blade. "It was like I was hit by a baseball. Then I was hearing shots, loud shots," Auger recalls. "I was sure it was a gun, I was sure it was the bikers. . . . He was here not to warn me, he was here to kill me."

The assassin fired seven times. One bullet missed the target. But the other six struck Auger in the back. Two grazed his spine. The shooter fired the shots through his umbrella, and police later said the umbrella might have deflected the bullets away from Auger's head. Auger turned toward his now fleeing attacker and then slumped to the ground. He was still conscious. He pulled his cellphone from his belt, extended the antenna and, as he looked up at the warm, sun-filled sky, dialled 911.

"Listen, I've been shot," he casually told a disbelieving operator.

"Where?"

"At the *Journal de Montréal*."

"Okay, stay on the line, sir, I'm sending help. . . . Who shot you?"

"I don't know. An armed man. . . ."

"Did you see him?"

"Listen, listen, madam, I didn't see anything."

"You didn't see anything?"

"I saw a guy with a gun. . . ."

"Armed with a rifle?"

"No, a revolver. . . ."

"You work for the press?"

"I'm a journalist, madam," he said, exhausted. "Stop talking to me. . . ."

Auger miraculously recovered and returned to work. The only tangible reminders are the bullet fragments still embedded in his back.

Police rallied to concentrate efforts on the Auger shooting. A police surveillance team later saw the man they believed to be the shooter join Mom Boucher for lunch at a downtown Montreal restaurant where the bikers celebrated the shooting. Police later found the getaway car, the .22-calibre pistol with silencer and the umbrella. They also arrested Charles Michel Vézina, fifty-three, an underworld gunsmith who sold the gun and silencer to the bikers. Evidence surfaced that he also sold the gun used to kill André "Dédé" Desjardins. And police believed that Joseph Ghaleb, who was a suspect in the murder of Desjardins, ordered the attempted murder of Auger either as payment of a debt to or a simple favour for Mom Boucher. (Four years later on a wet November morning, Ghaleb would be shot dead in front of his suburban Laval home.) Vézina pleaded guilty to gun charges in the Auger case and bargained a sentence of four years and eleven months. He was already on probation for an earlier weapons conviction. Police had everything but the shooter. Commander Bouchard says police know who he is but don't have enough proof to charge him.

The public reacted to Auger's shooting with a large protest march in Montreal and demands for strong anti-gang laws. The attempted murder of a journalist spooked everybody in the underworld as well, including the Mafia. They were terrified that the government would pass the same kind of racketeering laws that had proved so successful in the U.S. in convicting the heads of the New York mob families. They held a meeting with the bikers, and Mom Boucher was told in no uncertain terms that he had to stop the war with the Rock Machine. In a much-publicized move, on September 27, Mom Boucher met Frédéric "Fred" Faucher, the leader of the Rock Machine, for what the media referred to as "peace talks." The biker summit took place in a conference room at the courthouse in Quebec City. The two sides emerged about an hour later claiming they had agreed to a truce.

Faucher later called Rock Machine founder Salvatore Cassetta, who was in jail in the U.S., and told him that Boucher had offered to patch over the entire Rock Machine club. Cassetta cautioned against it claiming it was an Angel trick. He warned that sooner or later the Angels would wipe them all out in a massive purge. Yet all this talk about a truce didn't stop the bloodletting.

A month after the attempted murder of Auger, three masked men beat Francis Laforest, twenty-nine, to death in broad daylight. He was the owner of a neighbourhood tavern in the picturesque riverside town of Terrebonne, just east of Montreal. His killers were members of the Hells Angels affiliate called the Rowdy Crew. Three weeks earlier, Laforest had refused to allow them to sell drugs in his bar. They attacked him with baseball bats outside his house and left him to die on his front lawn.

Again, thousands of people took to the streets to protest police and government inaction. Leading the march this time was a recovered Michel Auger. "They believed that they were on top of the world," says Auger of the bikers. "The criminals had built up a system so sophisticated that they were the law. . . . We were the only country in the world where the gangs had a free ride."

Laforest would be one of nine Quebeckers murdered— and another sixteen injured—as innocents caught in the crossfire of the biker war. Serge Hervieux, thirty-nine, was married with two children and a steady job at a garage in suburban Montreal. On August 26, 1999, he was on the phone making plans for a surprise party for his sister when two men walked in and asked him if he was Serge. When he nodded, they shot him dead with a .357 Magnum. They were looking for his boss of the same name, who had ties to the Rock Machine.

And then there was Hélène Brunet, thirty-one. She was a waitress doing her regular morning shift at Eggstra, a north-end café, on July 7, 2000, serving coffee and juice to two biker loan sharks when she heard gunfire. One of the men, Normand Descoteaux, grabbed her as protection, but the assassin in the ski mask fired anyway. Brunet was hit in an arm and a leg; her right shin bone was shattered. The police refused to charge Descoteaux for using her as a human shield because it wasn't clear his actions were intentional. Brunet resorted to filing a civil suit against him, which is still before the court.

Elsewhere in Quebec, whole neighbourhoods rose up against the Angels. In St-Nicolas, a bedroom community just across the river from Quebec City, residents failed to persuade the local city council to force the Hells to remove a fortified bunker in their neighbourhood. "They told us, 'Don't be worried. It's only a small gang. They won't be noisy,'" bus driver Gabriel Guy says.

Then one afternoon a bomb blew up a Jeep just outside the bunker gates. It shattered windows for blocks around. Guy found chunks of the Jeep's engine in his driveway more than two hundred yards away. When the town still wouldn't budge, more than six hundred people formed a human chain around the bunker. Finally, police raided the building and closed it down.

"We were stronger than they were," Guy says. "They are nothing without their gang."

Other small towns stood up in a big way to the bikers. In Blainville, north of Montreal, the mayor went to court to force the local Hells to take down fortifications in their bunker. (Ottawa, Ajax, Durham and the Georgian Bay village of Victoria Harbour in Ontario were among other municipalities that took similar action with anti-bunker bylaws.)

Even in their private lives, police couldn't escape the mounting public pressure. "I was getting sick and tired of going to weddings and parties where people were saying, 'When the hell are you cops going to do something about this?'" André Bouchard said. Amid the chaos, however, he got one big break. On October 10, Crown prosecutor France Charbonneau won her gamble. Her determined appeal of Mom Boucher's acquittal in the prison guards' murders finally paid off. The Quebec Court of Appeals unanimously ordered a new trial for Boucher, ruling that Judge Boilard's instructions to the jury were replete with errors and so prejudicial that Boucher probably would have otherwise been convicted. Nearly two years after Boucher had walked free, Commander Bouchard had his chance to even up the score.

He was in his office when he got the call from the Crown minutes after the judgment came down. He wasted no time.

"Can I pick him up?"

"Yes."

But it wasn't going to be so easy. The ruling quickly reignited Quebec's smouldering police rivalries. The SQ wanted to arrest him. Bouchard wanted to arrest him. Neither side was backing down. Everybody wanted the satisfaction of cuffing Mom Boucher.

Bouchard was adamant. "Fuck if you think the SQ is picking him up. My boys are picking him up," he told his boss. "Those sons of bitches [meaning the SQ], they want to take him. We're taking him."

His boss was equally direct. "You arrest him, but make a deal with the SQ."

The Montreal police had twenty-four-hour surveillance on Boucher. He was in a restaurant south of Montreal meeting with his lawyers Gilbert Frigon and Benoît Cliche. All Bouchard had to do was give the order and the arrest would be made. But Bouchard was not the kind of guy to cross his boss. He called the SQ. They made a deal. Two homicide officers from Bouchard's team and two from the SQ would make the arrest. But where would they take him?

"We're bringing him here," Bouchard said.

No. The SQ stood firm. They were taking him to SQ headquarters at Parthenais in Montreal. Bouchard caved. But he extracted one last concession. "My guys cuff him."

Unmarked cars from Montreal police and the SQ descended on the restaurant at about 1 p.m. They waited patiently for Boucher to finish his meal and come out. Boucher's lawyers had already informed him of the judgment and told police he intended to give himself up. They were hoping they could control the arrest by delivering him to a police station. But as he left the restaurant, he was surrounded by cops, searched, cuffed and taken away. Boucher was calm. But when he got to Parthenais, he swore at the police. "He was pissed off," Bouchard recalled. Mom Boucher thought his acquittal had put the guards' murders behind him. He never dreamed the Quebec justice system, which had seemed so accommodating, would force him to go through the case all over again.

Police eventually took Mom back to his old suite of rooms at Tanguay Prison for women. "Mom Boucher," Serge Ménard, the Public Security minister, promised the public, "will get no special treatment in our prisons." It depends how you define "special." The government spent about $1 million building a ring road around the prison so guards can patrol the perimeter twenty-four-hours a day. The government also installed exterior and interior surveillance cameras and one-way windows so Boucher couldn't see the guards whose job it was to watch him. He had a kitchen and his own TV and exercise area. Boucher complained that the isolation was dispiriting. He was denied a transfer to Bordeaux Prison and would remain at Tanguay for the next eighteen months awaiting trial.

During that time, the world as he knew it would implode.

By mid-October, Wolverine detectives had turned their attention back to Project Ocean. First priority was to get inside 504, the apartment they were watching in east-end Montreal.

Breaking in was not a problem. The Hells were so confident of the secrecy of their operations that they had installed no surveillance cameras and left the apartment vacant and unguarded both at night and often during the day. Police made a key to the door, and SQ Sgt. Pierre Boucher and his technical team walked right in. There was no sign of life, no food or clothes and very little furniture. They quickly installed a camera and listening devices and left.

The next day Boucher and his fellow officers held their breath as they gathered around the audiovisual system, hoping they hadn't been detected. The chance of discovery was always a risk. Somebody could have seen or heard them and tipped off the Hells. If that were the case, instead of watching the bikers go about their daily business of crime, they'd watch them turn the day into a joke with bikers mugging for the camera.

The detectives soon realized they had nothing to worry about. Nobody suspected anything. As the camera rolled, the detectives' fears turned to astonishment and euphoria. They realized they had stumbled on something far more rewarding than they had ever dreamed. Instead of a stash house for dope, the police had tripped over a major Hells Angels bank accepting regular deposits of huge amounts of cash.

The camera revealed one other surprise. The Hells had a second apartment where they secretly stored the money. The runners knew nothing about it. It was designed to avoid a burn. Runners were seen entering 504, handing their bags of money to a man who turned out to be a relative of one of the Nomads named Robert Gauthier. The runner would give Gauthier a code denoting the source of the money and then leave. Gauthier would write the source code a note and slip it into the bag. Then he would check through the peephole to make sure the corridor was clear and the runners had gone, exit the apartment with the bag and return a few minutes later empty-handed.

Surveillance showed the second apartment was located one floor down at 403. Several nights later, Sergeant Boucher entered the fourth-floor apartment. Same thing. No food. No clothing. But this time he found two computers. He also found a large vault measuring about three by four feet hidden inside a cream-coloured dresser located in a bedroom. He and his team quickly installed bugs and a video camera.

The cameras and voice intercepts revealed how the bank worked. Runners made cash deliveries to apartment

504 every Tuesday and Thursday. Gauthier then took the money down to 403, where Stéphane Chagnon entered the amounts into a computer. Chagnon then put the money in the safe. Checks on Gauthier and Chagnon showed they were the brothers-in-law of two Nomads.

Several nights later, Boucher went back into 403. This time he took an RCMP computer expert who downloaded the computer hard drives. When they returned to headquarters, however, they found that the hard drives were empty of any documents. Why did the Hells have computers if they weren't using them? Several nights later Boucher went back inside 403. He set a hidden camera directly on the computers. The camera revealed Chagnon manipulating a disk or CD, Boucher couldn't tell which. Several nights later he went in again. A quick search turned up a Zip 100 disk hidden under the rug. He copied the disk and put it back.

This time there was no disappointment. The disk contained an extensive spreadsheet revealing multi-million-dollar cash transactions for multi-kilo purchases of cocaine and hashish. Numbers and code names were used to denote the sellers and the buyers. The dollar value of each payment as well as the date were carefully entered into the ledger. "It was a drug investigator's dream," O'Neill says.

And over the next three months it would get even better. Police would make keys for the vault, and Boucher would return to apartment 403 more than seventy times to photograph the piles of hidden cash and to update the spreadsheet by copying the Zip disk, which Chagnon obligingly kept hiding under the rug.

The vault in 403 acted mainly as a temporary warehouse for cash brought in that day. Chagnon packed it up at the end of each Tuesday and Thursday and transferred it to two other apartments in east-end Montreal for counting, stacking and distribution. Police installed listening devices and, in one case, a camera in these apartments.

Robert Gauthier's sister Monique, former wife of Nomad Michel Rose, did the counting.

The counting machines worked non-stop. Money was stacked in lots of $10,000, which in turn were packed into boxes of $500,000. Between $24 million and $36 million passed through the apartments on a monthly basis. The balance sheet as of January 2001, for example, showed $36 million in deposits plus $13.3 million in receivables, $3 million in delinquent accounts and $2.01 million in ready cash. Police dubbed it the Nomad National Bank.

"They had five money machines working twenty-four hours a day," says André Bouchard. "They were taking out the cash, putting it on the table, flattening it out so it wouldn't get stuck, and throwing it into these goddamn machines. It was almost like bubble gum to them. It was like a joke. They would laugh."

The Beaubien Street central bank and its various branches were among the most closely guarded secrets of the Hells Angels. Of the five people who ran the operation, only one could be called an outsider—meaning he was neither a biker nor did he have any family ties to bikers. Richard Gemme, forty, was a divorced insurance underwriter and part-time computer geek. He was studying for admission to Quebec's best business school, the Hautes Études Commerciales (HEC), when in 1999 two childhood friends who were bikers asked him to help fix some glitches in the Hells' new computer accounting system. Not only did he repair the problems, but he also stayed on to redesign the Hells' accounting spreadsheets to make them more user-friendly—a sort of Excel spreadsheet for dummies. His design allowed the Hells to keep track of every gram of dope they sold while maintaining separate balances for each Hells Angels chapter. At the end of each day, La Table always knew where it stood financially. Gemme also occasionally delivered money for the Hells and recruited friends to front as renters of the Hells' money-counting apartments. One lived thousands of miles away in Vancouver.

Despite the millions of dollars flowing through the Hells' bank, police never discovered exactly how the Hells were laundering their profits. At one point, police followed a pickup truck that carted away three boxes containing $1.5 million. The driver pulled into the driveway of an upscale suburban Montreal home belonging to a local businessman and left it unattended for several hours. Eventually, the boxes were hauled into the house. Police staked out the place for two weeks but never saw the money leave. Yet when police finally raided the house, the money was gone. Just one more load of money successfully washed away in the "Maytag of the North."

The spreadsheets revealed the speed at which the drugs were sold off. One $14 million shipment of 350 kilos of cocaine to the Hells was repaid within three weeks. The spreadsheets also indicated the Nomads supplied at least 2,000 kilos of cocaine a year and another 2,000 kilos of hashish to their own drug dealers and those in other chapters.

In December, the bikers closed down the apartment branches and concentrated all operations, including the money counting, in the Beaubien Street apartments. While it was easier for police to track depositors, the move raised concerns. Investigators worried the bikers might shut down the Beaubien bank and start up somewhere else without their knowledge. Still, they weren't ready to bust the bank quite yet because they had to fill two gaping holes in their investigation. First, they had to connect the money to drugs. Second, they had to break the code names and connect the accounts on the spreadsheet to the Nomads. Both were major hurdles. But sometimes you get lucky, which was what happened on January 24, 2001, when Sandra Craig walked into Wolverine headquarters.

Craig was the Bolivian cocaine importer whose husband, Raymond, had been murdered the previous August. Two months earlier, she herself had escaped an attempt on her life. For the Hells, it was simply business. Killing the Craigs was their version of eliminating the middleman. For Craig, calling up Wolverine was her version of revenge.

Craig met with O'Neill and SQ Sgt. Yves Trudel. Police agreed to take her statement under section 5 of the Canada Evidence Act, which meant her evidence could not be used against her. The first thing she did was pull a pile of papers out of her briefcase and show them to the detectives. The two officers looked at the papers and immediately realized they were identical to the accounting spreadsheets produced by the Beaubien Street bank.

"They gave me these papers," Craig said.

"Who gave you these papers?" O'Neill asked.

"André Chouinard and Michel Rose."

O'Neill was incredulous. "Excuse me, could you repeat that."

"André Chouinard and Michel Rose."

O'Neill can be an emotional guy. This occasion was no exception. Tears welled up in the policeman's eyes. Sandra Craig had just solved their two lingering problems. She was a drug supplier who could link the bank statements directly to the Nomads and her drug deals.

Sandra Craig recounted how the two Nomads had come to her home about a year earlier with the accounts and explained to her what they meant. "This is how much dope we got from you and this is how much money we paid you. Well, here we took off a couple of thousand dollars for expenses. . . ." Craig said she and her husband had supplied 1,700 kilos of cocaine over a period of about eighteen months to the Hells. Her evidence was confirmed by an old

Wolverine surveillance report that showed Rose and Chouinard meeting with an unknown woman on August 12, 1999. The woman turned out to be Sandra Craig.

With Craig as a witness, Project Ocean was complete. One week later, on January 30, police raided the Beaubien Street bank.

They were just in time. The Angels were moving their banking business. A lot of the counting was now being done in an east-end Montreal apartment on Place Montoire, where the bikers had three counting machines going non-stop. When police planted a bug, "All we heard were the counting machines, beginning early in the day and not stopping till the evening," Despatie says.

From the Place Montoire apartment, they seized $3,784,005 in Canadian cash and another $162,100 in U.S. currency. From the Beaubien apartment, O'Neill took away $720,000. At a third location, the police hauled in $879,115 in various bags. In all, that night the police seized $5.6 million in Angel drug profits. In the emptied Beaubien Street safe the police left their calling card—a small business card with the name "Wolverine."

"We left with tears in our eyes, giving each other high fives," recalls O'Neill. "We saw the money; we had the accounting to support that. To show that to a jury of regular Canadians—it's something real, it's something that you can touch."

The only person arrested that day was Stéphane Chagnon, the chief worker at the Nomads' bank. He was carrying two cellphones, three pagers—and a pocket phone book. The directory contained the codes on the banking spreadsheets used by some of the leading Nomads—"Renard" (French for "fox") was David "Wolf" Carroll; Walter Stadnick's code was "Gertrude."

Still, the police did not want to tip their hand. For the moment, they left the other fifty suspects in the banking operation untouched. Police could not afford to let the bikers know how far they had infiltrated their organization.

But there were signs the Nomads were panicking. Wiretaps intercepted Nomad André Chouinard calling Richard Gemme: "Some-times you've got to empty out your head, change ideas. You know what I mean?" Chouinard was trying to tell Gemme to destroy the computer records. The Angels didn't realize they were too late.

While Project Ocean struck deep into the Hells' drug and financial networks, Commander Bouchard was making headway on a completely different front.

Kane had helped police target suspects for many of the more than 150 biker murders since 1995. Since Kane's death, detectives Louis-Marc Pelletier and Michel Tremblay had been sifting through hundreds of white archival boxes loaded with witness statements, crime scene analyses and autopsy and ballistics reports. They were looking for anything that could link the murders to the long list of names Dany Kane had tapped as the killers. They were also looking for evidence showing a clear pattern of gangsterism— that the gang as a whole perpetrated the murders. They didn't just want to get the shooters. They wanted to get the bosses who ordered the killings. They re-interviewed hundreds of witnesses and re-examined every scrap of crime scene evidence. They were particularly interested in DNA. Any hair samples or other human body material such as sweat or skin flakes from gun handles, old Kleenexes found at the crime scene, clothing, spit, anything that might yield a clue was sent off to labs for DNA testing and fingerprinting. The tests took six weeks or more to complete. Eventually, they reduced thirty murder cases to thirteen, for which they had 174 witnesses and four pieces of DNA evidence. Now they had to find out to whom the DNA belonged.

Police started following the biker suspects. When they went into a restaurant and drank a cup of coffee, police seized the cup or plate of leftover food as evidence after the biker left. They were placed inside plastic evidence bags and sent off for testing.

In the end they recovered DNA evidence on four bikers, including Gregory Wooley, the notorious Rocker club president who police believed was one of the Hells Angels' principal hitmen. He was also the only black in the Hells Angels organization. But because the Hells forbid blacks membership, Wooley would never graduate to their full-patch ranks.

Wooley got into the business of killing at an early age. When he was seventeen, he gunned down a rival Haitian gang member. He was sentenced to only eighteen months because he was tried in juvenile court. His next murder charge came in 1998, with the murder of Jean-Marc Caissy. Dany Kane's former boyfriend Aimé Simard testified against him, but Wooley escaped conviction after the prosecutor had a nervous breakdown. Now, however, police were certain he wouldn't be so lucky. They had DNA from a toque he'd discarded in a subway garbage can linking him to a biker hit in downtown Montreal. They also had a witness who saw him put the toque and the murder weapon in a waste bin.

By February 2001, the detectives were confident they had accumulated enough evidence to prepare twenty-three charges of murder, attempted murder, conspiracy and gangsterism against forty-two bikers, including all the Hells Angels Nomads and Rockers. The charges included thirteen murders plus a global conspiracy on the part of the Hells and Rockers to kill members of the rival Rock Machine, Bandidos and allied gangs. Bouchard's detectives had also unearthed enough evidence to lay charges on three attempted murders, including two massive bombing plots.

Gangsterism remained the key element in Project RUSH—demonstrating that when the Hells killed, they killed as a gang. Proving this, however, remained a problem. Then the Nomads handed police a gift.

Wolverine learned that on February 15, 2001, the Hells Angels were holding a high-level meeting at a Holiday Inn in downtown Montreal. They didn't have time to bug the hotel room but decided to bust in on the meeting. It was hard to tell who was more surprised, the Hells or the police. Carefully laid out over the conference table were photographs of rival bikers—mostly Rock Machine and Bandidos, plus their pager numbers and addresses. Police also discovered that each of the Nomads was armed. It was a board meeting of Murder Incorporated lining up their next targets.

"We struck a gold mine when we went in there. This was amazing evidence for us," O'Neill says.

The Hells Angels didn't know what had hit them. But then, much to their surprise, police charged them only with minor gun offences. The bikers quickly pleaded guilty, figuring a few months in prison was nothing compared with a possible charge of conspiracy to commit murder.

The Angels laughed it off. They never suspected the joke was on them. The reason police had settled for minor charges was to keep the backup evidence for the raid confidential—otherwise, they would have been forced to disclose to defence lawyers their entire investigation. The police knew it was just a few weeks before the major sweep took place.

"They didn't see the train coming down the track," O'Neill says.

By mid-March, all the pieces were in place. Police had the Hells who weren't already in jail under blanket surveillance. Cameras, room bugs, taps on phones and pagers tracked their movements. Police felt they could take their time in organizing the arrests.

They finally chose Wednesday, March 28, for the take-down. By then, projects RUSH and Ocean would be finished, the proof catalogued, scanned onto CDs in thousands of PDF files and ready to go to court. Security remained tight. Only a few people knew the takedown date: the chiefs of the Montreal police department, the RCMP, the SQ and Wolverine. Initially they wanted to go at the beginning of the month. But they decided to code-name the arrests Springtime 2001 to impress on the public that this was a new beginning. So they waited for the spring season.

On Monday—two days before the bust date—Bouchard was ordered down to Wolverine headquarters for a briefing. There he and other section commanders first learned the date of the takedown and were given their marching orders—lists of targets and their locations, man-power, vehicles, staging areas. They also for the first time shared the details of their separate investigations. Everything came together in that conference room at Wolverine headquarters. All the pieces—the murders, the church meetings, the drug networks and the banking operations—fell into place, giving a complete picture of the Hells' criminal enterprise. "It was unbelievable," Bouchard recalled thinking.

Tom O'Neill, meanwhile, briefed hundreds of other officers in a huge amphitheatre. He ran through a two-hour Powerpoint presentation, complete with video excerpts of les messes, the biker business meetings, and scenes of bikers' cash-counting machines running over-time. Most police officers had never seen anything like it before; their jaws dropped.

"We thought about selling tickets and handing out pop-corn and pop," quips O'Neill.

But this was no game. O'Neill had to make sure the news about the high-level infiltration and pending bust did not leak out. So he made a direct, impassioned plea to his fellow officers: "We have kept it secret from our families, we kept it secret from our friends for over three years. We're asking you guys to do it for a few days out of respect for the integrity of the investigation and the hard work that's gone into this. We ask you to respect this and not to blow the cover on the operation."

Talk was cheap, though. Could two thousand cops keep a secret, never boast to their wives or girlfriends or drinking buddies? "Every day we were nervous, analyzing every phone call, fearful of a leak," O'Neill says.

Remarkably, it never happened. When police began banging down doors across the province, not a single biker had a whiff of what was coming. Quebec police had screwed up badly in the past. But in the end, when it counted most, they pulled it off.

As the city slept, a cold north wind brought distinctly unspring-like weather. It was still pitch black outside and frightfully cold just before 4 a.m., when RCMP Sgt. Tom O'Neill pulled into the Tim Hortons. This was the big day—Wednesday, March 28. Operation Springtime 2001. Two thousand police officers from an array of forces were going to swoop down and arrest more than 120 bikers in the biggest organized crime sweep in Canadian history.

O'Neill, as the Operations NCO, was in charge of coordinating the arrests. He ordered three dozen muffins and a bunch of coffees.

"You going to have a party or what?" the bleary-eyed girl at the counter asked.

O'Neill just smiled. "And I didn't want to tell her, Oh no, we're just having a big roundup today. We're arresting all the Hells Angels."

O'Neill made his way to the command centre on the fifth floor of the Parthenais headquarters of the SQ. He got into his chair and, except for bathroom breaks, would not leave for the next twenty-two hours.

Commander Bouchard arrived at his Place Versailles offices at 4:30 a.m. to organize his troops. Most of his men knew nothing about the planned raids. They had been told to be there and that's all. Bouchard's men would be in charge of arresting the forty-two bikers listed on his murder warrants. He briefed them on their assignments, distributed search warrants and described the logistics. At 6 a.m. Bouchard drove to Montreal police headquarters downtown, where he took over command central on the ninth floor. He had a team of about forty men and women working the radios. He had video and TV screens with feeds from the local TV stations. The cops had their own mobile video cameras so headquarters could watch what was going on. Liaison officers from the SQ and the RCMP worked at his side. A parallel communication centre at Parthenais oversaw the teams making arrests outside Montreal.

Montreal uniform cops met early that morning at the Claude Robillard Arena in the city's east end for a briefing. Forty police cars waited for them inside the stadium. Bouchard had a canine squad of only seven dogs to sniff for drugs, guns and explosives. He would have to spread them out, directing their handlers from one location to the next. Surveillance teams had already pinpointed buildings where guard dogs might be a problem. SWAT would be assigned to kill the dogs if necessary before police made their arrests.

The two thousand mobilized forces included officers from the SQ, Montreal police department, the RCMP, the Laval police and a few small city departments. Teams of immigration officers stood by to deport bikers from the

U.S. or Europe should they find any. The sweep targeted 142 bikers and associates, including 80 of Quebec's 106 full-patch Hells Angels, the entire Nomad chapter, plus all the Rockers and Evil Ones and 51 people accused as a result of Project Ocean. The main charges would be murder, conspiracy, drug trafficking, gangsterism, money laundering and weapons offences. In one day of coordinated raids throughout the province and in Ontario, they planned to take down almost the entire Hells Angels structure.

It went off like a charm. By the end of the day, 128 people were behind bars, primarily in Montreal. Police suspected that four bikers named on their arrest warrants were dead—such as Paul "Fonfon" Fontaine, the prison guard killer whom the Hells are suspected of eliminating after Mom Boucher's second arrest. Police seized about $500,000 in cash and froze $7.5 million in other assets, including Michel Rose's boats and Mom Boucher's farm in Contrecoeur and his two South Shore houses.

From his jail cell, Mom could only watch as the empire he had spent years building crumbled in a single day. Since the start of Boucher's murderous biker war a decade earlier, there had been at least 157 murders, 167 attempted killings and 16 disappearances. In the year 2000 alone, at least 10 of the 49 homicides in Montreal could be attributed to the biker war—one out of every five deaths. Now at last, it appeared the bikers would pay for their crimes.

When the raids were over, Bouchard drove to his office at Place Versailles to oversee the interrogations. He felt great. Everything had gone as planned. Now he was going to have some fun. He decided to start a betting pool among the officers: Which prisoner would crack first and agree to become a *délateur*—a government witness? Police officers browsed through the list. Some bikers were off the betting sheet right away. There would be no deals with them.

Nomads like René Charlebois. Police had videotaped him giving them the finger, playing the hotshot. And now Charlebois was in an interrogation room crying like a baby and was the first one to want a deal. But Bouchard's attitude was " 'Fuck you, no deal for you.' I got a deal with a lower one that we know can get these big guys. No giving a free pass to these schmucks."

Bouchard bet on Wooley, guessing a black man had nothing to lose. He wasn't going anywhere in the Hells hierarchy and his racist Angel overlords would probably rat him out anyway. "We've got him cold and his lawyer knew it. We've got DNA. I mean, he was dead. What more do you need?" Bouchard reasoned. But he was wrong: "Son of a bitch. He was the only one really who never even said a word."

In the end nobody won the pool. Police and prosecutors weren't interested in making deals. They decided their cases were so solid that it was too late for deals. But they still needed DNA from some of the suspects. Biker lawyers had often warned their clients not to smoke, eat or drink anything during an interrogation and if they did, not to leave anything behind. By law, police are not allowed to offer an accused food or drink or cigarettes if the intention is to get fingerprints or DNA. That's considered a violation of constitutional rights. But if the accused asks for a cup of coffee and leaves the cup behind, that's a different story. Police can seize that.

The bikers hadn't eaten in a long time. Smokers hadn't had a cigarette. They also needed water to counter the dehydrating effects of the muscle-building steroids they constantly took. So the cops went into the interrogations smoking like chimneys and eating burgers and fries and drinking lots of water. Some bikers gave in. "Hey, can I've a burger?" "Sure, sorry, forgot my manners."

Most bikers were careful not to leave anything behind. Police watched on video screens as bikers left alone in the interrogation rooms ate their cigarette butts. One biker ate a whole Styrofoam cup. He asked for a glass of water and the cops gave him a Styrofoam cup. Chomp, chomp, chomp. Down it went.

One biker proudly refused to take anything. "If you think you can get my fucking DNA . . . you're a bunch of assholes!" He glared at the police as he pulled a Kleenex out of his pocket. "If you think you can get me to give you fucking DNA, you're full of shit, you sons of bitches." (Honk!) "Fuck you, you bastards." (Honk!) He tossed the Kleenex into the garbage and police had their DNA. Bouchard laughs. "You look at these guys. They're not all the sharpest pencils."

Tom O'Neill left his command headquarters at two the next morning—Thursday, March 29. He was exhausted and drained but still slightly elated by the adrenalin rush. Twenty-two hours earlier, he had been the first one in; now he was the last to leave. He turned off the lights and smiled.

"Nobody got hurt. The majority of the bikers were arrested. It was the best day of my police career," he says. "But the work had only begun."

For starters, there were some who got away. Three Angels were vacationing in the Mexican sun while police arrested their colleagues.

Surveillance had failed to locate Wolf Carroll at his home in the Laurentian ski resort community of Morin Heights. Phone taps revealed he was vacationing in Ixtapa, Mexico. In the weeks leading up to Operation Springtime 2001, Tom O'Neill learned that two other Angels were also in the region known as the Mexican Riviera—Nomad André Chouinard and Yves Dubé, a member of the Montreal South chapter charged in Project Ocean.

That meant trouble. O'Neill was not about to ask the unreliable Mexican police for help in apprehending the vacationing Angels. Corruption among Mexican authorities was endemic and legendary. O'Neill knew there was a chance the Mexican targets would slip away, but it was a risk he was willing to take: "It's an acceptable loss in a way, because we thought we would get them after."

It was a gamble the police lost. They didn't inform their Mexican counterparts until the morning of Wednesday, March 28, about the arrest warrants for Dubé, Carroll and Chouinard. The authorities there promptly rounded up seven "undesirables" and deported them. But only one was an Angel: Yves Dubé. André Chouinard's wife and son flew home. But there was no sign of Chouinard himself, or of Wolf Carroll.

The Hells Angels' international network through Europe, the Americas and Australia gives them plenty of places to hide. Police believe the likely refuge for a Canadian Angel on the lam is Brazil, with beaches, booze, bikers—and no extradition treaty with Canada. Chouinard's run from the law would last just over two years. He snuck back into the country and on April 18, 2003, police picked him up in a small Eastern Townships village outside Montreal.

But to this day, David "Wolf" Carroll remains on the run. A police affidavit claims he had a million dollars stashed away in Antigua. O'Neill's only hope is that the fugitive might get homesick. For Wolf, the Dartmouth boy who became the Nomad overlord of the Nova Scotia drug scene, the fall from power must be devastating. "He is very, very close to his son and he loves his girlfriend," O'Neill says. "It is almost worse than being in jail. You can look over your shoulder for only so long."

Tom O'Neill also had two Ontario arrests to supervise—Donald "Pup" Stockford and Walter "Nurget" Stadnick. Picking up Stockford in his family home in Ancaster went off without a hitch. The vice-president of the Quebec Nomads turned out to be quite a pack rat: police carted away plastic-coated cards identifying members, prospects and pager numbers for the Nomads and other chapters; coded lists of the Nomads' twelve favourite restaurants in the Montreal area; minutes of meetings in a brown briefcase; and a 2000 tax return for the Nomads Quebec Inc., identifying Mom Boucher as president and Stockford as vice-president.

Stadnick proved more of a challenge. Three days before Operation Springtime 2001, several Hamilton police officers huddled in a conference room around a speakerphone. On the line from Quebec, Tom O'Neill was revealing to them for the first time the details of the Dany Kane investigation; he stunned them by announcing that police had secured search and arrest warrants for Stadnick.

"You can hear a lull," he recalls. "They'd been trying to get him for years."

"You say there are murder charges—is that first degree, or second degree?" one Hamilton officer asked.

"Murder—first degree," said O'Neill.

The Hamilton police could hardly believe what they were hearing; they asked O'Neill to read the charges. One by one, the Quebec RCMP sergeant went through all thirteen of them—each one for first-degree murder.

There was another hush in the room. Then one officer blurted out, "We love you guys. You're the best!"

Invigorated by the prospect of nabbing such a long-time target, the Hamilton regional police offered twenty-four-hour surveillance of Stadnick's house. It did not take long to establish that his home was unusually quiet.

"Doesn't look good. We haven't seen him around," Steve Pacey said on the phone to O'Neill. The burly Hamilton biker cop more than anyone wanted to see Stadnick behind bars. "Do you guys have any intelligence that he is away?"

"Well, we don't know," was all O'Neill could say.

Checks at border crossings and airports eventually revealed that Stadnick was vacationing with his common-law wife, Kathy Anderson, in a plush resort in Montego Bay. O'Neill contacted the RCMP's liaison officer in Jamaica, Richard Sauvé, who quickly made the six-hour trip by car from the island's capital to the tourist sun spot. At the Wyndham Rose Hall Golf and Beach Resort, Sauvé caught sight of their man.

"I saw him—he's sitting by the pool," Sauvé told O'Neill. "He's with his girlfriend."

O'Neill did not want to approach Department of Justice officials in Ottawa too soon to ask them to help coordinate any actions abroad, for fear that some overexcited bureaucrat or secretary would let slip the crucial date. Only on Wednesday morning, as the raids began in Quebec, did the RCMP get the paperwork authorized.

In the cold Hamilton dawn that day, Steve Pacey was standing just outside Stadnick's home at the end of Cloverhill Avenue on Hamilton Mountain. A heavily armed tactical team went in first, with Pacey close behind. They rushed up the outside porch stairs, kicked in the door and tossed in what police euphemistically call "distraction devices"—percussion grenades that explode with loud booms and blinding flashes of light. They need not have bothered. No one was home. Police searched through the well- furnished house, the kitchen and dining room, up past the china cabinet on the second floor, into Stadnick's bedroom. No sign of Walter and his wife. But police found plenty of evidence.

Stadnick was a man concerned about his security: they seized three miniature surveillance cameras, including one hidden in a dummy smoke detector, and a bulletproof vest found in a gym bag. Apparently, Stadnick had been a busy Nomad organizer. Police found eleven plastic-coated Hells Angels cards with telephone numbers and names. Inside a bag labelled "Important Papers" they found more cards and brochures on the U.S. racketeering law.

They also seized plenty of personal items: photos of Stadnick, wearing a vest with the inscription "Filthy Few"; two Airmiles cards and several credit cards; ten bottles of fine red wine and a crystal wine decanter.

Pacey walked into Stadnick's office, sat down at his desk and turned on the biker's computer. With expert skill, he tracked the digital footprints Stadnick had left, searching through the computer's history to see the Web pages and files the Nomad leader had last accessed. He confirmed to O'Neill the resort Stadnick had chosen in Jamaica.

But if Pacey thought he had finally outsmarted Stadnick, the biker had one final surprise for him. In a small night table right next to Stadnick's bed was striking evidence that the bikers had been keeping just as close tabs on the cops as they had on him. In the drawer, Pacey found surveillance pictures of himself. No other cops—just Pacey.

"Well, obviously I was the target of that picture," Pacey says. "It was a little surprising. Just me."

Meanwhile down in Jamaica, police believed Stadnick was quietly trying to slip away. On Wednesday afternoon, police spotted him in the hotel lobby with his bags packed. They were convinced he had found out—through a phone call or on the Web—that Quebec police were sweeping up his buddies back home. Stadnick's wife later insisted they were simply changing hotels. In any event, the RCMP's Richard Sauvé kept them covered. "If it wasn't for him, we would have lost Stadnick," O'Neill says.

Police tracked Stadnick to the nearby Ritz Carlton, where a Jamaican SWAT team eventually moved in to make the arrest. Facing extradition on thirteen counts of murder, Stadnick was held as a high-risk offender—never left alone or permitted any visitors. "Walter was put in a hellhole cell overnight and then transported to the prison in Kingston, Jamaica," his wife reported. By Monday, April 2, Stadnick—dressed in khaki jeans and a black shirt with paisley print on the front—walked into a courtroom with his hands shackled behind him. Ever the diplomat, the diminutive biker told the Jamaican court he knew nothing about the charges against him in Canada but was eager to return home to contest them.

Tom O'Neill flew down a week later with a partner from the Montreal police to pick up Stadnick. Prison conditions in Jamaica were a "bit like *Midnight Express*," O'Neill says, so he assumed Stadnick would be grateful to see them.

"So, Walter, would you like to stay here for a couple more weeks?" the Mountie joked. "That could be arranged."

"Couple more weeks—I'd be running this place!" Stadnick shot back.

Indeed, as Stadnick walked through the prison, the other prisoners yelled to him: "Yo, Walter! Yo, Walter!"

"I thought a white boy in a Jamaican jail, they're going to be frying him up," says O'Neill. "But he made himself some friends in there and he was real cocky."

As they boarded the small, seven-seat RCMP plane for the long flight home, O'Neill turned to his prisoner. "There's two ways we can do this: the hard way and the easy way," he began. "The hard way—I put the cuffs on you, I leave them on you and I shackle you to the seat for the whole ride. The easy way—you don't screw around and we take the cuffs off. But I tell you: you do anything stupid, you're putting my security at risk, you're putting the pilot's security at risk and you're putting your security at risk."

"I won't give you any trouble," Stadnick said.

Wearing a short-sleeved buttoned shirt and loose-fitting cotton pants, occasionally nibbling small sandwiches, Stadnick had plenty of time to chat with his police companions. "He's talking to us about everything, he's very open," O'Neill recalls. "He talked about his days as a Cossack; his parents; he was even willing to talk about the Hells Angels—anything that doesn't incriminate him."

O'Neill noticed Stadnick was constantly on painkillers, still popping pills years after his horrific accident. The biker had redone some of his tattoos after he'd burned his hands and arms; O'Neill wondered if that was painful.

"There's no feeling," Stadnick explained. "It was easier to do it after than before."

O'Neill asked Stadnick what kind of guy he was.

"I don't drink much and I don't do drugs," the biker replied. "I'm kind of a quiet guy."

Half an hour later, O'Neill looked at one of Stadnick's tattoos: "Filthy Few" it said, reputedly earned only by those who have killed for the Angels. "I've heard other people tell me what it is all about," O'Neill said gingerly. "But I'd like to hear it from you."

"Oh, that's because I like to party when I stay out late with the boys," Stadnick said.

"A while ago you told me that you're a quiet guy, that you don't drink and you don't do drugs?" O'Neill asked.

The Nomad clammed up. O'Neill recalls his prisoner was always very calm. He never got excited—except when the police broached the case. "You might want to come over to our side," they suggested at one point.

Stadnick went silent. He turned his head and seemed to stare at nothing. He took his napkin to his lips and wiped the corners of his mouth as he finished his sandwich. He refused to play the policemen's game, declining any more conversation about the arrests.

Still, the Nomad leader was confident about his future. He would not be behind bars for long, he told his police escorts. At most he felt he'd be inside for a year.

He didn't think there was any evidence against him.

O'Neill explained they had video and audio surveillance, including church meetings of the Rockers, the puppet gang for the Nomads.

"The Rockers, I hardly knew those guys," Stadnick said. "They all spoke French. I didn't understand."

"You remember Dany Kane, don't you?" asked the Mountie.

"Yeah," said the Nomad.

"Well, he was one of our agents."

Once again, Stadnick turned silent.

Back in Ontario, the police brass could not resist gloating now that Stadnick was behind bars. Niagara Regional Police Chief Gary Nicholls told reporters that the Angels "will feel this loss." Heaving a premature sigh of relief, Nicholls predicted that Stadnick's arrest might hinder the Angels in setting up their Niagara chapter.

The police chief had little idea how wrong he was. In just over a year he would face a biker invasion beyond his wildest nightmares in his honeymoon dream capital. Police could gloat over the fact that they had at long last jailed Stadnick and his fellow biker leaders in Quebec. But that was like a doctor's boasting that he had excised a small tumour in the lungs when the cancer had long since spread throughout the body.

In B.C., the bikers were stronger than ever. In Manitoba, the seeds that Stadnick had sown over the past years were bearing fruit. And in Ontario, Stadnick's home province, the Hells Angels carried out the biggest recruitment coup in their history—reducing the police from Ontario to helpless bystanders.

It was far, far too early to claim victory.

PART IV

FROM SEA TO SEA

THIRTEEN

The Golden Horseshoe

"Bike clubs keep one young at heart. . . . Criminality is not a prerequisite to becoming a member. If a member engages in a criminal act he does so under his own volition and is subject to the laws of the land."

DONNY PETERSEN, ONTARIO HELLS ANGELS
SPOKESPERSON, JUNE 2002

It began with the sewing machines. Outside the four-storey fortress that served as the Hells Angels' clubhouse in Sorel, about fifty miles northeast of Montreal, the police from Ontario and Quebec watched in amazement as the bikers hauled in two industrial-size sewing machines—so heavy that it took four men to carry them. This was going to be a patch-over of historic proportions.

The festivities took place on a cold, damp Friday night, December 29, 2000. On guard outside the bunker were members of the puppet gangs: the Rockers from Montreal and the Rowdy Crew from Sorel. One gang member passed around new cellphones to the young bouncers on security detail. Not far from them stood members of the anti-biker squads from Quebec and Ontario, armed with video and still cameras.

By late afternoon, the buses from Ontario started arriving. Other bikers pulled up in late-model sport-utility vehicles. The Hells Angels were engineering a mass corporate takeover—signing up all the Ontario members of the Satan's Choice, Last Chance and Lobos and all but thirteen of the Para-Dice Riders, as well as individual members from their stalwart rivals, the Rock Machine and the Outlaws motorcycle gangs. Eleven of the Ontario men would become prospects; all the rest—179 bikers in total—were about to become instant Angels. What the HA was getting was nothing less than Ontario—Canada's richest province and the country's richest drug market.

Steven "Tiger" Lindsay, a Para-Dice Rider for thirteen years, stopped in front of George Coussens, the Toronto cop who had shadowed the PDRs for years. "How ya doin', George?" he said.

Donny Petersen, the most public spokesman for the Ontario bikers, also nodded to some of the officers and smiled. Other bikers seemed less amused. Lorne Brown, one of the Para-Dice Riders' hard-liners who until then had always resisted the Angels' overtures, rushed by the police lines. One of the officers could not help taunting him by chanting the biker's oft-repeated vow: "I'll live and die a Para-Dice Rider." Not amused, Brown stomped by without saying a word.

But inside the clubhouse, Brown did what all his fellow bikers had come to do: they discarded the once-cherished patches of their former clubs. In exchange, the industrial sewing machines pounded away, attaching the red-and-white winged skull crests made exclusively in Austria to the black leather jackets and vests of the new Ontario Hells Angels.

Outside in the cold, the police could only stamp their feet in the snow. Then, a few hours later, the newly minted Angels started filing out of the clubhouse, many of them clutching their new clothes, still in plastic bags under their arms. "They were coming out, so proud, like they made the NHL," remembers Coussens. "But [there were] others with eyes glancing back and forth nervously. You could see some of them going, 'Oh boy, what am I into?' "

Bewildered Angel converts were not the only ones unnerved that night. So were the Ontario police. "We went back to our hotel room and had a couple of beers," one officer recalls. And the conversation quickly turned to what Coussens aptly called the "new world order."

"This is a significant date in the history of biker gangs in Ontario," Coussens told his fellow officers. "The game has changed."

The police, frankly, were stunned. Only once before in the history of the Hells Angels—in 1999 in Germany when they patched over 220 members and 44 prospects—had the exclusive biker club signed up so many former opponents in a single ceremony. For years, the Ontario police had been warning that sooner or later the Hells Angels would muscle into the province. But the speed, size and sweep of their takeover took even veteran biker watchers by surprise.

Don Bell headed the Provincial Special Squad, formed in June 1998 to counter the bikers and eventually reorganized in 2000 as the Biker Enforcement Unit (BEU). He says police assumed the Hells Angels would try to recruit a select group of leaders from rival groups.

Instead, the Hells Angels seemed to be scraping the bottom of the biker barrel. Police considered the Satan's Choice and Para-Dice Riders as sophisticated gangs worthy of Hells attention, but the Last Chance and Lobos were second-string, doped-up bands full of what cops call "mumblies"—losers and users. "We always felt the Hells Angels were—I hate to say it—of a different status," Coussens explains. "But when they started doing this, we thought, Why are they taking all these mumblies? We thought you guys were a little better than this."

The answer, clearly, was business. The Hells Angels were desperate because their arch-rivals, the Texas-based Bandidos, allied with the Hells' long-time Quebec foes, the Rock Machine, had suddenly moved into Ontario in a big way. By November, the Rock Machine had seventy-five members, with two chapters in Quebec and now three in Ontario. When they became probationary members of the Bandidos, it was a humiliating slap in the face to the Angels. The Bandidos—with about five thousand members and more than one hundred chapters in ten countries—were the only serious world rivals for the Hells. And now they had accomplished what the Angels had failed to do in two decades: establish an official presence in Ontario.

The Hells Angels had to strike back—and fast. They did, with Walter Stadnick leading the way. First, the Hells moved to secure their western flank. On December 16, in Stadnick's second home province of Manitoba, the Hells Angels waived their own rules and officially patched over Ernie Dew and his gang members after only five months as prospects instead of waiting the traditional year. Next, they secured the centre—the rich drug trade of Ontario.

Police started spotting Quebec bikers—mainly from the Sherbrooke chapter—in talks with Ontario gangs. Stadnick was never far from the scene. On December 16, Ontario police caught sight of him along with Donald "Pup" Stockford, his fellow Hamilton resident and Quebec Nomad, meeting with members from the Satan's Choice, the Para-Dice Riders and other clubs. The Angels came up with an offer the Ontario bikers could not refuse. The Bandidos were giving their new recruits only prospect status: trade in your patch, sign up with us for a year as a Bandido-in-waiting and then—with luck—you'll make it into the club. But the Angels proposed a straight patch-for-patch swap. Trade in your PDR colours for an HA patch, no questions asked.

"They're loyal to each other until they die—and then the next day they're swapping patches with guys who are their sworn enemies," says Andy Stewart, who for three years coordinated investigations for Ontario's Biker Enforcement Unit. "I think it all boils down to money. That's what drives these guys. Why stay with such a small group when you can go to the Hells Angels and become part of an international gang that has contacts all over the world?"

The Hells Angels had carried out the biggest biker takeover in Canadian history instantly making the Golden Horseshoe of southern Ontario the power base for the biggest biker gang in the world. The Hells Angels had bested their Bandido foes: overnight, the Angels had gone from no chapters in Ontario to a dozen, more than four times the number of chapters and five times the number of members as the Bandidos. From the Satan's Choice, they got entrenched chapters in Thunder Bay, Sudbury, Simcoe County, Keswick, Kitchener, Oshawa and Toronto East. The Para-Dice Riders gave them strong clubs in Toronto Central and Woodbridge. From the Lobos, they got a shabby chapter in Windsor, and the weak Last Chance delivered Toronto West. And a group of defectors from the Outlaws and the Rock Machine formed a Nomads chapter in Ottawa.

Walter Stadnick, the visionary from Hamilton who had become a Quebec Nomad and a Manitoba mentor, had won. Though he would not be free very long to savour his victory, he could end the year 2000 satisfied that he had accomplished his goal: the Hells Angels would enter the twenty-first century with an empire that was, at long last, coast to coast.

It did not take long for the Ontario police to notice changes in their long-time biker targets once they'd put on a Hells Angels patch. On a superficial level, many of them literally cleaned up their act, trimming their hair and beards, trading in their scruffy clothes for proper business attire. In the wake of a decade of violence in Quebec, they knew their PR image needed polishing. They also needed a salesman—and they found him in Donny Petersen.

Petersen was a natural choice as the group's front man. His official title was Ontario secretary-treasurer; he was one of the Angels' three national spokesmen along with Ricky Ciarniello in Vancouver and Mike McCrea in Halifax. His marketing ability was on display when four hundred Hells Angels from across Canada rolled into Toronto on the weekend of January 12, 2002, to celebrate the club's first anniversary in Ontario. The bikers took over the Holiday Inn on King Street in the heart of the city's entertainment district.

Police in Toronto had asked store owners around the hotel to display a sign warning "No Gang Colours." Petersen countered with a public letter, insisting they were "a motor-cycle club and not a 'gang.'"

"You will find us courteous and accommodating," the Angels wrote, even offering references from entrepreneurs happy with the bikers' patronage. "The economic spin-offs of our convention will be yours to partake, if you choose."

While restaurant owners competed for biker dollars, curious onlookers gathered outside the Holiday Inn, hungry for autographs from the Angels, photographs and even sex. A hopeful twenty-six-year-old told one local paper, "I've always wanted to meet a real man."

Then into this PR minefield stumbled Toronto's mayor, Mel Lastman. On Friday evening, the mayor circled the Holiday Inn in his limousine on his way to a dinner with Roman Catholic cardinals and bishops. Later, he dropped his police security guard and scurried back to the hotel. Lastman said he was talking to the hotel manager when a Hells Angel, Tony Biancaflora, came up to him. "He put out his hand and I shook his hand," Lastman said, although witnesses reported that the mayor shook hands with several other bikers as well.

The elected leader of the largest city in the country told the *Toronto Sun* that his welcome by the Hells Angels was "fantastic. When I came in, they were yelling, 'Hey, Mel! Hey, Mel!' They greeted me with open arms." On national TV news, the mayor assured Canadians across the country: "You know, they are just a nice bunch of guys."

The next day, a photograph of the mayor's handshake from Hell was front-page news from one end of the country to the other. The Angels, of course, were delighted. On a billboard outside their clubhouse in London, Ontario, they thanked Toronto and its mayor for their "support." Editorialists, cartoonists and political commentators across the country lampooned the hapless Lastman. In Quebec, where bikers meant blood and hearses, not buffoonery and handshakes, the *Journal de Montréal* splashed the picture on its cover, with the headline "The Mayor of Toronto: The Friend of the Hells." Josée-Anne Desrochers, the mother of the young boy killed by a biker bomb, called on Lastman to resign. "I find it degrading," she said. "Is the government with us or is it the bikers who are with the government?"

On a roll, the Angels tried to score more PR points on Saturday: as television cameras rolled, they handed out $20 bills to homeless people. But Donny Petersen's marketing spin may have been too successful. Days after the biker party left town, the Ontario government turned around and dumped the very public biker from its advisory committee. The government made it clear it was now changing its mind for one reason only: "[Y]our appointment . . . has been revoked because of your association with the Hells Angels," Queen's Park said in a letter.

Eager to defend his rights—and not unmindful of the public relations opportunity the incident provided—

Petersen promptly filed a civil lawsuit against the Ontario Ministry of Training, Colleges and Universities, insisting that his constitutional right to free association had been violated. "My membership in a motorcycle club has always been and continues to be an important part of my personal belief system in individual freedoms and defiance of arbitrary and unlawful authority," he said in his court filings.

Building a sanitized image for public consumption was one thing. Internally, the Angels had a serious case of indigestion: in their rush to take over Ontario, they had swallowed a lumpy mishmash of new recruits. True, at the top of the pyramid were polished biker veterans like Petersen and Andre Watteel, the Satan's Choice club president from Waterloo who was a successful businessman.

But at the bottom of the pile were scruffy boozers and bums who never would have made it past the rigorous screening process—from puppet to hangaround to prospect—that the Hells Angels usually imposed. In a biker world that supposedly prided itself on club loyalty, the Angels were now composed of opportunists who seemed to change colours at will. One biker from London, Billy Miller, earned the nickname "Velcro" among cops because he changed patches so often: in the space of eighteen months, he shed his Outlaws vest for Rock Machine colours, then a Bandidos T-shirt and now a Hells Angel patch for the North Toronto chapter. A well-functioning criminal underground is built on trust and partnerships, but many of the Ontario Angels had no idea who their fellow bikers were in a neighbouring city or even a neighbouring chapter.

"I think a lot of them are still in shock; they're still figuring out who's who in the zoo," says George Coussens. "You got guys hugging each other and they don't even know the guy. They're learning who they can trust: 'Who's the coke guy I can make in Kitchener? Who's the guy for stolen parts in Keswick?' "

If there is any chapter that wields more corporate clout than others, it is Toronto Downtown. The dreary stretch of Eastern Avenue, just past the Don Valley Parkway is lined with rundown flats marred by chipped green and blue paint and rusted iron fences. The brown brick two-storey building at 469 Eastern stands out because it's the only house in the neighbourhood with a front door shielded by a cement wall, a security camera mounted on top; and, in the middle of the front wall, a small red-and-white neon sign: "Hells Angels Toronto."

It is here, in the former Para-Dice Riders clubhouse, where a lot of the negotiations took place to win the Ontario bikers over to the Angels. The presidents of the other chapters now gather at the Toronto clubhouse for their regular business meetings. Downtown Toronto is also probably the wealthiest chapter in the Hells' new Ontario fiefdom; it is certainly the largest, with thirty-one members.

The chapter is home to such prominent ex-Para-Dice Riders as Donny Petersen. The current president is another long-time PDR, John "Winner" Neal, whose two sons—dismissed by police as "punks"—are also in the chapter. Neal prefers the comforts of Barrie to Toronto's shabbier east end and has a car dealership called JLN Sports and Auto Centre.

The only chapter that comes close to rivalling downtown Toronto in wealth and clout is Niagara Falls. The drug and stripper trade is bustling in a town that thrives on cash-heavy tourists from both sides of the border, and everyone wants a piece of the action. Just ask Det. Sgt. Shawn Clarkson of the Niagara Regional Police. A towering figure at six feet six inches, he still looks like the high school basketball star he once was, except for the 250-pound girth and slight policeman's paunch. A local boy, he signed up for a badge in 1988 at age twenty-three; now pushing forty, he has his hands full keeping tabs on the bikers. "There's always been large consumption and trafficking of cocaine here," he says. "There are many attractions down here—tourists, casinos—and it keeps on growing."

Traditionally, Niagara was Outlaw territory. From their base in St. Catharines, nine Outlaws had ruled their turf, aided by a dozen enforcers in a puppet group called the Black Pistons. But the Angels muscled their way in. They set up a prospect chapter in Welland, headquartered in a sprawling clubhouse less than twenty minutes from the falls. The largest and most secure clubhouse in the province, it seems oddly out of place on a quiet country road, next to acres of crops, an ostrich farm and a driving range. Explicitly modelled after the castle-like clubhouse in Sherbrooke, Quebec, the two-storey building is garishly red and white, surrounded by a high-security fence and surveillance cameras.

As in Quebec, the HA in Niagara Falls have control of the sex trade as well, getting the strippers to deal their coke. Many of the women come from Quebec, plying their trade in the strip bars, which the bikers—and the tourists—like to frequent.

Down the highway in Hamilton, the task of keeping watch on the bikers in the Steel City falls to Steve Pacey. Including Walter Stadnick, there are eleven Angels who call Hamilton home, but no chapter: instead, they're members of clubs in Kitchener, Toronto and, of course, Quebec. "Hells Angels influence is subtle, behind the scenes. It isn't so much in your face," says Pacey. "I think that's just the way Walter does business."

Prominent in Hamilton and many other centres across the province are puppet clubs. Some chapters have their own support group. In Niagara Falls, about a dozen young toughs call themselves the Dogs of War. In Toronto, the downtown chapter has the Redline Crew, a name reminiscent of Stadnick's Redliners in Winnipeg. Elsewhere, the Angels briefly experimented with a series of clubs named Demons (again recalling Stadnick's failed Demon Keepers, led by Dany Kane). The Ontario Angels had their biggest success with the aptly named Foundation. The idea was to have a single feeder organization implanted in various cities, filled with young, all-too-eager punks sporting tattoos and black vests.

In Hamilton, the Foundation gave the Angels a visible presence without the hassle and higher police alert that comes with setting up a formal HA chapter. The Foundation celebrated their arrival in Hamilton with an appropriate flourish. When rock star Ozzy Osbourne and his band came to town in March 2002, the Hells Angels and Foundation puppets—in full colours—got backstage passes. After the show, Ozzy and the band members boarded a bus with the bikers and went back to the Foundation clubhouse.

Getting their new house in order was just the beginning for the Ontario Angels. They also had to confront their rivals for the riches of the Golden Horseshoe. In their December 2000 patch-over, the Angels had swallowed up two of their largest competitors, the Para-Dice Riders and Satan's Choice. A third group, about fifty biker veterans known as the Vagabonds, remained on friendly terms. That left two formidable obstacles to the Angels' monopoly over Ontario: the Bandidos and the Outlaws. There was no doubt the Angels were going to take on their opponents. The only question was how: by all-out war as they did in Quebec, or by a more subtle, made-in-Ontario method.

Like smooth corporate takeover artists, the Angels relied first on friendly persuasion and pressure. If that didn't work, they used guns and muscle. To ensure their victory, the Hells would turn to a recent convert named Paul "Sasquatch" Porter.

At a staggering 425 pounds spread over a lumbering six-foot-seven-inch frame, Porter was—as one cop delicately put it—"a big piece of humanity." But it wasn't his size that interested the Angels; it was his pedigree. Porter had started as a close friend of Mom Boucher's in the early 1980s, but like many of Mom's pals he'd signed up not with the Hells Angels but with the Rock Machine. For years, that made him an arch-enemy of the Hells and he had the bullet wounds to prove it.

From 1990 to 1994, he was known as *le boss de la Main*, controlling the red-light district at the bottom of Montreal's famed Boulevard St-Laurent. He was arrested but never convicted on drug charges. Says Benoît Roberge, the Montreal police detective who tracked the Rock Machine: "He didn't do business with a lot of people. He was afraid; he didn't take chances: he preferred to sell fewer drugs and make less money if that meant staying out of prison."

Sasquatch could keep the police off his back—but not Mom's avenging Angels. On May 31, 1997, while driving along a Quebec highway near the small town of L'Épiphanie, Porter nearly had his own religious awakening when an Angels hit squad sped by and let loose an explosion of gunfire. A bullet scratched his left arm and nestled in the bulletproof vest he was wearing. "It wasn't my time to die," he said.

Ten months later, in March 1998, the Angels tried again by opening fire on Porter's vehicle along Highway 25 near Lachenaie, but they failed again to stop the Rock Machine behemoth. Porter moved to Ontario to get back at the Angels by expanding the Rock Machine there: it was Porter who sponsored the Machine's beachhead chapter in Kingston in June 2000. But the Hells' vendetta against him crossed the provincial border as well.

The next month, Porter and many members of his gang were to attend a bike "Show and Shine" at the Canadian Thunder motorcycle store in Georgetown owned by Joe Halak, a fellow Rock Machine member. Someone decided to add some spice to the celebrations by hiding a bomb in a *Toronto Sun* newspaper box right next to the store. Only by accident was the explosive device discovered: a Sun distributor stumbled upon it when he had to change a defective newspaper box. The remote-controlled bomb, packed with 2.2 kilos of C-4 explosive, was filled with several thousand four-inch nails. It was strikingly similar to the ones used by the Angels against their enemies in the Quebec biker war; the plastique also came from Quebec. Had it detonated during a packed bike show, it would have caused heavy damage to Porter and his pals and perhaps many other bystanders.

Still, Porter didn't flinch. In October, he was there alongside other Rock Machine leaders when they sat down in Montreal with Mom Boucher to talk about a Thanksgiving truce. But two months later, Sasquatch gave the Angels a large Christmas present—himself. He defected to his long-time enemies and joined the mass patch-over in late December 2000. It was just what the Angels needed if they were going to win their upcoming war to wipe out the Rock Machine in Ontario. "He had a lot of intelligence [on the Rock Machine]," says Dan Gore of the Ottawa police. "Porter knew everything—their houses, their summer cottages, their families." The Hells Angels rewarded this betrayal by giving Sasquatch the presidency of the Nomad chapter based in Ottawa.

It was not hard to see why Sasquatch figured life would be easier—and probably longer—by going over to the other side. He had survived three murder attempts; four of the other eleven founding members of the Rock Machine in Quebec had not been so lucky. The HA had assassinated them and their associates by gunshots or car bombs—one so devastating that the police could only identify the victim by means of a small piece of skin with a tattoo on it.

Porter also brought many of his former Rock Machine partners with him. The most notable was André "Curly" Sauvageau (who'd earned his nickname because of his bald head). Like Porter, Sauvageau had been a long-time pal of Mom Boucher's—they'd once dated a pair of sisters. From Toronto, Porter persuaded about ten members of the Bandidos chapter to jump to the Angels. Four hold-outs refused and simply retired; within two weeks the chapter had collapsed. In Ottawa, Porter recruited two of his close friends, Johnny Spezzano and Steve Burns, both of them former Outlaws whom Porter had lured to the Rock Machine, only to now drag them into the Angels. Spezzano was such an eager convert that he shaved his head and had the Angel Death Head logo tattooed on both sides of his scalp.

Porter's conversion of an army of Bandidos and Outlaws was testimony to the fact that, in the Golden Horseshoe at least, profits spoke louder than patches. "You would never, never see in the United States an Outlaw becoming a Hells Angel. It just wouldn't happen," says Don Bell. "Whereas here, if the Hells Angels offer a better financial opportunity, they're going to make the jump."

The HA had tried sweet-talking their enemies and, with Porter's help, had scored some success. But it was too limited for the ambitious Angels. Now it was time to revert to the language of guns. Alain Brunette, like Porter, had left Quebec to help build the Kingston chapter of the Bandidos. Brunette had been Porter's right-hand man during their Rock Machine days in Montreal along the Main, but unlike Porter, he refused the Angels' siren call. "They killed all my friends, my brother bikers. And now they want me to change sides?" he told Roberge. "I'm not a prostitute."

So the Angels tried a more direct approach. On February 13, 2001, Brunette was driving in the right lane of the highway near Mirabel airport north of Montreal. Suddenly a car pulled alongside him in the centre lane and four shots rang out, shattering the side and rear windows, putting a bullet hole in the car door and several into Brunette's upper body. Wounded badly but not fatally, Brunette swerved his car around and sped away.

By year's end, Brunette was telling the Angels, "We just want to live in peace." They weren't listening. In Oshawa, a twenty-five-year-old Bandido member named Eric "The Red" McMillan had the misfortune of running into a number of Angels at a local strip club. They slashed him with a knife from his chest to his belly and repeatedly shot at him while he managed to stagger to a nearby car. The Angels were out for Bandido blood, and they sent Daniel Lamer to collect it. Lamer worked for the Rockers, the enforcers for the Quebec Nomads chapter. At thirty-seven, Lamer had spent more than half his life as a gun-toting criminal. Now the Hells Angels wanted him to kill Bandidos leader Alain Brunette.

Early in March 2002, Lamer headed to Kingston to do the hit, only to discover his target had gone on holiday. On Sunday morning, March 10, he drove down the 401 to try again. His driver was Marc Bouffard, a member of the Rockers. Around ten-thirty, as the hit squad raced past Morrisburg—just over an hour's drive from their target— an OPP patrol car pulled them over for speeding. Lamer stepped out of the car and opened fire, armed with two guns and wearing body armour. One of his bullets hit an officer's bulletproof vest and grazed his head. The police returned fire; their bullets hit Lamer five times and killed him, saving Alain Brunette's life once again.

Biker blood, unfortunately, was not the only blood to be spilled that week, as the Angels tried to wipe out their

Bandido rivals. Four days later in Quebec, Yves Albert, a thirty-four-year-old father of two, was putting gas into his car at a station not far from his home in the bedroom community of St-Eustache, just north of Montreal. Two men in a van suddenly pulled up and riddled his body with bullets. He died almost instantly. It was a terrible case of mistaken identity. The Bandido gang member they had wanted to kill from a nearby town had a car of the same make and colour; even three numbers of the licence plate were the same. The biker war in Quebec had claimed yet another innocent victim.

Back in Ontario, what the Angels began, the police finished off. On June 5, about three hundred police officers swooped down on homes and clubhouses of the Bandidos in Toronto, Kingston, Montreal and Quebec City, arresting Alain Brunette and twenty-five other gang members. In Ontario, they issued arrest warrants for sixty-two people and seized nearly two hundred kilos of hashish, eight kilos of cocaine, four firearms and a silencer. It was the Quebec police that initiated and led the operation against the Bandidos, but it was the Ontario Angels who reaped the benefits: the Bandidos were effectively wiped out as a serious force in the province, reduced to about ten barely active members in the Kingston area.

With the Bandidos crippled, the Hells Angels in Ontario had only one more serious rival to contend with: Mario "The Wop" Parente and his Outlaws. The Outlaws had almost as many chapters, but with between seventy and eighty members only half the number of soldiers as the Angels. During a secret meeting in the Niagara region, the Angels offered to patch over all the Outlaws in the province, but only a handful took the bait.

Animosity was sharpest in the London area where the Outlaws had a power base. On January 7, 2001, four members of the Jackals, an Angels puppet gang, had come calling just after midnight at the home of the former local president of the Outlaws whose house also served as a clubhouse. A shootout erupted, with twelve shots piercing the night and one just missing a passing motorist. The four Jackals fled, but not before one of them crumpled to the ground, seriously injured with two bullets in his stomach.

The Outlaws were rapidly losing strength in southern Ontario: plans to expand in Niagara Falls collapsed because of internal dissension, they lost some key players to the HA and others simply quit the biker scene. Then—as with the Bandidos—what the Angels started, the police finished, wiping the Outlaws out as a force in the province. On September 25, 2002, the police began a sweep that eventually netted fifty-two current or former members of the Outlaws—virtually everyone in the gang—as well as seventy-eight weapons, including a machine gun, rifles and handguns, and $1.6 million worth of drugs. "Project Retire" was the culmination of three years of undercover work, relying on a single informant. South of the border, the FBI raided several Outlaw clubhouses, nabbing the international president in Indianapolis and the national vice-president in Michigan. In Hamilton, police arrested Outlaw leader Mario Parente, charging him with trafficking.

Three months after wiping out the Bandidos, the police take out the Outlaws leaving untouched the Hells Angels, the largest and highest-profile biker gang. Even some police admit that, in the short term at least, their crackdown helped the Angels. "That's a shitty way of putting it, but I guess there's no getting around that. That's the end result," says one biker cop.

Less than two years after they turned the Ontario biker world upside down with a massive patch-over of smaller clubs, the Angels stood supreme and unchallenged: their only indigenous rivals, the Outlaws and the Bandidos, vanquished—in part by defections, HA terror and police crackdowns. "Only two people are left in the ring now—us and them," says biker cop George Coussens about the Angels. "But I can't help feeling they're going to get better and tougher to catch."

Where once Coussens had to deal with undisciplined Para-Dice Riders who did little to prevent the police from watching them, now the police were facing Hells Angels who devote a lot of energy and expertise to watching the cops. Mark Dafoe, who became the leader of the new Richmond Hill chapter, walked right up to Coussens once and began snapping pictures with a tiny digital camera.

"What are you doing that for?" Coussens asked.

"That's for my bros out west," Dafoe replied, indicating that the Angels exchanged information across the country about their enemies.

Dafoe also had cameras mounted on the front and back of his bike. And many bikers were now taking to carrying small tape recorders in their vests to capture any exchanges between them and the police for possible use in any legal proceedings.

"They're smartening up," says Coussens. "It's a different world I'm in."

Tighter, more professional security is in evidence everywhere. In nearby Oakville, a puppet clubhouse on Speers Road has a surveillance camera set up outside—hardly unusual for a biker locale. But a Hells Angels member from the Downtown Toronto chapter lives right next door—and he has installed cameras and hidden microphones behind blacked-out windows in his house so he can intercept police conversations.

Hells Angels supporters have also infiltrated the post office, phone companies and even police offices. In

November 2002, a janitor who cleaned the offices of York Region police detectives lost her job when her close relationship with a Hells Angels biker came to light—not through police work but simply a phone tip to the cops.

Ontario responded—slowly at first but steadily in recent years—by setting up the largest, most expensive police task force in the country dedicated to fighting bikers. Since 1998, Ontario has had a Provincial Special Squad with forty-four officers from eighteen police agencies around the province specifically to deal with the rise of the bikers. In August 2002, the government upped the budget to $5.6 million, doubling the number of officers to 108. The agency got its new name, the Biker Enforcement Unit, and a new logo: a handcuff locking a pair of motorcycle wheels. Ontario wanted to avoid the disastrous infighting and the joint command structure that crippled the Wolverine squad in Quebec and CLEU in British Columbia. Instead, the BEU has a single chain of command: it's an OPP-run operation from the top down and Don Bell runs a tight ship.

The BEU public relations machine likes to throw out numbers. In 2002, the force laid 446 charges against 37 bikers and 110 associates. Three-quarters of the charges were for weapons or drug offences. Still, the statistics talk about charges, not successful convictions. Many cases are dropped or get plea-bargained to lesser offences.

The harsh truth is that so far—almost three years after the Hells Angels became the dominant biker gang in Canada's largest province—only a handful of Angels are behind bars or facing serious charges.

Late in December 2002, police did charge Billy Miller, the president of the North Toronto chapter, along with two other chapter members, with weapons offences and participation in a criminal gang. And in Thunder Bay, police also charged Peter Manduca, a thirty-eight-year-old Angel and reputed karate expert, with conspiring to kill two businessmen. After his first trial ended in a mistrial, he was acquitted in April 2003 and is no longer with the gang.

Donny Petersen, the Angels' public spokesperson, had made much of the fact that although his brothers in Quebec had been jailed for bombings, shootings and murder, the Ontario organization was clean: "The Hells Angels in Ontario is not a criminal organization," Petersen was fond of saying. "Nor has such a finding been made in any court."

But late in 2002, Petersen lost his appeal before the Superior Court of Ontario over his dismissal from the government motorcycle advisory committee. In a two-to-one decision, the court ruled that the government did not infringe on Petersen's Charter rights to freedom of association. In words that were sure to sting the biker who had once addressed the Empire Club, the judges wrote, "Members of the public have been exposed to widely disseminated information tending to show that the Hells Angels Club is closely connected to organized crime and that many of its members have been convicted of serious criminal offences."

These days, the once talkative front man for the Angels is less comfortable when reporters pose unscripted questions about his club's violent track record and their mounting criminal charges. Donny Petersen turned down several requests to speak at length to this book's authors. "No matter what I say, it always gets mixed with dead babies," he told us during one conversation. Instead, Petersen prefers issuing carefully styled public statements. In a letter to the *Ottawa Citizen*, he repeated the mantra that being a Hells Angel "is a fun and adventurous life that appeals to many. . . . Bike clubs keep one young at heart. The Hells Angels and the biker sub-culture represent freedom and individuality."

But Petersen chose his words carefully when it came to the sticky issue of crime. "In a multicultural society such as ours, it is my opinion that no one person or group could possibly dominate the drug culture," leaving open the door that the Angels were active but not dominant in the drug trade. He went on to say, "Criminality is not a prerequisite to becoming a member. If a member engages in a criminal act he does so under his own volition and is subject to the laws of the land." It was a curious admission that the Hells Angels were more than just a social club of fun-loving biker enthusiasts. After all, the local president of a Kiwanis Club or a local cycling team would hardly think there were even enough criminals in his or her group to spell out the rule that the crimes they committed were on their own time. Yet Petersen felt it necessary to stress that a Hells Angel caught on the wrong side of the law was not acting under club orders but "under his own volition."

Apparently, a lot of Petersen's friends were following their volition wherever it led them. The Biker Enforcement Unit released statistics indicating that 83 percent of members of the biker gangs had criminal records, most of them for serious drug, weapons and violence-related offences.

FOURTEEN

Wild, Wild Winnipeg

———

"You could put us all in jail, and there'll be seven more guys
here. We're not going away. You gotta realize how big this
motorcycle club is."
ERNIE DEW, PRESIDENT, MANITOBA HELLS ANGELS

It started with a family feud and bloody street shootings; it
escalated into bombings and the intimidation of witnesses;
it reached its peak in 2002 with the attempted murder of a
police officer; and by the time it was over police in
Winnipeg and the Manitoba justice minister were scrambling for answers.

If Ontario was a sprawling biker battlefield, Winnipeg
was more like Dodge City. In Ontario, Stadnick and the
Quebec Angels had inspired the creation of about a dozen
chapters; in Winnipeg, there were fewer than a dozen members. But that didn't make them any less dangerous. The city
had always been Walter Stadnick's second home: by early
2001, even though the Quebec Nomad leader was behind
bars, the bikers he had groomed, inspired and won over to
the Hells Angels banner were wreaking havoc in a manner
the province had not seen in years. Pressured by the public
and politicians, police and prosecutors responded with a zeal
that sometimes only made matters worse.

The spiral of violence began with a chance encounter on the first day of summer in 2001. Rod Sweeney was about to cross the railway tracks near the Lutheran church and the Seventh-day Adventist school. The Hells Angels member was just down the street from the bikers' own place of worship—their well-secured clubhouse on Chalmers. Many people in the neighbourhood of Elmwood knew Rod and his big red tow truck.

As did Kevin Sylvester.

Out of the ashes of the biker wars of the past decade, Sylvester was one of the few surviving Spartans, the rivals of the Los Brovos who went on to become Angels. A loose cannon even by biker standards, he had once been kicked out because he was "over the edge." He was involved in more than a dozen shoot-outs, was stabbed in prison and nearly died after being shot by another biker.

Sylvester had never forgiven Sweeney and the other Brovos for the disappearance and presumed murder of his brother Darwin, the Spartan leader. So on June 21, 2001, Sylvester spotted Sweeney's tow truck and quickly pulled his Harley up alongside.

"I dunno, I just lost it, lost my temper. I pulled out the gun and shot him," he later explained. Sylvester said he was knocked off his bike as Sweeney flung open his door, but that still did not stop Sylvester from firing five more shots into the truck.

"Not in front of my son!" Rod yelled. The two-year-old—blood splattered all over him—was in the truck.

Sweeney was hit four times: on the left side of his head, his shoulder, arm and knee. He made a dash from the car; Sylvester says he thought about shooting him in the back before deciding against the idea. He turned instead to the little boy.

"He was strapped into the seat. He was terrified. He had blood on him but didn't look like he'd been hit," said

Sylvester. He promptly sped away from the scene.

Remarkably, except for some nerve damage to his left hand, Rod Sweeney made a full recovery. His son was uninjured.

The next day, somebody took a shot at Glen MacEachern, a Hells Angels hangaround, in the parking lot outside a strip joint frequented by bikers. He also was only wounded, but the Angels could not let such brazen attacks go unpunished.

"If somebody drives up beside you with your kid in your vehicle and opens fire and point-blank shoots you, you expect to get away with that?" says Manitoba Hells Angels president Ernie Dew.

It did not take long for the Angels to exact their revenge. Five days later, at 10:25 p.m., gunfire erupted again in Elmwood. Michael Carroll, a friend of the Sylvesters, lay bleeding but not dead on his doorstep as a green car sped away. The assailants had fired seven bullets, two while he was lying on the ground. Police would eventually charge Ian Matthew Grant, one of the Zig Zags of whom the Angels thought highly enough to tap as a prospect member, with the attempted murder. Nicknamed "The Terminator," Grant, only twenty-eight at the time, stood an imposing six foot five inches, with blondish cropped hair and a hint of a moustache.

Before the month of July was over, there would be five drive-by shootings. Sylvester's home was firebombed no fewer than three times: On July 2, two Molotov cocktails exploded against the front of the house. Two men returned the next day and set the kitchen alight by throwing another Molotov cocktail. Two weeks later, Sylvester's detached garage was in flames.

There was little doubt the Angels were behind the arson. They next tried an ambush. A few days later, Sylvester spotted a truck following him in busy traffic. He floored the gas pedal, ran several red lights and even jumped the median into oncoming traffic but could not get away. Two gunshots struck his window and tail light, but he wasn't hit. Ian Grant, along with Dale Donovan, a prospect who would become a full HA member in less than two years, and a hangaround named Sean Wolfe, would eventually all be charged with conspiracy to commit murder.

The Angels stepped up their intimidation. On Monday, July 30, Sylvester appeared in court for a bail hearing on charges stemming from his shooting of Sweeney; a biker in full colours was there to watch. The next day, the bikers sent someone to the courthouse to request the bail documents, with Sylvester's new home address.

That afternoon, the bikers made one more try. Kevin Sylvester, in a four-door silver Cavalier, spotted a black truck with tinted windows. Two men were inside; in the driver's seat was Dale Sweeney, Rod's brother. Several shots suddenly rang out from Sweeney's vehicle, directed toward Sylvester.

"I ducked down and took the first right I could," Sylvester recounted.

The attempted assassination exploded in the heart of the city on Portage near Broadway, and it was a miracle that the biker feud claimed no innocent bystanders. Summer students at Gordon Bell High School were close enough to hear the gunshot explosions.

Sweeney sped away, but police picked him up a few blocks away, along the same street down which his truck had fled. They also found a bag with a gun inside on the same route. The full-patch biker matched the general description witnesses gave of the assailant, and his black truck matched the attacking vehicle. He was arrested on a charge of attempted murder.

It was a circumstantial but not implausible case. In their fervour to nail their first Hells Angels member on such a serious charge, authorities rushed to make a deal with Sylvester, the intended victim, in the spring of 2002. It was a deal they would soon have cause to regret.

As the summer of 2001 drew to a close, the bikers and their hangarounds were riding high, convinced they owned the city. They could be seen strutting proudly at Fort Garry Place on boxing night in mid-September. On the bill was one of their own: Ralph Moar Jr., the boxer who had been charged in the December 2000 drive-by shooting of the 15-year-old who had been mistaken for a gang rival.

At a large round table in one corner of the hall, sitting like a king surrounded by his loyal knights, was Danny Lawson. The vice-president of the Manitoba chapter was the only one sporting the full-patch colours of an Angel, his Mohawk haircut and dark eyes adding to his fearsome look. At his side sat a giggly young blonde.

Next to him sat Darren Hunter, the Hells Angels' sergeant-at-arms, a red baseball cap twisted backwards on his head, his blond hair neatly cropped. Police say Hunter keeps to himself: "You don't see him losing his head," says Ray Parry. But Hunter has no love for the police. "Don't talk to me. I hate the fuckin' cops," he has been known to say.

Shane Kirton, thirty-three, was the other full-patch member on hand, a bouncer at a local bar who liked to wear his Hells Angels colours on the job. A beefy man with a brown goatee and a gold chain dangling from his neck, he had just been charged with assaulting a police officer— with his belly. Two Zig Zags hovered around the Angels: Sean Wolfe and Ian Grant.

By the end of the year, the police had saddled half of the twelve members of the local HA chapter with an array of charges, ranging from drugs to attempted murder. Three were out on bail, three behind bars. In December, a Zig Zag member was sentenced to four years in prison for the drive-by shooting that put a bullet in the head of a fifteen-year-old a year earlier.

But if the Angels were hurting, they didn't show it. They unveiled their new clubhouse on Scotia Street, in the comfortable West Kildonan district. The spacious home was a step up the social ladder from their old headquarters in blue-collar Elmwood. Tucked away at the end of a street lined with elegant homes, the 2,865-square-foot house backed up against a quiet river. A large sign warned visitors "No Trespassing."

The fancy digs reflected a new-found prosperity and maturity for the Manitoba Angels. They were no longer the greasy, unemployed bikers of yesteryear.

Chapter president Ernie Dew has been a licensed mechanic for twenty-two years, skilled enough to boast that even police come to him to get their cars fixed. He has three young children with his current wife of seventeen years and two older children in their twenties from a previous marriage. He says his son, twenty-five, did a year of law at university, and his daughter, twenty-one, wants to specialize in forensic medicine.

"I'm a family man," says Dew. "Back in the old days, nobody worked. Get out of the sixties, guys; we're not in the sixties any more. Everybody's well dressed. You don't see hair down to your ass. There's a big change. We all get older and we all get wiser."

And richer.

Dew lives in St. Andrew, a pleasant suburb on the outskirts of Winnipeg, across the street from fellow Angel Bernie Dubois's successful scrapyard business. Dubois has a red brick home with arched windows over an entranceway lined with potted plants and a statue of a lion. In his backyard, there are two vintage cars, including a white Rolls-Royce.

The prospect members are not starving either. At fifty-two, Ron Stirling is one of the oldest bikers—"this is a man having the world's worst mid-life crisis," one police officer quipped—who lives in an upscale neighbourhood just down the street from an RCMP inspector.

A favourite biker hangout is Teasers, the strip bar attached to the Chalet Hotel at a highway intersection in the northeast corner of the city. The parking lot, next to the grain elevators, is always packed. Sean Wolfe, a hangaround, worked at Teasers as the chief bouncer. And Angel prospect Billy Bowden has been seen at the owner's office.

At the other end of the city, the bikers enjoy the atmosphere of the Concord Motor Hotel, an even seedier hangout. Mario Raimondi, listed as the owner of the motel, has put his name on court documents to post bail security for biker Dale Donovan.

The top brass and the politicians could pretend that everything was under control. But Det.-Sgt. Ray Parry, now in charge of the biker unit, was too experienced to get cocky about the bikers and their network of support cells. "You take a cell out and you still have nine others operating within days," he says. "You can take a top dog down, but that doesn't mean you've taken the whole operation down. They've got the people groomed. It's all about money." And in the New Year, the bikers would have a few more surprises for the police.

The year of 2002 began with a bang—literally. And it nearly cost the life of one Winnipeg police officer.

On a cold winter night in February, a concrete brick came crashing through the front window of a small home belonging to Esther Schmeider, a member of the Winnipeg police's anti-gang squad. She turned on the outside lights in time to see two people scamper away.

When police arrived, they found several gas-filled Molotov cocktails on the lawn. There was little doubt the hoodlums intended to set her home ablaze and that she was a target because of her biker work. Just two months earlier, her van had exploded in flames in her driveway. Police were outraged. Danger—even death—is an accepted part of their job. But there are unwritten rules, even in the world of crime. And one of those is *don't get personal.*

"There was a clear definition of roles," says Ray Parry. "Now, officers are being followed around, intimidated. We didn't see that before."

Parry went to see Ernie Dew, local chapter president and one of the old-style guys. Dew was adamant: "This is not a club thing; it has nothing to do with the club," he assured the cops.

Dew says he tries to tell the younger hotheads in the organization to cool it. "They don't like to hear a lot of stuff I got to say. I was the same way when I was younger. I didn't like to listen to nobody."

And perhaps the Zig Zags and other biker supporters were not listening to him. The police were willing to believe the attack on the officer's house was not officially sanctioned by the Hells Angels club, but someone in the biker hierarchy ordered it. They had a pretty good idea it came from the puppet group, the Zig Zags. "They're younger, smarter, better educated," says Rick Lobban. "They're more violent. They have grown up on movies and the mystique of the gun. They think they are invincible."

Two Zig Zags strolled into the local 7-Eleven in the Elmwood area of town, a neighbourhood the bikers traditionally claim as their own. They reportedly grabbed some candy without paying and threatened the hapless clerk on their way out.

Police charged one Zig Zag for uttering threats against the clerk—but that seemed to provoke more gang-related intimidation. On March 26, three masked men tossed a Molotov cocktail into the store, but it failed to ignite. Four days later, two men returned and hurled two lit Molotov cocktails into the store, setting the entrance ablaze, igniting a customer's pant leg and causing $15,000 damage to the store.

Three days later, the bikers and their associates cranked up their terror campaign, graduating from convenience stores to the courthouse. This time it involved a Hells Angels associate named Robert Coquete, a Zig Zag who carried out dirty work for the Hells Angels. At a New Year's party in 2000, Coquete got into a fight with a rival gym owner named Joe Soares. Police charged Coquete with assault.

Coquete, a professional kick-boxer, was used to throwing his weight around for the bikers. Now that Coquete himself was in trouble with the law, the Angels seemed willing to return the favour. On April 2, when Coquete was to start his new trial, his alleged victim got a rude awakening at 1:30 that morning. Shotgun blasts blew out Joe Soares' living-room window. Soares's elderly parents, also at home, luckily escaped injury.

The next day, Tyler and John Chidlow, who worked as security guards during the New Year's Eve party at Fort Garry Place, testified. It did little good. The judge acquitted Coquete, ruling that the evidence suggested his fight with Soares might have been consensual. Still, the bikers weren't done with their own justice. That afternoon, the Chidlows' house was firebombed; Tyler Chidlow went to hospital suffering from smoke inhalation.

As they had in Quebec, the bikers seemed determined to assault the justice system itself. Many of the attacks went unreported, says detective Ray Parry: witnesses were followed; there would be late-night phone callers who'd hang up; and outright threats were made. In one earlier case, police said cocaine dealers offered a bounty for the execution of a woman who had acted as informant against them. One of the accused put a gun to her neck and said,

"This is how the Hells Angels kill rats and agents." The woman was put under witness protection.

The police soon arrested several men for the firebombings at the 7-Eleven convenience store and the shooting at Soares's home, including Harold Amos. He was later charged with gangsterism for his alleged affiliation with the Zig Zags. Police suspected Amos was acting with or at the behest of someone higher up in the organization. But proving it was not going to be easy.

The same problem confronted police in Vancouver, Toronto and Montreal. Without well-placed informants, it was almost impossible to penentrate the criminal dealings of the Angels or their puppet groups. "Members of the HA go out of their way to insulate themselves from prosecution by hiring other people who hire other people," says one Winnipeg officer.

Winnipeg police had neither the money nor the manpower to run major infiltration projects with wiretaps and surveillance. So they had to fall back on the luck of the draw: whatever snitches or squealers would come forward—and they were not always reliable. Their first chance came with Robert Coquete.

Three days after he was acquitted of the assault charges, Coquete was boarding a plane in Calgary, apparently on his way to Europe. He never made it. Police nabbed him and hauled him back to Winnipeg on new charges, including robbery, kidnapping, extortion and assault.

Then something strange happened. Police released Coquete two days later, but his address on court documents was now given as the second floor of the Public Safety Building—the cop shop. In other words, Robert Sousa Coquete had turned.

Coquete for the first time gave Winnipeg cops a peek inside the workings of the lower levels of the Manitoba

Hells Angels. A videotape of Coquete's confession shows him wearing a grey Nike sweatshirt pullover, blue track pants and white sneakers. He ambles into the bare interrogation room, keeps his hands folded on the table and spins nervously in his chair. But he was to prove an unreliable informant and the Winnipeg police and prosecutors would soon discover he was no Dany Kane or Stéphane Gagné.

On the weekend of May 4, Toronto police arrested Ian Grant on a Winnipeg warrant on eleven charges, including conspiring to commit kidnapping and drive-by shootings. Three weeks later, two more bikers were behind bars, including Sean Wolfe, twenty-five, for a drive-by shooting against the Mirs in November 2000.

Without the resources of a Biker Enforcement Unit as in Ontario or Wolverine in Quebec, the Winnipeg police were going to have little luck getting to the higher-ups in the Angels' Manitoba empire. So instead the police hoped to destabilize their operations by going after their underlings, the fast-rising prospects, the pivotal links between the full-patch members working behind the scenes and the thugs on the street doing the dirty work.

The police boasted to the press that "they have worked their way up the biker gang hierarchy with the intent of getting the whole 'house of cards' to cave in." But the police and the prosecutors held only one high card in their hand—Robert Coquete. But in another case they were about to learn that using one biker to go after another one can sometimes lead to a nasty crash.

The Winnipeg cops had turned one violent biker, Robert Coquete, into a snitch against his one-time pals. Now they were going to try to use one attempted murderer to nail another one.

In the spring of 2002, Manitoba police had in their custody two people who had tried to kill each other, with little concern for any innocent bystanders. Kevin Sylvester had opened fire on Rod Sweeney while his young son was sitting next to him in his truck. Rod's brother Dale, police say, later shot at Sylvester while he was driving down a busy downtown street. They could use either gang member as a witness against the other. They chose ex-Spartan Sylvester to go after Hells Angel Dale Sweeney. In exchange for his testimony, Sylvester would get a new home and identity as part of the witness protection program, an insurance settlement and a letter of endorsement for early parole.

And jail time? Normally an attempted murder rap, even with a plea bargain, would net a double-digit prison sentence. Instead, the Crown was so eager to nail a Hells Angel, they settled for two years less a day.

"I'm figuratively choking on this right now," the judge could not keep from saying at Sylvester's sentencing. "I'm going to hold my nose and go along with this."

Now they had to hope Sylvester could deliver the goods. When Sweeney's trial got under way in early June, the Hells Angels member flew in some high-priced talent for his defence—Alan D. Gold, a skilled and combative attorney who was the former president of the Criminal Lawyers Association. Gold's strategy was simple: put Sylvester on trial instead of his client.

And at times it appeared to be working. Noting that Sylvester had been in the middle of about a dozen gun battles over the course of his career, Gold wanted the jury to consider there might be many people besides his client who would want Sylvester dead. "You seem to be one of the most shot-after people," he said.

Sylvester claimed on the stand that he got rid of the gun he used against Sweeney by asking an unnamed nephew to throw it off a bridge into the river. But Gold revealed that ballistics reports showed the same gun was used the following night to shoot Hells Angels associate Glen MacEachern outside the Teasers strip club.

It was a bombshell—an embarrassing fact that the police had either overlooked or hidden. Either way it was a disaster, seriously undermining the credibility of the prosecution's victim and key witness.

Flustered, Kevin Sylvester insisted on the stand that he knew nothing about the MacEachern shooting, claiming the gun was already in the water.

"This is like winning the lottery for you, isn't it?" Gold said at one point. "Except you wrote your own lottery ticket. You're getting an unbelievable deal from the government in exchange for your testimony."

What was remarkable about Sylvester's sweetheart deal with the Crown was that he was not able to identify his assailant. Sylvester never pointed to his Hells Angel enemy sitting in the defendant's chair to declare, That's the man who shot me. The Crown instead used Sylvester only to supply the motive: biker revenge. Dale Sweeney tried to kill Kevin Sylvester because Sylvester had tried to kill his brother Rod.

Mr. Justice Perry Schulman of the Court of Queen's Bench took the case under consideration. Dale Sweeney would have to wait until the fall to find out if he had a lucky angel on his shoulder.

Not having had much luck in cracking down on the Hells Angels for serious crimes, the police at times seemed downright petty. They once pulled over Jeff Peck, habitually in prison on drug or other charges, when he was out on parole. The excuse? A noisy muffler. Peck threw the ticket on the road in disgust; the cop promptly charged him with littering.

At one point, Winnipeg's finest managed to hide a tracking device on Ian Grant's truck in order to follow his movements. Grant uncovered the gadget when he took his truck in for repairs and refused to give it back to police. The chagrined police responded by charging him with theft of the very gadget they had planted.

Hells president Ernie Dew also found himself the target of police zeal and mistaken identity. In mid-April, police arrested him for the beating of a thirty-six-year-old patron with a claw hammer, chairs and a microphone stand at a bar several months earlier.

"You're not serious, are you?" Dew told the cops when they came to his door.

Dew insisted he was home with his children the night in question, just after New Year's. Indeed, the complainant said his attacker was a long-haired man in his late twenties or early thirties weighing about 180 pounds. Dew, with his thinning short hair, looks distinctly middle-aged—all 240 pounds of him.

The Crown knew they had a shaky case. So shaky that they did not oppose a judge's ruling to allow Dew—on bail—to travel to Spain for a World Run of Hells Angels. It was a ridiculous situation: the leader of the Manitoba Hells whose parole stipulations forbade him to associate with his local comrades getting permission to go to an international biker extravaganza. The Crown dropped the charges against Dew shortly afterwards, and the police looked foolish.

Except for their erroneous and embarrassing accusation of the bar brawl, the police have nothing on Ernie Dew. The most serious rap they have been able to pin on vice-president Danny Lawson is having prescription drugs without a prescription. They arrested Mark Bohoychuk, secretary-treasurer, on an extortion charge. Four of the six remaining full-patch members who do not hold executive positions were tied up in the justice system for most of 2002, but none of them faced serious time. Jeff Peck was still in jail on a minor drug bust.

But if Winnipeg police were dreaming that their sweep against the bikers in the spring of 2002 would bring them closer to toppling the men at the top, they got a rude awakening by the fall.

On the last day in September, Hells Angel Dale Sweeney stood before Judge Perry Schulman, accused of attempted murder for the daylight shooting of his hated rival, Kevin Sylvester. A conviction would be the most serious legal blow Manitoba had struck against the Angels since their arrival in the province three years earlier. But it was not to be.

Instead, Judge Schulman directed his blows against the police and the prosecution. "Members of the Winnipeg Police Service assumed that Sweeney was guilty from the start and made no effort to investigate the possibility that someone else committed the offence," Schulman declared. He blasted the police for failing to seriously question their star witness—a witness he found less than useless.

"I have found his evidence to be worthless," the judge said. "I place no reliance whatever on his evidence." Schulman also lashed out at the sweetheart deal the Crown signed with Sylvester, "which provided him with a wonderful benefit even though he provided police with no information other than that which they believed they possessed."

In the end, Schulman ruled that Sweeney was the driver of the black truck that followed Sylvester, not the passenger who fired the bullets. He said the gunman might have just been trying to "wound, maim or disfigure" Sylvester, not necessarily kill him. He acquitted Dale Sweeney of attempted murder but convicted him of the lesser charge of being a party to the discharging of a firearm.

For all the trouble and embarrassment the police and prosecutors experienced in making a pact with Sylvester, their Hells Angels target got only six years in prison. With his pre-sentencing time in custody, Sweeney would do only three years. Gold returned to Toronto, but it would not be his last venture outside Ontario to defend bikers.

The small sign on the glass door restricted entrance to adults over eighteen, but few paid any attention. At the entrance to Old Joe's Sports Lounge were two Sega arcade games: pretend Harley-Davidson bikes were attached to video screens to simulate a crash-and-burn ride. But the pool hall was a lot closer to real bikers than most people suspected.

Tucked in the corner of a yellowish brown brick building on a busy street in Winnipeg's north end, the two-storey sports lounge was separated by a music shop and a furniture store from a plain building that housed the riding office of Gord Mackintosh. Before he became the province's justice minister, Mackintosh—as a backbench member of the Legislative Assembly—unsuccessfully opposed the granting of a liquor licence to the pool hall, no doubt fearing the consequences on local youngsters.

He knew only half of it. In real life, Old Joe's was a crack sales centre, run by the sister of one of the most senior Hells Angels. In August 2002, police arrested two men and Dawn Marie Deane, the forty-nine-year-old sister of Bernie Dubois, the veteran biker who went from the Redliners to the Brovos to the HA. Dawn Marie had a $70,000 interest in the pool hall. A nine-month under-cover operation revealed she was selling not pool games or Coca-Cola but cocaine. A police agent made thirty-nine purchases of crack at her thriving store—at times so busy that he had to wait in line.

Police searched her brother's home but came up empty-handed. His sister, however, turned out to be an aggressive business planner and considered expanding her operation to include a delivery service. "This is quite common in Winnipeg, where cocaine is delivered to your doorstep just like a pizza," said the prosecutor. Deane was sentenced to four years.

The seedy underworld of crime and coke had landed right next door to Manitoba's justice minister. In his spacious minister's office at the legislative buildings, he could only shake his head in disgust.

"It is a cancer," he says. "And the solution to cancer is often complex and difficult, and any politician who says that I have a one-line answer to organized crime is just not giving the straight goods at all. I would love to have the one-line answer, but if there was one there wouldn't be thousands of Hells Angels in the world."

Old ways of policing and prosecuting won't work, he insists: the gangs are organized, so the justice system has to be better organized to challenge that. "I think there has to be a different thinking brought to bear," he says as he pounds the table.

To his credit, Mackintosh has moved quickly to give the province a biker bunkers law, formally known as the Fortified Buildings Act. He wanted to avoid the situation in Quebec where municipalities were left to fend on their own against intimidating fortresses built by the Angels. Manitoba's law imposes a province-wide ban on buildings that have bombproof doors, concrete barriers, steel bars and other fortifications.

The province is moving on other fronts as well. Mackintosh set up a new witness security program to give more protection to people who have to testify against bikers. The province also created a specialized team of seven prosecutors to work closely with the police on biker and gang cases; there is also a prison gang suppression unit and a special squad of six probation officers who monitor high-risk gang members. The city of Winnipeg, meanwhile, drafted a by-law to make it illegal to wear gang colours, crests or logos at city-backed events. And city police have pressured downtown nightclub owners to place certain customers, many of them Hells Angels associates, on a sort of blacklist—a tactic civil liberties lawyers dismissed as "questionable."

Still, Mackintosh concedes "the very nature of organized crime" has made it hard for his prosecutors and police to cripple the real power of the Hells Angels. "Its underground nature, the multiple players, the layers—the people doing things for other people—the intimidation tactics and the organizational structure of the Hells Angels itself has made it a very serious challenge across the world," he says. "That makes it very difficult to sometimes instill confidence on the part of the public that there's action."

For months, Mackintosh promised to set up a joint police strike force dedicated to fighting the bikers. But he has been blocked by an intense rivalry between the RCMP and the city police. While the Hells methodically eliminate their rivals, critics charge that the police agencies have spent more time fighting each other than the bikers. The street cops who pound the pavement scoff at the Mounties who get flustered when the bikers are smart enough to dump a body beyond Winnipeg's city limits. The RCMP, for its part, chides the local cops for not concentrating on gathering intelligence to get the big picture—and eventually the big guys at the top of the Angel hierarchy. Until Mackintosh can settle the power struggle, the police forces will remain divided and dispirited.

The local street cops, meanwhile, complain they are underequipped to handle the biker threat. They don't have digital cameras to record the comings and goings of various bikers from across the country and then e-mail the intelligence to their counterparts in the rest of Canada. Overtime budgets are tight—booking Saturday work needs three weeks' advance notice—but the bikers don't stop their business on weekends.

The Winnipeg police department also has a standing policy of rotating most of its officers from various units every one to three years. That helps to prevent burnout and brings in new blood. It might work fine in homicide or robbery where each case usually has a different culprit. But police rotation breeds instability in anti-gang work while the same veteran bikers sharpen their skills over the years.

"The Hells Angels don't rotate, and they're not afraid to develop an old boys' network," says Lobban. He notes that only two of the five original anti-biker cops back in 1997 are still on that beat. And many of the best and brightest on the force are quitting. "I'm seeing guys my age and junior to me pulling the pin. You're resource strapped and you can only allocate so much, so why would you stay?"

Lobban himself has been pushed out. After almost two decades of experience with bikers, he left the gang unit to head up the detective squad in District 6, a largely middle-class section in south Winnipeg. Ray Parry stepped into Lobban's shoes as the head of the biker unit though he too would be gone within a year. On the third floor of the Public Safety Building, the flow charts with the latest gang intelligence are posted on the bulletin board. They list the members of the Zig Zags and other gangs, colour coded to indicate who is in tightest with the dominant Hells Angels.

"There is no rivalry, no predatory group," notes Parry, a hint of respect if not admiration for his long-time biker foes creeping into his voice. "It's a business, it's about making money and they're very efficient about how they do it."

Several miles to the north at an auto repair yard on the outskirts of the city, Ernie Dew laughs.

"I read in papers that I make a million dollars!" he bellows. "Not true. If it is I'm still waiting for my cheques. I haven't seen it. I make ten dollars an hour here. I'm not made of money."

Dew sits in a cluttered corner of the small trailer that serves as an office for the mechanics. He wears a baseball cap and an oil-stained shirt; black-framed glasses hang from a chain around his neck, and a thick gold wedding band with diamonds sparkles on his finger. His eyes are silver blue, his moustache still shows a hint of blond. But his body can't hide the four decades of rough living and riding. He has a long scar on his stomach and an ugly purplish abscess runs from below his left knee to the ankle—a worrying sign of a serious infection that developed from a compound fracture after a motorcycle accident.

On the phone, he cajoles and sweet-talks a nurse, setting up another appointment for an operation to try to save his leg. It's hard not to see the charm and easygoing nature that even the cops admit is a trait of the Hells Angels leader. "He's a personable guy," says Ray Parry.

Tacked to the wall behind him, like a proud family photo, is a picture of his $40,000 Harley-Davidson Road Glide. Ernie Dew has come a long way from the Keystone minibike he cherished as a teenager.

He put $9,000 of engine work into the brand-new bike even before he rode it. "I ripped the engine up, stoked it right to the nuts, as big as she'll go," he says like a proud father. "I want it standing ass end when it comes out."

Dew agrees to sit down for a brief interview, telling one of this book's authors: "go ahead, ask whatever you want." When asked about the overriding view that the Hells is a criminal organization, he says: "There's bad and there's good in every group. I don't care where you go."

"But a lot of normal people don't have weapons charges, they don't have guns, they haven't been charged with shootings," he's told.

"We've got a bad reputation, I'll tell you that," Dew concedes. "But it's a lot better these days than it has been.

We want to be recognized as the same as everybody else. We are a motorcycle club."

But what about the drive-by shootings, the turf war for drugs, he is asked. "Can you see why people say: 'These people control the drug trade, this is not your regular Saturday night club?'"

"I don't see where you get off saying we 'control' the drug trade. I don't agree with that," Dew replies.

"Do you just disagree with the verb 'control'?"

"I'm not saying that we have any part in it. There are probably people in the Hells Angels that do deal drugs. It's not just one group of people."

Dew himself says he recently spent eighteen months in prison for conspiracy to traffic. "We've had our share of shit fly here," he says. "You want to put me in jail, put me in jail. Jail doesn't scare me."

But Dew is upset with what he sees as frivolous prosecutions and harassment of bikers. He says his own arrest for the alleged bar brawl that embarrassed police when all charges were dropped cost him $7,000 in lawyers' fees. Now he's talking of launching civil lawsuits against the police.

"They've used the courts to cost us piles of money, so now we're going to turn it around," Dew says with a big smile. "We're trying to turn the tables and fight back."

The interview is over. And the president of the Manitoba Hells Angels has a final word of warning:

"You know what? You could put us all in jail, and there'll be seven more guys here. We're not going away. You gotta realize how big this motorcycle club is."

FIFTEEN

B.C. Bonanza

"There were some very wealthy Hells Angels in B.C. primarily
because they have been left untouched by law enforcement."
INSPECTOR ANDY RICHARDS, ORGANIZED CRIME AGENCY

In British Columbia, you can find a home with a river view,
then get your lawn landscaped while you do your grocery
shopping or enjoy a fine meal in an Italian restaurant, call
your date on your cellphone if he or she is late and even
book tickets for your holiday—all through businesses run
by the Hells Angels. Few British Columbians realize just
how extensive the Angel business empire is: a walk along
East Hastings in Burnaby will take you past a popular café
and two clothing stores owned by bikers.

"These guys have buckets of cash," says Sgt. Larry Butler
of Vancouver police's Outlaw Motorcycle Gang Unit.

The B.C. Angels make up the third largest contingent of
bikers in Canada after Quebec and Ontario, but they are
Number One when it comes to wealth and stature. What is
remarkable about the West Coast Angels is not their total
cash flow; Mom Boucher and his Quebec Nomads were
probably raking in as many, if not more, millions from their
East Coast drug trade. In Quebec, though, the Angels had

not tried to infiltrate the mainstream economy and the stock exchange. At least not like the B.C. bikers.

"They're baby boomers: they've come up in the criminal game," says Pat Convey, who tracked the bikers for years as an RCMP officer in Victoria. "These guys have learned as they've gone on. They've become wealthier because they've become smarter and became smarter because they've got enough money to seek appropriate advisers."

Those advisers include well-heeled lawyers, accountants and businessmen who help the Angels carry out some of the most extensive money-laundering schemes in the country. The Angels may not have completely discarded their riding leather for three-piece suits, but many of them have moved into a startling array of businesses. Meanwhile, plenty of corporate sharks seem only too willing to swim with the bikers. In B.C., the gap between Harleys and Howe Street is not as wide as most would imagine. Sasha Angus, in charge of cracking down on fraud and enforcing the rules at the B.C. Securities Commission, says: "We understand the biker gangs are behind a lot of stuff we've seen. But they don't always leave their calling card."

By far the richest club in B.C. is Vancouver East End. The clubhouse on East Georgia is surrounded by a large brown fence and ten neatly trimmed bushes. The white two-storey stucco building has a small bay window in the front.

Club president is John Bryce. "He's a very easygoing guy," says a fellow biker who has known him since high school. "When he explodes, he explodes. But he was always cool." Cool enough to keep a clean criminal record and amass a fortune. Bryce runs a bike store on Parker Street in Burnaby called Hi-way Choppers, and if that is his only source of income, the bike business must indeed be booming, for John Bryce lives exceptionally well. In addition to his business property and private residence, Bryce also owns four homes in the 1700 block of Caledonia in North Vancouver and another house in Maple Ridge. His mother, sister and a close associate live in three brand-new houses built at the same time on Wall Street in East Vancouver. Bryce's own home at 341 Springer sits atop a majestic hill in Burnaby that overlooks the entire Vancouver area and is currently valued at $538,000.

In the driveway you might see the new green Ford Excursion that he leases, but Bryce also has two Harleys and several classic cars, including a 1933 Ford Coupe and a 1966 Chevelle. Antique cars seem to be a bit of a passion for the B.C. bikers, who have gone far beyond the two-wheel Harleys. Ron Cameron has a '34 Ford Convertible and a '47 Ford Coupe. Carlo Fabiano has ten cars, one a vintage '61 Chevy Impala.

It is a tribute to the wealth and stature of the East End bikers that like their leader Bryce, few remain in the working-class east end of the city where so many of them grew up. Several join Bryce in Burnaby's comfortable corners; others live well in North Vancouver, West Vancouver and Maple Ridge.

Not surprisingly, the bikers are into bike stores—three different members operate major cycle businesses in Burnaby, Nanaimo and Maple Ridge. Also not surprising is the Angels' interest in the lucrative sex trade. Rob Alvarez from the East End chapter has a business licence from the city to run Rhythm Productions, a company that with a few beds and cameras puts porn on the Web. Alvarez says that though his company is new, he has been eager to "get to know the movers and shakers" in the business.

Robin Lee already had experience moving and shaking her various body parts. The wife of Damiano Dipopolo, another East End member, she ran a soft-porn Web business. Her slick Web site offered videos and pictures of her scantily clad body as well as a wide selection of other "Canadian Hotties." The Angels also controlled two of the three stripper agencies that run most of the live action in the bars and strip joints across the province.

But the B.C. bikers are much more diversified than bikes and sex, investing heavily in many profitable ventures, including major real estate holdings from apartment buildings to supermarkets; construction and waste disposal. Two cellphone stores—Planet Cellular and Tele Tel Communications—are run by HA members or associates. Rocco Dipopolo, a one-time East End prospect and still close to the club, runs the EuroSport Café on East Hastings; his brother Damiano owns another restaurant on Commercial Drive. The Angels always had traditional leather and bike clothing stores, but now they are also branching out into mainstream fashion. Nomad member Tony Pires has Antonio Clothing in Aldergrove; Werner Gonzalez of the Haney chapter runs Pronto Moda on Hastings; and just down the street, Damiano Dipopolo also owns Digstown clothing, with hip black-lined windows and the latest cuts from Ecko and J.Lo.

The B.C. bikers are also involved in the entertainment industry: Kim Harmer of the Mission chapter runs 81 Transport, which services the movie industry. When superstar Shania Twain gave a concert in Vancouver in 1999, two full-patch East End members, Damiano Dipopolo and Carlo Fabiano secured backstage passes and sat on the stage, just out of the audience's line of sight, dressed in their full HA colours.

Bikers also played the stock market. Ernie Ozolins, at one time the leader of the Haney chapter, always had cash to spare. A confidential police report reveals he was arrested twice in 1993 with "very large amounts of cash on his person," once as much as $185,000. He owned several Harleys, a black Porsche and a BMW. Ozolins was good friends with Martin Chambers, a former Vancouver lawyer and real estate dealer with long-standing ties to the bikers. By his own admission, Chambers had visited the Haney clubhouse at least twice and considered Ozolins "one of my closest friends" with whom he had "many business ventures." Chambers would eventually be arrested in one of Canada's biggest money-laundering stings run by both the RCMP and the FBI and was sentenced to sixteen years in a U.S. prison in the fall of 2003.

In 1997, Ozolins and two freelance criminals with close ties to the Hells Angels got involved in a pump-and-dump scheme, jacking up the price of a bogus mining company before bailing out and pocketing the profits. Ozolins did not live long enough to enjoy the rewards. He was executed at home with his girlfriend on June 2, 1997, in a murder that remains unsolved to this day.

One of the longest serving and wealthiest East End members is Lloyd "Louie" Robinson. Robinson is the half brother of the East End chapter president, John Bryce (they have the same mother), but many feel he is the real brains and driving force behind the chapter. Robinson was one of the West Coast Hells Angels with the strongest ties to the Italian Mafia from back east. His closest connection was a Toronto boxer named Eddie Melo, a protégé of the Montreal Mafioso Frank Cotroni and the Commisso family in Toronto. When Melo came out west, Robinson took his Mafia pal to the Angels' clubhouse. Robinson also made frequent trips to Toronto, meeting Melo in Yorkville hangouts like Remy's or the legendary Pilot and—according to RCMP surveillance teams—also talking directly many times with the Commissos.

A big man in his mid-forties with dark, curly hair, Robinson has earned a reputation as someone not to be crossed. In September 1989, Hilmar Suessmaier, the forty-eight-year-old owner of the Metro nightclub on West Georgia, tried to eject a customer for causing a disturbance. He was so badly beaten that he died three days later. Based on witnesses' testimony, police arrested Robinson. The Crown later stayed the charge for lack of evidence. Again in April 1996, police charged Robinson and a Hells Angel colleague, Gino Zumpano, with extortion. And once again, the Crown dropped the charges, saying there was not sufficient likelihood of getting convictions.

Robinson has always had a sharp eye for business. Like other bikers, he has had his fingers in the stripper business. In Vancouver in the early 1990s, the bikers had influence over two of the three companies that dominated the trade. Elie Bruneau, president of the Haney chapter, owned Deluxe Entertainment (and still runs it to this day). Robinson ran That's Entertainment with an ambitious promoter named Ken Lelek—and their partnership would help launch the modern world of Internet porn and gambling. That's Entertainment was owned by 399413 Alberta Ltd. Annual reports for 1993 and 1994 named Lelek and Robinson as directors. By 1995, only Lelek was listed but both men remained business associates.

The revolution began at Number 5 Orange, one of the many strip bars in Vancouver's Eastside. The Number 5— promising "Cold Beer" and "Hot Babes"—is only six buildings away from police headquarters.

That's Entertainment approached some young computer wizards and proposed putting pictures of the girls on CD-ROMs so bar managers could decide whom they wanted to hire. That's old technology, the techies said; let's put this on the Internet.

They filmed the strippers at two different locations: at Number 5 Orange and also at the Carrall Street offices of a new company Lelek helped create in May 1995 called Starnet Computer Communications.

"A LIVE Video feed from a strip club!" announced one of its first Web sites, Sizzle.com. "You're not just reading text or looking at photos; you can SEE and HEAR your fantasy woman—LIVE!—it's as though you're right there with her!" The publicity sounds exaggerated today when streaming video and live action is commonplace on the Net, but back then this was revolutionary. Porn, as usual, was pioneering technology that would later seep down into the rest of the industry. "Sizzle.com was the first company in the world to broadcast a LIVE video feed from an exotic show lounge via the Internet," Starnet boasted.

Making breakthroughs with video technology was one thing, but Vancouver's Web porn pioneers also had to come up with new ways to handle money over the Internet. Initially, they ran the credit cards through Number 5 Orange. Starnet then perfected its own credit card interface—a secure, on-line banking system—and got a contract with the Bank of Montreal to handle the transactions.

Within no time, Starnet had porn customers in more than sixty countries clicking onto a plethora of Web sites. Sizzle.com proclaimed itself "the dirtiest site on the Net." Redlight.com bragged it was "home of nasty shit." The company also expanded into gay sex with Chisel.com, a "gay sex super site—so live it hurts."

By 1997, the company had moved into an even more lucrative frontier—on-line gambling. It obtained a licence from Antigua—a convenient offshore haven—and developed some of the world's best on-line gaming technology. Customers flocked to the cyber casinos to play blackjack or poker; sports enthusiasts put down bets on everything from hockey games to soccer matches.

The gambling and on-line sex added up to a surefire win for Starnet. For the fiscal year of 1997, Starnet reported revenues of $1,996,535, which nearly tripled by 1999 to $9,773,000. Starnet's nerve centre in Vancouver covered

27,500 square feet with 280 workstations, twenty-two servers and three eight-foot satellite dishes on the roof. At one point, Starnet had the largest bandwidth pipeline in the city—pushing more Web traffic than anyone else in the province. On paper, at least, Starnet's value peaked at close to $900 million. Business was so good that Starnet applied to be listed on the prestigious NASDAQ exchange.

But there was trouble brewing. Starnet's explosive success caught the eye of Mike Ryan. A twenty-four-year veteran of the RCMP, Ryan had been working on commercial crimes since 1984. He was a different kind of cop—more accountant than action hero. In 1991, Ryan managed to find time to graduate from Simon Fraser University with a bachelor's degree in business administration; in 1995, he picked up a law degree from the University of British Columbia.

Two things intrigued him about Starnet's amazing rise to fame and fortune. First, he knew that Lelek had ties in the stripper business with biker Lloyd Robinson. Second, he was dubious about claims that the company was doing much of its Web business out of the tiny island of Antigua. "It was hard to make phone calls out of that place. You cannot run a company of that size with that bandwidth out of Antigua. You've got to have something here," he says.

Thus in late 1997 was born Project Enigma.

For the next two years, Ryan and his fellow Web sleuths kept digging in a hunt that was as high-tech and as lowdown and dirty as you can get. Ryan's people downloaded Web sites, tracked IP addresses and compiled Web domain hierarchies—but they also scoured through the garbage outside the homes of company executives.

"When we started it they had eight Web sites—then it mushroomed," Ryan says. By the end the cops were trying to monitor several hundred Web sites. They set about amassing evidence that Starnet-affiliated Web sites—even those registered offshore—were part of a gambling business coordinated and directed from Vancouver, and therefore in violation of Canadian law. Posing as gamblers, RCMP officers wagered on dozens of matches: an NHL game between the Canadiens and the Senators, an NFL match between the Packers and the Bears, even a Scottish 1st Division soccer game between Aberdeen and Dundee.

By the end of the summer of 1999, they were ready to attack. Early on Friday morning, August 20, police smashed into the offices of Starnet Communications International. They hauled away 154 boxes of documents, 74 computers and hard drives and a computer server with more than 100 gigabytes of data—the equivalent of 100,000 books. At the CIBC bank on Burrard Street, Starnet officials rushed in and tried to transfer $6,697,000 out of bank account number 0321516 to Antigua. Bank employees refused and police were able to freeze the assets.

At the time of the police raid, Starnet insisted it had long since outgrown its ties to Lelek and, through him, the connection to Lloyd Robinson and the Hells Angels. On paper, it was true that Robinson had ceased to be a director of That's Entertainment since 1995 and Lelek had stepped down as director of Starnet by the end of that year.

But when police searched Lelek's house, they found business records that indicated the men were still close. "We see a division of revenue: Lelek/Robinson," says one police source. According to the source, they found cancelled cheques issued over a period of time, made out to Robinson, and a trust agreement, drawn by a lawyer used by Robinson, stating that Lelek held a chunk of Starnet shares in trust for the Hells Angel.

While Lelek was neither a formal officer nor a director of Starnet when the police swooped down, he clearly remained intimately involved with the company. RCMP search warrant documents stated that throughout 1998 and 1999, company officials were sending Lelek copies of the minutes of directors' meetings and important e-mails. Lelek also held a large block of shares in Starnet through an offshore trust.

Ryan did not have the resources to investigate what he considered the real enigma behind Starnet—who exactly owned the company during the heyday of its porn and illegal on-line gambling? What if the sex and gaming were only sidelines—albeit extremely profitable ones—and the real game was that the bikers and other organized crime groups used Starnet's technology to launder money?

Starnet got its start from a $2.2 million private placement—a market tool that allows companies to not disclose their backers—from what corporate documents described as seven sophisticated offshore investors. "I would call them the Secret Seven," says Ryan, noting their identities to this day remain unknown. Starnet then sold licences to anyone who wanted to operate an offshore gaming site—and fork over $100,000. The RCMP succeeded in tracking the ownership of only about eight of the sixty-odd licence holders.

"We could never find out who the owners of the [other] offshore trusts were," says Mike Ryan. "We don't know how many are bikers. What's to stop an organized criminal from anywhere in the world having their nominee go into Starnet, buy a Web site, get it up and running and collect revenue for criminal purposes through that vehicle?"

In one case, the police tracked a single client who placed more than $5 million in bets in a ten-month period. "Now that's somebody with a significant gambling problem," quips Ryan. "Or it's a money launderer." Ryan's investigation also found offshore companies and trusts placing huge bets. "What offshore entity on the Grand Caymans or the Bahamas finds it necessary to place wagers on the Internet?" Ryan asks.

But questions of the Mountie on the money trail would go unanswered. Two years later, almost to the day—on August 17, 2001—the company pleaded guilty to one count of keeping a device for gambling or betting. It paid a fine of $100,000 and forfeited $6 million deemed to be the proceeds of crime. No individuals were ever charged. With its legal problems behind it, Starnet—now a legitimate company called World Gaming—moved its gaming operations offshore and sold its on-line porn business to an offshore company. The Web sites such as Sizzle and Redlight—still boasting "absolute filth since 1996"—operate out of the same humble Carrall Street address where the company began.

Lloyd Robinson, meanwhile, continues to prosper. Today the Hells Angels veteran owns a home on the mountainside of West Vancouver on Cammeray Road, valued at $1,330,000. Over the years, he has been a shareholder in Robinson Investments, JLK Holdings and Genesis Resources; he also had ties to Treasure Island Resources Corp., whose directors included chapter president John Bryce's sister. He also bought a private placement and held an option on shares in a gold and silver mining and exploration company.

The Starnet bust was a rare success—and a partial one at that—in an otherwise bleak landscape of police failures to counter bikers in British Columbia. Just four months after the Starnet conviction, a jury in New Westminster took less than two hours to acquit Haney Hells Angel leader Elie Bruneau on three charges of trafficking in cocaine. The judge found the informant run by an RCMP investigator so unreliable he warned the jury to be wary of his testimony. Little wonder Rick Ciarniello, the HA West Coast secretary, was fond of boasting: "We might point out to you that no members of the British Columbia Hells Angels are in prison."

"There were some very wealthy Hells Angels in B.C.," says Andy Richards, who first took on the bikers as a Vancouver police officer in 1991. "Primarily because they have been left untouched by law enforcement and they've been given a decade essentially to run free and amass criminal wealth."

Plagued by rivalries, incompetence and a general under-estimation of the threat posed by the bikers, the police in B.C.—especially the RCMP—did little to take on the Hells Angels until their power made them virtually impregnable. The Mounties division in British Columbia is the largest in the country—one in four of the force's 22,000 members are stationed west of the Rockies. "Who else had the money and resources to look at the bikers?" asks one police veteran in the province. "The RCMP did nothing until very recently—almost twenty years after the fact of the Hells' coming to the province."

For about ten years the RCMP in B.C. did have a Special E squad, set up to monitor the drug trade and, by default, the bikers. Many felt its mandate was too broad, its resources spread too thin and its focus too concentrated on intelligence over action: "They were expected to cover all the [biker] rides. They could tell you what colour underwear a biker was wearing on a certain day," says one biker cop. "But they weren't given enough resources to conduct any enforcement initiatives."

When the Mounties disbanded their squad, the B.C. bikers were left to the largely ineffective CLEU, the Coordinated Law Enforcement Unit that had been in place since 1974. Municipal police forces and the RCMP were supposed to pool their best resources to combat organized crime, but, in the words of one insider, "it became a dump-ing ground for the various police departments . . . of injured people, alcoholics, people in the twilight of their career being put out to pasture."

Richards, like many police officers, remembers the frustration in the early nineties of trying to get the top brass to take the bikers seriously. "I recall being at meetings where people were making the arguments that we need to start looking at these guys from a meaningful enforcement perspective, and the idea was pooh-poohed by senior RCMP members," he says.

Even back at RCMP headquarters in Ottawa, some senior officials will admit—albeit privately—that the B.C. division seemed shockingly reluctant to take on the bikers. "They were afraid of their own tails," says one officer close to the biker investigations. Indeed, on at least two separate occasions, the RCMP walked away from golden opportunities to infiltrate the bikers even when they had the chance delivered to them on a platter.

In one incident in 1996, a senior member in one B.C. chapter came forward to offer his services as an informant. He had been wronged by another member, ripped off and made to look like the bad guy. He had recently been kicked out of the club, but provided the police with valuable insight into recent club history. In particular, he described in detail a recent cocaine-importation conspiracy.

The Mounties balked. "Ah, we don't have money to pay these guys," one Mountie remembers senior brass in B.C. complaining. When Ottawa offered to come up with the cash, the B.C. Mounties devised other excuses: "Ah, it's not the money any more; he's got too many members in his family to protect," they said. In the end, nothing came of the potential informant.

The second missed opportunity, in the summer of 1998, was even more disturbing. An active member of a B.C. chapter—"one of the movers and shakers" in the trafficking of cocaine, as police describe him—found himself in trouble. A drug deal had gone sideways, and he became a cannibal for the debt: pay up or die. "He needed $80,000 overnight to pay his drug debts. He got fucked by some members of the HA," says an RCMP officer familiar with the case. "That's all he had to do to keep going. And he could have fed the police things because of his position."

The HA member did not trust the RCMP so he called Vancouver Crime Stoppers to say he had information on the bikers. "Get me out of this temporary jam here and I'll work with you," he told the Vancouver police when they got in touch with him. "It had great potential," says an officer involved. "He was willing to work with us and could have put away multiple full members of the HA in jail."

The police approached the RCMP for funds to run the operation. Again, the top brass dithered. Over the next four to five days, they manufactured delay after delay and excuse after excuse. "This was a gift that walked in the door," says one angry officer. "And he began to lose confidence in the police—understandably so." Fed up and scared, the biker went into hiding, leaving police with nothing.

"Two times HA members came knocking at the door. Two times!" says a senior Mountie in disbelief. "We lost both guys because of some idiots." He puts his finger to his forehead in a feigned gesture of suicide. "Give me a gun!"

One of these potential informants could have become the Dany Kane of B.C., helping to infiltrate into the highest reaches of the secretive club and bring down its top members. But the RCMP turned its back. In the minds of many frustrated and bitter cops, these two screw-ups confirmed what many joked was the real motto of the RCMP in B.C.: "Big files, big problems. No files, no problems."

The paralysis plaguing the RCMP in B.C. came to a head in 2001, when the force had a chance to nail drug dealers for an astounding $330 million worth of cocaine. Instead, in one of the biggest disasters in the war against organized crime in recent years, the Mountie brass blew the case.

The tale starts with Philip John Stirling, a fisherman in his mid-fifties who lives in Metchosin, a tiny suburb of Victoria. He is, by all accounts, an expert marine navigator who knows the Pacific waters—and the smuggling routes—very well. "He's a good mariner," says Pat Convey, who got to know Stirling during his thirty-five years as a Mountie, working mainly narcotics on Vancouver Island. "He can pilot a ship and park it on your front lawn."

In 1989 he was sentenced to five years in a cocaine smuggling conspiracy. He openly boasted to reporters that around 1999 he'd got the inside track on a massive cocaine importation deal between the Hells Angels and Colombians. He offered to snitch for the RCMP in return for witness protection and the tidy sum of $1 million. By law, the Mounties cannot confirm or deny if anyone was their informant; privately RCMP sources admit they struck some kind of deal with Stirling—and it looked promising.

But the top brass effectively sabotaged the operation. The first upset came right at the start when Richard Barszczewski, then an inspector in charge of the RCMP's Drug Enforcement Branch in B.C., suddenly nixed the deal his men had made with Stirling. Today, Barszczewski refuses to divulge any details: "The case is still an ongoing investigation," he says.

But his officers in the field were furious. Pat Convey was one of the hands-on agents working the file. With his trim white hair, leather jacket and blue jeans, Convey looks a lot fitter than his fifty-five years. "It was going to be a good international bust. Then the wheels fell off," he says. "And they just kept falling."

There was nothing Convey and his colleagues could do but tell Stirling the plan was cancelled. But Stirling apparently went ahead with the drug deal anyway. Late in November 2000, Stirling had bought a $100,000, eighty-eight-foot vessel called the *Western Wind*. Stirling says when he left port he was planning only to go fishing when his onboard computer registered a threatening e-mail ordering him to make his way to Colombia to pick up the drugs. The police say they later found no record of such a message.

What is not in dispute is that by early February 2001, after a detour off the coast of Colombia to pick up the cocaine, the *Western Wind* was heading back to Victoria—much to the shock of the RCMP. The Mounties had a disaster on their hands: there was a huge cargo of cocaine sailing toward British Columbia—and the waiting arms of Hells Angels. But the RCMP was caught with its pants down because Barszczewski had scuttled any deal with Stirling. The RCMP notified the Americans so that at least the boat could be stopped. As soon as it crossed into U.S. waters near Cape Alava, Washington, American authorities boarded the vessel and, according to court documents, found 101 bales of cocaine concealed in two modified fuel tanks located near the bow.

At the Seattle office of the U.S. Customs Service, they were excited. This was the biggest cocaine bust the region had ever seen—and now they had a chance to hit back at organized crime. Rodney Tureaud was the special agent in charge of the Seattle office. When he moved to the cold Northwest from the South, he had set himself several goals—he wanted to seize a helicopter and a plane for smuggling (which he did) and a dogsled (which he didn't). He also wanted to nab a biker. "I wanted to get some colours. I wanted to arrest a Hells Angel and put his ass in jail and get some colours." Maybe this would be his chance.

Meanwhile, in the choppy waters of the Strait of Juan de Fuca, the boat and its coke were in police hands. Pat Convey from the RCMP had raced down and was now on board; he and the Americans realized they could turn the situation around: they could put pressure on Stirling, caught red-handed with his boat overflowing with illegal drugs.

Police told Stirling he could face arrest—or lead them to his Hells Angels buyers back on land. Again, in the eyes of Convey—and now the American agents on board—it looked like a surefire way to nab the big-time importers. "These types of things are like eclipses—they don't come every year. You have to take advantage and you have to respond," says one American law enforcement officer involved in the case. "You don't have time to call to Washington or Ottawa and ask, 'Mother, may I?'"

But the Mounties did ask for permission. And again, Barszczewski nixed any plans to proceed. Without Barszczewski's sanction to offer Stirling witness protection, any deal was off. The police officers on board the *Western Wind* were stunned. "It would have been a success if not for Richard Barszczewski," says one Canadian police officer, noting it was Barszczewski who pulled the plug not once but twice on the operation.

Barszczewski again declines to give his reasons: "It's not right for me to talk about it," he says. But he does suggest that even if the Mounties had followed the shipment to port, they would not necessarily have nabbed the ringleaders. "In a mother-ship operation, getting the main organizers of that kind of event on the site for arrest is extremely rare."

It is not a rationalization that sits well with the Americans. "The people on the ground level who are working the case should have been allowed to go forward with it," says Tureaud. "You don't stop doing a case. That's covering your ass."

Frustrated, the Americans could do little but escort the vessel back to port. U.S. federal prosecutors opted not to bring any charges against anyone—in part, because the Mounties refused to divulge any information about their ties to Stirling as an informant. In the end, the U.S. officials destroyed the 5,500 pounds of coke, letting Stirling and his crew go, but seizing the boat. Curiously, Stirling filed papers in the U.S. District Court in Tacoma opposing the forfeiture on the grounds that at least at one point he was working for the police: "[He] was acting at the behest of the government of Canada in furtherance of legitimate law enforcement goals."

That bold admission should have been a death sentence from the Hells Angels, who, after all, lost the most when their coke never arrived. "I'm surprised he's still alive," says Pat Convey. "He still owes people for two and a half tons of coke." Presumably, the Hells Angels have concluded that dead men don't pay their debts. Stirling—still an expert navigator—could perhaps be useful another day, for another drug delivery. "That's worth something. Why would you get rid of a good item and something that is working well?" Convey speculates.

Yet nearly three years after one of the biggest cocaine seizures in history, not a single person has been arrested or charged.

Rodney Tureaud retired from the U.S. Customs Service without ever getting the biker or the dogsled he wanted as a catch. He still can't contain his outrage at the botched case. "It was a travesty. For two or three small rocks of crack cocaine—you're talking about something you can put on one fingertip—you go to jail for ten years or more. And we catch them with a boatload of two and a half tonnes of cocaine and then we turn them loose? It's baffling. We had an opportunity to make a significant impact on organized crime in Canada. It's an insult to everybody in law enforcement on both sides of the border."

As for Richard Barszczewski, the inspector whom many blame for blowing the *Western Wind* operation, he got a promotion—he's now superintendent in charge of RCMP support services, which puts him in charge of witness protection, informants and undercover operations.

And he adamantly refuses to see the Stirling affair in a negative light.

"The success is that two and a half tonnes of coke were taken off [the market] and even though at the current time there are no charges, it was a real big hit," the senior Mountie says.

Pat Convey, for one, is convinced that Stirling could have led the police to the highest echelons of the drug importing networks. "There are a lot of questions on this case—and not a lot of answers," says Convey. "Almost everybody involved said why? Why did the wheels come off?"

If the RCMP was having difficulty making drug busts, the Vancouver homocide squad was not having much more luck nailing bikers for murder. Not for the lack of trying; bikers tended to leave bodies on the streets, but not clues. Two killings in the months that followed the *Western Wind* debacle showed how tough it could be.

All it took was one bullet. With his blood and life trickling out of him, Donny Roming lay crumpled on the street on a cool night in the spring of 2001, not far from the fancy bar in Vancouver's Yaletown that he liked to frequent. Four shots were fired; one lodged in Roming's upper-right chest. Two suspects hopped into a vehicle and dashed over the Granville Bridge. A couple of patrol officers saw the muzzle flashes and heard the crack of gunfire. They ran to the scene but were too late to save Roming.

In death, the boisterous member of the Nomad chapter of the B.C. Hells Angels looked a lot less imposing than he did in life. Over the years, he had beaten both weapons and drug charges. He was a known cocaine importer and trafficker. Now, at forty-three, he was a corpse.

Homicide cop Mike Porteous knew this would be another dead-end investigation. He wouldn't need an informant to tell him what happened, and it wouldn't take long for investigators to get a pretty good idea of who shot whom and why. But officially, Roming's murder would go unsolved. Just like the other twenty or so gang murders in the past five years.

And the solve rate?

"Zero," says Porteous glumly. "We're zero for twenty. Our normal solve rate on murders would be probably 70 percent. The lion's share that are unsolved are organized crime."

Roming was one of the founding members of the East Enders, the support group for the Hells Angels. He started off as a low-level trafficker, worked as a bouncer and methodically worked his way up through the hierarchy. Once a full-patch Angel, Roming took control of a lot of street-level coke in the east-end bars of the city. Roming was also one of the enforcers who helped to push the bikers' competitors out of the stripper business. He beat one owner, a 67-year-old man, so badly the victim had to be hospitalized.

John "Slick J" Rogers also grew up in the east end, but he took a different, more independent path to drug wealth. He used to be involved in drug activity with the Hells Angels, but he splintered off and ended up being quite successful. The two men were on a collision course.

Late on the Friday night of March 9, 2001, Roming and a friend were out on the town with his pals, bar-hopping in a limousine. They ended up at the Bar None, a nightclub on Hamilton Street. Roming's friend got into a spat with the Rogers gang. The name calling and bravado spilled onto the street. By then it was 1:51 a.m. Roming had plenty of alcohol in his blood and a full patch on his back: as a senior Hells Angels member, he could hardly take these insults lightly.

"He was not as big as most of the others, but because of who he was he played a front-and-centre role," says Vancouver homicide cop Mike Porteous. "He figured his chances were pretty good."

A bad miscalculation. One of the Rogers gang produced a gun. Roming was not impressed—he pulled out his own weapon. His opponent fired a warning shot in the air, but the Hells Angel did not back off: Roming fired and missed; the shooter fired and hit Roming in the chest. The Nomad fell to the street in the middle of the intersection.

"Oh, my God, you just killed him!" one of the men cried out.

The Rogers gang fled in nearby cars, but the Hells Angels crowd rushed into action. Roming's gun disappeared, as did many of the shell casings at the crime scene. By the time two homicide detectives—Gary Vath and Rick Tod—arrived on the scene, Roming's companions who'd witnessed the shooting suddenly developed selective amnesia. Case number 01-48397 was going nowhere.

But the homicide investigators also knew the Hells Angels were not going to let the police do their work for them. Two weeks after Roming's funeral, the police were keeping watch on the East Vancouver home of John Rogers's brother—a residence frequented by Rogers and his friends. They noticed a man in black clothing lurking behind the house. He got into a Budget rental car and circled the block one more time before driving away.

The man was Ricky Alexander. At forty-six years of age, Alexander had a shaved head and a reputation vicious enough to frighten even many bikers. "He's a scary fuck. Really scary," says one close friend of the bikers. His criminal record includes armed robbery, break and enter, and drug trafficking. Alexander was especially close to John Bryce, the leader of the East End chapter. During the war against "The Russians" in the early nineties, when the Angels' foes shot up their clubhouse, Alexander was the first person Bryce called.

So police put Alexander under surveillance—and, not disappointing them, he returned to the house in East

Vancouver. A heavily armed team swept in and arrested him—a dramatic confrontation with a touch of comedy.

"You're under arrest for attempted murder," the officer in charge said.

"Attempted murder of who?" Alexander asked.

"I don't know."

"You're arresting me for attempted murder, and you don't know who I'm supposed to have killed?"

Nevertheless, when police searched the vehicle, they found two handguns—a semi-automatic and a long-barrelled .22 revolver—plus the business cards of various bikers. But it was the two pieces of paper in the glove compartment they found most revealing.

"It was a hit list," says homicide detective Gary Vath.

In Alexander's neat handwriting—peppered with more than a few spelling mistakes—were the names of John Rogers and the three gang members who were present at the Roming shooting. Doubtless thanks to the Hells Angels' intelligence network, Alexander had a startling amount of personal information on the men: not just descriptions of their cars and their addresses but buzzer codes for apartments; where they worked out; where they tanned; and details about girlfriends, mothers and fathers, even their pets.

At trial, Alexander pleaded guilty to carrying a loaded prohibited weapon but denied he was up to anything nefarious for the Hells Angels or that he had a "hit list." His lawyer said his client didn't know what he was going to do with the information he gathered from his surveillance and insisted the loaded gun in his waistband was for his own protection.

John Rogers, on the other hand, knew he was living on borrowed time: late Sunday, April 29, when he drove out to a gas station on the corner of Oak and 67th streets, he was wearing a bulletproof vest. He carried a gun and had two more in his car. As he exited the store to return to his car, an Asian man walked up and fired a bullet into his chest. Rogers's bulletproof vest only delayed his death. The first bullet ricocheted off the vest and up into his chin. He fell to the ground. His assassin fired another slug into his side and one more into his skull.

The police had no doubt his death was retaliation for the slaying of Donny Roming, even if the Hells Angels knew Rogers was not even on the scene when the Nomad died. "It's all about saving face for them, so they take care of him in a gangland style," explains Porteous. The message has been sent: 'This is what happens to people who mess with us,' and they move on.

There was one glimmer of bright news on the biker front in early 2001: two determined biker cops were able to score the province's first major legal victory against the Hells Angels. Two full-patch members were convicted on drug charges—commonplace in other provinces but a rarity in B.C. It was a costly and lengthy operation and even the police admit the big fish got away. But the investigation also helped lead to the formation of a new police agency that for the first time might have a chance at piercing the Angels' armour.

The story began back in 1995 with an informant. Robert Molsberry was a doorman at the Number 5 Orange Hotel bar—the downtown strip joint used by the Starnet entrepreneur Ken Lelek and East End Angel Lloyd Robinson to launch a porn empire on the Web. Molsberry also put in some time at Marble Arch, another bar where the booze and the girls were cheap and the coke was a pretty good bargain as well. Molsberry had a small piece of the action, selling as much coke on the side as he could. But then trouble started.

The street-level traffickers at Marble Arch told him this was "East End territory." That control was administered through two Hells Angels associates, Francisco "Chico" Pires and Ronaldo Lising. Both men had been members of the East Enders, a farm team for the powerful East End chapter of the Hells Angels. They then graduated to direct association with the East End chapter. Pires was a prospect member on the verge of getting his full patch; two of his brothers were full members—Tony was a B.C. Nomad, George was with the East End chapter. Ronaldo Lising was climbing up the ranks behind him and would get his prospect status soon afterwards.

Molsberry learned from his fellow dealers that they were forced to buy their product from Lising and Pires at $1,500 an ounce—about $400 above the market price. The Hells Angels associates "had threatened to kill any one of them who dared purchase cocaine elsewhere," according to court documents. Molsberry complained to the bikers that their price was exorbitant, but he was no fool. A Vancouver native, he had grown up with some of the East End guys and knew they were not to be messed with. Over the next four to five months, until April 1996, Lising and Pires supplied Molsberry with coke on about twenty-five occasions—usually an ounce or two, once as much as five ounces—for a total of about forty.

Things began to unravel for Molsberry in the summer of 1996. His coke stash was stolen and he fell into debt with the Angels. Molsberry went into hiding at a friend's apartment in Vancouver's west end. But on July 6, 1996, Pires and Lising tracked him down and threatened him. Desperate, Molsberry called the police. The patrol officer who arrived passed his name on to the biker cops.

The case fell to Andy Richards. As a beat cop, Richards had been frustrated for years at the unwillingness and inability of police to penetrate the biker empire; then, in the early nineties, he had led a two-year investigation into biker control of the stripper business that ultimately collapsed for a lack of witnesses willing to testify. Now he saw his chance. He teamed up with Al Dalstrom, another biker cop veteran dispirited with the way police were ignoring the Angels. They decided to use Molsberry not as the RCMP had worked Kane—to gather intelligence—but as Roberge had deployed him: to hit specific targets with an eye on big arrests.

That was the easy decision. The trickier one was to figure out how to run the Molsberry operation, dubbed Project Nova. Logically, it should fall to CLEU, the Coordinated Law Enforcement Unit. But both Dalstrom and Richards had come to the conclusion that CLEU was clueless. When they asked CLEU for a secure phone Molsberry could use, the agency came back with a phone that turned out to be registered to the RCMP.

So instead Richards and Dalstrom got some funding to cobble together an ad hoc team outside CLEU. They paid Molsberry $2,000 a month and $25,000 at the end of the investigation—"peanuts in the agent world," as Richards puts it—and the hunt was on.

For the next six months, they ran Molsberry as an agent, supplying him with the cash to pay off his debts and make numerous new drug buys. For six more months after that, they ran what police call a "full-blown wire" on Pires and Lising—complete wiretaps on their phones, as well as hidden microphones and cameras in Molsberry's apartment. They intercepted more than four thousand conversations over a fifteen-month period. The massive electronic surveillance offered a tantalizing peek into the murky world of Hells Angels drug operations—their thirst for profits, their codes and sometimes even their folly.

To shield their drug deals over the phone, Pires and Lising employed an ever-changing series of codes. "Meeting to eat" meant meeting to buy coke; eventually they changed that to "lunch" or "dinner" or "beer." Sometimes "oh zee" signified an ounce (oz.) of cocaine.

"Grab a couple of oh zees, man," Pires told Lising on March 11, 1997, prompting his partner to exclaim, "Fuck, where do you come up with these codes of yours, man?"

At times, though, the elaborate code system broke down—sometimes with comic results.

At 6:41 a.m. just three days after Christmas, Lising—never one to take a holiday from business—was speaking to another distributor. He was trying to get him to deliver to Haney chapter member Vince "Stocky" Brienza "a case of beer"—an ounce of coke.

"Hey," Lising began the pre-dawn call.

"Hey," came the bleary reply.

"Give Stocky a case of beer," Lising told him.

"Huh?"

"Give Stocky a case of beer," Lising repeated.

"What?" said the befuddled associate.

"Give him one," barked Lising.

"Well, no, I don't have a fucking case of beer," the man insisted. "If I had one, I'd give him one."

"Listen," the Hells Angels prospect cut in, losing patience. "Do you know what I'm talking about? You don't know, do you?"

"Oh, okay," came the reply.

"You're a dumb fuck, aren't you," complained an exasperated Lising. "You're gonna make me do this on the phone."

"No. Okay."

"Understand now?"

"Yeah, I do."

"Just one case."

"Okay."

The white Christmas cheer was finally on its way.

In the modern age of instant technology, the Hells Angels associates also developed a simple pager language. The digits "55" at the end of a pager message indicated the caller was a prospect for the East End (EE) chapter—*E* being the fifth letter in the alphabet. Multiple 55's meant urgency. When Lising paged one partner with a "5555555555," he got a call back within two minutes.

By the summer of 1998—two years after they first met Molsberry—they were ready to move. With a delicious sense of timing, the police waited to make the arrests until July 23, when Hells Angels from across the country were gathering in Vancouver to celebrate the fifteenth anniversary of a number of B.C. chapters. They charged Pires and Lising—by now full members—and several other Hells Angels associates.

The police nearly lost their case by losing their key witness. The bikers put out a $50,000 contract on Molsberry. The police had spirited him out of the country, but his hunters were able to track him down—using cellphone records and cloned pagers, the police suspect, thanks to the Angels' connection with cellphone companies. Molsberry was whisked away in time and, shaken but not silenced, testified against his Angel drug suppliers in open court in 2000.

Richards at first had a rough time finding a federal prosecutor in town willing to take on the HA. "They all said no—they were concerned for personal safety." In the end, the deparment went outside the province. They called on Peter Hogg, a federal Crown attorney who, in 1999, won a conviction against two men for shipping $2 million for organized crime across the country. Hogg didn't hesitate to take the job, even though the provincial track record in convicting bikers was abysmal. "I know we've had trouble," he told his team. "Let's do a good job on this."

And they did. Molsberry's testimony—supported by the massive number of wiretaps—was enough to convict Lising and Pires. They were sentenced in January 2001 to four and a half years in prison for trafficking in small amounts of cocaine. But only at the end of the trial did the prosecution reveal the two were HA members. "There was this palpable gasp from the jurors," recalls Hogg. The bikers, naturally, have appealed and even if they lose, will likely spend less than a couple of years behind bars.

In a province where prosecutions, much less convictions, of the Hells Angels were rare, the media were desperate for good news on the biker wars. "Hells Angels convicted for the first time" read one headline. Even the police will admit that after deploying twenty-five officers for two years at a cost of a million dollars, it was a partial victory at best. Richards and his team had tried to target a full-patch member much more senior than Pires and Lising, someone who was supplying them at the multi-kilo level. But they ran out of time and money. "They've been untouched for so long. The Hells Angels carry a big stick," Richards says. "They have a pretty easy run out here—and it's just now that we're beginning to target them effectively."

But Project Nova did teach the police in B.C. two important lessons for cracking the Hells Angels fortress. First, as the biker cops in Quebec, Ontario, Manitoba and now B.C. were learning, given the level of sophistication and secrecy within the Angels, police need well-placed spies and snitches—wiretaps alone are not sufficient. "At the end of the day, you need to penetrate, get into them with someone who is trusted, do hand-to-hand business," says Al Dalstrom. "And it takes dollars and real commitment to run agents into the Hells Angels."

Money and commitment that municipal police forces don't have. That was the second important lesson of Project Nova. Richards and Dalstrom both came from the Vancouver police department, and the two-year operation stretched its resources to the breaking point. Like Winnipeg, Vancouver was seeing just how costly and time-consuming it was to combat organized crime.

But if the Vancouver police could not handle the Hells Angels alone, who could? There was a recognition that nobody else in the province—including the RCMP—had been able to do it thus far," says Richards. "It's a matter of getting the right combination of investigators and experts together and funding it properly. We just have to give them the model to work with."

That model became the Organized Crime Agency (OCA). The B.C. government finally abolished the hapless CLEU in October 1998; five months later, in March 1999, a new, streamlined organization was born.

The OCA's headquarters lay tucked away in an industrial park on a small island near New Westminster. While not exactly a secret location, the grey, nondescript building blended in with the other warehouses and offices. There were no signs identifying the site as the new nerve centre in B.C.'s war against organized crime: just a chain-link fence topped with rolls of barbed wire and a security gate with a single intercom.

Inside, about 170 people were busy trying to crack through the walls of organized crime. The OCA became a magnet for some of the best and brightest of the biker cops. Pat Convey, the RCMP veteran fed up with how the force blew the *Western Wind* coke bust, signed up with OCA a month after that disaster. Mike Ryan, who started the Starnet probe with the RCMP, finished it with OCA. Fifteen officers worked full time on the Hells Angels, including Vancouver police veterans like Andy Richards, who held the rank of inspector at the OCA.

It was hard not to see OCA as a slap in the face of the RCMP. The RCMP were supposed to handle major crimes in B.C. such as drugs and money laundering. In effect, the creation of OCA was saying the RCMP was not doing its job. But the OCA's chance to take on the bikers would be short-lived. By 2004, the Mounties would win the turf war and the OCA would be merged into the RCMP.

While the OCA and RCMP battle it out, the street level cops still have a job to do. The black radio in Larry Butler's office is in the shape of a Harley-Davidson. Posters and stickers promoting the Vancouver Hells Angels cover his filing cabinet. With his squat muscular body, short, blondish hair, black T-shirt, jeans and the earring in his left ear, Butler, like many biker cops, could be mistaken for a biker were it not for his badge. Sergeant Butler runs the Outlaw Motorcycle Gang Unit of the Vancouver Police Department (VPD) out of an east-end building.

His assignment is simple but daunting: monitor the East End chapter—already the most powerful and wealthy in the province—and keep the streets safe; gather intelligence and arrest any bikers if they break the law. For all that he has a unit of three: himself and two detective constables. The city's anti-graffiti squad has more officers, leading the biker cops to joke that if only they could find some offensive scribblings on the Angels' clubhouse, they could perhaps get the manpower for a raid.

It is tough, often unrewarding work. In the summer of 2002, John O'Shaughnessy walked into a police station, claiming he had been beaten by Juel Stanton, an East End HA, in a dispute over a marijuana-growing operation. Butler knew Stanton only too well. A grim-looking man with short hair and a goatee, Stanton was a full-patch member with a full temper to match.

After a three-week investigation by more than a dozen officers, police arrested and jailed Stanton on several charges of aggravated assault, extortion and confinement. But a year later, on July 22, 2003, a judge acquitted the biker on all charges, dismissing the alleged victim as a "manipulative liar." One more victory for the B.C. Angels.

The police could take some solace from the fact that two days later Organized Crime Agency announced the arrest of a B.C. Nomad, Glen Hehn, on charges of possessing 51 kilos of cocaine for the purpose of trafficking. It was the biggest drug bust yet against a full-patch member.

The cockiness and confidence of the West Coast Angels is typified by the Nomads. Set up in 1998 by Donald Roming and other East End bikers, the B.C. Nomads have none of the clout and power that Mom Boucher's squad did in Quebec; they do not rule over other chapters. Still, they do see themselves as a cut above the rest.

"They're too eager," one former friend of the bikers says of the Nomads. "Everyone wants to have a BMW. They don't want to wait five to ten years."

Jamie Holland doesn't have a Beemer, but the twenty-nine-year-old Angel is the proud owner of a 2002 Porsche—not to mention a brand-new Harley and a Ford Expedition. Typical of the hungry young Nomads, Holland started off as a prospect, doing security for Nomads Bob Green and Gino Zumpano. Now a full-patch Nomad himself—and as usual with no known occupation or means of support—he bought himself a $600,000 suite at the Wall Centre in downtown Vancouver with a panoramic view of the city. But Holland's cockiness may have got the better of him. Late in 2002 he got into a fight outside a bar. A gun popped out of his waistband; he pleaded guilty to weapons charges. He got slapped with an $8,000 fine, forty-five days in jail, a five-year ban on carrying firearms—and was also ordered to stay away from Bob Green, one of the founders of the Nomads who was with him at the bar.

Yet, for all the bikers' wealth and comfort, few British Columbians realize how much power the bikers wield in their province. Even politicians in the law-and-order government of premier Gordon Campbell seem blissfully unaware.

SIXTEEN

No Safe Harbour

———

"We have been absolutely shocked by what we have heard. What
became apparent to us was that there was a whole underground
system of governance in some ports that
the police were aware of but did not have the resources
to address."
LIBERAL SENATOR COLIN KENNY

Damiano Dipopolo was used to having things his own
way. The long-time Hells Angel from the East End chapter in Vancouver was a successful businessman: he ran a
cellphone company for several years and then managed a
clothing store and a café, while his wife operated a polished Web porn site. So, in early 2002 when Damiano
strolled onto the Vancouver port, he did not expect to get
hassled. He didn't formally work on the docks, but his
twin brother, Rocco, a fellow biker, had been a longshoreman for years and had a union ticket. Dozens of Angels
and their associates worked on the waterfront, and
Damiano knew the bikers could roam around the docks
with impunity.

Damiano walked up to one of the ships that had
arrived and met one of the crewmen. He then got into his
car to leave. At the security checkpoint, an unsuspecting
guard dropped the boom gate: Dipopolo, after all, did not
have authorization to be on the premises. The Hells Angel

simply revved his engine and rammed through the gate.

The following day a couple of enforcers—some young Hells hangarounds—came down to have a little chat with the overly enthusiastic security guard. "The next time Mr. Dipopolo comes, don't you dare think about dropping the boom gate down," they told him in no uncertain terms. "He comes down here and does what he wants, when he wants—got it?"

Five years after Ottawa disbanded the ports police, the Angels still rule the roost down by Vancouver's waters, and their power has since grown. Latest police estimates put the number of full-patch members and associates working there at forty-three. "No one organized group controls the waterfront," says Peter Bell. "But because these guys have people in the right places, it enables them to do more."

Bell is a senior strategic intelligence analyst for the Organized Crime Agency in B.C. On the wall behind his desk are large charts detailing international drug routes. A former detective-sergeant from Queensland, Australia, Bell came to Canada with a noticeable Aussie accent and an insatiable curiosity about how the criminals keep getting away. He threw himself into an eight-month study of organized crime infiltration in the Vancouver ports. The result: a thirty-five-thousand-word report that is grim and disturbing. It says the bikers and other organized crime groups have their people working not just on the docks but also in trucking, maintenance, laundry and garbage services on the waterfront. Garbage? Why not—in January 2001 about eight kilos of coke were smuggled through the refuse taken off vessels in Prince Rupert.

Bell says at least eight of the bikers at the port are foremen—that means they can send people where they want to, and decide who can park on the port and where. "We see a gathering of players when a certain vessel arrives," Bell explains. For two days during the summer of 2002, for example, there was a migration of people who normally work at the Delta and Vancouver ports to the Fraser Surrey operation. One senior foreman, a known biker associate with twenty years' seniority at the Vanterm container facility, suddenly went to Surrey to work as a junior foreman for two days. Other known biker allies were on hand— drivers, gantry operators, the ship's chandler and checkers. "It stinks," blurts out Bell. "It sends alarm bells off to us; we knew something was going on." But without advance intelligence and the time to mount an investigation, it's difficult for the police to do much besides watch.

Even when they try, they are stymied by biker intelligence. Bell says that in one sting operation at Vanterm, the police seized 150 kilos of coke, replaced it with harmless white powder and waited to see who would show up to pick up the drug shipment. Suddenly, at 10:22 that night, the lights went out, plunging that particular area of the port into darkness for precisely seventeen minutes. By the time the lights came back on, the culprits had made off with the shipment. The smugglers didn't get the real drugs, but the cops didn't get the smugglers.

Al Debruyn, the president of the White Rock chapter and port foreman who wore his colours at the opening of the Robert Banks superport, has moved up in the world: he is now the senior longshoremen training officer. Police have seen him in regular chats with an executive of a container shipping company at the port. "You see a senior executive on a $300,000 salary wearing a three-piece suit sitting down with a biker once or twice a week having a coffee," says one law enforcement source. "They could just be shooting the shit—'How's it going?' It could be completely innocent. But you know, if you hang around with shit, some of it sticks to you."

Peter Bell, for his part, is also critical of what he sees as port management's lax attitude to security. The port screens only 121 out of the 27,000 people who work on the waterfront for security clearances. Port security now lies mainly in the hands of a small intelligence unit of eleven people called the Joint Forces Operation (JFO). Each police force also has its own units on the ports. Sgt. Jock Wadley heads the Vancouver police department's waterfront team of fifteen. "Two boats to patrol two hundred kilometres of shoreline," he says, pointing to the small craft tied up near the police outpost. "There is a whole area that's left unguarded."

"No Access Beyond this Gate" warns a small sign at one of the terminals, called Centerm. The gate was wide open and there was no security guard; anyone could walk or drive right through. Wadley says the companies have promised tighter fence security, but no dates have yet been set for the improvements.

In a noisy Greek restaurant along the waterfront, Gary Fotia and Mike Toddington sipped mediocre coffee just a few blocks from the docks they used to patrol. Five years after they lost their jobs as ports police, the two men took little comfort in realizing they had been right about the HA threat—even if their bosses refused to listen. Toddington sued the port corporation for wrongful dismissal and won an out-of-court settlement, adamantly refusing to agree to a non-disclosure clause. He still battles on, using his post as the executive director of the International Association of Airport and Seaport Police to warn the public about the criminal threats at the port.

Fotia, the young boy who gazed out on the docks and dreamed of becoming a cop only to see his crime-fighting days on the waterfront turn into a nightmare, helps Toddington out when he can. "We did not have resources to finish [going after the HA] because the rug was pulled out from under us," Fotia says. "The public has to know what's going on down there."

In Montreal, the public finally did get a glimpse of what was going on down at the ports. And, as was to be expected with almost any police success against the bikers and their allies, it came thanks to an informant—two of them, in fact. For nearly three decades, police had tried to nail Gerry Matticks, the gregarious Irishman who ruled the waterfront. Now, thanks to Dany Kane and another snitch, they finally got him.

When Kane's tips led the police to the Nomads' banking operations and Project Ocean in the fall of 2000, one of the regular accounts on the computer spreadsheet was code-named "Boeuf"—Maurice "Mom" Boucher's nickname for Matticks. Later, in a biker notebook, police discovered a code sheet that put Boeuf next to Gerry Matticks's name and his cellphone number. That was another big clue, but it wasn't the only one.

One of the people police spotted making regular trips to the Beaubien Street apartment that served as the Nomads' financial hub was a former vitamin-store owner named Elias Luis Lekkas. On a monthly basis, Lekkas would leave the apartment with bags stuffed with cash— lots of it, usually $500,000 in small bills. Then he would drive to a large rural estate owned by Matticks to count the money. Lekkas agreed to squeal against his former boss and on August 6, 2001, a handcuffed Gerry Matticks gave a single-word answer when asked in court if he pleaded guilty: "Yes."

The evidence revealed that on a waterfront that port boss Dominic Taddeo had boasted was one of the most secure in the country, Matticks had brought in a staggering 33,363 kilograms of hash and 260 kilograms of cocaine in eight shipments in just over a year. Matticks pleaded guilty once he was assured that he would not be extradited to the U.S., where he would face a much tougher sentence. In Canada, he got twelve years; he could be out in as little as two years.

Six months later, Matticks got more bad news. In an early-morning raid, fifty police officers from three different forces arrested his son Donald and fourteen other men. Police alleged that Donald had orchestrated the importation of $2.1 billion in hashish and cocaine between 1999 and 2001—44 tonnes of hashish and 265 kilograms of cocaine. The drugs went to the Hells Angels, for distribution across the province and likely Ontario and New Brunswick as well. With Donald working as a checker on the waterfront it was not hard for the gang to divert containers onto trucks and into a warehouse off port grounds.

If the arrests were any embarrassment to port officials, they didn't show it, shrugging it all off by distancing themselves from the corruption: they noted Donald Matticks was not technically an employee of the port but was paid through a hiring body known as the Maritime Employers Association. "Montreal is no worse than any other international port," a spokesman said lamely.

In fact, for years it *had* been worse, but the port bosses consistently denied there was a problem. When Liberal Senator Colin Kenny led a fact-finding mission to the Montreal port, his group was stunned. It was like a scene out of *On the Waterfront*, he recalls. "We were looking at each other, wondering when Karl Malden was going to appear," he says. "[It] shocked the hell out of us." Kenny's inquiry found that very little was being done to control crime in Montreal since the loss of the ports police unit. Security guards, provided by a company hired by the Port Authority, are unarmed. They have no power of arrest. The companies are easy for organized crime to penetrate.

Kenny's visit to Montreal was part of a cross-country investigation with other members of the Senate's standing committee on national security and defence. His official report was devastating. "We have been absolutely shocked by what we have heard," he told reporters. "What became apparent to us was that there was a whole underground system of governance in some ports that the police were aware of but did not have the resources to address." Customs officers testified that bikers and other criminals can make whole containers disappear from the ships, smuggling them directly out of the port or hiding them for later looting.

Among Kenny's findings in Montreal were that about 15 percent of stevedores have criminal records, as do 36.3 percent of checkers and fully 54 percent of the employees of a company contracted to pick up garbage. In Halifax, a sample of 500 longshoremen turned up 187, or 39 percent, with criminal records, while in the port of Charlottetown 28 of 51 (almost 54 percent) had criminal records. In Toronto, Hells Angels members are working as ramp or ground handlers at Pearson airport, smuggling large quantities of drugs from aircraft. Two retired police officers told Kenny's committee that Air Canada "stonewalled" police attempts to pose as employees in order to infiltrate a group of Hells Angels who were working for Air Canada cargo. The airline denied the charge. (Canada's Auditor-General Sheila Fraser would later estimate that as many as 4,500 people associated with biker gangs and other crime groups are operating at the nation's five major airports.)

Kenny and his team recommended compulsory background checks on employees, national standards for security perimeters around the harbours and a public inquiry on the ports. The government eventually came up with more cash but little else.

Just months after the Senate made its findings public, a big bust in Halifax revealed the extent of organized crime infiltration in the port and how little attention the authorities had paid to the problem in the past decade. In July 2002, the RCMP and local police mounted a series of coordinated raids in Nova Scotia, Quebec and Ontario, arresting over thirty people and seizing $95 million in drugs, $8.2 million in assets (including cars, trucks, jewellery and furniture) and $216,000 in cash. The drug haul included 317 kilograms of cocaine, 428 kilograms of hashish, 676 kilograms of marijuana, 159 kilograms of hash oil and 3,700 marijuana plants.

The operation began more than two years previously when the RCMP in Hamilton got a tip. "We identified an individual in Halifax who would act as a facilitator, someone who had people placed in strategic positions," Staff Sgt. Kevin Payne told reporters. That man was Paul Arthur, a crane operator who lives in the coastal village of Ketch Harbour. Other port workers charged were longshoreman Robert Langille and port clerk Laurence Coady. All three insist they are innocent, and are awaiting trial.

The group freelanced, according to police, offering easy access to the ports for interested parties in Quebec and Ontario. One key customer in Montreal was Steve "Bull" Bertrand, a close friend of Mom Boucher's. A case of forty-nine kilos of cocaine was earmarked for him. When it arrived at the Halifax port on February 8, police say the port workers in on the scheme were able to tip off the bikers that customs officials were planning to check all containers on the ship. Bertrand was advised he hadn't "won the lottery" that day. He later pleaded guilty to drug charges and was sentenced to seven years and a $100,000 fine—which he paid right away.

The bust also revealed the continued collaboration between the Angels and the Mafia. Police charged Jose

Guede, a Montreal lawyer who works in the law office that represents Mafia boss Vito Rizzuto, with brokering the cocaine deal with the Colombians. The RCMP named Rizzuto as part of the conspiracy to import the cocaine but said there was not "sufficient evidence to proceed to an arrest."

The RCMP, naturally, boasted the Halifax port bust had "just dealt a severe blow to organized crime." But no one in the RCMP seemed to notice that the three port workers identified in Halifax had all been on the watch list of the ports police a decade earlier. Paul Arthur was at the centre of the ring Eric Mott had identified as far back as 1993; Robert Langille was also on his chart; as well as Laurence Coady, the partner of Debbie Milton—the woman close to the Hells Angels who was the focus of much of the ports police investigations.

"There are no words to explain how angry it makes me," says Bruce Brine, who was fired by the ports and could not convince the RCMP that he and his team had even done organized crime investigations. "The RCMP says there is nothing to support the allegations I made back then, and yet here are all these arrests happening that confirm the intelligence work we had done ten years earlier."

One can only imagine how many drug shipments could have been prevented if authorities had listened to Mott and Brine in the early nineties instead of firing them.

In January 2003, Ottawa unveiled a $172.5-million package to beef up port security, including eleven new mobile X-ray scanners for containers and tighter screening of dockyard workers. No one disputed the need for high-tech gadgets—if only to increase the number of containers checked from the current pitiful rate of 3 percent. But nothing can replace human intelligence.

It is people who do real policing, not machines. In Halifax, regular policing down by the docks is now reduced to as little as two patrol officers from the local police department. From the Dartmouth side of the harbour, Bruce Brine gazes out over the waters that flow by Halifax. The former superintendent of the local ports police is still shattered from his firing and nervous breakdown in 1995. He has spent most of the subsequent eight years trying to win back his reputation. After the RCMP refused his request for a criminal investigation, Brine appealed to the force's Public Complaints Commission, arguing that the investigators had never contacted key witnesses in the case. He has also filed a complaint against the ports in front of the Canadian Human Rights Commission.

"We were doing good work; I was honest," he says, a thin film of water forming in his eyes. "They took my life, they took my badge, my livelihood, my credibility."

All he wants is a letter of apology and his ports police shield back—Badge 131—so he can retire with honour.

PART V

HELL TO PAY

SEVENTEEN

Mega-Headaches

———

"I am a woman of conviction. I don't play."
CROWN PROSECUTOR FRANCE CHARBONNEAU

By the spring of 2002, Maurice "Mom" Boucher had been isolated for eighteen months within the concrete walls of Tanguay women's prison awaiting his murder trial. Guards watched as Boucher spent most of the day nervously pacing round and round his cell. He refused to eat most of the prison food, prepared by female prisoners, fearing it was contaminated. Instead he ate candy bars and put on about twenty pounds. He had had no contact with his Hells Angels brothers and could only watch as police rounded up his fellow gang members—including his son Francis—in Operation Springtime 2001. But Mom had beaten the murder rap once, and he knew that the government was going to trot out the same tired and discredited stool pigeon, Stéphane Gagné. Mom had seen this movie before and the bad guys had won; surely they would win again.

But anybody who thought Maurice Boucher's second trial would be a carbon copy of the first didn't know France Charbonneau.

Montreal's courthouse is a modern rectangular monolith of granite and tinted glass that towers over the old city. Lawyers and clients congregate in whispering groups in poorly lit corridors and in small, closet-size rooms next to the courtroom entrances. This is the marketplace where lawyers haggle over pleas. The commodity is a guilty plea. The currency is jail time. About 85 percent of all cases are plea bargained. But there would be no deal for Maurice Boucher.

"The courtroom is my living room," says Crown prosecutor France Charbonneau. "It's my home." As both Mr. Justice Pierre Beliveau and defence lawyer Jacques Larochelle were soon to find out, nobody was going to push her around in her own home. No bikers would be allowed to enter the windowless courtroom, as they had in the first trial, to intimidate the jury. She got the court to bar anybody sporting a logo. You couldn't even get in with a Lacoste golf shirt unless you removed the alligator. No logos, no insignia. No knuckle-busting Hells Angels rings or tattooed arms. Not in her living room.

To further protect jurors from intimidation, she had carpenters construct a wall of frosted glass blocking the audience's view of the jury. She knew journalists would protest if she did otherwise, so she made sure the press could see the jurors from their designated seats. The result was that only a few bikers showed up. And even then, they didn't stay long. Boucher, erect and watchful in the prisoner's box, was on his own.

Gone too was the polite atmosphere that pervaded the first trial. Charbonneau had no intention of showing deference either to the judge or to the defence. Her job was to prosecute a man she regarded as a killer. She wanted to create an atmosphere that reflected the seriousness of her mission. There would be no familiarity, no tension-breaking jokes or easygoing banter. There would be no calling Boucher "Mom." He was to be Mr. Boucher or Maurice Boucher. This was war and there would be no prisoners. "I am a woman of conviction," she says. "I don't play."

While Charbonneau's main target was Maurice Boucher, she also had Larochelle in her sights. Charbonneau had studied him throughout the first trial and was not impressed. She put him in the same category as the lawyers who used to order her to get coffee when she worked as a legal secretary. They gave her the confidence to go to law school in the first place; she figured she could do better than these *grands seigneurs*. Now, twenty-three years and eighty murder trials later (with only one loss), Charbonneau decided to tear away the credibility of Larochelle. Not just put Boucher on trial. Put his lawyer on trial too. Charbonneau planned to watch Larochelle like a hawk. She was certain he'd blow it somewhere along the line. She just wanted to make sure she caught the moment.

The last jury had believed Larochelle when he portrayed star witness Gagné as untrustworthy. Charbonneau therefore ordered the police to re-examine all the evidence. She hoped they would find additional proof to corroborate Stéphane Gagné's testimony. They pored over wiretap transcripts and viewed hours and hours of surveillance tape. What they found was both rewarding and disturbing. Police investigators had failed to fully analyze photographs, videotapes of Hells Angels rallies, wiretap transcripts, phone records and surveillance reports. Because investigators rely on civilian analysts to log tapes, they found the civilians had overlooked important evidence.

They discovered, for instance, that sections of Gagné's testimony were confirmed on surveillance videotape. Gagné had testified that he was with Boucher and Tousignant on December 5, 1997, when they drove to Sorel for the twentieth-anniversary celebrations of the Quebec

Hells Angels. Investigators dug up a police video showing the three men arriving in Boucher's Dodge Ram and making faces at the cops, exactly as Gagné had described. They also found a video showing Boucher and Gagné leaving the Sorel bunker in Boucher's SUV, just as Gagné had testified.

Unlike the first trial, Charbonneau succeeded in getting tapes of two telephone conversations between Boucher and his friend Daniel Foster into the court record. Foster was the car dealer who Gagné said supplied the surveillance and getaway cars used in the guards' murders. The tapes showed that on June 4 and June 27, 1997, police picked up two telephone calls. In one, Foster says he's in the process of buying the cars. In another, he carefully suggest he and Mom get together to "calculate the cost of the cars you bought this month." Charbonneau had confirmation that Foster regularly supplied Boucher with used cars, just as Gagné had claimed.

The tapes also supported Gagné's description of the Hells hierarchy and proved his close association with Boucher. Nobody had bothered to check the tapes for confirmation of that. Now, for the first time, Charbonneau had them in hand. But that wasn't all.

Perhaps most important, Charbonneau also had a new witness who further confirmed Gagné's story. Police had picked up Serge Boutin, the Hells drug lord in downtown Montreal. As Boutin later told Charbonneau, he didn't mind being charged for drugs; that was part of the business. But now he was charged with the murder of police informant Claude Des Serres in February 2000 in a Laurentians chalet. Facing twenty-five years in prison, Boutin agreed to plead guilty to a charge of manslaughter with a seven-year sentence in return for his testimony. Charbonneau would use him to confirm much of what Gagné said about the Hells hierarchy and Boucher's position at the top. He would also testify that Paul Fontaine had gone into hiding after Gagné's arrest. Charbonneau hoped to show that two of Boucher's closest biker associates—Fontaine and Toots Tousignant, both of whom were involved in the guards' murders—disappeared after Gagné became a *délateur*. A jury would find that curious.

One important witness, however, refused to testify. Nancy Dubé, the furniture store clerk who had seen Gagné burn the getaway car after the Rondeau murder, had had a sudden change of heart. It happened one day when Mom Boucher walked into her store. He circled round her, eyeing her like a wolf. Then he left. "She almost died of fright," Charbonneau later said as she explained Dubé's absence to the judge.

Charbonneau also failed to get into the record an attempt to bribe her key witness, Stéphane Gagné. Gagné signed an affidavit stating that before the trial a lawyer secretly offered him $1 million to be paid to his family if he refused to testify against Mom Boucher. This is partially confirmed by one of Kane's reports. He noted on May 9, 2000, two years before Boucher's second trial, that Robitaille had confided to him that the Hells had "bought off" Gagné and he was back on side. According to Kane, Robitaille told him that even if Gagné were to change his mind and disclose the bribery to the court, it would be good for the Hells because it would destroy Gagné's credibility. Gagné, however, immediately informed police about the bribery attempt and signed an affidavit naming the lawyer. Judge Beliveau ordered Gagné's affidavit sealed, and the jury was never told about it. Nor was the lawyer ever charged because it was basically Gagné's word against his.

Trial opened on March 26, 2002, amid tight security. Charbonneau, who had received death threats and was named on a hit list that police found in a Hells bunker, had twenty-four-hour police protection. Police set up surveillance cameras around her house and wired her windows. Every day during the trial, they chauffeured her in a convoy to and from the courthouse; the stress would eventually take its toll—not during the trial but afterwards.

Throughout the trial Boucher remained impassive, rarely speaking to his lawyer. Other than the odd smile directed at a police officer testifying against him, he revealed almost no emotion.

The trial did not go smoothly. It was four weeks of acid and vinegar. Charbonneau fought for every inch she gained; Larochelle tried to rally, but it was clear he was uncomfortable with the Crown's aggression. Charbonneau even turned on Judge Beliveau, upbraiding him for smiling. "You find this funny," she barked at one point. But she was all over Larochelle. Not a sarcastic gesture or comment went unpunished. If he sighed or shrugged, oohed or aahed as he cross-examined Gagné, she repeatedly objected to his sarcasm. Her unrelenting watchfulness seemed to jar his usual poise. He became loud, forgivable for a defence lawyer but also careless. That's when her strategy paid off and she enjoyed her finest triumph.

Larochelle had been battering Gagné for days, trying to show that his original confession differed markedly from his testimony. Gagné had agreed that he hadn't told Sergeant Pigeon the whole story the morning of his interrogation. But he said he had not slept for more than twenty-five hours; he was exhausted and not thinking straight.

"I've seen the video." Larochelle was almost triumphant. "And you don't look tired."

Charbonneau couldn't believe her ears. It was as if Larochelle had just shot himself not in the foot but in the head. Anyone who had seen the video would have known that Gagné looked completely exhausted. So what was Larochelle thinking? Had he not seen the video? A loud thud suddenly filled the courtroom as she slammed the palm of her hand on a pile of papers. "Let's see the video." All eyes turned to Larochelle. He was clearly shaken. But there was nothing he could do. The video was brought in, and there was Gagné almost falling asleep in his chair.

Larochelle's credibility had taken a severe blow, and for the rest of the trial Charbonneau feasted on his mistake. During her final arguments to the jury, she mercilessly accused him of attempting to distort the truth: "If I had not vigorously objected—an objection which my colleague so delicately described as a fit of hysterics—if I had not insisted that you see the video for yourselves, wouldn't you have been convinced, as Mr. Larochelle had wanted, that Gagné lied when he said he was tired? Was that the search for truth, the search for a just and fair trial?"

Despite valiant efforts to convince the jury that Gagné was a liar trying to save his skin, the credibility of Boucher's aristocratic lawyer seemed to be the main issue.

The jury began deliberations April 25. They were out for eleven days, three of which they spent reviewing tapes of the final arguments. But by the ninth day they told the judge they were deadlocked. Beliveau told them to keep trying. Eleven jurors had made up their minds; one held out—apparently confused about the concept of reasonable doubt. Beliveau explained the legal meaning, and two days later the jury announced it had reached a verdict.

Just before noon on Sunday, May 5, 2002—fifteen years almost to the day after Mom had become a Hells Angel—the jury pronounced Maurice Boucher guilty on all three counts, two for the murders of Diane Lavigne and Pierre Rondeau and one for the attempted murder of Robert Corriveau. Boucher remained motionless save for a slight pursing of his lips.

Charbonneau couldn't hold back her delight. Smiling broadly, she congratulated her partner Yves Paradis. She looked for Larochelle. He had gone. At the end of the first trial, Charbonneau and her fellow prosecutor Jacques Dagenais had shaken hands with a victorious Larochelle. Two years later, a defeated Larochelle did not return the compliment.

Diane Lavigne's sister, Hélène, who had been in court almost every day, cried and leaned her head on the shoulder of a police investigator. She always carried mementos of her sister—an earring, a medal and the card from the funeral home. "I talked to her. I told her, 'You have to do something,' but I was still scared," she told reporters. "At least justice was served." Léon, Lavigne's father, who was too ill to attend the trial but showed up for the sentencing, was more blunt: "I really want to thank the jury," he said. "They really must have balls to decide something like that."

Hélène Brunet, the waitress who had taken four bullets when the bikers decided to use her as a human shield, said the jury gave her hope that justice would be done for the other innocent victims in the biker war.

In his jail cell in Ste-Anne-des-Plaines, Stéphane Gagné heard the news on TV. "I shouted, 'Yes!' and went to the prison yard to work out and get some sunshine," he told Michel Auger of the *Journal de Montréal*. That night he celebrated his triumph over his former boss by drinking a Pepsi and watching the hockey game on TV.

Commander André Bouchard was on the golf course getting ready to tee off when his pager rang. It was a 911. "What the fuck, 911!" he complained. A scratch golfer with a four handicap, he didn't like being disturbed, and a 911 usually meant the end of his game. He called in and was immediately transferred to the offices of the prosecution.

"What?" Bouchard was impatient.

"Guilty," said the voice at the end of the line. It was one of his detectives. "Guilty on everything. They nailed him."

"Give me France."

Bouchard congratulated the prosecutor. "She was crying on the phone," he recalls. "They had a party at her house. We were all invited to go down and have champagne." The police commander who had spent three decades fighting the bikers—and the last decade going up against his nemesis, Mom Boucher—decided to let the lawyers celebrate on their own.

Bouchard finished his round.

The conviction of Mom Boucher in May 2002 was the Quebec Hells Angels' Stalingrad, the point at which the tide of war turned against them. The government had not only put away the highest-profile leader of the most powerful underworld crime syndicate in the country, but it had also reversed an alarming string of courtroom defeats. Now, the emboldened prosecutors turned their sights on the forty-two Hells Angels and Rockers arrested the previous year during Operation Springtime 2001.

What became known as the "mega-trials" began in April 2002 in a new $16.5-million courthouse built next to Bordeaux prison. The building has the highest security of any courthouse in Quebec. Surrounded by a chain-link fence topped with barbed wire, the bunker-like yellow-brick structure is patrolled twenty-four hours a day by security guards and equipped with the latest in security cameras and metal detectors. The building's two identical courtrooms are together the size of a regulation hockey rink. Defendants sit on elevated bleachers behind a wall of soundproof glass listening to witnesses through speakers or earphones—evoking uneasy images of the Nuremberg war crimes trials. The courtrooms are so big that each lawyer is outfitted with a microphone and a flat video screen through which he or she can watch witnesses and view evidence. It is a high-tech operation designed to ensure everything runs smoothly. What designers didn't count on, however, were the biker defence lawyers, who ground out a relentless series of rearguard actions like some desperate retreating army.

The bikers faced charges of murder, conspiracy to commit murder, drug trafficking and gangsterism. Mom Boucher was charged separately on ten additional murder charges. The trials promised to be another gruelling test of the country's first anti-gang legislation, which had been on the books since 1997. This was the challenge: how to prove that someone in a well-structured and layered gang was guilty of a crime simply because he or she was a gang member. To date, most trials under the law had been costly and cumbersome. The most famous debacle came in Manitoba, where the government built a special $3.5-million courthouse to try thirty-five members of the Manitoba Warriors gang. But the expensive facility was never used: almost all the defendants pleaded guilty to cocaine charges in exchange for the Crown dropping the anti-gang charges. "Anyone want to buy a courthouse?" the justice minister said in June 2000, only half-jokingly.

Police and prosecutors were beginning to realize that there was no magic solution. So when Quebec's first megatrial opened in the spring of 2002, there was understandable concern that the complicated proceedings in the new high-tech courthouse at the northern tip of the island of Montreal would, like the mess in Manitoba and Edmonton, turn out to be another recipe for disaster.

A trial of over forty defendants was unmanageable. So the Quebec prosecutors' attack plan was to divide the Hells Angels into groups loosely organized around their status within the Hells hierarchy and the seriousness of the crimes. The first mega-trial involved thirteen Hells Angels Nomads and Rockers charged with thirteen murders; the second featured seventeen Rockers, each charged with gangsterism, drug dealing and conspiracy to murder.

Mr. Justice Réjean Paul, a gruff man with a booming voice and a huge bushy moustache, presided over the first. Thirteen was his unlucky number. Despite valiant efforts on his part, the trial quickly became a circus.

The trial proceeded at a snail's pace as the thirteen defence lawyers seemed to tag-team every witness. Paul's efforts to speed up the proceedings often fell on deaf ears as many defence lawyers simply ignored him. By the third month, they had heard 74 witnesses—which sounds like a lot, except that there were 750 witnesses scheduled in all. At that rate, the trial would drag on for a year and a half. One visiting lawyer left the proceedings saying he was "ashamed of his profession."

The defence team comprised some veteran courtroom sappers, some of whom had had their own run-ins with the law. One had been almost disbarred when he got into a barroom brawl. Another had escaped cocaine charges. Others were related to Hells Angels members. The grittiest of them all was Réal Charbonneau. A large, rotund man with a Friar Tuck hairstyle, Charbonneau had been found guilty of obstructing justice by trying to persuade a government witness to sign a false statement in 1986. Police had armed the witness with a body pack and recorded the entire conversation. Charbonneau was nailed with an eighteen-month sentence but persuaded an appeals court to overturn the verdict and order a new trial. He then argued that because his main defence witness, a shady gang lawyer named Sidney Leithman, had been murdered (apparently by Colombian cocaine traffickers), he couldn't get a fair trial. The judge agreed and acquitted him.

Now Charbonneau was representing Hells Angel Paul "Smurf" Brisebois on two murder charges and one attempted murder—and from the start, it was trench warfare between him and Judge Paul. Charbonneau frequently interrupted the judge and ignored his orders. At one point, Paul told him his cross-examination was illegal and ordered him to sit down. Charbonneau objected and using a rudely exaggerated Québécois *joual*, he sneered: "*Aïe, chui pas fini moé là, là,*" meaning "Hey there, I ain't finished yet, okay." After five months Paul had had enough. He did what he had never done in twenty years of sitting on the bench—he threw a lawyer out and charged him with contempt of court. "I am fed up having to systematically bring him to order almost every time he opens his mouth," Paul told the court.

Charbonneau's client Brisebois sat in the prisoner's box, smiling as the battle unfolded, winking in amusement at a female friend in the audience. He realized his chances were probably better if he went on trial alone. When the judge gave him the choice between finding another lawyer, representing himself or starting afresh, Brisebois knew which door to choose. He elected to have a new trial, separate from the others. So the mega-trial of thirteen was now down to twelve.

A more serious and costly debacle was taking place down the hall in the other mega-trial involving the seventeen Rockers. Once again it all came down to one man: Judge Jean-Guy Boilard. The same judge whose erroneous instructions to the jury had scuttled Mom Boucher's first murder trial was back once more—and once more, he would wreak havoc on biker justice.

The trial got off to a rocky start when lawyers objected to the Crown's disclosure of the evidence on 177 computer disks. These included the equivalent of 693,000 pieces of paper. In addition, the Crown had 274,000 conversations caught on wiretap, 256,000 police logs and 211 surveillance videos. The defence wanted all of it on paper. Lawyers claimed the disks could be manipulated and documents hidden. The Crown argued that the disks were secure and easy to navigate. Prosecutors said it would cost millions of dollars and take months to photocopy and to organize hard-copy documents. Defence lawyers brought in a witness from Vancouver who claimed to be a computer security expert. When police investigated him they discovered he was a paving contractor who had once testified in court as an expert in asphalt. Police also discovered he had connections with the Hells Angels in British Columbia.

The defence lost their bid, but then seven defence lawyers threatened to walk out if they were not paid $1,000 a day—double the normal legal aid rate. Not to be outdone, Boilard met their expectations and more. He tripled the rate to $1,500 a day, declaring that "no work of intellectual value can be done outside of that," because the trial was "mammoth, colossal, a new species." Quebec's justice minister—astonished that a judge would simply overrule fees legislated by the government—threatened to reverse the ruling but never did.

The lawyers for the bikers were ecstatic. Many of them had never seen such a profitable pay package. The longer the trial dragged on, the more money they made. Boilard predicted the case could last eight months. At the maximum weekly pay of $9,000, the legal aid lawyers could assure themselves of at least $288,000. Legal aid lawyers in the other megatrial before Judge Paul also demanded more money and were awarded $5,500 a week, more than twice what they normally earned. Suddenly, there wasn't much incentive for a speedy trial. Both cases dragged on like wounded snails. The trial presided by Judge Paul soon took on a country club pace. Court time was about four and a half hours a day. As the summer of 2003 approached, the judge urged the prosecution to plea bargain with the Hells. He awarded the lawyers days off to play golf and seven weeks off for summer holidays.

Meanwhile, in Judge Boilard's courtroom, the mega-trial hit a mega-wall.

The die had been cast more than a year earlier on June 21, 2001, when defence lawyer Gilles Doré pleaded a two-day bail hearing before Boilard. Doré could be a fairly scrappy lawyer when he wanted to be, and back then he wanted a biker client up on seventeen murder charges to be freed. It was an outlandish request in anybody's court, but Boilard found it particularly annoying. "An insolent lawyer is rarely helpful to his client," he told Doré, eyeing him over his glasses. Boilard chastised Doré for his "bombastic and hyperbolic rhetoric," called him "impertinent" and claimed his bail hearing procedure was "completely ridiculous." Doré complained to Boilard about his abuse in a personal letter. Boilard then denounced Doré for writing a personal letter to a judge presiding in one of Doré's cases. If Boilard thought he had had the final word, though, he was wrong.

Doré wrote a lengthy complaint to the Canadian Judicial Council, the body that oversees the conduct of federally appointed judges. One year later, on July 15, 2002, three judges of the council's complaints committee wrote Boilard a letter of reprimand in which they called his remarks an "offensive and unjustified . . . personal attack on a lawyer . . . [that] has tarnished your image and undermined that of the magistrature as a whole." Although the letter carried no sanctions and simply asked Boilard to stop badmouthing lawyers, it would have devastating effects on the biker mega-trial.

A copy of the letter was leaked, and by the weekend the story of Boilard's rebuke was all over the press. On Monday, July 22, Boilard was back on the bench. But he wasn't happy. To a shell-shocked court, he announced he "no longer [had] the moral authority, and perhaps the required aptitude, to continue my role as arbitrator in this trial."

Even if Boilard was convinced that the council's letter had undermined his status in the trial, he could have asked if the defence lawyers had any objections to his staying on; if none of them spoke up they could hardly use the incident in any appeal. But Boilard chose not to proceed that way. Instead, in a huff, he announced he would take time off to consider his retirement and walked off the bench, leaving everyone in the courtroom breathless—and, a first for most biker lawyers, speechless. That afternoon he was busy mowing his lawn.

Back in court, Boilard left behind a fiasco. After fifty days of testimony, the pleadings of ten defence lawyers and four prosecutors and the assistance of three police investigators working full time, the trial simply turned to dust. The jurors had sat through 123 witnesses, examined 1,114 exhibits and viewed 56 CD-ROMs. All for nothing. Judge Pierre Beliveau, fresh from the Mom Boucher trial, was brought in to clean up Boilard's mess. But he couldn't do it. He dismissed the jury and ordered a new trial.

The radio call-in shows buzzed. The media had a field day. Montrealers—who thought they had seen everything in a decade-long biker war—couldn't decide if they should laugh or cry. The only good news, thought many, was that at least the new judge, furious at the defence lawyers, had cut their legal aid fees in half, to $750 a day.

It was not until January 2003—seven months later—that a new trial could get started. During the intervening time, six of the seventeen bikers pleaded guilty to charges of drug dealing and gangsterism and got sentences ranging from three to eleven years. A seventh biker was excused because he said he was dying from a variety of diseases including cirrhosis of the liver caused by hepatitis B, diabetes, hypertension and the after-effects of two heart attacks. Doctors predicted he wouldn't last ten months. His lawyer attempted to have the court quash the charges against him. But almost a year later, the biker appeared to have made a miraculous recovery. Police found him looking healthy and fit as he bounded into a video store to rent a movie.

Judge Boilard, meanwhile, had decided not to retire. Within a few months of quitting the trial, he was back on the bench with renewed confidence that he could perform his functions as a Quebec Superior Court magistrate—his moral authority apparently still intact.

By the start of 2003, the mega-headaches were just beginning, for both prosecutors and bikers—and not just in Quebec. In London, Ontario, the courts were already backed up dealing with the more than fifty Outlaws swept up in Project Retire in 2002. The judicial system also had to grapple with the more than sixty Bandidos in Ontario and another two dozen Bandidos in Quebec rounded up that same year.

And while the Quebec courts were still trying to digest the two mega-trials against the Hells Angels, a third marathon trial loomed—this one for the anglos. Two prominent Quebec Hells Angels—Nomads Walter "Nurget" Stadnick and David "Pup" Stockford—opted to be tried apart from their fellow Angels. The two anglophones from Ontario requested a trial in English; they were joined by a third Nomad, a bilingual francophone named Michel Rose. All three face multiple counts of conspiracy to murder, drug trafficking and belonging to a criminal organization; Stadnick and Rose also face several first-degree-murder counts.

Rose made sure he had high-powered help. He first called on a lawyer who had represented him in the 1970s—Marcel Danis, a former cabinet minister in the Mulroney government and now a vice-rector at Montreal's Concordia University. Danis appeared four times as Rose's temporary lawyer until he put Rose in touch with Toronto's Edward Greenspan.

Greenspan is one of Canada's better-known trial lawyers: his clients have included Broadway producer Garth Drabinsky; Robert Latimer, the farmer found guilty of second-degree murder for gassing his twelve-year-old daughter; and Gerald Regan, the former Nova Scotia premier who won acquittals on charges of rape. Now he had to defend a biker charged with killing several rival bikers and murdering an innocent man who had the unfortunate luck to have the same first name as a Hells target. Greenspan vowed he would fight all the way to the Supreme Court to keep his client from being tried in the mega-trial courtroom, where a glass partition separated defendants from their lawyers. "This is fundamentally intolerable in a free and democratic society," Greenspan said. "I can't talk to my client except through glass."

Meanwhile, Stadnick and Stockford were not about to skimp on their legal arsenal either. They recruited Alan D. Gold of Toronto, the former president of the Criminal Lawyers Association and no stranger to the biker judicial wars. In December 2000, he had helped draft Mom Boucher's ultimately unsuccessful bid to the Supreme Court of Canada to reverse the Quebec Court of Appeal's quashing of his first acquittal for the murder of the prison guards. In 2002, Gold flew to Winnipeg to go to bat for several Angels charged in shootings and beatings.

Gold and Greenspan began an aggressive defence from the start. They demanded that the massive pile of evidence— more than 500,000 pages and ten CD-ROMs—be translated into English, a task the government estimated could cost as much as $23 million. Greenspan, professing to be computer illiterate, also requested that the CD-ROM material be printed out. The Quebec courts said no; both lawyers sought leave to appeal to the Supreme Court of Canada.

But in January 2003 the country's top court refused to hear their appeal, giving no reasons, as is the custom, for its refusal. So it was back to Montreal for the setting of trial dates. Going up against the legal heavyweights Greenspan and Gold—who between them have six decades of courtroom battles—is a relative newcomer. Crown prosecutor Randall Richmond is a slight, soft-spoken man who looks more like an accountant than a courtroom brawler—which perhaps is appropriate, given his expertise in money laundering and commercial crime. There is such an age difference between the Crown and the defence that when Richmond was still in law school twenty years previously he remembers admiring Greenspan, who back then was already "the foremost defence lawyer in the country." Still, Richmond is no neophyte and was not chosen for this job simply because he's one of the few fluently English-speaking provincial Crown attorneys. He's also the deputy chief prosecutor for organized crime in the province and has a number of successful biker prosecutions under his belt. He insists he is not intimidated by his "definitively impressive adversaries." On the contrary, he says he's thrilled at the chance to take them on.

Walter Stadnick, the man who two decades earlier had the vision to build the most profitable criminal network in the history of outlaw biker gangs, had throughout this period avoided prison with the help of high-priced lawyers and old-fashioned luck. But he had never before faced such serious charges. Nor had he ever faced the grim determination of the quietly plodding and grindingly meticulous Randal Richmond.

At least in public, though, the Nomad veteran was not nervous. He had told his arresting officers, calmly but confidently, that he would not stay in jail very long this time either.

EIGHTEEN

Between Heaven and Hell

———

"The bikers are law enforcement's collective failure.
In the seventies they were street thugs, disorganized crime.
We have watched them grow into multinational organizations.
There was a time and a day when they were not as organized
and we just watched them grow."
RCMP SUPERINTENDENT GARRY CLEMENT,
PROCEEDS OF CRIME

The carnival atmosphere of Niagara Falls, Canada's capital of make-believe, novelty shops, wax museums and pink honeymoon suites, was the perfect place for the Hells Angels 2002 Canada Run.

The Hells Angels had eighty of their Quebec members facing multiple murder, gangsterism and/or drug charges, more than half of their Manitoba chapter were in court or behind bars, three B.C. members were dead or missing and two others busted for coke, the Halifax chapter was teetering on collapse because of arrests for trafficking and murder—but, heh, the Angels had come to party. It was pure fairyland.

The annual Hells Angels Canada Run—previous rides had rolled into Halifax, Edmonton and Winnipeg—was a sort of yearly mating ritual between the bikers and the police. The bikers don their colours, the police theirs. The police try to show the public their tax dollars at work; the bikers try to convince the taxpayers that it's all a waste of their hard-earned money.

Some serious business does get done. Usually, executive meetings are held on the first day of these biker conventions. Representatives from each of the Angels chapters across Canada sit down for a meeting—a sort of war council. For the police, it's an all too rare chance for biker cops from across the country to meet in person and exchange intelligence. For the beleaguered Angels, it's a chance to score some much-needed PR points.

"The purpose of our Canada Run is recreational and speaks to the main purpose of the Hells Angels, which is to socialize and enjoy our motorcycles," Donny Petersen, the Angels' public spokesperson in Ontario, wrote in a statement to a local paper.

Climb on our make-believe carousel, Petersen seemed to be saying, and see where it takes you.

With their bulky bulletproof vests and thick, heavy boots, the men in blue filed out of the Legion Hall, looking more like an army battalion than police officers. Walkie-talkies, pagers and cameras dangled from belts, almost but not quite obscuring their guns.

It was noon on Tuesday, July 23, just hours before the main biker contingents were to hit town. The police had commandeered the Legion Hall as their command centre. Don Bell surveyed his men from the BEU making last-minute preparations with their partners from the RCMP and police forces across the country. The local police were taking no chances, cancelling all holiday leave, even at the height of summer.

The Angels took over two entire Days Inns, one of them not far from the wax museum. Tourists gawked as, hour after hour, platoons of expensive Harleys rolled into the parking lot. More than a dozen cops stood watch, dutifully filming every biker. One young BEU officer scribbled down the licence plate number of every vehicle as it entered or left the parking lot. Meanwhile, from one of the first-floor corner rooms, the Hells Angels had their own spy team, snapping pictures of the police and journalists.

The atmosphere was almost friendly. Many of these bikers and biker cops know each other on a first-name basis.

"How ya doin', guys?" One biker waves as he jaunts by the officers.

"Don't look so serious—cheer up!" says another biker.

As the Harleys began filling up the parking lot, the club names on the back of the leather jackets paid tribute to the Hells' national reach and unchecked growth. The Bacchus club from Albert County, New Brunswick. The Nomads from British Columbia. The latest chapter from Toronto's Richmond Hill.

The younger, itchier prospects and hangarounds milled about on the curb. They seemed almost embarrassed by the fact that their black vests were bare—no Hells Angels patches or club names. They tried to compensate with garish tattoos and loud banter.

A handful of Quebec bikers pulled into the parking lot.

Someone taunted them about being far from home. "*Vous êtes loin de chez vous.*"

"Non," said Stéphane Trudel defiantly. "*On est chez nous.*" It's true that he was on home turf. A former Montreal biker, he was now with the Nomad chapter in Ontario.

Later that afternoon, Donny Petersen rode in wearing full leathers. When he took off his helmet, his neatly trimmed beard and cropped hair hardly ruffled.

"We have your suite ready, sir," the clerk at the front desk, almost awestruck, said politely.

Petersen dropped his gold CIBC card on the counter and thanked her. He was less cordial to a journalist.

"Naw, I have nothing to say," he declared after a polite handshake. "Every time I talk to the media, it gets twisted."

"We expect them to be on their best behaviour," Don Bell, Ontario's top biker cop, warned at a press conference. "It's just a ploy on their part; it's part of their marketing strategy. They are not motorcycle enthusiasts. They are criminals." In a direct challenge to Donny Petersen's sales pitch, Bell countered with his message: "[They say] they are here to enjoy the Niagara region and they contribute to the economy. The money they are spending is gleaned from illegal activities and we don't want that money."

But just two blocks away from where Bell was trying to woo the public, Frank Marchese, the owner of Paesano's restaurant, was busy hustling bikers strolling by his eatery. To his glee, three bikers from B.C. and then three more from Trois-Rivières ambled in for lunch.

Inside, Frank's sister Jennie and his niece Melanie kept busy serving the special guests. In stilted English, a Quebec biker—with tattoos all the way down his arms and stringy hair to his shoulders—began flirting with young Melanie, asking first for her name, then her phone number.

"What, are you crazy?" Melanie's mother retorted, wagging a finger at the biker. "She's a baby—she's sixteen!"

Everyone laughed, and the incident failed to spoil the jovial mood. "They were gentlemen," said Frank Marchese of his constant biker clientele that week. "And great tippers: 30 percent."

At the end of the four days, the Hells Angels departed quietly from the Niagara Peninsula—as quietly as the din of hundreds of Harleys can allow—leaving behind a lot of big tips and happy restaurant owners. By any calculation, they had bested the police in their PR skirmish, and the smiles on their faces showed they knew it.

Coincidentally, six thousand religious pilgrims also had happened to be in Niagara Falls that week, prompting more than one wag to quip that the town found itself between Heaven and Hell. The faithful had flocked to see

Pope John Paul II at the World Youth Day celebrations in Toronto, although that did not stop some of them from snapping pictures of themselves in front of the police and the bikers.

One visiting Catholic priest even saw the hand of divine providence in the Angels being in Ontario at the same time as the Pope. "We are in the business of saving souls. If we can't do that for everyone, then what is our ministry all about?" he told a local paper. "So maybe it is a grace [for the bikers] to be here at the same time as the Holy Father."

Except that the frail pontiff soon flew home, leaving behind only memories of his blessings from heaven. But as they roared away from the falls of Niagara, the hearty Angels made it clear they were going to keep rolling down the road to hell for a long time to come.

Niagara Falls was not the only PR coup for the Angels.

The Hells Angels have opened stores across the country that sell clothing, stickers and other material in support of the club. These authorized souvenir shops operate in Toronto, Durham, Welland and Oshawa in Ontario; in Edmonton; and in Haney, British Columbia. In Winnipeg, the bikers tried to turn a tattoo shop in the fashionable Exchange District into a support store; Darren Hunter, a full-patch member, was one of the company directors. They were blocked on a technicality, so they moved and set up River City Choppers not far from the provincial justice minister's constituency office.

The Angels also operate at least ten official Web sites—four for Ontario clubs, two for the East Coast, another couple for the West and two more in Saskatchewan. (The Quebec Hells have not taken to the Internet like their counterparts elsewhere and do not have a Web site.) There are videos and photos of HA gatherings, e-mail support pages and news bulletins. One Ontario page links to a Web site called Know Your Cops that posts pictures of biker cops. The sites also sell support clothing (all credit cards accepted) and collect money for the bikers' legal defence fund. "We are arguably within the top fifteen branded names in the world," Donny Petersen told *The Globe and Mail*. "The public recognizes our logo more than the biggest Canadian corporations.'"

"There's a big PR battle going on between us and the police, and I think we're winning," says Ernie Dew, the president of the Manitoba Angels.

The uncomfortable reality is that while the HA did not get their start in this country, they've become as Canadian as maple syrup. Police and tabloids often stigmatize criminal gangs as "the other" or "foreigners," be they Chinese triads or Jamaican street gangs. But the Angels are firmly rooted in their communities: in Quebec, with a handful of exceptions, they are uniformly francophone; in Halifax most of them are down east boys; in Manitoba and Alberta they are prairie boys.

How did the Hells Angels grow to be the strongest organized crime threat in Canada—not just in Quebec but across the country? The simplest answer is that police and politicians ignored the bikers for too long. Despite ample warnings that the Hells were determined to dominate organized crime throughout the country, nobody took action until it was too late. In Quebec, where bombs went off with the regularity of a Northern Ireland, it took the murder of an eleven-year-old boy in 1995 to prod the police into action. There was no serious crackdown until public outrage forced the government to act in the wake of the car bomb that killed Daniel Desrochers. And even then it wasn't until government ministers found their own names on a biker hit list in 1999 that their complacency vanished and the judiciary soldiered forth with grinding determination and a fistful of cash. In other provinces, it took several more years for authorities to catch on to the danger and begin to assign proper resources. But by then this once ragtag group of bikers had succeeded in building a national organized crime empire.

"In the seventies they were street thugs. We have watched them grow into multinational organizations. My own opinion is that the bikers are law enforcement's collective failure," concludes Garry Clement, the RCMP superintendent in charge of proceeds of crime.

Once politicians and police brass finally woke up to the biker danger, rivalry among police forces hampered any effective action. The squabbling came from petty jealousies, competition for scarce dollars and cop egos that can be bigger than their guns.

Only Nova Scotia and Ontario managed to escape the worst of police rivalries. Ontario had the unified BEU. In Halifax, they stuck the best biker cops together as past of the Metro Integrated Intelligence Unit. And it is just that—integrated. Inside their cramped offices on Oxford Street, the men huddle around desks and computers. You cannot tell who is a Mountie and who is a Halifax cop—and the officers don't care, either. But infighting and jealousies paralyzed Quebec's Wolverine squad for several years. In British Columbia, the OCA and the RCMP are often barely on speaking terms. In Winnipeg, tensions between the RCMP and local police have prevented the creation of any joint strike force. A two-and-a-half-year investigation with a high-level informant in one province—for security reasons, the location has to remain secret—was sabotaged when the RCMP and regional police disagreed over how to proceed. They were close to arresting no fewer than three full-patch Hells Angels members and a couple of prospects for multiple kilos of cocaine. It would have been the biggest HA bust in the province's history but instead the case was abandoned in

January 2003, leaving bad blood on both sides of the police fence and letting all the bikers slip away.

There also continues to be an absence of national police coordination in the fight against the bikers. "The bikers have a national strategy and they invoke their will. Why can't the police put their act together?" asks Sgt. Rick Lobban in Winnipeg. On paper, the "National Strategy to Combat Outlaw Motorcycle Gangs" has existed since 1996. It calls for everything from a "national vision" to the "regular exchange of information." It is supposed to be coordinated by the Criminal Intelligence Service Canada (CISC) in Ottawa, with three Mounties, including Jean-Pierre Lévesque, working full time on the bikers. But Lévesque soon found himself alone: one of his colleagues was shifted to work on East European gangs; another left and was eventually replaced by someone who in turn also left. The RCMP had more people at head office taking care of the musical ride and Mounties on horseback than criminals on motorcycles. Only by the beginning of 2003 was there hope of bringing back a full three-member team.

There is no money for what are called "Tier 3" officers—the front-line biker cops like Larry Butler in Vancouver or Steve Pacey in Hamilton—to meet more than once a year. Bikers meet more often to exchange tips and lessons than police officers do. Biker lawyers, some of whom attend biker parties and join them on motorcycle runs, constantly advise their clients on the latest police tactics and keep them abreast of relevant cases and laws. This information is then distributed throughout the HA organization. They collaborate better than the prosecutors taking on the Angels. Back in 1998, Lévesque set up what he called the Legal Advisory Workgroup (LAW), made up of the most active biker prosecutors. They began meeting about twice a year, starting with eighteen prosecutors. "They exchanged judges' decisions on wiretaps, bikers, what's new in the provinces. They started to love it—it was great." But when an official in the federal ministry of justice got wind of the fact that a police officer—a sergeant, at that—was coordinating Crown attorneys, he put a stop to it. The LAW group hasn't met since December 2000.

Police computers from different jurisdictions do not even talk to one another effectively. All police forces across the country have access to the Canadian Police Information Centre (CPIC), the country's computerized police information database. It handles over a hundred million queries annually from fifteen thousand points of access. But CPIC lists only criminal records, not intelligence files: if an Ontario police officer pulls over a biker from Alberta and punches in his name, he'll come up empty if the biker has a clean record. Even if he has a rap sheet, CPIC won't tell the officer about the biker's known criminal connections and modus operandi.

The RCMP stores its intelligence files in its own National Criminal Database. But only RCMP officers have access to it. Most other police forces put their intelligence information into a separate national system called ACIIS, for Automatic Criminal Intelligence Information System. In Quebec, they have a third database called G-11. The three systems do not communicate with one another or share information. For years, there has been discussion about setting up one central database, but so far that has not happened.

Even when police do make arrests, Canadian laws and courts do not always help. "When you get caught in Canada, you don't get jail time. If you get caught in the States, you'll rot in jail," says one RCMP drug officer. A low-level gang member in the U.S. caught trafficking even small amounts of cocaine can get ten years or more; in Canada he might face less than half that and would be out of jail after serving only a sixth of his time. What would you rather do—tough it out behind bars for a couple of years or turn in a Mom Boucher?

At the start of 2002, a new federal anti-gang law came into force. Known as C-24, it tried to improve on the 1997 anti-gang measures. For one thing, it makes it easier to prove gang membership. Instead of the old "5-5" rule that obliged the Crown to prove that no fewer than five members of a gang had been involved in criminal activities over a five-year period, the new law reduces the legal definition of a criminal organization to only three members. It also widens the target: it is now an offence for a person to be knowingly associated with a criminal organization. Even an accountant or a bodyguard could be prosecuted for doing a job for the gang that would be legitimate were it done for anyone else.

In the wake of the biker assault on the justice system, the new law also targets anyone who has intimidated police, judges, witnesses and even journalists—the attempted assassination of Michel Auger was still fresh in everyone's mind. The previous law made no distinction between a gang leader and a regular biker; the new law singles out leaders. Sentences are tougher, too. Anyone who instructs another person to break the law is liable to a sentence up to life imprisonment. But now those convicted of organized crime offences would have to serve at least half their sentence before being eligible for parole.

The new anti-gang law came into force too late to be applied in the Quebec mega-trials. So, oddly enough, its first test will come over a minor scrap over a satellite dish in Ontario. The local Hells Angels chapter in Woodbridge were not satisfied with a receiver installed at their clubhouse. Three men visited the businessman who sold them the dish. On January 31, 2002, police arrested and charged the three with extortion. Then came a surprising twist: police and prosecutors decided to up the ante by charging the three men with participating in a criminal organization, naming Steven "Tiger" Lindsay and Raymond Bonner as member of the Hells Angels. It was a gamble—pinning such a heavy charge on such a minor offence. The prosecutor will have to prove not only that Tiger and his fellow Angel are guilty of uttering threats and extortion but that they did so as members of a criminal gang. In effect, he will be putting the Hells Angels on trial. The defence, meanwhile, will try to put the new anti-gang law on trial.

Even with the best of laws, the more sophisticated HA crimes, such as their highly successful money-laundering schemes, have gone largely untouched. A lot of biker money is used in loansharking, a common method to clean up money. Dany Kane talked about Mom Boucher having $10 million on the street. Loansharking is intimately tied to gambling and casinos. Casinos, with huge cashflows and quick turnovers of money, are one of the easiest places for criminals to launder their bounty, a sad irony considering many casinos are government-owned. Canada has long been ridiculed as an embarrassingly easy place to launder money thanks to lax rules and anemic enforcement. "For years we were one of the weak links in the chain," admits Superintendent Garry Clement, the RCMP's top man in charge of Proceeds of Crime. "We just didn't have the systems in place."

By the middle of 2002, Canada finally had in place FIN-TRAC—a new federal agency mandated to track money laundering. Analyzing millions of bank transactions, FIN-TRAC is supposed to pass on what are called Suspicious Transactions Reports to the RCMP. But so far only a handful have crossed the desk of the Mounties.

What's worse, privacy concerns forbid the police to access FINTRAC's database. In other words, if a police officer knows a Vancouver biker and drug importer is making regular trips to an offshore bank, he cannot request to see that biker's financial records. On the other hand, a Mountie can directly access the American database, known as FINCEN. A Canadian police officer can spy on what a Canadian money launderer is doing with his money in the States, but what that same Canadian biker is doing with his money here is out of bounds.

Indeed, there have been few investigations specifically aimed at the money-laundering operations of the Angels. The immense wealth of the biker gangs remains out of reach. And that means even when bikers go to jail, they know when they come out, their money and their resources are there for them to pick up where they left off. "The arrest of Mom Boucher was a great coup, and law enforcement in Quebec should be very proud of that," says Clement. "But what did we take down financially? How did we hurt that infrastructure? And that's really what's going to thrive for years to come."

The final reason for the bikers' enduring strength in Canada is that the Angels themselves have ensured they are not an easy target—even by organized crime standards. Organized crime, because it is sophisticated and layered, is difficult to penetrate and prosecute. The Hells Angels offer a special challenge because there are long lineups of young recruits—loyal and disciplined—willing to take up the colours. There is no godfather, no single boss whose elimination would bring down the empire. The HA are more like McDonald's: close down one franchise and the others can still flourish.

The Angels have the best of both worlds: a national and international network for cooperation, without the entanglement of a top-down pyramid structure. The Angels chapters are like terrorist cells that could teach Al Qaeda a few lessons about insulation and protection. Police in Vancouver could arrest the leaders and half the members of the Nanaimo chapter, and it would scarcely put a dent in the operation of the others. Even in Quebec, where their ranks have been decimated, two senior Hells quickly filled the breach left by Mom and his Nomads and are rebuilding the organization.

That means each cell has to be penetrated and destroyed—and the only way to do that is with informants. They can be small-scale snitches caught in a squeeze like Robert Molsberry in Vancouver or Robert Coquete in Winnipeg or big-time squealers like Stéphane Gagné, who ultimately brought down Mom Boucher for the murder of the two prison guards. Or, better still, they are agents, like Dany Kane or the as yet unnamed infiltrator of the Outlaws in Ontario, who burrow to the top of a biker gang and feed the police with a constant stream of information.

But without an inside spy—before or after the fact—it is virtually impossible to take down as secretive and disciplined a group as the Hells Angels. Yet good, reliable, well-placed informants are hard to find—and when one of them, like Dany Kane, comes calling, the arrangement is just as likely to blow up in your face.

"These are long, expensive files. It takes money and it takes will—the commitment to stick with these files," Andy Richards, of B.C.'s Organized Crime Agency, explains.

Yet with few exceptions, that commitment has rarely been there.

The Hells Angels are a bundle of contradictions. They control much of the country's cocaine trade but will expel members for abusing drugs. They profess to be anti-authoritarian rebels but enforce some of the strictest, most restrictive club rules of any organization. They openly wear their gang colours and yet run one of the most secretive underground empires.

That makes speculating on their future a perilous venture. "Predictions? They're not hard—they're impossible," says Andy Stewart, after several years with Ontario's BEU. Few people, for example, could have predicted how quickly they expanded in Ontario after the patch-over of 2000, or how quickly they collapsed in Quebec after Operation Springtime 2001.

Given their independent, cellular structure, the Angels are weakest now where they had only one cell or chapter and the police hit hard—notably Halifax and Winnipeg.

The most troubled HA operation in the country is Halifax. In April 2001, police arrested full-patch member Neil Smith and three other men on first-degree murder charges. Sean Simmons—not unlike a few biker pals—had worked down at the port as a checker; he was a small-time drug dealer who at one point had wanted to join the Angels but ran afoul of his heroes. According to later court testimony by a police informant, Simmons was killed in part because he had slept with a mistress of chapter president Mike McCrea.

Then, on December 5, 2001, the Halifax Hells got an early wake-up call. More than two hundred Mounties and regional police officers swept down on their clubhouse and numerous homes as a climax to a ten-month investigation dubbed "Operation Hammer." They arrested three full-patch members on drug charges—Mike McCrea's brother, Clay, Art Harrie and Jeff Lynds. The hammer came down with full force on January 29, 2003. Clay McCrea and Harrie got six years each for trafficking, after pleading guilty to selling two hundred grams of cocaine to an undercover agent. Lynds got three years for offering to sell a thousand tablets of ecstasy. The judge also banned them from possessing firearms for life.

And then, as a further slap in the face to the bikers, the judge accepted the Crown's request to seize the Dutch Village Road clubhouse, in effect making Ottawa the proud owner of a somewhat used Hells Angels hangout.

In August of 2003, Angel Neil Smith was found guilty of the first-degree murder of Sean Simmons, the man gunned down in a Dartmouth apartment three years earlier. He got life in prison and joined three other full-patch members in jail on other charges. So the Halifax club had only three members left standing, and for the fourth time since its creation, the Halifax chapter's official status was in peril.

McCrea was forced to resign as world secretary; he rarely makes himself as available to the media as he once did and is currently taking computer courses full time. "He has too many things to worry about; he's barely keeping above water," says the RCMP's national biker watcher, Jean-Pierre Lévesque.

On the run, hiding somewhere and watching his empire collapse from a distance, David "Wolf" Carroll has got to be dispirited. All the plots he orchestrated have come to naught, and his once-proud Angels are in disarray in his East Coast kingdom.

Manitoba has also been initially shaken by the jailing of several of its members and prospects: By the start of 2003, three full-patch Manitoba Angels were in prison or facing charges. Five associates —Ian Grant, Sean Wolfe, Ralph Moar, Harold Amos and Dale Donovan— were also facing three dozen charges, including membership in a criminal gang, the Zig Zags. Still, Ernie Dew and the rest of the biker veterans have shown determination. They eventually promoted Donovan, Grant and Billy Bowden to full-patch status, bringing their membership up to thirteen.

In the two other prairie provinces, the bikers have five chapters flourishing, two in Saskatchewan and three in Alberta—in Edmonton, Calgary and Red Deer. Alberta, though, ran into trouble when a drug bust nabbed about half of their Calgary chapter in March 2001. In November 2002, two Hells Angels bikers from Edmonton were charged with the first-degree murder of a former Medicine Hat nightclub bouncer.

The Hells Angels remain the strongest in B.C. and Ontario, and it is likely that the pillars of their organization will remain—and grow—in these two key provinces. In B.C., they have the money; in Ontario, they have the numbers.

"They're a powerful group and still in expansion mode," says Larry Butler of the Vancouver police department's biker unit. Already bursting with fifteen full-time members, seven prospects and three hangarounds, the East End chapter is fast-tracking a new chapter in Kelowna. They have set up a satellite club in that upper-crust city in B.C.'s interior, with six prospects, led by East End member Guy Stanley, who lives there. With the Kelowna boys as full patch members, the number of chapters in B.C. would rise to eight and mark the first time the bikers' geographic grip has extended beyond the Lower Mainland and Vancouver Island.

Ontario, for its part, can boast about 260 Hells Angels members, prospects and hangarounds—about half of the total HA forces in Canada. To the original eleven chapters and the Nomads that emerged after the instant patch-over of 2000, the Angels steadily added new chapters: North Toronto in February of 2001; Niagara Falls in July of that year; Sudbury in September 2002; and, most recently, London in July of 2003. One of the original chapters in Richmond Hill dissolved, its members going to other chapters. That left the Angels with an impressive fifteen chapters in Canada's largest province. As of mid-2003, fewer than a dozen Ontario Angels were behind bars.

Given that Ontario is Canada's richest province—and the richest drug market—there is little doubt that the balance of power within the Hells Angels will shift here over the coming period. Quebec chapters sponsored and mentored the Ontario bikers, but the arrest or flight of English-speaking Nomads like Walter Stadnick, Pup Stockford and Wolf

Carroll weakened Quebec's grip considerably. "I think their influence is eroding by the week," says Toronto biker cop George Coussens. "The Ontario guys are snubbing them."

The Quebec Angels, meanwhile, are down but not out. For all the noise and publicity, the Operation Springtime 2001 sweep saw the arrest of more than 120 bikers—but fewer than 60 of them were full-patch members of the Angels and their puppet groups. That left about 70 full-fledged Angels and dozens of supporters still free to do business. "We didn't finish them off, but we set them back years," says the RCMP's Tom O'Neill. The decapitation of the Nomads left the biggest drug market—Montreal—a wide-open battlefield. Three chapters surrounding the city—St-Basile-le-Grand, Sorel and Sherbrooke—are trying to make sure the Angels don't lose too much ground to the Mafia and other gangs. Sherbrooke, historically one of the power centres along with Mom Boucher's Nomads, remains a force to be reckoned with.

Benoît Roberge of the Montreal city police predicts that the Quebec Angels will restructure quietly and remain low-profile. "I think the majority of the Hells will say that the Nomads went too far—especially in attacking the judicial system," he says. "There's a difference between business and terrorism; in the short term [what Mom did] seems really tough, but in the long term it's not good for business."

Mom Boucher is not finding life behind bars easy. As of May 2002, Boucher's new home was the federal maximum-security prison in Ste-Anne-des-Plaines, north of Montreal. His first few weeks were relaxing enough: he played volleyball and on June 25 he even got some career counselling—though it was not entirely clear what advice the prison system would give to an unemployed Nomad leader who will not see the other side of the penitentiary gates until he is seventy-three years old. Like most prisons in Quebec, the Ste-Anne complex is divided into biker wings: E block for the Hells, F block for their Rock Machine enemies and D block for everyone else. As long as he was with his entourage, Mom was safe and could play at being king, albeit a deposed one.

But over the summer, prison authorities transferred Boucher to the Special Handling Unit (SHU) within the prison, where his neighbours would include Clifford Olson, the serial child-killer from British Columbia, and Allan Légère, dubbed the Monster of the Miramichi for four murders in New Brunswick. No other bikers were there; Boucher found himself alone and exposed. Once the most feared man in Quebec, Boucher himself was now nervous. He glances anxiously down both sides of his cell-block before venturing out.

Boucher, the man who once ordered killings at will, had good reason to be jittery. On August 13, 2002, an inmate from Saskatchewan attacked him with a knife. Six other inmates came to Boucher's aid, beating his assailant and stabbing him with his own weapon. Less than a month later, there was another attempt on the biker kingpin's life.

In early September, Boucher was waiting for his lunch. The inmate making the deliveries of the trays through an opening in Boucher's cell took out a homemade gun: the tube of the zip gun was the kind of roll found in paper towels; the detonator and "bullet" came from parts of a television set.

Surprised by the attack, Boucher fell on his rear—not the most dignified position for a Hells Angel crime lord. He quickly scrambled to stand up and smile, hoping to save some face. Indeed, only his pride was hurt.

There was much speculation about the attacks. Press leaks indicated that the first man was a Native from Saskatchewan, the second a friend of his who was involved with the Indian Posse, one of the Native street gangs. It was possible Boucher was the victim of gang warfare and reprisals. Over the summer, there had been growing tension in the Stoney Mountain Penitentiary in Manitoba. A member of the Zig Zags, the Hells Angels' enforcers, threw a Native gang member down a flight of stairs; an Indian Posse inmate retaliated by stabbing an Angels supporter. The Native gangs certainly had the prison network and the bravado to take on the former Nomad leader.

Still, the assaults showed how far Mom had fallen. Unlike a Mafia don who could still run his empire from behind bars, Boucher had few friends and little family to call upon on the outside. Though he undoubtedly has a fortune in drug profits stashed away somewhere, his power has waned considerably—at least for the time being.

Several other prominent Hells Angels are still at large— most notably Mom's fellow Nomad Wolf Carroll. In Vancouver, the murders of Angels Donny Roming and Ernie Ozolins remain unsolved. In Winnipeg, police still have at least three unsolved biker-related murders and one disappearance on the books.

Aimé Simard, the killer who turned informer against Dany Kane and other bikers, was serving a life sentence for three counts of second-degree murder. But he was finding life behind bars, well, hell. Shunned by other inmates as a squealer, he tried to commit suicide by swallowing pills and slashing his wrists. "I feel hunted," he told Montreal's *La Presse* newspaper. The hunt ended on Friday, July 18, 2003. Simard was found dead in his cell at the Saskatchewan Penitentiary in Prince Albert, reportedly stabbed 106 times. One of the five suspects was a biker associate, sparking a wave of panic among other informants, especially Stéphane Gagné, who had dared to cross the Angels.

After her exhausting and stressful victory over Mom Boucher, Crown prosecutor France Charbonneau did not take on any new trials for the next year and a half. In February 2004, she was appointed as a Quebec Superior Court judge. André Bouchard, the Montreal police commander, is approaching retirement and trying to give up smoking. Tom O'Neill, the RCMP sergeant who coordinated the Operation Springtime 2001 arrests, transferred out of the Wolverine squad and now heads a terrorism unit for the RCMP in Montreal. In Winnipeg, Ray Parry got promoted to full sergeant and followed his veteran partner Rick Lobban out of the anti-gang unit. Most of the other biker cops across the country are staying put—for the moment.

"Nobody really comes banging down your door to say what a great job you did," says one. "I liken it to being a janitor: nobody really knows how dirty it was before you got there—they just see the dirt you missed. They have no idea what it would have been like if you weren't there."

For many ordinary citizens, there are still many dirty spots to clean up. Hélène Brunet, the Montreal waitress used by one biker as a human shield in a shootout, is still speaking out against biker violence. She got in touch with the mother of Daniel Desrochers, the eleven-year-old whose death in a biker car bombing sparked the first wave of public outrage, and the mother of Francis Laforest, the bar owner clubbed to death for standing up to the bikers. Together, they have spoken at media events and meetings.

One tabloid dubbed them the "Elles Angels."

Long after Kane's suicide in a garage in August 2000, his ghost still haunts the biker world. It haunts the corridors of prisons, where Mom Boucher and dozens of his followers languish behind bars because of the secrets he told. It haunts the corridors of court houses where lawyers and judges are still hearing cases and appeals sparked by his spying.

Kane's ghost haunts the police and the bikers, because everyone in this deadly game knows he is out there. Across the country—on the docks of Vancouver, in the strip bars of Winnipeg, in the casinos of Niagara Falls, on the streets of Montreal and in the back alleys of Halifax—they're all looking for him.

The police are trying to find him, recruit him, groom him and send him back in to infect and destroy.

The bikers are trying to spot him first and crush him like a virus.

Everyone is hunting for the next Dany Kane.

and it would have to begin again from scratch. He urged a settlement. Finally, almost a year after their mega-trial had begun, the deal was struck.

When it was over, however, the police officers in the court showed only a hint of a smile. They knew the sentences were flimsy. As leaders of the Hells Angels, four Nomads—Normand Robitaille, thirty-five, René Charlebois, thirty-eight, Gilles Mathieu, fifty-three, and Denis Houle, fifty—got the stiffest sentences: twenty years for drug trafficking, gangsterism and conspiracy to commit murder. But with the two-and-a-half years they had already served counting for double time and Canada's lenient parole laws, the four could be out on the street again in only seven-and-a-half years. The five other guilty men, all Rockers, got fifteen years. They could be out in three.

The Crown refused to settle with three of the original accused—Rocker Gregory Wooley and Nomad prospects Jean-Richard Larivière and Pierre Laurin—against whom they had direct evidence of murder, including fingerprints and DNA. Laurin eventually got a life sentence for conspiracy to commit murder, drug trafficking and gangsterism, but will be able to apply for parole after serving ten years behind bars. Wooley's trial ended in a hung jury and Larivière is awaiting the outcome of his trial.

Almost six months later, on March 1, 2004, Quebec's other mega-trial—against three Hells Angels and six Rockers—reached a landmark conclusion. This was the first time a mega-trial had gone all the way to a jury verdict and thus it was the first real test of the anti-gang law. "I look at people who get up at seven, are stuck in traffic, work for ten bucks an hour, then come back at night. They are the fools," one of the accused had once said dismissively. But the jurors found the nine bikers guilty of gangsterism and drug trafficking; eight of them were also convicted of conspiracy to commit murder. They face life in prison.

That same day, across town in another courtroom, two Nomads from Ontario—Walter Stadnick and his pal Donald Stockford—began their trial. A third English-speaking Nomad who was to be tried with them, Michel Rose, had pleaded guilty to conspiracy to traffic drugs, conspiracy to commit murder and gangsterism. He was sentenced to twenty-two years in prison. But Stadnick and Stockford opted for "no deal," instead to take their chances with a trial before a judge alone. It was the wrong decision.

When proceedings first began, Stadnick walked into the courtroom handcuffed and humbled. For years as a biker kingpin he never had to worry over as much as a parking ticket. Now he was facing twenty-three counts of murder, conspiracy to commit murder, drug trafficking and gangsterism. And on June 23, 2004, Superior Court Judge Jerry Zigman convicted Stadnick and Stockford, his long-time lieutenant, of everything but the first-degree murder charges. Judge Jerry Zigman sentenced each man to 20 years in prison plus $100,000 in fines. If the bikers didn't pay up within two years, another 18 months would be added on to their jail time. It was a far cry from the $2-million in fines Crown Prosecutor Randal Richmond had requested. Still, it was clear the new anti-gang laws had won again.

Meanwhile, Stadnick's high-ranking colleague Maurice "Mom" Boucher is appealing his conviction for the murder of the two prison guards. Boucher also is awaiting trial for thirteen outstanding murder charges. But if the former biker leader was hoping to get some help from his trusted lawyer Benoît Cliche, he was out of luck.

Just two days after he had appeared in court defending the Nomad leader in early November, Cliche himself was arrested as part of a roundup of thirty-one people associated with the Hells. Cliche was the hapless biker lawyer whose failure to return Stéphane Gagné's frantic calls after his arrest helped turn the assassin into a stoolie for the cops.

Police charged Cliche with gangsterism, trafficking cocaine and conspiracy to traffic cocaine, alleging he helped Hells associate Steve Bertrand, thirty-seven, to move large quantities of cocaine while Bertrand was behind bars at the federal job-training penitentiary in Laval.

The biggest surprise occurred May 27, 2004, when, on a warm Thursday night in Quebec City, police arrested Nomad Paul "Fonfon" Fontaine for the prison guard murders and dozens of other serious crimes. Police had believed him dead. In fact, he had been hiding out for seven years.

In all, of the ninety-one bikers who had faced charges in the aftermath of the police crackdown of Springtime 2001, almost eighty pleaded guilty or have been convicted. By late February 2004, Quebec police initiated a new round of arrests—laying drug, gangsterism and other charges against forty more bikers, including a dozen full-patch members of the Montreal South chapter and Jacques Emond, the powerful leader of the Sherbrooke chapter. These were the bikers who had filled the vacuum left behind by their imprisoned colleagues.

Now that they themselves are behind bars, the question is, Who will rise up to take their place?

The anti-gang law also got a boost in the rest of the country. In Ontario, Steven Lindsay and another member of the Hells Angels had been arrested in a minor extortion case but their case assumed national significance when the Crown added gangsterism charges under the revised federal anti-gang law. The bikers' lawyers argued the anti-gang legislation violated the Charter of Rights because it is too vague and infringes on the right to associate. But on February 27, an Ontario Superior Court judge agreed with the Crown that the new law was necessary "to combat organized crime across the country."

But while there were successes on some legal fronts, authorities were still having difficulty determining and locating the bikers' vast riches.

In Quebec, justice officials have continued efforts to round up Hells Angels properties but have so far failed to find the motherlode, which likely is stashed offshore. Nomad Denis Houle was forced to hand over his estate in the Laurentian Mountains worth more than $300,000, plus jewellery worth $65,000 and about $30,000 in cash. But authorities agreed not to seize his home, which in any case was heavily mortgaged.

In Vancouver, proceeds-of-crime cops were rubbing their hands with glee after Martin Chambers, the disgraced biker-connected ex-lawyer, was nailed on money laundering charges. He was nabbed in the States, where wiretap rules are more lax and sentences a lot stiffer. They ruefully noted that Chambers got sixteen years for laundering $700,000 of what he thought was cocaine money, while in Canada a money-launderer who funnelled $20–30 million and about thirty tons of drugs got two years less a day and didn't spend a single day in jail.

Crime still pays in Canada and organized crime pays a lot better.

The B.C. Angels, always Canada's richest, were certainly not wanting for money. Jamie Holland, the young Nomad with a taste for fancy cars, could be seen showing off his new Mercedes. He and fellow Angel Gino Zumpano also paid $800,000 cash through a holding company to purchase a nightclub in Vancouver's trendy Gastown. Ever eager to show a hip face to the public, several members and prospects of the East End chapter, including veteran biker Damiano Dipopolo, appeared in a video alongside the popular rap group Swollen Members.

The B.C. bikers had much to sing about as their membership numbers also kept swelling. On January 21, 2004, they held a lavish party at the East End clubhouse. Among the new inductees as full-patchers was John Punko, the aptly named thug who got an eight-month sentence for making a death threat against one of the prosecutors in the cocaine bust of Angels Ronaldo Lising and Francisco Pires.

But as B.C.'s Hells Angels expanded, the province's Organized Crime Agency (OCA) would not live to see its fifth birthday. Created in 1999 to target bikers and organized crime—in part, because the existing police structures weren't doing that effectively—the OCA was disbanded by early 2004. The BC government announced it was abolishing the crime agency, moving the OCA's operations under the umbrella of the RCMP. For the cash-strapped BC government, it was in part a way to try to fight crime on the cheap: instead of footing the bills for the independent OCA, they fold it into the federal RCMP, knowing that Ottawa pays 30 percent of the RCMP's budget in BC.

The good news was that many of the OCA's best biker experts—former Mounties such as Pat Convey, as well as Inspector Andy Richards—stayed on board, working with the RCMP's Combined Forces Special Enforcement Unit. The police in British Columbia seemed determined to put their in-fighting behind them and the top brass at the RCMP were showing a renewed interest in battling the west coast bikers.

When *The Road to Hell* was first published in the fall of 2003, the bikers, not surprisingly, were less than pleased. "The boys were amazed at how deep you got," says a biker source. "They don't like all that dirty laundry out there." He calls himself "Ears" and though he had a falling out with the Halifax chapter he maintains close ties to the Angels. Ears told the *Halifax Daily News* that several Hells

Angels members met in Toronto and Montreal and were so angered by some of the book's revelations they were literally "spinning guns on the table tops."

The reaction to the book by some police bosses was more disturbing. Some of the police officers who either gave us interviews or whose intelligence reports were cited in the book—in Quebec, in British Columbia and at RCMP national headquarters—faced internal investigations or reprimands.

What they told us is part of the historical record of this country. For Canadians to comprehend their history and to evaluate the strength and weaknesses of their criminal justice system, they need law enforcement officials to share their stories without fear of retribution. For there can be little doubt that law enforcement headaches and screw-ups continue.

In Montreal, it was revealed that a veteran RCMP drug investigator working on a major Hells Angels case had jeopardized the lives of undercover cops by discussing sensitive information with a neighbour in 1997. It turned out the neighbour's father was a close friend of Mom Boucher. The officer was transferred to the Mountie's VIP protection unit.

In Winnipeg, police launched an internal investigation into why they failed to notify an innocent young man of a pending hit. Kevin Tokarchuk, twenty-four, was shot to death in his garage on May 24, 2003—exactly one year after the killing of the Hells Angels' Zig Zag gang member Trevor Savoie. Kevin's brother, Daniel, was eventually found guilty of killing Savoie. A tipster had warned police that Kevin had been fingered for vengeance but somehow Kevin was never notified.

Then in June of 2004, a much awaited mega-trial against five Hells Angels associates facing a total of 36 charges, including conspiracy to commit murder, fizzled out. The Crown stayed the charges against the five Zig Zag members largely because their star witness, biker-turned-snitch Robert Coquete, was proving to be difficult and unreliable. What's worse, Crown attorney Bob Morrison sent a letter to defence lawyers stating that some police officers "may have committed criminal acts" during the investigation. Details of those acts have yet to be disclosed.

In Saskatchewan, a CBC inquiry uncovered the fact that prison officials were warned that Aimé Simard's life was in danger weeks before the biker informer was stabbed to death in his jail cell in July 2003. Simard himself had asked for a transfer out of the Saskatchewan Penitentiary just two days before he was killed.

Silencing the critics of the police—especially those on the inside—only backfires. The cracks on the road to hell cannot be so easily paved over.

Julian Sher
William Marsden
Montreal
January 2005

Chronology of Key Events

1948	The first chapter of the Hells Angels is set up in San Bernardino, California.
1957	Ralph "Sonny" Barger sets up the Oakland chapter in California, and the HA soon moves its international headquarters there.
December 5, 1977	The first Canadian chapter of the Hells Angels is set up in Sorel, Quebec, when thirty-five members of the "Popeyes" club patch over.
August 14, 1979	Laval, Quebec, chapter formed.
1982	Walter "Nurget" Stadnick, from Hamilton, Ontario, joins the Hells Angels in Quebec.
July 23, 1983	Three British Columbia chapters formed in Vancouver, White Rock and Nanaimo.
December 22, 1983	Vancouver East End chapter formed.
September 1984	Stadnick badly burned in motorcycle accident.
December 5, 1984	Chapters formed in Sherbrooke and in Halifax, where David "Wolf" Carroll builds his base.
May 1, 1987	Maurice "Mom" Boucher becomes a full patch Hells Angel.
June 13, 1987	Haney Chapter formed in B.C.
1988	Stadnick becomes national president.
September 1989	Police arrest Vancouver East End member Lloyd Robinson for the murder of a nightclub owner but eventually drop the charges.
1990	Biker war between Quebec Hells Angels and rival Rock Machine begins to claim growing number of lives.
1992	Vancouver police launch Project Eliminate to go after Hells Angels active in the stripper business but fail to bring any charges.

1993	Halifax ports police constable Eric Mott shows his new boss Bruce Brine his intelligence files detailing biker connections in the port. Two years later, Brine is fired.
April 1, 1994	Dany Kane, working for Stadnick and Carroll, is arrested in Ontario as a leader of the Demon Keepers.
August 1994	Vancouver ports police issue their first major report unveiling "a massive billion-dollar-plus drug import industry" with the Hells Angels at its centre.
October 17, 1994	Kane, once outside of prison, calls RCMP Sgt Jean-Pierre Lévesque. He becomes RCMP Source C-2994.
December 9, 1994	Mom Boucher forms the Nomads, which would become the most powerful HA chapter in Canada.
August 9, 1995	With the biker war at its peak in Montreal, a bomb kills eleven-year-old Daniel Desrochers, sparking public outrage.
September 23, 1995	Quebec sets up the Wolverine squad, a special task force bringing together the Sûreté du Québec, the RCMP and local police forces.
February 27, 1997	Kane and his lover Aimé Simard murder Robert MacFarlane in Halifax.
March 1997	Mike Toddington, head of the Vancouver ports police, is fired but he sues successfully for wrongful dismissal.
April 30, 1997	Kane is arrested for the murder of MacFarlane.
June 26, 1997	Stéphane Gagné and André "Toots" Tousignant murder prison guard Diane Lavigne.
July 1997	Ottawa dismantles the ports police, despite warnings from major police forces, some of its own advisers and the provinces.
July 27, 1997	The Angels form chapters in Edmonton and Calgary.
July 24, 1997	Police detain about 150 bikers, most of them from B.C., at a roadblock outside Calgary, but an Alberta judge blasts the police for violating the "fundamentals of justice" and failing to prove the HA were involved in crime.
September 8, 1997	Stéphane Gagné and Paul "Fonfon" Fontaine murder prison guard Pierre Rondeau.

October 9, 1997 — Donny Petersen of Ontario's Para-Dice Riders addresses elite Empire Club in Toronto.

October 18, 1997 — Walter Stadnick and Angels from across the country flock to Winnipeg to help Los Brovos celebrate their thirtieth anniversary.

December 5, 1997 — Police arrest Stéphane Gagné, who agrees to become a government witness against "Mom" Boucher.

December 18, 1997 — Mom Boucher is arrested and charged for the prison guard murders.

June 1998 — A special squad is formed in Ontario to investigate the bikers and is reorganized in 2000 as the Biker Enforcement Unit (BEU).

Summer 1998 — The RCMP in B.C. reject the offer of an active member of a local chapter to turn police informant, the second time in two years they decline the opportunity to infiltrate the HA.

July 23, 1998 — Burnaby chapter set up in B.C.

November 27, 1998 — A jury acquits Mom Boucher of the prison guard murders.

December 18, 1998 — A judge declares a mistrial in the MacFarlane murder case. Kane is freed.

March 11, 1999 — The Organized Crime Agency of British Columbia (OCABC) is established.

Spring 1999 — Wolverine starts Project RUSH, which is designed to sweep up the entire HA network in Quebec.

August 23, 1999 — Montreal Det. Sgt. Benoît Roberge and SQ Sgt. Robert Pigeon recruit Kane as an informant.

October 31, 1999 — HA rival Randy Mersereau disappears in Nova Scotia; Kane tells police Carroll wanted him dead.

March 10, 2000 — Kane confesses to his crimes and signs a contract to become an agent-source.

June 2000 — Kane tells police of a plot by Wolf Carroll and the Halifax Angels to kill Kirk Mersereau.

July 21, 2000 — Hells Angels absorbs Manitoba's Los Brovos as the local gang becomes a prospect chapter.

August 8, 2000 — Kane commits suicide.

September 2000	Start of Project Ocean in Quebec.
September 10, 2000	Kirk Mersereau, an enemy of the HA in Nova Scotia, and his wife are executed in their home.
September 13, 2000	Quebec journalist Michel Auger survives a biker assassin's six bullets.
October 10, 2000	Quebec Appeals Court overturns Mom Boucher's acquittal and orders a new trial. Boucher is re-arrested.
December 16, 2000	The Hells Angels patches over Ernie Dew and his Los Brovos gang members after only five months as prospects—instead of waiting the traditional year.
December 29, 2000	The Hells Angels establishes itself as the pre-eminent gang in Ontario by patching over 179 members from other clubs and creating a dozen new chapters.
January 22, 2001	Almost five years after the police begin Project Nova, two full-patch members, Ronaldo Lising and Francisco "Chico" Pires, are found guilty of trafficking in cocaine, becoming the first B.C. HA members convicted of a serious crime in years.
March 28, 2001	Operation Springtime. Police in Quebec arrest more than 120 bikers in province-wide sweep.
August 6, 2001	Gerry Matticks, the kingpin who ran the smuggling operations in the Montreal ports, pleads guilty to drug charges and gets a twelve-year sentence.
December 5, 2001	In Operation Hammer police sweep down on the Hells clubhouse in Halifax and make numerous arrests on drug charges.
January 12, 2002	Four hundred Hells Angels from across Canada roll into Toronto to celebrate the club's first anniversary in Ontario, embarrassing Mayor Mel Lastman when he is photographed shaking the hand of a biker.
January 31, 2002	Ontario HA member Tiger Lindsay is arrested with another member and charged with extortion, but the Crown also makes it a test case for Canada's new anti-gang law.
April 2002	The biker mega-trials begin in Montreal.

May 5, 2002	A jury finds Mom Boucher guilty of the prison guard murders. He gets life in prison.
June 5, 2002	Ontario and Quebec police arrest most of the Bandidos in Toronto, Kingston, Montreal and Quebec City.
July 22, 2002	The biker mega-trial in Montreal is aborted after Superior Court Judge Jean-Guy Boilard resigns.
September 26, 2002	Ontario police arrest most of the members of the Outlaws in Project Retire.
January 29, 2003	Three Halifax HA members are sentenced to three to six years after pleading guilty to cocaine charges. Their clubhouse is forfeited.
July 18, 2003	Aimé Simard, Dany Kane's lover who also turns police snitch, is found face down in a pool of blood in his jail cell in the Saskatchewan Penitentiary. He died of multiple stab wounds in what police suspect was a biker-arranged killing.
August 2003	Halifax Hells Angel Neil Smith is found guilty of first degree murder and gets life in prison, joining three other full-patch members in jail on other charges and putting the Halifax chapter's official status in peril.
September 2, 2003	Nomad Walter Stadnick, along with fellow Hamilton-area biker Pup Stockford, start pre-trial hearings in Montreal on multiple charges of murder and gangsterism
September 11, 2003	Four Hells Angels Nomads and five Rockers plead guilty at a Montreal mega-trial to conspiracy to commit murder, gangsterism and drug trafficking. They get 15 to 20 years.
November 5, 2003	Quebec police arrest Benoit Cliche, the hapless lawyer for Mom Boucher. His arrest was part of a roundup of 31 people associated with the Hells Angels. Cliche is charged with gangsterism, trafficking cocaine and conspiring to traffic cocaine.
February 25, 2004	Quebec police initiate a new round of arrests—laying drug, gangsterism and other charges against 40 more bikers, including a dozen full-patch members of the Montreal South chapter.

February 27, 2004   Canada's anti-gang law withstands its first legal challenge when an Ontario judge rejects claims by lawyers representing two Hells Angels members charged with extortion that the law violates the Charter of Rights.

March 1, 2004   In the first biker mega-trial in Canada to make it all the way to the jury stage, Montreal jurors find three Hells Angels and six Rockers guilty of gangsterism and drug trafficking and conclude eight of them were also guilty of conspiracy to commit murder.

April 7, 2004   Paul Wilson, a Halifax associate of Nomad Wolf Carroll, pleads guilty to the murder of Robert MacFarlane. Police informer Dany Kane helped carry out the hit.

June 24, 2004   A much awaited mega-trial against five Hells Angels associates in Winnipeg facing a total of 36 charges, including conspiracy to commit murder, fizzles out when the Crown stays the charges against the five Zig Zag members.

September 13, 2004   Quebec Nomads Walter Stadnick and Donald Stockford are each sentenced to 20 years in jail and $100,000 in fines for drug trafficking, gangsterism and conspiracy to commit murder.

November 29, 2004   Joseph Ghaleb, Hells Angels money launderer, loan shark, and the man police believe ordered the attempted murder of journalist Michel Auger is gunned down in front of his suburban home in Laval, Quebec.

December 5, 2004   Two hundred Hells Angels from across Canada and the world gather in Sherbrooke, Quebec to celebrate the 20th anniversary of the local club and the 27th anniversary of the Montreal (Sorel) chapter.

Acknowledgements

———

Investigative books rely on the help of many people. This book is no exception. But given the nature of the Hells Angels, some of those names understandably will have to remain anonymous.

Many of the interviews and documents quoted in the book were originally in French. Great care has been taken to be as accurate as possible; some quotations have been edited slightly for clarity or grammar. Our special thanks to Isabelle Richer, Marie-Hélène Loranger, Janet Bagnall and Jackie Daigneault-Collin for their help with translations and transcriptions of court transcripts, surveillance videos and tape recordings.

Journalists across the country kindly shared their analyses and opinions, and we appreciate them all: In Halifax, we were aided by Dean Jobb and Patricia Brooks of the *Halifax Herald*, and especially Phonse Jessome, who covered the Angels for the CBC. In Quebec, Paul Cherry of *The Gazette* did research into the Hells Angels' criminal records. In Ontario, Linda Guerriero of CBC's *the fifth estate* helped track down many leads. Peter Edwards from the *Toronto Star* and Bill Dunphy and Paul Legault of the *Hamilton Spectator* aided constantly. In Winnipeg, the CBC's Melanie Verhaeghe was especially helpful, along with Krista Erickson, as were Bruce Owen and Mike McIntyre of the *Winnipeg Free Press*. In Vancouver, Kelly Ryan of the CBC, Neal Hall and David Baines of the *Sun* and *Stockwatch*'s hard-working Brent Mudry in particular lent a hand, while freelance journalist Mike Laanela did legal research. And in the United States, Mike Carter of the *Seattle Times* shared his expertise, and Erik Schelzig covered the Miami courts for us.

Cal Brocker in Toronto and Bill Cotter in Vancouver provided insight into money-laundering and police work.

The deepest gratitude of all journalists covering the bikers goes to lawyer Mark Bantey for fighting all those publication bans. For the long hours he spent with us dispensing legal advice, we are forever indebted.

Our thanks to Michael Levine, our agent, and Alison Reid, our copy editor. Our deepest appreciation goes to our editor, Diane Martin, for her patience, perspective and editing skills. Whether it's the life of Pi or the life of "Mom," she shows remarkable insight.

We also thank our families for their support and help, especially our wives and fellow journalists, Lisa and Janet.

Julian Sher
juliansher@canada.com

William Marsden
wjmarsden@hotmail.com

Index of Proper Names